THE SLAVE TRADE OF EASTERN AFRICA

The Slave Trade of Eastern Africa

R. W. Beachey

10 East 53d St., New York 10022
(a division of Harper & Row Publishers, Inc.)

Published in the USA 1976 by
Harper & Row Publishers, Inc
Barnes & Noble Import Division

ISBN 0-06-490326-5

© Rex Collings Ltd 1976

Typeset by Malvern Typesetting Services
and printed in Great Britain
at the University Printing House, Cambridge
(Euan Phillips, University Printer)

Contents

PREFACE		vii
1.	From Antiquity to the Coming of the Portuguese	1
2.	The Southern Slave Trade on the East African Coast	11
3.	The Northern Slave Trade based on Zanzibar	37
4.	The Anti-Slave Trade Patrol on the East African coast in the Nineteenth Century	67
5.	The Clarendon Committee 1869: Select Committee 1870/71: the 1873 Treaty	94
6.	Egypt and the Sudan	121
7.	Northeast Africa and the Middle East	148
8.	The Slave Trade in the Interior of East/Central Africa	181
9.	The Last Phase of the Anti-Slave Trade Campaign	220
10.	Sir Arthur Hardinge and the Abolition of Slavery	242
	RECOUNT AND SUMMARY	260
	NOTES	263
	BIBLIOGRAPHY	298
	MAPS	308
	INDEX	311

Acknowledgements

I wish to express my thanks to the Colston Society for permission to reproduce a Paper delivered at the Colston Symposium, University of Bristol, in 1973, and which appears in Chapter IV of this book substantially as presented there.

My deep gratitude is expressed to Professor G. S. Graham for reading the manuscript and for many helpful and shrewd comments; and to Dr G. S. P. Freeman-Grenville for allowing me to draw on his intimate knowledge of the East African and South Arabian coasts and for expert assistance in providing maps for this book.

Preface

This study was originally intended to cover the slave trade on the East African coast in the nineteenth century. The ramifications of this trade however led to an ever-widening field of research, embracing most of Eastern Africa and extending into the Middle East: a much larger world than originally contemplated, and one in which there is a singular lack of written sources on the slave trade.

In contrast to the flow of monographs, Ph.D. theses and books, a veritable mountain of literature, that exists for the West African/Atlantic slave trade, a blanket of silence has covered that on the eastern side of the African continent. The self-reproach and polemics, the political and ideological twist given to so much of the writing on the West African/Atlantic slave trade, finds no comparable fertile field in which to flourish on the eastern side of the continent. There is here no ideological or political cause to serve by such an approach, no lingering bitterness. It is difficult today, when surveying the Eastern African scene, to visualize the dimensions and reality of the slave trade which dominated so much of the life of that world in the nineteenth century.

In a brief recount and summary at the end of this book, an estimate is made of the total number of slaves exported from Eastern Africa in the nineteenth century. It is based on incommensurate data and approximate averages; it is no more than tentative, and open to supersession and quantitative exactitude. But to be within a substantial percentage, whether 10, 20, 30%, minus or plus, of the real number is no more or no less than has been done for the West African/Atlantic slave trade with its infinitely more copious documentation and tabulated data.

The main merit of this study, I would hope, is that it may stimulate further research into the slave trade of Eastern Africa at the regional level. As far as I know, this is the first attempt to treat with it at an overall level. It is a starting point.

1
From Antiquity to the Coming of the Portuguese

It is an easy transition, geographically and culturally, for a traveller crossing over from Arabia to the Horn of Africa, despite the intervening waters of the Gulf of Aden. The same topographical features of the Arabian coastline are prolonged down the east coast of Africa. Long stretches of white sand edging the shoreline; spectacular high cliffs looming up out of the haze, and suddenly dropping down to eddying bands of surf; the light and shadow that play tricks on the eye, when the heat of midday drops down in shimmering bands, causing the gaze to droop; and the lone straggling figures, man and beast, crawling along the white line of the desert's edge: to the last sandy hillock and lone rock sentinel, they are the same, whether Hadhramaut coast of Arabia or Benadir of Somaliland.

South of Lamu, where the desert shoreline shades into tropical verdure, and the graceful coconut palm and dark green of mangrove smudge the water's edge, the illusion of familiarity persists. For the men who planted Arab colonies on the East African coast carried their culture and religion with them. Intertwined with the cloying perfume of frangipani, resinous tang of camphor, pungent smell of spices, guttural of Arabic, and rapid onomatopoeia of Swahili, there mingles and combines the spell of Islam, so as to assure a homecoming to the traveller from the East. Semi-decaying towns, white mosques, crowded bazaars, narrow streets, elaborately carved doors and latticed windows, all add the final touch of the Orient.

The East African coast presents little or no physical obstacles to invaders of her shores, and for thousands of years they have come in on the monsoon. Contact between the Middle East and the East African coast probably existed long before the Greek, Hippalus, in the first century A.D., recorded information on the movement of the winds and currents of the western Indian Ocean.[1] The lateen sail, a characteristic feature of the Arab dhow which traversed the western Indian Ocean, was in use in the Persian Gulf by the first millenium B.C.[2]

During the classical period probing expeditions down into the Red Sea, by the Greek sailor, Scylax, in the fifth century B.C., and Philo, Admiral of Ptolemy I Soter, in the third century B.C., were in search of the elephant for military use.³ Under the second and third Ptolemies (285-221 B.C.), penetration was extended southward; so that by the end of the third century B.C., Greek merchants acquired a familiarity with the coast as far south as Cape Guardafui. Contact with the East African coast south of Cape Guardafui, during the classical period, arose from merchants being blown off course. Eudoxus, returning from India in the early first century B.C., was carried south of the Cape; and Diogenes was carried by the monsoon down to the Zanzibar Channel; while Theophilus, who duplicated Diogenes' feat, was in turn surpassed by Dioscurus who, it is averred, reached Cape Delgado.⁴

These incursions southward into the Indian Ocean brought increasing knowledge of the East African coast. The geographer, Strabo, in the first century A.D., refers to the Aethiopians, a term applied to Africans generally, and to numerous ships which sail annually into the Indian Ocean from the Red Sea;⁵ while Pliny, the Elder, who states in his compendium on human knowledge that half the nations live by traffic and merchandise, possibly had in mind this increasing commerce of the western Indian Ocean.⁶

It is not easy to identify the role of East African slaves in this commerce, but reference to African slaves in general appears to be as old as recorded time. Pre-historical graves of Lower Egypt show that a Libyan race of ten thousand years ago enslaved an earlier Bushman or Negrito population, and in ancient Egypt the institution of slavery was an established feature. During the era of dynastic Egypt and down to Roman and Byzantine times, the Sudan was periodically raided for slaves. It was traditional practice in ancient Egypt, from the time of the dynasty of Fenerefu onwards, to raid for slaves in the lands to the south, the Bilades Sudan (land of the Blacks), and these raids are recorded in the annals of Thutmose III and Amenhotep II. And similarly, sailings from Egypt to the land of Punt (northern Somaliland) during the Eighteenth Dynasty, had as their object the obtaining of male and female slaves.⁷

Slaves were always in demand in the Alexandrian market. There are portrayals of negro slaves on Alexandrian terracottas, showing them as rather pathetic figures, visibly unhappy folk in the damp cold and dank climate of Alexandria.⁸ A first century mosaic of Pompeii depicts a negro slave at a banquet; and does not Seneca refer to 'one of our dandies with our outriders and Numidians'.⁹

Eunuchs and ivory are mentioned as subject to duty at Alexandria in Ptolemaic times.[10] Slaves made up a large proportion of the population of the Greek and Roman world. Their main supply arose from prisoners of war. The campaigns in Europe and Asia threw an almost unlimited number of these on to the market. A single raid on Epirus brought in 15,000 slaves, and the fall of Carthage meant wholesale enslavement for its inhabitants. The flow of slaves from the outlying portions of the Empire was unceasing. Ten thousand slaves a day could be disposed of in the great slave market at Delos in the Mediterranean.[11]

There is however no specific reference to a trade in slaves from the East African coast until the time of the *Periplus of the Erythraean Sea*, dating from the early second century A.D., and by an anonymous author from Alexandria.[12] The *Periplus*, a form of supercargo's guide, picking out points of information on trade and geography of the East African coast,[13] tells us that it was politically 'subject under ancient right to the sovereignty of the Power which held the primacy in southern Arabia'; and it was frequented by 'Arab captains and crews who trade and intermarry with the mainlanders of all places and know their language'. There is mention of slaves of the 'better sort' brought to Egypt in increasing numbers. The Periplus affirms the far-flung nature of East African trade at this early date. In addition to slaves, cinnamon, ivory, tortoiseshell and ambergris are exported from the East African coast.

From the time of the *Periplus* down to the tenth century were the 'dark ages' in the history of the East African coast; there is scarcely any contemporary reference to it available for this period.[14] Ptolemy's *Geography*, which sums up knowledge available at about the fourth century A.D., adds little to what the *Periplus* tells about the coast. Nikon, on the Somaliland coast, which the *Periplus* refers to as an anchorage, is designated by Ptolemy as a trading station; the promontory, Prason, is sited at Cape Delgado; while the great mountain, a short distance inland from the coast, is probably Mount Kilimanjaro. And the Nile derives its source from the Mountains of the Moon and great lakes of the interior. The voyage of Cosmas Indicopleustes, a Greek merchant, to Ceylon in 525 AD., sheds little light on the East African coast, although indirectly referring to it as 'Zingion'.[15] No new information on the East African coast appears until the writings of Arab chroniclers in the tenth century, and reference to it in Chinese medieval sources.[16]

But it was probably during these 'dark ages', this literary hiatus, that there took place a slow movement of Bantu peoples up the East African coast. Although the *Periplus* makes no mention of black inhabitants of East Africa, al-Masudi, writing in the tenth century, refers to their being present in the region of the Juba river; and Chinese writings of the medieval period, in referring to an island in the west, possibly Zanzibar, state that its inhabitants have bodies as black as lacquer and with frizzled hair, while in the land of Popali, in the southwestern Ocean, there are a people (probably akin to the modern Masai) who 'stick a needle into the veins of cattle and draw blood which they drink raw, mixed with milk'. These people were frequently raided by the Arabs who purchased their womenfolk from them at high prices.[17] African slaves were taken to the Ta'ashi (Arab) countries where they were used as 'gatekeepers . . . It is said they do not long for their kinfolk'.[18] At Mo Lin, probably Malindi, the inhabitants are reported as being black, and these black slaves were worth their weight in aromatic wood in China.[19]

That a long-standing trade in East African slaves with the Persian Gulf area existed even before the rise of Islam may be deduced from the large number of black slaves present in the Euphrates valley by the ninth century.[20] In 869, when Ali ibn Muhammed raised his banner of revolt at Basra, promising freedom to all slaves, those employed in the saltpetre industry in the lower Euphrates swarmed to his side. They captured and sacked Basra, annihilated its inhabitants, and for ten years they ravaged the area of the lower Euphrates. Their pillage only ended with the capture of their main fortress at al-Mukhtara in 883.[21] The number of persons who perished in these servile wars is estimated at over half a million. Additional evidence of large numbers of East African slaves in the Persian Gulf area is shown in that the princes of Bahrain at the mid-eleventh century possessed 30,000 negro or Abyssinian slaves, and they were employed in agriculture and gardening.[22] That there was also probably a long-standing slave trade with India, probably in Ethiopian slaves, is evident in that slaves were in sufficient number to rise to prominence under Rukn ud-din Barbak, ruler of Bengal (1459-74); and during the period 1486-93, they set up a temporary regime of their own in Bengal.[23]

Contact between the Arab world and East Africa appears to have increased with the rise of Islam. According to the Portuguese writer, de Barros,

> The Arabs before they adopted the faith of Mohammed had sailed from their native shores to the ocean. They behaved as peaceful strangers only concerned with trade and did not more than buy

and sell and return to their home country. However, after they absorbed that infernal doctrine, which they upheld with the arms whose use Mohammed and the Khalifa who followed him had taught them, they became much bolder and went much farther.[24]

Messianic zeal may have been a propelling force in the spread of Islam, but it was more likely to the schisms and dissent generated within Islam that the flight of its votaries to East Africa must be ascribed. The great division between the Umayyads (supporters of Uthman, the third Caliph) and the Alids (supporters of Ali, the fourth Caliph) resulted in refugees betaking themselves, by the easiest escape route possible, on the course of the monsoons to East Africa. The Swahili histories of Lamu and Pate, and the late nineteenth century Arabic Kitab al-Zanuj, support a tradition that, in the reign of the third Umayyad Caliph (685-705 A.D.), Syrian colonists settled in East Africa; and the ninth century Arab historian, al-Baladhuri, refers to two brothers, Sulaiman and Said, who, when the army of Abd al-Malak conquered Oman at the end of the seventh century, fled to East Africa and settled at Lamu; and the Almozeid, followers of the martyred Husain, son of Ali, after an unsuccessful revolt in Iraq in 740 A.D., fled to East Africa, and settled between Kismayu and Lamu.

The pattern of this early settlement on the East African coast was probably one in which several groups of immigrants from the Persian Gulf region, from the ninth century onwards, established small isolated trading centres in Pemba, the Lamu archipelago, possibly in Zanzibar, and at points on the southern Somali coast. Evidence from recent excavations at the town of Manda, on an island north of Lamu, tends to support the tradition of early migrations from the Persian Gulf area. Manda, probably founded in the ninth century, retained commercial ties with the Persian Gulf; and was an important centre for imports of glass and pottery. Later immigration from the Persian Gulf region was likely to have been responsible for the growth of trade on the southern Somaliland coast, especially at Mogadishu.[25]

The gold trade which developed in the twelfth century between Mogadishu and the Sofala country, on the southern portion of the East African coast, resulted in Shirazi merchants, or those of mixed blood, settling at Mafia and Kilwa, centres of the gold trade. And from them emerged independent sultanates at Mafia and Kilwa. Kilwa's prominence in the thirteenth and fourteenth centuries arose largely from her control of the trade in gold and ivory. Kilwa's trading connections extended far afield, to the Persian Gulf, India and the Far East. In the fourteenth century this trade tended to shift to the southern Arabian coast, probably to Aden, a town well placed for trade in the western Indian Ocean.[26]

Recent excavations in the Lamu archipelago and re-assessment of documentary and epigraphic evidence would indicate that the town of Pate was non-existent or very unimportant before the fifteenth century. Pate's prominence from the sixteenth to the eighteenth century appears to have coincided with the period of Portuguese domination at Kilwa, and consequent transference of Omani trading activities from there to Pate.

By the tenth century the Arabs were established along the coast and on the offshore islands; from Malindi in the north, to the Ruvuma river in the south. Kilwa, Sofala, Mogadishu, Malindi, Mombasa and Zanzibar became centres of Arab influence, and marked points where trade from the interior debouched at the coast. Al-Masudi, who visited there in the early tenth century, and al-Idrisi, the geographer, writing in the twelfth century, testify to the extensive seaborne commerce of the Zanj coast.[27] The Arabs controlled a large trade in ivory and amber; iron was an important article of trade; and slaves, it might be hazarded, were a constant factor in trade. In the *Kitab al-Ajaib al-Hind*, by Buzurg, a Persian Gulf sailor, probably written about the middle of the tenth century, reference is made to a captain from Oman who, in 922 A.D., lured a negro king on board his ship near Sofala and took him back to Oman along with two hundred slaves. And it is stated that

> The visitors to this country steal their children enticing them away by offering them fruits. They carry the children from place to place and finally take possession of them and carry them off to their own country.[28]

Al-Idrisi also refers to ships leaving Oman to bring back slaves from East Africa.[29] Ibn Battuta, who visited Kilwa in the fourteenth century, noted that its Sultan led frequent expeditions against Africans on the mainland. Slaves were apparently plentiful at Kilwa, for the Sultan and his son presented twenty of them to an indigent fakir from the Yemen.[30] At Mogadishu, ibn Battuta was waited on by a eunuch: the town was the centre of supply for slaves to Aden.

This trading activity and veneer of Arab civilization was confined to the East African coast and offshore islands. There is no evidence of Arab penetration inland. The interior was an unknown world, probably inhabited by a nomadic Hamitic people and with isolated pockets of the original Bushmanoid. Coast and interior were separate and different worlds, and the wall of isolation between them was not breached until the nineteenth century. But the Zinj coast never formed a unified whole, apart from the unity that Islam impressed on it, and trade shared in common. Arab influence was most noticeably reflected in the emergence of a so-called Swahili population, the result of intermarriage between Arab and African. This Swahili population although nominally Islamic, and continually affected by Arab and Indian Ocean influences, remained deeply Africanized.

A new era in the history of the East African coast commenced with the discovery of the Cape route to the East by the Portuguese. In 1498 Vasco da Gama, after rounding the Cape, visited the main Arab towns on the East African coast as far north as Malindi. The Portuguese were surprised at the civilized nature of Arab rule. It was a contrast to what existed on the main periphery of the rest of Africa. There were fine stone buildings, mosques, a developed architecture, and many peoples from the Indian Ocean world were in residence. Kilwa had recently been minting its own coinage. Trade connections extended as far away as Cambay. Mombasa was

> Very large and beautiful, and built of high and handsome houses of stone and whitewash, and with very good streets ... It has its own king, himself a Moor. The people are attired in silk and gold in abundance. It is a town of great trade, and has a good harbour, where there are many ships, both of those that sail for Sofala, and those that come from Cambay in India and Malindi, and others which sail to the islands of Zanzibar, Mafia and Pemba.[31]

Sea commerce was freighted in vessels whose sailing qualities equalled those of Portuguese ships. The Arabs possessed an impressive navigational skill and knowledge of the Indian Ocean.

There was also, the Portuguese noted, a trade in African slaves. They were employed on the coast as native troops, domestic servants and labourers. At Kilwa they were more numerous than the 'white Moors', and were 'engaged on farms growing maize and other things'.[32] At Mombasa the Arabs employed a force of 500 archers, 'all negro slaves'.[33] And farther north, at the Somaliland ports of Zeila and Berbera, the Arabs carried on an active slave trade in 'Abyssinians' whom they sold to the people of Asia.[34]

Portuguese control had followed rapidly on da Gama's visit. In 1505 they sacked Kilwa and Mombasa, and in 1517 burnt Zeila. The destruction of a large Muslim fleet at the battle of Diu in 1509, the fall of Muscat in 1508, and of Hormuz in 1515, affirmed Portuguese mastery of the western Indian Ocean. By 1529 they were challenging Ottoman power in the Red Sea. Portuguese supremacy brought a rigid monopoly of trade. From official stations, Kilwa, Mozambique and Sofala, and subject towns, Mombasa, Zanzibar and Lamu, where local sultans paid them tribute, the Portuguese ruled the coast. They were quick to seize the Sofala gold trade. The slave trade, however, at least during the earlier period of Portuguese rule, never attained great importance. At a time when the annual trade in gold was running at ten thousand mithqals, and ivory exports at over £50,000 yearly, slaves receive scarcely a mention. The Portuguese kept numerous domestic slaves on the upper Zambezi, and residents at Sena and Tete possessed as many as 800 each.[35] A pattern was already being established for that state of affairs which Livingstone was to observe on the upper Zambezi in the mid-nineteenth century.[36]

There are records of slaves falling into English and Dutch hands from Portuguese ships captured on the way to India; and in a defeat of the Portuguese in 1535, at al-Shihr off the Hadhramaut coast, the Turks acquired numerous domestic slaves as booty. At Diu, in India, the Portuguese employed 600 Africans as soldiers in the mid-sixteenth century. An account of Portuguese trade with India in 1596 states that

> Many slaves, both men and women, are carried thither because they are the strongest in all the East countries to do their filthiest and hardest labour wherein they only use them.[37]

But on the whole, there is no substantial evidence to show that there was a great demand for African slaves in India. In a land teeming with cheap, low class labour it could hardly be expected that there would be great need for foreign slaves. Nor is there evidence to show that the Portuguese carried on a slave trade with the Middle East world. Indeed their Christian religion would have debarred them from selling slaves to Muslims. For did not slaves usually adopt the religion of their masters?

There was however a small trade in slaves round the Cape. Portuguese ships returning from India might put in at Mozambique ports for water and supplies; and they would fill their half-empty holds with slaves. Records of various shipwrecks off the southeast coast of Africa in the early seventeenth century indicate that numbers of slaves were included in these losses. But this trade was never on a large scale, and Mozambique was too distant and the Cape passage too hazardous, for an East African slave trade to compete with that from Angola and Guinea in the markets of the New World. Even after a law was passed in 1645 allowing the export of slaves to Brazil from East Africa, the trade did not develop. The long haul round the Cape still made it too expensive a proposition. It was not until a later age of faster ships, and diminished supplies of slaves from West Africa, that the East African slave trade with the New World attained substantial proportions.[38]

The paramount interest of the Portuguese always lay in India. Even when the Turkish commander, Amir Ali Bey, carried fire and sword down the coast as far as Mozambique and temporarily captured Mombasa in 1589, thus forcing the Portuguese to look to the security of their East African defences, it was the seaway to India which the latter felt was threatened. The great fortress of Fort Jesus on Mombasa Island—constructed in 1593-96 and portraying in its architecture the high points of Rennaissance fortification combined with Indian defence work, a symbol of Portuguese pride and strength for the next 150 years—and the lesser forts along the coast and at Zanzibar, were meant to complete the line of defence on the sea route to India.

At the height of their power on the East African coast there were probably never more than one hundred Portuguese civil and military personnel stationed there. The Portuguese always placed considerable reliance on Arab, Swahili and Bantu underlings for the defence of their key points on the East African coast. Correspondence between Lisbon and Goa for the period testifies to the subordinate role assigned to Portuguese interests in East Africa in relation to India, for it is singularly lacking in reference to East Africa.[39] It was the trade in cinnamon, silks and precious gems with India, and the transit trade with the Far East, that dominated Portuguese calculations; and these far outweighed any attractions that East Africa might offer.

And, keeping these Portuguese priorities in mind, their achievements on the East African coast were not unimpressive. The massive Roman simplicity of Fort Jesus and the Vasco da Gama pillar at Malindi, which marks the point from which the great Captain set out on the last lap of his journey to the fabled Indies, are mute reminders of Portuguese challenge to the world of the Crescent.

But the Portuguese, like the Arabs who preceded them, confined their activity to the coastal strip. There is no evidence of Portuguese penetration inland, not even a few miles from Fort Jesus. That they might link up their possessions on the Swahili coast with their interests in Ethiopia was apparently contemplated,[40] and this if achieved would surely have outranked all other Portuguese feats in the western Indian Ocean world.

But by the seventeenth century, Portuguese supremacy in the Indian Ocean was increasingly challenged by the Omani Arabs,

Dutch, British and French. The Persians, assisted by an English squadron, wrested Hormuz from them in 1622; they were ejected from Muscat and the Arabian seaboard in 1650; and, following a series of assaults in which negro slaves from Muscat were employed, the Arabs took Fort Jesus from them in 1698. An attempt by the Portuguese to regain control of the Fort resulted in a seasaw struggle in which it changed hands a number of times, until the odds were finally settled in favour of the Arabs. By the mid-eighteenth century the Portuguese had withdrawn from the East African coast north of the Ruvuma river, and the Arabs were left in sole control. Arab and Portuguese could now, unfettered by external interference, farm their respective portions of the East African coast for slaves.

2
The Southern Slave Trade on the East African Coast

I. THE PORTUGUESE SLAVE TRADE

Confined to their province of Mozambique, following the loss of their northern strip of the East African coast, the Portuguese might well have developed it on lines of modern efficiency, intelligently exploited its resources, and established model plantations, as did the Germans in their East African colony prior to World War I. In the eighteenth century there were promises of a better approach. In 1752 the administration of Portuguese East Africa was separated from that of Goa, and under an able governor, Francisco José Maria de Lacerda e Almeida, appointed in 1772, there was some stiffening in official standards, and attempts made to reform the administration. Anticipating the isolation of Portuguese possessions if the British seized the Cape and extended their rule northwards, Lacerda projected a chain of Portuguese forts from Mozambique to Angola on the West Coast; this would give Portugal a firmer control over the interior. He opposed the slave trade and rejoiced when slave-dealers lost money in their ventures. Was this not divine retribution for enslaving fellow humans created in the image of God?[1] There was nothing further removed from the stereotyped figure of a sleazy Portuguese official, so often caricatured by the British, than Lacerda. His death, while journeying into the interior of central Africa in 1798, marked the end of a brief and enlightened period in the annals of Portuguese rule in East Africa.

Throughout most of the nineteenth century the Portuguese seemed to have lost the will to rule their East African colony.

> Over their coastline extended the withering blight of a feeble and obsolete system of protection which seizes all vessels attempting to trade on that coast without licenses from the Portuguese government and so driving the inhabitants into the slave trade, which the Portuguese have not the power to repress[2]

Crassons de Medeuil, Captain of a French slaver, visiting the Portuguese East African coast in the 1790s, noted the sparseness of its inhabitants, and that the Portuguese 'always made a mystery of their section of the coast'. It had not been surveyed. Parts of it were unknown and had never been visited by Portuguese officials.

It was an enormous seaboard, from Delagoa Bay in the south to the Ruvuma river in the north, 1300 miles as the crow flies, and nearly 2000 miles if following the tortuosities of the coastline. There was little tangible evidence of Portuguese rule along it during the early nineteenth century. Lourenco Marques, on Delagoa Bay, reflected little of its former importance as a military and trading station, apart from a decaying fort and a few rusty cannon. It did not become the main outlet for the large transit trade with South Africa until late in the nineteenth century.

Inhambane, 200 miles farther north, on the Mirama peninsula, a small strip of land held on sufferance from the natives, was rarely visited. Sofala, ancient outlet for the gold trade from the kingdom of Monomotapa, was now in ruins, with a few black troops quartered in its little fort. Quelimane, on the north bank of the river QuaQua, near the great delta of the Zambezi, despite having a fetid climate, was the main port and trading centre of the southern portion of the Province.[3] Its inhabitants comprised a native population of three to five thousand, and a few hundred militia (mostly paroled convicts, mulatto and black), miserably clad and worse fed.[4] The few Europeans in Quelimane were a dispirited lot, hardly mustering enough energy to move out from their acacia-shaded boulevard which skirted the river's edge . . . 'their sickly appearance and tottering gait sufficiently indicated the slender thread on which their existence hung.'[5] Beira, on a tongue of sand near the mouth of the river Pungwe, the site of a forgotten Arab settlement, made no pretensions as yet to being the great port it was to become at the end of the century.

North of Quelimane for over a distance of 700 miles, apart from a small stockade at the mouth of the river Angoche, there was nothing to indicate Portuguese rule until Mozambique, the capital and largest town, was reached. Occupying a small sandy coral island, garrisoned by a few hundred sickly soldiers, and with a population of a few hundred Europeans and half-castes, the same number of free Africans, and about 5000 slaves,[6] Mozambique was declining in trade and importance, but it was not quite the heap of ruins the British were so fond of making it out to be. It was a clean and solidly built town, with double-storied houses, in excellent repair and superior to those at either Mombasa or Zanzibar. Public buildings were impressive, especially so the palace of the governor, which had formerly been the Jesuit college of Sao Paulo. As in most other towns along the East African coast, Banyans (Indians) were in residence as traders.

One hundred miles north of Mozambique was Port Amelia, on Pemba Bay, dating from the early days of Portuguese rule and now decrepit. Another hundred miles north was Ibo; dating from the early seventeenth century, it was the northernmost point of any civic importance on the Portuguese East African coastline. It was on one of the small group of islands making up the Kerimba archipelago, with a shallow but sheltered harbour. Its two forts, now derelict, were quite in disuse.

On the basis of the shadowy peripheral control as indicated above, the Portuguese made grandiose claims to a vast hinterland.[7] And from these few points along the coast, described by British observers as 'decaying towns' where all was 'ruin and dirt and devilment', they carried on a precarious and ramshackle administration. Malagasy slave-hunters and mainland Africans raided with impunity near Mozambique town; in 1840 the Mapazetas overran the country near Delagoa Bay, until they were bought off; and the Zulus on the right bank of the Zambezi exacted tribute in the form of useless muskets from the Portuguese in return for forbearance in their raiding. The Portuguese officials appeared to have neither the will nor power to oppose these raids.

It was Portuguese obstruction of legitimate commerce, their 'unwarranted assumption' of the coast from 'English River to Cape Delgado', and 'exaggerated obstructive tariff and differential duties', which tended to shut out the natives from any trade but that in slaves.

James Prior, surgeon on the frigate *Nisus*, when visiting the East African coast in 1811-12, reported a flourishing slave trade at Mozambique. Ten thousand slaves were annually exported from here to South America and the islands in the Indian Ocean. 'Indeed throughout the East, the common term for an African is *Mozambiques*'.[8] During 1817-18, twelve ships, with over 4000 slaves on board, sailed from Mozambique for Rio de Janeiro. And it is estimated that 10,000 slaves annually were exported from Mozambique to Brazil and another 7000 annually to the French islands in the Indian Ocean, during the period from 1815 to 1830. By 1830 Quelimane was possibly the most important slave port in Africa, with export of slaves running to a high of possibly 10,000 annually for some individual years in the 1820s.[9] By 1837 the export of slaves to Brazil and Cuba from Portuguese East Africa was running at about 15,000 annually.[10]

Captain Owen, in the course of his survey of the East African coast, 1822-3, observed that:

Quilimane is now the greatest mart for slaves on the east coast. They are purchased with blue dungaree, coloured cloths, arms, gunpowder, brass and pewter, red coloured beads in imitation of coral, cutlery, and various articles. The free blacks of the country and banyans carry on the trade inland for the merchants ... From eleven to fourteen slave-vessels come annually from Rio de Janeiro to this place, and return with from four to five hundred slaves each on an average ... To contain the slaves collected for sale, every Portuguese house has an extensive yard, or enclosure, called a Barracon, generally surrounded by a lofty brick-wall.[11]

Not all slaves were exported from Mozambique, for there was a strong local demand for them. The colony's economy rested on a slave basis, and the institution permeated all sectors of social life. The academic distinction between 'slave' and *'colono'*, the latter being the tribesman dwelling on the *prazero* and supposedly a freeman in that he paid a head tax, was meaningless. For the *'colono'* was subject to his landlord, and obliged to work at his behest; he was a slave for all practical purposes, if not in theory.

The great estates, the *prazeros*, provided a fertile field in which the slave trade could flourish. They derived from an imaginative if somewhat unorthodox plan by the Portuguese government in the seventeenth century, to establish a Portuguese plantocracy in their East African possession.[12] The richest part of Mozambique was parcelled out into about one hundred estates, each three leagues by one league in area, and bestowed for a term of three lives in the first instance on Portuguese ladies, who were to marry only men of Portuguese blood. Male offspring were excluded from the succession; a daughter inherited under the same obligation as her mother. This somewhat unusual device to secure a pure Portuguese lineage failed to achieve its aim. Grants of land exceeded the original stipulation; Tambara for example, in the Sena district, extended in size almost to that of Portugal itself. Tenants often held more than one area. Portuguese males were reluctant to take up estates which might be lost to them through failure to bear daughters. And Portuguese planters, cut off from home, or saddled with chronically ailing wives, turned to African mistresses. They ignored the injunction to live on their *prazeros*, leaving them in charge of half-caste managers (sometimes sired by themselves), and these became well-entrenched local figures, usurping power, setting the authorities at defiance, and ceasing to pay tithes to the latter. They constructed formidable stockades on their estates, and gathered round them large numbers of house and field workers. They became a power in the land. The *prazero* of Senhor Morgads, one of the largest in the colony, contained 30,000 inhabitants, mostly slaves. Its vast square storehouses, thick walls, pieces of cannon, servants' quarters and slave huts resembled the feudal domain of another age. A typical example of the large, unruly *prazero* owner was Bongo, who pursued the slave trade almost unchallenged, and defeated government forces sent against him in 1867-8.

In addition to slaves employed on the *prazeros* large numbers were used along the coast as cane-cutters, wood-cutters, machila-bearers (porters), and as general labourers. Kept in subjection by a rigid separate code of laws, infraction of which might result in reduction to the status of outright slavery, the threat of exportation could always be used with good effect to extract good behaviour from them.

Despite a restrictive limitation of their freedom, the life of slaves under Portuguese rule was not the terror critics and humanitarians claimed it to be. The Portuguese tended to treat their slaves in much the same fashion as the Arabs. During capture and events leading to enslavement, and the trek to the coast, suffering was undoubtedly great. But once settled down on the *prazero* there descended on slave and master alike an ennui, an acceptance of master-slave relationship which tended to shade any marked cruelty. Slavery was part of the normal pattern of life. Africans were reported to have come from the interior and voluntarily offered themselves as slaves in return for a few pieces of clouty (cloth); and slaves who had deserted their masters were later known to return to them.

The slave trade in Portuguese East Africa was abetted by dishonest officials and half-caste underlings. Officials dependent on the colonial treasury for their salaries, recouped their meagre earnings by conniving at the slave trade. The profits to be made out of the slave trade were such that it was the general feeling in Mozambique that the Governor-General paid for his appointment in Lisbon, and 'even appointments at Ibo and Quelimane are sold'.[13] Captain Beaver, of the *Nisus*, during a visit to Mozambique in 1812, noted that its governor, Don Antonio Manuel de Mello Castro e Mendoza, had just completed a three-year term of office without seeing anything of his territory, fearing to venture outside his official residence lest he be struck down by fever or sunstroke; and he was now retiring to Madeira with a fortune of 300,000 dollars (about £80,000).[14] This was something similar to the Nabob in British India tradition.

Although well intentioned and showing zeal on first appointment, a Portuguese governor, once surrounded by unprincipled rogues, soon succumbed. In 1850, Mascarhenas, Governor of Ibo, informed Wyvill, Commander-in-Chief at the Cape, of his intention to stop the slave traffic; a few months later, when his aid was requested in the task, Mascarenhas disclaimed all knowledge of the traffic, and ultimately was so open in his toleration of it that it was too much for even the hardened sensibilities of Lisbon, and he was recalled. Commander Bunce maintained that Portuguese authorities were fully aware of the extent of the slave trade in their territory. Vessels trading in the Mozambique Channel on the Portuguese side had first to go to the port of Mozambique to be cleared and pay dues; and it was notorious that Portuguese slavers lay outside creeks and rivers, making a private signal 'which their agents answer on shore', and slaves were then sent out to them in launches.[15] There was the well-known case of the *Eolo*, a Portuguese slaver captured by HMS *Orestes*, in March 1850. Unaltered in appearance, and under the command of the *Castor*, she was sent up to Mozambique from the Cape. She anchored in Pemba Bay, and a Portuguese launch, mistaking her for a slaver, came off to see if she wanted slaves. Five hundred at 20 dollars apiece could be obtained, given three or four days' notice. When the high price was queried, the reply came, 'a good many people have to get their share out of it . . . the Governor of Mozambique, and the officer in charge of the Portuguese cruiser'.[16]

In British eyes most Portuguese officials were venal. In 1846, Governor Abreu de Madeira, of Quelimane, was relieved of his post because he was in league with slave dealers, and about the same time the Governor of Mozambique absconded on a slave ship to Rio de Janeiro. Governor-General Duval, 'a great friend of the English', whose probity no English officer ever doubted, did not escape the imputation of having made 60,000 dollars out of the slave trade.[17] Major Tite, Governor of Ibo, after commencing his career with high intentions, succumbed, and bribed an interpreter on a British cruiser to withhold information on the slave trade.[18] Major Carvalho, also Governor of Ibo, an officer in whom the Governor-General, Almeida, placed the utmost confidence, after 'two months on his death-bed, made a will'. Among his requests was one that his effects remain untouched for two years. It was explained that this was impossible, and he died intestate. Examination of his property revealed 20,000 dollars in gold, and a list specifying shares due to public officers at Ibo on account of various slave-trade transactions. Wyvill reported in 1852

> I regret that the Portuguese authorities instead of repressing this traffic, afford every facility for its continuance. I learn that the

Governor of Inhambane permitted a slaver to lie at anchor off that port for three weeks and capture 1000 slaves in December 1851, and the Governor of Ibo connived at the trade.[19]

Thus nominally ranged on the side of Britain in the matter of anti-slave trade treaties, and assiduous in official assertions of good intent, Portugal never threw her weight fully behind an anti-slave trade crusade, nor appointed officials with zeal for the cause.[20] Livingstone did not condemn the Portuguese outright. 'The Portuguese home government has not generally received the credit for sincerity in suppressing the slave trade which I conceive to be its due.' But it was frustrated by men on the spot.[21] In addition there was no pricking of public conscience in Portugal by evangelicals and powerful anti-slave trade societies, often with corresponding members in the colonies, as was the case in nineteenth century Britain.

An additional obstacle to an effective anti-slave trade campaign came with the independence of Brazil in the early 1820s. Following recognition of her independence by Portugal and Britain in 1825 and 1826 respectively, and despite her pledge to honour anti-slave trade treaties signed with Portugal, Brazilian slavers operated and claimed freedom from interference south of the line; they ignored the decree of 1836 which prohibited export of slaves from Portuguese possessions, and continued to run under the Portuguese flag. Brazil, along with Cuba, was rapidly becoming one of the greatest slave-importing territories in the New World. Thomas Fowell Buxton, quoting from official and private sources, placed the total import of slaves into Brazil in 1837 at 78,000, and for Cuba at 60,000.[22] Captain Cook, who commanded a vessel on the East African coast in 1836-8, estimated that 15,600 slaves were carried to Brazil and Cuba from the ports of Quelimane and Mozambique in one year, and Lieutenant Bosanquet of HMS *Leveret*, at about the same time, placed the figure at 12,000 annually.[23]

On the Mozambique coast, with the finest known harbours on the East African periphery and most of its navigable rivers, far removed from European surveillance, slavers operated unmolested. The American, Richard P. Waters, visiting Mozambique in February 1837, noted that

> This city is a depot for slave vessels, which collect slaves on the coast, at different places, I can see from the deck of our Vessell that the decks of these Slavers are filled with Slaves, mostly with children from 10 to 14 years of age. This sight called up many unpleasant feelings. What can I say to those engaged in this trade, when I remember the millions of slaves which exist in my own country.[24]

Portuguese involvement in the slave trade to Brazil and Cuba drew from Palmerston in 1835 that angry and oft-quoted comment

> The ships of Portugal now prowl about the ocean pandering to the crimes of other nations; and when her own ships are not sufficiently numerous for the purpose, her flag is lent as a shield to protect the misdeeds of foreign pirates.[25]

In an attempt to check this trade, Britain in 1839, in high-handed fashion, arrogated to herself by unilateral act the right of visit and search for her warships over Portuguese vessels suspected of slaving, and treated those convicted as guilty of piracy. An outcry was aroused in Europe over this unprecedented measure. To abate it, an international conference of the great powers was convened, the result of which was the Quintuple Treaty of 1841, whereby Britain, Austria, Prussia, Russia and France agreed to seizure of vessels fitted out for slave-trading. Portugal was not party to this treaty, and held out for another year, until, by the Equipment Clause Treaty of 3 July 1842, she agreed to right of search if conducted in the 'mildest manner', and when there was strong suspicion that a vessel was equipped for slave-trading.[26]

But not only was Brazil not party to this treaty, but the problem of distinguishing Brazilian from Portuguese slavers remained. During the second half of 1842, fourteen slavers sailed from Quelimane for Rio de Janeiro, and 70,000 slaves were exported from Quelimane over the period 1819–47.[27] Ephraim A. Emmerton, in June 1843, while at Quelimane, saw gangs of slaves fresh from the interior, thin almost as skeletons.

> They had an iron ring round the neck and a chain went through it, thus connecting together 40 or 50 in a line. At night they were shipped off in boats to be taken down the river to barracoons erected near its mouth where they were kept. When the coast was clear of cruisers, then they were hurried off on board a vessel kept in waiting for them and taken to Rio de Janeiro for sale.[28]

The Aberdeen Act of 1845 which empowered British cruisers to seize Brazilian slavers, laden or empty, north or south of the line, and bring them before British Admiralty courts, was highhanded action and justified only on grounds that Brazil herself had agreed to treat the slave trade as piracy, and put it down with full rigour. But any gains that the Aberdeen Act brought were offset in 1846 when Britain introduced gradual equalization of sugar duties in the United Kingdom, ending the monopoly enjoyed by the British West Indies in the British market, and giving an impetus to sugar cultivation in Brazil and Cuba, and with it an increased demand for slaves. A slave purchased in Mozambique for £3-5-0 could be sold for £41-1-0 in Rio de Janeiro; and there was no stigma attached to the trade. According to the captain of a captured Brazilian slaver it was 'looked on rather as a sphere of spirited and skilful adventure than as a discreditable line of enterprise'.[29]

The task of countering it reposed almost entirely on the small British naval anti-slave trade patrol.[30] Support from Portugal was practically non-existent, apart from permission in 1847 to enter Portuguese ports, bays and creeks for the pursuit of slave ships. But when attempts were made to ferret out the haunts of the slavers there was such an outcry over wrongful seizures that cruisers in capturing generally adhered to the rule of the red flag (Arab) or none at all, 'as being the safest plan, because many of our captains have had to pay very heavy sums as indemnification for the illegal capture of Portuguese vessels'.[31]

In the face of these discouragements it was no surprise that the report of the Commissioners at the Cape for 1848 showed no abatement in the slave trade.

> The usual proportion in the number of Negroes imported into Rio de Janeiro during the last twelve months has been furnished by the slave dealers in the Mozambique.[32]

Commodore Wyvill of the Cape Command had much experience of the slave trade in the Mozambique Channel; he had previously been captain of the *Cleopatra* in the 1840s,[33] and had acquired more familiarity with the Portuguese coast than Portuguese officials themselves. He now directed Commander Bunce in the *Castor* to sweep the coast near Ibo, and sent the *Brigantine* and *Penguin* to patrol the Mozambique Channel. Especial attention was given to the Angoche river area. It was an important centre for the export of food stuffs, rice, millet, corn and beans, and above all slaves. A settlement of Arabs had set up a permanent depot there, and their barracoons, large sheds encompassed by a stake kraal, were capable of holding 4000 to 5000 slaves. With the large stores attached they represented a capital investment running to many thousands of pounds. It was from barracoons such as these that Portuguese slavers, hoisting Portuguese or American flags, as circumstances dictated, or as whalers in disguise, obtained many of their slaves.

Bunce searched out and burnt these barracoons, punished local chieftains who were involved in the slave trade, and destroyed their villages. At Masani, over a hundred Arab slavers had settled. Bunce dispersed them, seized their stores with £40,000 worth of piece goods, and freed a number of slaves. And Wyvill rounded out Bunce's work when, in 1849, he obtained treaties from local chiefs at Angoche by which they promised to desist from slave-trading. But this was work that the Portuguese should have been doing, and the fact that the British were pursuing their anti-slave trade campaign along the Portuguese periphery even to the extent of making treaties with local chiefs to check the slave trade, without any protest from Portuguese officials, was an indication as to how little the latter knew, or possibly cared, about what was happening on their coastline. But Wyvill and Bunce's brief but forceful campaign against the Angoche slavers was short-lived in its results. Captain Sulivan, visiting there a few years later, reported revived activity of the slavers.[34]

British naval forces were pitifully inadequate for the task facing them. From the Cape to the Equator, and as far east as 60° longitude, was included in the Cape Command. The demands made on its dozen ships were excessive. Five vessels alone were on patrol at St Helena during the exile of Napoleon there, until his death in 1821. Not more than one or two ships ever got as far north as Quelimane. Two vessels could not effectively keep watch over the whole East African coast and western shores of Madagascar. Burton maintained that it was not until 1843 that a British cruiser, the *Cleopatra*, from the Cape patrol, made an official visit to Zanzibar.[35] Proposals to strengthen the naval patrol in the early fifties were forestalled, partly owing to the outbreak of the Crimean War, but more to lack of conviction on the part of the Treasury at home that the anti-slave trade patrol was warranted. Thus in 1854, Commodore Talbot had only three vessels to deploy between Delagoa Bay and Zanzibar, over 1300 miles of coastline; and this number was further reduced to none, when the *Dee* was laid up for refit, and the *Crecian* and *Dart* were recalled to the Cape.[36]

Slavers were well informed as to the movements of these few British cruisers. When the *Dart* for example, in 1853, identified a number of slave depots on the coast, advance information to the slavers resulted in only two suspected ships being overtaken and these had to be released owing to inadequate evidence of slaving. Time and again a cheerful note of optimism in the Slave Trade Commissioners' report at the Cape proved premature; next season's story was one of a renewed slave trade.[37]

Curtailment of the slave trade round the Cape came not as a result of the anti-slave trade patrol's activity, but rather as a result of happenings in Brazil. The appearance there of yellow fever in 1849–50 was attributed to the arrival of slaves from East Africa.[38] A public outcry against their import resulted in a radical drop in numbers of slaves brought in by slave vessels. An annual figure of imports of 60,000 as at 1850 was soon reduced to a few thousands by 1853.³⁹ Material concern as to health and well-being had achieved what a moral campaign could never have attained. By 1865 the price of a 'healthy adult slave' at Bahia in Brazil had risen to £172.10.0; and for a slave with a skill or profession, it was £200.⁴⁰ Circumstances in Brazil were also working against the slave trade. In 1871 the Brazilian government decreed the abolition of slavery by a series of phased steps. In 1888 total and immediate abolition was decreed, and under this legislation 700,000 slaves were emancipated.

The practical cessation of the Brazilian marked by the mid-century, the opening of Mozambique ports to foreign trade, the registration and progressive emancipation of slaves in Portuguese possessions, and the prohibition of their export as free labourers should have ended the slave trade at Mozambique. But these decrees were ignored in the face of a new and rapidly developing and most lucrative market for slaves in Cuba. When Spain in 1817, in return for payment from Britain of £400,000, prohibited the slave trade north of the line, it should have ceased in the Spanish colony of Cuba. But effective evasion by Cuban planters, connivance of Spanish officials there, and the restrictive nature of 'right of search' as conceded by Spain under her 1835 treaty with Britain,⁴¹ enabled the slave trade to Cuba to flourish unchecked.

It was increasingly carried on under the American flag. The Equipment Clauses Act of 1847 had rendered the Portuguese flag less valuable for slavers, and they had sought protection under the flag of another power where right of search was not admissible. The United States had declared against the slave trade in 1807, and affirmed her opposition to it by the Treaty of Ghent, but insistence on freedom from search for vessels under her flag continued to be a point of the highest honour. The Americans had fought a war with Britain on this issue, and Britain was the power which would most frequently invoke right of search if the principle were conceded. The United States had a fast-growing merchant marine on the high seas, national pride was involved, and she would not concede what in the last resort was the real test of a nation's sincerity in the anti-slave trade cause, namely, right of search over vessels flying her flag. This American attitude possibly influenced France, a power equally sensitive to British naval supremacy, in taking a stand against granting right of search.⁴² These two powers, and Spain to a lesser extent, posed in this matter of right of search a most serious obstacle to an effective anti-slave trade campaign at sea throughout most of the nineteenth century.

And it took on a much more serious character when combined with the appearance in the 1860s of large, fast, American-built clippers, similar to the famous schooner *America*, and created for the naval patrol a problem of the first magnitude. Designed in construction and size to stand up to the boisterous waters of the Cape, and sailing under French, Spanish, and, more often, American colours, they heralded a new phase in the slave trade. Their owners were usually commercial houses in Marseilles and Barcelona, and a high capital investment was placed in these ships. Their loss could be a grave financial shock to their owners. The loss of five out of its fleet of six clippers in the early 1860s poised a Marseilles firm on the brink of collapse.[43] The *Manuela* of 700 tons, captured off Johanna by the *Brisk* in 1860, was capable of carrying 900 slaves, and following adjudication at Mauritius she was sold to the British Admiralty for £2560, a large sum for those days.[44] A large clipper, a Spanish slaver, destroyed by the *Penguin,* was capable of carrying 1000 slaves. The *Espérance*, fully fitted out, with slave-irons and provisioned with 150 large casks of water, which had cleared Barcelona six months previously, had come up to the island of Mafia when she was detained by the *Lyra* in 1860. She caused a sensation when towed into Zanzibar harbour. The Arab dhows were diminutive beside her.

In the annals of the clipper slave trade on the East African coast the name of a Spaniard, Buona Ventura Mass (or Bonaventius Mass) is of interest in this last phase of European involvement in the slave trade on the east coast of Africa. Formerly in French consular employ, and later agent of Vidal Frères of Marseilles and Barcelona, he acted as intermediary in a series of slave trade transactions on the East African coast in the late 1850s and early 1860s. In 1857, he arranged the collection of 800 slaves from Lamu for shipment to Havana; in 1858, he was implicated in a deal with Sultan Majid for the collection of 600 slaves from the east side of Zanzibar. In 1860, after laying up for a year at Aden, he arranged the collection of 3000 slaves at Lamu and Kilwa for four large clippers.[45] At the end of 1860 he advanced 5000 dollars to an Arab at Kilwa to supply 600 slaves for Réunion, and arranged with the Governor of Lamu for 300 slaves for a Spanish vessel, the *Formosa Estrella*. When the latter was captured by HMS *Persian* in December 1860, the uncollected slaves were taken by Arab slave dealers to Arabia, but not before 250 out of the original number had died.[46] Buona Ventura Mass, after a brief appearance in Portuguese East Africa in February 1861, vanishes until his name finally crops up in connection with the *Margaraita Quintera* (formerly the notorious Spanish slaver

Ciceron) transporting coolies from China.

The protection under the American flag enjoyed by these clippers, even possibly more than their fleetness, caused Commodore Wise of the African squadron, to complain bitterly of the 'shameful prostitution of the American flag . . . under that ensign alone is the trade now conducted'. But the abuse was about to be drawn to a close. When Lincoln became President in 1861, and Seward replaced Cass as Secretary of State, the Act of 1820 which declared slave-trading to be piracy and meriting punishment as such, was given teeth; and the need for British support in the Civil War resulted in a change in American policy towards the slave trade. By the Washington Treaty of 7 April 1862, the right of search was conceded to within 200 miles of the American coast, 30 leagues of the Cuban coast, and 200 miles of the African coast. Slavers, however, soon circumvented the latter restriction by resorting to the coast of Madagascar, which was outside the two hundred-mile limits. This loophole was removed in 1863, when territorial limits of African waters were extended to take in those of Madagascar.[47]

The extinction of the Cuban slave trade followed quickly on these moves; and when legislation was enacted there to phase out slavery its end was soon in sight. In 1885 the British consul-general at Havana reported that 'in a year, or at most two, slavery even in its mildest form, would be extinct.'

The effect of the decline of the Cuban market was quickly reflected in East Africa. Captain Bowden, after cruising in the Mozambique Channel for three months in 1865, had not seen 'a single European slave vessel'. An extensive slave trade was still carried on, however, across the Channel by Arab slave dhows. This branch of the slave trade was most pernicious and difficult to eradicate, for the Portuguese were slow to end the institution in their territory, and it was from here that the Arabs obtained their supplies. Thus Earl Russell in July 1862 contemptuously remarked that

> Portuguese colonial possessions on the Eastern Coast of Africa, instead of becoming, as they might have been, flourishing colonies, are now only monuments of Portuguese misrule.[48]

When Playfair, British consul at Zanzibar, visited the Portuguese coast in 1863, he observed that despite the decree of April 1858, which set abolition at twenty years hence, with an interim period during which Africans could not be enslaved, the general populace was wedded as ever to slavery and its 'unholy gains'.[49] Apart from the governor-general 'not a man has a free servant'.[50] Refractory slaves were forced to labour on public works without recourse to a legal tribunal, and Playfair noted that they were subdued and respectful, not like the 'cheery slaves at Zanzibar'.

He also observed signs that the Portuguese were at last bestirring themselves in suppressing the slave trade. They were now keeping closer watch on the San Antonio river area, a favourite haunt of slavers, and they had recently destroyed several slave dhows at Velhace and Mocambe. The Governor-General, de Almeida, had alerted the British to the movements of the Spanish slaver, *America*, and to Arab dhows resorting to unfrequented parts of the coast. With unwonted zeal a Portuguese gunboat had chased a slaver across the Channel from Conducia Bay to Madagascar, and they had brought two captured slavers before the Mixed Commission Court at the Cape in 1865. Portuguese ports were now open 'without any restriction to the commerce of all nations', and accusations that they connived at the slave trade were vehemently rebutted by the Portuguese.

It was, they said, carried on by Arabs, subject to the Sultan of Zanzibar, and Britain had a special relationship with that personage. Why then did she not put pressure on him to debar his subjects from engaging in the slave trade? And as for Portugal, she controlled only one side of the Mozambique Channel, and was doing her best to stamp out the slave trade on her coastline. The British charge that slaves 'swarmed' at Mozambique was meaningless, for how could one distinguish between free and unfree persons? And was it not generally known that Governor-General de Almeida had been especially selected for his post as an 'upright and honourable character who exercised zeal and vigilance' in checking the slave trade?[51] He had induced slave dealers to turn to legitimate commerce, and had expelled Arab slavers from Angoche.

Evidence of the effectiveness of Portuguese measures against the slave trade was apparent in the glut of slaves at Ibo—owing to inability to export them—and in the drop in number of slaves shipped from Portuguese East Africa round the Cape, from a figure of 15,000 to 20,000 annually, to 1200 to 1500 annually, over the three-year period 1860 to 1863.[52] Only one European slaver, a Spanish brig, collected slaves north of Pemba Bay in 1864. Sir Bartle Frere, who visited Portuguese East Africa in 1873, could affirm this improved character of Portuguese administration. The former high duties on their coastline had been relaxed, and restrictions on foreigners entering their territory had been removed. The Portuguese had recovered from the series of disasters which had overtaken them when their troops had been defeated on the

Zambezi, when Angoche had been in control of Arab slavers, and when the Portuguese themselves had hardly dared venture out of their main town, Mozambique. Governor-General de Almeida was now anxious to co-operate with the British, and had launched expeditions against the powerful half-caste, Bongo. Frere thought the Portuguese had 'turned the corner'.[53]

Inland there was a different story to tell. For here the slave trade continued unabated in scale and in intensity. Slaves were going to Kilwa from whence they were shipped northwards. The attention of the British anti-slave trade patrol was increasingly directed to the northern coast. In the year ending September 1866, only one of its ships visited Mozambique; the remainder, *Lyra*, *Penguin*, and *Pantaloon*, were stationed between Muscat and Aden.

II. THE SLAVE TRADE TO THE FRENCH ISLANDS IN THE INDIAN OCEAN

French involvement in the East African slave trade dates from the occupation of the islands of Bourbon and Ile de France by the French East India Company in 1664 and 1715 respectively. Under an able governor, La Bourdonnais, appointed in 1735, sugar cultivation was encouraged, and the islands became one of the main sugar producing areas of the world, comparable to the British West Indies, drawing their labour, as in the case of the latter, from Africa. The Seychelles, a small group of islands farther north, annexed to France in 1744, also depended on the same source for labour for the prosperous spice plantations developed there.

French possessions in the Indian Ocean turned easily to East Africa for slaves. Ile de France is only 500 miles from Madagascar, and 1100 miles from the African mainland, and with the encouragement of French authorities it was easy to develop the trade. Following the withdrawal of the Portuguese to the south of the Ruvuma river by the mid-eighteenth century, the French roamed unhindered along the northern strip of the East African coast, and for the remainder of the century were the main European traders there. In their search for slaves they ranged along the coast as far north as the Juba river,[54] were the main clients of the slave market at Pate, frequented the Lamu archipelago, and raided canoes, seizing their occupants as slaves.[55]

The French trade in slaves loomed so large at this period that a French trader, Morice, conceived a plan in 1776 of placing it on a more regular basis, by acquiring from the Sultan of Kilwa the exclusive right to purchase from there 1000 slaves annually at a price of 20 piastres apiece, together with a promise that 'No other but he shall be allowed to trade for slaves, whether French, Dutch, Portuguese, etc . . . until he shall have received his slaves and has no wish for more'.[56] Morice anticipated that the export of slaves from Kilwa would ultimately rise to many thousands a year, and, stabilized at a price of eight dollars per head, would play an important part in French commerce in the western Indian Ocean.

But Morice's scheme never got under way. It smacked too much of restriction and monopoly. And French authorities at Port Louis were averse to alienating the Sultan of Oman who claimed sovereignty over the East African coast. Negotiations were already under way with him to recruit labourers from his East African ports, at five piastres apiece. Morice's scheme seemed unnecessary, and was soon shelved. Another French trader, Joseph Crassons de Medeuil, attempted to revive it, following two visits to Kilwa in 1784-5 to sound out its inhabitants in the matter. He found them friendlily disposed 'towards establishing this type of trade in a manner likely to commend itself to the Ministry'. Kilwa's harbour was 'vast and safe', could hold a 'prodigious number of ships', and the immediate country produced slaves, 'superb specimens' if selected with care.[57]

Crassons noted that 4193 slaves had been transported from Kilwa in twenty-eight months, and at forty piastres per slave this represented 167,720 piastres, a sum which could be saved for the French if the trade were in their hands.[58] And when another French trader, Dallons, after visiting East Africa in 1799, pointed out in his *Reflections on French commercial relations with East Africa* that local governors at Kilwa and Zanzibar, despite the treaty of 1781 with the Sultan of Oman, were charging the French 11 to 12 piastres per slave, it seemed sensible to circumvent these exactions by acquiring Kilwa.

But Crassons' and Dallons' plans, like that of Morice before them, came to nothing. For the French revolutionary wars had now intervened, and the law of 1794, which decreed freedom for slaves in French possessions overseas, voided any arrangements that Crassons and Dallons might make.

But the law of 1794 was fiercely opposed by local authorities at Bourbon and Ile de France, and the slave trade continued to flourish there. Compensation might have reconciled planters to the loss of their slaves, but this would have been contrary to the spirit of the Declaration of Rights of Man and a Citizen; men were 'naturally free', and slaves must enter into their inheritance at once, without question of payment of compensation to erstwhile owners. An attempt by the French government in 1796 to enforce abolition on the islanders was successfully resisted, and during Napoleon's consulship they were virtually masters of their own fate. The French government, engrossed in the struggle in Europe, tamely acquiesced in this non-compliance, and the slave trade to the two islands continued practically uninterrupted.

By the end of the eighteenth century their slave population stood at over 100,000, against a white and coloured population of 20,000. And it was further sustained when, in 1807, the French concluded a treaty of 'Amity and Commerce' with the Sultan of Oman, whereby they were accorded favoured nation privileges in his East African dominions. For the next few years French slavers roamed along the East African coast picking up cargoes of slaves unmolested. Portuguese slave ships at Mombasa, Zanzibar, and Kilwa were only half the number of French ships there. Captains Tomkinson and Fisher, of HMS *Caledon* and *Racehorse*, visiting Zanzibar in 1809, noted the activity of French slavers there.[59] And James Prior at Kilwa in 1811 observed that its inhabitants spoke French 'tolerably well';[60] at Mauritius the French had maintained a 'constant intercourse' in slaves, ivory, and gold dust.[61]

But this predominant French influence along the East African coast began to wane following British occupation of the Seychelles and Ile de France in 1810. There was no lessening, however, of the slave trade to these former French possessions in the Indian Ocean. At this date the slave population in Ile de France still stood at 60,000, and in the Seychelles at 2500.[62] The Abolition Act of 1807 was not registered in the courts of Mauritius, nor published in the local Gazette when Britain took over that colony. This omission, and the fact that the capitulation terms of 1810 secured for the inhabitants of Mauritius inviolability of their laws and customs, was interpreted by them as assuring the continuation of the slave trade. The matter was not righted until 1813, when the 1807 act was extended to Mauritius. But in the interval the slave trade prospered; and received an added boost when, following surrender to the British at Tamatave, on the east coast of Madagascar, French planters there were allowed to bring their slaves to Mauritius.

The Treaty of Paris in 1814 left Ile de France (Mauritius) and its dependencies (the Seychelles and former French ports in Madagascar) in British hands, but restored Bourbon to France. Slave smuggling into the latter island continued despite legislation against the slave trade by the French government.[63] The force of this legislation was weakened by the mild penalties for its violation, and by the French government stoutly refusing to grant to other powers right of search over vessels flying the French flag. Apart from a spurt of vigour in 1818-19, when eight French ships were brought to Bourbon for adjudication, the French evinced little concern at the slave trade at Bourbon. When Castlereagh addressed the French government in the matter in July 1818, quick rejoinders came. Were the British not aware that their own vessels were involved in the trade, and that recently 'un bâtiment anglais' had been caught transporting slaves to Bourbon? And that at Mauritius, now a British colony, 4,000 slaves had been landed in less than a year, apparently with the acquiescence of its Governor![64]

Sir Robert Farquhar, Governor of Mauritius, an official of the East India Company, like many British officials with long experience in the East whose finer perceptions as to the iniquity of the slave trade had become somewhat blurred, did not see eye to eye with humanitarians and abolitionists at home, and could not get excited about an anti-slave trade campaign. He was also absorbed at the time in a plan to make Madagascar a British possession, and in inducing planters from Mauritius to settle there. It was only after the French successfully resisted Farquhar's designs on Madagascar, and sustained their claim to ports there, on the grounds that these had not been specifically referred to in the Treaty of Paris, that Farquhar concentrated on affairs in Mauritius.[65]

The slave trade at Mauritius was carried on by desultory smuggling rather than by open-scale methods. Slave vessels lay ashore, landed their slaves at night in fishermens' boats and by raft, while lookouts on shore turned a blind eye to their operations. Farquhar, sympathetic to the needs of the Mauritian planters, half-heartedly supported an anti-slave trade campaign. It was only when government and public pressure at home became overwhelming that he took more stringent measures against the slave trade. It was to this end that he turned to Radama, chief of the Hova tribe in Madagascar, a shrewd and enterprising ruler, well in touch with the outside world, and desirous for its plaudits and to be considered as an enlightened ruler. His father had been one of the largest slave-holders in the island; Radama would reverse this position. He fell in line with British wishes. By a treaty of October 1817, he decreed

> the entire cessation and extinction, through all the dominions of King Radama and wherever his influence can extend, of the sale or transfer of slaves or other persons whatever, to be removed from off the soil of Madagascar into any other country, island or dominion of any other place, potentate or power.

An English agent was to reside at Radama's court to see that the

THE SOUTHERN SLAVE TRADE 29

treaty was observed. Radama was to receive from Britain an annual subsidy of £2000 and military goods.[66] There was thus initiated at Radama's court a British military and (following the introduction of the London Missionary Society in 1827) Protestant tradition, lasting well into the late nineteenth century. In the same year Farquhar made a similar agreement with the King of Johanna in the Comoro islands. And in 1818 the export of arms and gunpowder from Mauritius into Madagascar was prohibited so as to check intertribal warfare and slavery. In 1819 Governor Milius of Bourbon, in consequence of Farquhar's prompting, prohibited the export of horses for slave-raiding cavalry in Madagascar, and Milius would have gone farther than even his own government in meeting British requests for right of search over vessels flying the French flag.[67] In a further spate of activity against the slave trade, as though to make up for his former lethargy, Farquhar renewed in 1820 the 1817 treaty with Radama, sent an agent to the island of Rodrigues to check on a notorious slavers' nest there, and in 1823, as a result of another treaty with Radama, acquired for British cruisers the right to seize slave ships in Madagascar waters.[68]

But these measures failed to halt the smuggling of slaves into Mauritius. The Black River area on the west side of the island was a favourite spot for their disembarkation. European vessels were involved in the trade; the *Industry* and *Coureur*, under French colours, were captured in 1821, and the notorious brig, *Brazileno*, under Spanish colours, evaded capture until the mid-nineteenth century.[69] This illicit trade maintained the slave population of Mauritius at almost full strength, and in the Seychelles enabled it to increase during the 1820s. The lucrative and developing cotton industry in the Seychelles depended on slave labour. Vessels lying up there during the hurricane season covered their losses during their enforced stay at the Seychelles by carrying on a shuttle service in small numbers of slaves between the islands. So abundantly supplied with slaves were the Seychelles that, during the great cholera epidemic of 1819-20 which decimated the slave population in Mauritius, many slaves were shipped from the Seychelles to make up the losses in Mauritius.

The attempt to maintain a vigilant and effective blockade of Mauritius against the slave trade was weakened by the hurricane season, when the British naval patrol withdrew to the north.[70] The loss of HMS *Delight* in the hurricane of 1824, owing to an inability to close her hatches on the large number of slaves taken on board from a captured slaver, was an unusual episode, but appears to have confirmed the Navy in the wisdom of withdrawing from Mauritius during the hurricane season. But slavers disregarded the hurricane danger, and made the most of the unguarded sea lanes; and when, in 1825, Mauritius sugar, long at a disadvantage in the British market, was placed on an equal footing as regards duty with that from the British West Indies (largely as a result of Farquhar's work as Member of Parliament following his retirement to England), sugar production in Mauritius received a boost, and with it an increased demand for slaves. Their numbers stood at 76,000 in Mauritius in 1825, a slight drop only from the figure of 80,000 in 1819. In a debate in the House of Commons in 1826 it was pointed out that in the previous year ten times as many slaves had been detected and freed in Mauritius than in all other British colonies combined.[71] Mauritius, along with Zanzibar, was the great slave-holding emporium of the Indian Ocean.

The Anti-Slavery Society was assiduous in its attack on the institution of slavery in Mauritius, and the British West Indies sugar interests, from less worthy motives, accused their competitors of unfair advantage in using slave labour. Pressure from humanitarian groups and abolitionists resulted in the appointment of a Commission, the so-called *Eastern Inquiry,* under Major Colebrooke to report on the slave trade in Mauritius.

The immediate result of its inquiries was the passing of an Ordinance for the Protection of Slaves in Mauritius; and in its report (June 1829) the slave trade in Mauritius was scathingly denounced.[72] Cargoes of young men and women 'usually in the proportion of one female to three males' were openly landed in Mauritius, and there had been 'extraordinary attempts to escape before quitting Africa', despite being chained together on board ship. Small pox and overcrowding on slave vessels caused great mortality among slaves. And in Mauritius, when landed from crowded vessels, they were ranged in warehouses, with price labels suspended from their necks. It was all too reminiscent of the worst days of slavery in the British West Indies, and more reprehensible in that it was in open defiance of anti-slave trade laws. The *Eastern Inquiry* recommended immediate abolition of slavery in Mauritius. The majority of slaves were held there illegally anyway, in that they had been imported after 1813, at which date the slave trade had been declared illegal. The Inquiry recommended the appointment of consuls at Zanzibar, Réunion and Madagascar, to keep watch on the slave trade, and expressed a pious hope that 'right of search' would be conceded by all powers.

The *Eastern Inquiry's* recommendations, especially that of immediate abolition, raised a storm of protest among the planters of Mauritius. Abolition, they claimed, would ruin the island, economically and socially. In England, Farquhar, stung by the 'sneering and insolent remarks on the tenderness of my early friendship for the slave trade', challenged the Anti-Slavery Society's statement that female prisoners in Mauritius were whipped in public, and worked in chains. The Commissioners, said Farquhar, had craftily 'strung together isolated incidents over the island for a period of 18 years' to make an artificial case against himself and the planters.

In the face of the *Inquiry's* assault, the planters sent off a deputation to London to argue their case against abolition, and failing that to obtain adequate compensation for loss of their slaves. Despite tenacious defence of their interests the deputation was unsuccessful in staving off abolition. But it won the case for compensation. The two million pounds paid for loss of their 70,000 slaves under the decree of 1834 was sufficient to underwrite the prosperity of the sugar industry in Mauritius.[73]

An alternative source of labour had now to be found. Temporary recourse had already been made to India in 1834, and the planters increasingly looked in that direction for a permanent labour supply. Under arrangements made with the Indian government in 1842, recruitment was placed on a regular basis, and by 1856 60,000 Indians had been transported to Mauritius. On arrival there they were contracted out for a period of five years, at a wage of five rupees per month, and with rations of rice and ghee included. On expiry of their contract they might remain in Mauritius for a further term of employment, in which case they might choose their own master.[74] In these arrangements of the 1840s lies the explanation of the predominating Indian population in Mauritius today, and also the explanation of the peaceful transition from slavery to post-slavery conditions, more successfully achieved in Mauritius than in perhaps any other part of the British Empire in the nineteenth century.

In the nearby French colony of Réunion (formerly Bourbon), the monopoly accorded to its sugar in the French market and the development of a prosperous vanilla industry, maintained a keen demand for labour, and a continuing slave trade to meet it. There was no unremitting pressure from humanitarians in France, as was the case in Britain. And the small French anti-slave trade patrol based on Réunion rarely bestirred itself.[75] French officials never fully addressed themselves to the task of suppressing the slave trade. The Frenchman, Guillain, marvelled at the sustained zeal of the British in pursuing this thankless cause, and they did so not from any 'Machiavellian egoism of which that great nation is accused'.

Although not completely disassociated from desire for material gain,
> one must none the less acknowledge an incontestable merit, a manifest greatness, in a people which, as one whole body, government and governed alike, is passionately bent on redressing the social crime of Slavery, and pours out its money, its ships, and its sailors and involves itself, day after day, in quarrelling and bloodshed in order to achieve its noble mission.[76]

Guillain failed to detect these qualities in his own countrymen.

Their slavers openly resorted to Port Louis for repairs, and in their search for slaves pressed the Sultan of Zanzibar for bases on the northern portion of his East African coastline. Failing to get these, they challenged his sovereignty over the island of Nossi Bé which he claimed under a treaty with Queen Seneeko of Madagascar, and ran up the French flag there. And they continued to run 2000 slaves a month into Réunion during the 1820s.[77] Hamerton, British consul, arriving at Zanzibar in 1841, noted the activity of the French there in obtaining slaves.[78]

But the planters of Réunion, like those of Mauritius, were facing changing times. French anti-slavery societies, inspirited by the example of their English contemporaries, were turning to the attack.[79] And planters on Réunion were beginning to look to an alternative source of labour, and one less open to vilification than the slave trade. There thus grew up the so-called *free labour* or *engagé* system. Its origins lie in a convention signed by France with the Sultan of Oman in April 1841, whereby recruitment of labourers from his African dominions was permitted.[80] Following an Act of May 1849, decreeing emancipation of slaves throughout French dominions, and a refusal by the British to the recruitment of coolies from India, the French *engagé* trade developed on a regular basis. It became a substantial branch of French commerce in the Indian Ocean.

Africans from the mainland, Madagascar and Zanzibar were now brought to the coast, crammed in barracoons, held until arrival of a French vessel, hauled aboard, and asked if they were willing to serve as workers in Réunion or the Comoros for five years. Their reply, usually in the affirmative, was a mere formality. Their fate was already sealed.[81] French, Arab, and American vessels were involved in the trade. Those of Regis and Company of Marseilles in two years landed over 25,000 labourers on Réunion. When the Sultan of Zanzibar, despite an attempt by Admiral de Hell and the French consul at Zanzibar to make him change his mind, refused recruitment of *libres engagés* from Zanzibar (he received no duty on their export), the French resorted to the eastern, and uninhabited, side of that island. Hamerton's protests, and representations by Britain to France in the matter, brought an order from the Governor of Réunion for 'a stop to every undertaking having for its object the indirect trade in negroes'.[82]

But the order was ignored. Arab slavers were not bound by it, and they were increasingly turning to this new and profitable branch of commerce. At Lindi, Arab slavers a few miles inland held slaves in readiness, awaiting the arrival of and signal from a French buyer at the coast. The shipping of *engagés* was pursued under a veneer of respectability, for the French were meticulous in maintaining certain formalities and in seeing that a French official presided over transactions. It was a lucrative business. A slave obtained on the mainland for eight to ten dollars, manumitted at Johanna for 30 to 40 dollars, could be re-engaged as a contract labourer, and disposed of on Réunion for 80 to 120 dollars. The short sea journey lessened the risk of apprehension, and the apparent respectability of the trade made it an attractive proposition for those not quite steeled to the risk of the raw slave trade at sea.

High profits led to overcrowding in vessels, many times the usual number of persons being carried. A small dhow captured off Madagascar with 272 African labourers on board was equipped to carry less than half that number. The French steamer, *Mascareignes*, in three trips carried 1300 labourers to Réunion; her normal cargo was 150 persons. The French barque *Aurélie* carried 200 Africans to Réunion; her normal list was one-third of this number.[83]

Portuguese officials connived at the trade. The governor of Mozambique provided 250 labourers for the French ship *Laura* in 1856;[84] in the same year, as a result of local famine at Quelimane, 1500 *colonos* were shipped from there as free labourers to Réunion.[85] Portuguese authorities, in 1855 and 1856, decreed the prohibition of the *engagé* system in their territory. But sorry results followed. In 1857 the vigorous governor, de Almeida, siezed a French barque, the *Charles et George,* with 110 Africans on board. The vessel was condemned and her captain punished. There was an immediate outcry from France. The vessel was ordered to be released. The Portuguese refused. A diplomatic crisis ensued, and in October 1858 two French warships entered the Tagus river in Portugal. English support failed to materialize. And Portugal freed the *Charles et George.* It was a costly lesson, and henceforth the Portuguese were wary about interfering with the contract labour system.

Following the *Charles et George* incident, French officials were more stringent in their control over recruitment of engagés. But their impressment continued, as Livingstone observed in 1860, when at Johanna in the Comoros he witnessed the escape of one of these 'free' labourers from the *Mazurka*, a vessel which under French supervision had recently collected them from Kilwa. And in 1858, the French pressed the Sultan of Johanna to permit the erection of a reception depot there for African labourers, with a residence for a French officer to preside over their shipment to Réunion. Despite a 2000-dollar inducement, and the promise of five dollars for every labourer collected, the Sultan remained true to his treaty with Britain.[86]

The French then resorted to Madagascar for their labourers. The British cruiser, *Castor*, visiting there in late 1858, reported French vessels picking up 'free' labourers from local chiefs, at the rate of 3 muskets or 3 kegs of gun powder per man. One chief was supplying 1800 labourers annually under this arrangement. And Colonel Rigby, British consul at Zanzibar, on arrival there in 1858

> found a most active slave trade carried on at Zanzibar itself, and along the coast by French vessels . . . the French vessels went escorted by French men-of-war, and slaves were taken to Réunion and Mayotta . . . There is a French ship here now full of slaves, they all wear a wooden ticket round the neck . . . they pretend that it is not a slave trade, that the negroes are only engaged to serve for a term of years and go willing . . . On reaching the deck of the French ship the ceremony of engaging the slaves as 'free labourers' is gone through by an Arab interpreter, who asks them in the presence of the delegate (a French official) whether they voluntarily engage to serve for five years at Réunion. The interpreter assures the delegate that the slave is willing to become a 'free labourer' at Réunion in every instance. The Delegate cannot speak the native language and does not know what question the slave is asked, nor the nature of his reply, but being assured by the Arab that the slave is willing to go to Réunion, the French delegate is satisfied.[87]

Rigby's efforts to end the *engagé* trade in Zanzibar brought severe recriminations from the French. They insisted that it had nothing to do with the slave trade, and claimed immunity from search and interference for their vessels in the Sultan's ports, under an 1834 agreement with the ruler of Muscat. Strong remonstrances from the British over the *engagé* trade, however, came to the notice of Napoleon III, and he, ever sensitive to human suffering, took action.[88] In 1859 the *engagé* trade was abolished. But in June 1860, in consequence of the 'want of labourers in Réunion', it was renewed with a stipulation that *engagés* must be carried only in vessels under French officers, and that a five-dollar fee for certification as 'free' men, and 30 dollars for engagement for each man, must be paid at point of shipment. French officers were to take scrupulous care that only 'free men' were exported.

Under these arrangements 10,000 Africans were exported from the East African coast between Kilwa and Cape Delgado in 1860; and from Quelimane, in 1861, a Portuguese dealer shipped 4,000 free labourers to Réunion. At Ibo, a few hundred slaves were usually to be found crowded in the old fort, awaiting the arrival of a French vessel.[89] During the early 1860s a French brig, the *Caridat,* was on station in the Mozambique Channel to tender to French vessels seeking *engagés.*[90] *Engagés* themselves were under no illusion as to their status; those who escaped 'preferred death to remaining'.[91]

When, in 1856, Britain permitted recruitment by the French of labourers from British India, and the French government announced stringent measures to control the *engagé* trade, it was expected that it would lessen. But evidence before the Select Committee on the Slave Trade, 1871, showed that it still persisted at Quelimane and Mohilla. The main culprits were now the Arabs, and captures made by the British naval patrol showed the elaborate preparations they were taking to pursue it. The dhow *Salamanti* captured off the Comoros in 1866 was well stocked with betel-nut, rice, corn, arms and ammunition; she carried double the number of persons permitted under a pass issued by the British consul at Zanzibar; and she possessed three flags. One of them was French.

In this unorthodox and final phase of the slave trade to the French colonies, old familiar ruses were employed to evade capture. Craft were run ashore at Madagascar to avoid seizure, the French flag was used to give immunity from search and capture, and slaves were translated into *engagés*, usually under the guise of a grant of freedom. In Madagascar well-to-do classes continued to purchase their slaves from Arabs who brought them across the Mozambique Channel. The run could be made in three to four days, and slaves were landed on one of the many fine bays on the northwest side of Madagascar. One or two such crossings could be made in the interval between the northeast and southwest monsoon, and the trade developed into a regular pattern, as a lucrative side-line for Arabs who came down from Arabia, unloaded their wares at Zanzibar, arranged for next season's supply of slaves, then proceeded to the Mozambique Channel, usually in late December when the prevailing winds were westerly and the British naval patrol was far to the north. They could then run across the Channel unmolested, before their return northwards to Zanzibar. Slaves purchased on the African side of the Channel at seven to 20 dollars apiece could be sold in Madagascar for 28 to 30 dollars.[92] At Maintyrana, on the northwest side of Madagascar, where a settlement of 500 Arabs made the slave trade their main business, 2000 slaves were landed in one year, 1869. The town was approached by a secret water passage, navigable only at high tide, through which slaves could be run unseen.[93]

Arab involvement in the slave trade at Madagascar was reported by Commander Parr, who visited the Portuguese coast in October 1864. He found numerous parties of slaves held on shore, awaiting arrival of Arab dhows to carry them across to Madagascar.[94] The Sultan of Johanna, in the Comoros, no longer true to his treaty engagements with the British, was permitting slave dhows to land there. The Sultan of Zanzibar was sharing in the profitable trade; a dhow belonging to him, and carrying 75 slaves, was captured by HMS *Columbine* in November 1871. The slaves, purchased in Mozambique for 16 to 20 dollars apiece, were to be landed in driblets on the Madagascar coast, between Cape Amber and St. Andrew.

Sir Bartle Frere, visiting Madagascar in 1873, estimated that up to ten thousand slaves annually were still landed there by Arab slavers. Queen Ranavolana II's proclamation against the slave trade had small effect in Madagascar. It was not until the French government decreed the abolition of slavery in Madagascar, as from June 1896, that the smuggling of slaves into that island ceased. But so strongly did the tradition of slavery linger on in Madagascar that even after that date, when ex-slaves became numerous and troublesome, it was found convenient to declare them vagabonds, and thus force them to labour on public works.

3
The Northern Slave Trade Based on Zanzibar

Little is known of the nature of Omani rule on the East African coast during the eighteenth century following the withdrawal of the Portuguese.[1] There were perhaps few continental shorelines so removed from the main currents of European activity, apart from the few French slavers resorting there. The coast had few physical attractions, no great rivers giving easy and quick access to the interior, and stories of savage tribes inland frightened off the more timorous. The coast scarcely figured in the colonial rivalry of the great powers. It remained a backwater, only faintly disturbed before the Napoleonic wars.

That the local Swahili were restive under Omani rule is evident from their exodus to Mafia, and from letters to Goa from the Sultan and notables of Kilwa, pleading for the return of the Portuguese as preferable to the Omani.[2] But the Swahili gradually settled down under their new masters, filled local offices as that of Jumbe, and merged with the Omani community. A shift in importance of towns along the coast took place. Pate became dominant in the Lamu archipelago, Malindi and Mombasa, once key points under Portuguese rule, now declined into relative obscurity, but Kilwa acquired a new importance as the centre for a vigorous slave export.

There is little evidence of British contact with the East African coast during this period. Captain Lancaster (later Sir James, and director of the East India Company) of the *Edward Bonaventure,* which remained at Zanzibar for three months in 1581, undergoing repairs and provisioning, had recommended the island

> [for the goodness of the harbour and watering and plentiful refreshing with fish and sending sorts of fruits of the country, as cocos, and others, which are brought us by the Moores as also for the oxen and hennes, is carefully to be sought for by our ships, as shall hereafter pass that way.][3]

But few British ships resorted there over the next two centuries.[4] East India Company ships tended to strike northeast at about the latitude of the Comoro islands after rounding the Cape. There was little inducement to run up to Zanzibar, in the face of an adverse wind, or at the expense of lengthening the journey to India. And English slavers had ample business on the west coast without resorting to East Africa for slaves, and facing the long haul around the Cape. A change is discernible at the end of the eighteenth century. The Napoleonic wars, renewed French diplomacy in the Middle East, the invasion of Egypt, the real or imagined threat to India, all brought need for more accurate information on East Africa. Alexander Dalrymple (cartographer to the East India Company) in his *General Collection of Nautical Publications 1772,* had summed up information to date on the East African coast, and this was now supplemented by information gained from Commodore Blankett's voyage of 1798-1799, and incorporated in the India Directory of 1809.[5] Austin Bissell, first lieutenant on the *Daedalus* under Blankett, who published an account of the voyage in 1806, noted that 'There had not been an English ship in Zanzibar within the memory of the oldest inhabitant', and that an active slave trade was carried on there by the French, and many Zanzibarians spoke French as a consequence.[6]

That Zanzibar was an active slave trade centre was also attested to by M. Dallons, who visited there in 1799, and noted that its revenue depended largely on the export tax on slaves. A slave market flourished in the town, and slaves were disposed of 'amid the shouts of public auctioneers'.[7] Captain Smee and Lieutenant Hardy, in the *Ternate* and *Sylph*, who visited Zanzibar in 1811, also observed the slave trade there. The governor, Yacout, an able and rapacious eunuch, with a 'ruling passion for power', received ten dollars for every slave he sold to the French. The revenue of Zanzibar, 60,000 dollars per annum, was largely derived from the slave trade. Out of the island's total population, estimated by Smee at 200,000, three-fourths were slaves. Between six and ten thousand slaves annually were shipped to the Middle East countries. The slave market was the centre of the town's activity.[8]

These reports on the slave trade at Zanzibar awakened little interest in Britain at a time when the overriding concern was the war with France. Correspondence however took place between the Bombay government and Said of Muscat in 1812 and 1815, over the matter of his subjects carrying slaves to British India, and on the depredations of pirates and slaves in the Persian Gulf. In 1820, in an attempt to check the latter, treaties were made with the principal sheikhs of the 'Pirate Coast'.[9] But the naval squadron of the Bombay Marine (the East India Company's navy), to which was assigned the task of implementing these treaties, noted that the main culprits in bringing slaves into the Gulf were the Omani Arabs, who were not covered by the treaties, and who, in Zanzibar, were selling slaves to the Portuguese and French, and feeding the illicit slave trade in Mauritius.

The African Institution drew attention to this in March 1821, when it requested the East India Company 'to interpose their powerful mediation with the Imam of Muscat for the entire abolition of the slave trade at Zanzibar'. The Company, in reply, affirmed its 'most cordial concurrence in the benevolent views entertained by the members of the Institution'.[10] In the same year the Governor-General of India, Lord Hastings, consulted with Governor Farquhar of Mauritius in the matter. The connection between the slave trade in Mauritius and the role of the Omani Arabs in Zanzibar was now clear. Rumours reached Farquhar in early 1821 that the French had recently deployed twenty-four slave vessels fully fitted out by a Nantes firm for slaving in East African waters, and plans were under way to set up a slave depot on the small island of Providence, between Madagascar and the Seychelles. To check on these rumours, Farquhar deputed Captain Fairfax Moresby, of HMS *Menai*, to cruise between Madagascar and Zanzibar in 1821. Moresby reported that the proposed base at Providence had not materialized, but there was ample evidence of a brisk slave trade by the French at Zanzibar. Eight ships under French or Arab colours had sailed from there within a three-week period, each carrying from 200 to 400 slaves. The French brig, *Le Succes*, 'a most beautiful vessel', captured by Moresby, had 340 slaves on board, and there were 20,000 more awaiting sale in Zanzibar. French agents now looked to that island as the slave market of the morrow.[11]

British officials were also concerned over the northern Arab slave trade with British India. Its origins were ancient, for the same monsoon which carried East African slaves to the Middle East also took them to India. The trade was small, and references to it scattered, such as 430 *black* boys reported to be in Bombay at the end of the eighteenth century,[12] that the Third Ceylon Regiment, in 1811, had 800 Africans in its ranks (they had been purchased at Goa at 30 dollars apiece, and then inducted into the regiment), and an official report in 1812 that Arab slavers brought in about 100 slaves annually to Calcutta. A statement in the *Calcutta Journal* in 1823 claimed that Calcutta was a mart where Africans were sold to the highest bidder, and 150 eunuchs had been brought there in the current season by Arab slavers.[13] In Bombay African slaves had long been a familiar sight, for it was the practise from the early nineteenth century to land them there from captured slavers, and they were subsequently cared for by the Church Missionary Society at Nassick near Bombay. Slaves continued to be imported into Karachi as late as 1842. Thus the slave trade to India was sufficient to be an irritant to humanitarians in India and they sought legislation to end it.[14]

Legislation against the slave trade in India had been enacted in Bombay and Bengal in 1805, 1807, 1811, and 1813,[15] but despite this, smuggling of slaves into India continued. The great act of 1833 which ended slavery elsewhere in British possessions was unfortunately not extended 'to any of the territories in the possession of the East India Company or the island of Ceylon or the island of St. Helena'.[16] Thus, so long as the institution of slavery was permitted in India, efforts would be made to supply that market. It was not until the decree of 1836, forbidding the import of slaves into Sind, Kutch, and Kathiawar, and the abolition of the legal status of slavery by the act of 1843, that the slave trade to India ceased.[17]

To effectively end the Arab slave trade with the French and British India, there was need to strike it at its most vital points: Zanzibar and Muscat. This joint goal might be attained by an approach to Said, ruler of Muscat. Said had emerged as ruler of Oman after the death of Sultan bin Ahmed in 1804, following a disputed succession. He was an able and vigorous ruler, an element of stability in the Arab world. It was to him that the British now looked. The time was propitious for such an approach, for Said was now aware of the dominant role of Britain in the western Indian Ocean. The establishment of a British military base at Perim in 1799, a treaty with the Shah of Persia in 1800, a treaty of amity and commerce with the Sultan of Aden in 1802, and the capture of widespread French possessions in the Indian Ocean in 1810 left no doubt as to with whom primacy of naval power lay.

But it was no easy matter to wean Said from the French. They were well entrenched in the Persian Gulf—their influence there extended back to the early eighteenth century.[18] And although that influence had waxed and waned following the outbreak of the war with England in 1793, France attempted to step it up, and sent various missions to the Middle East. In 1795 a French consulate was established at Muscat. To offset French influence at the Sultan of Oman's court, especially that of a French physician acting as confidential adviser to the Sultan, the East India Company, in October 1798, made a treaty with the Sultan in the form of a maritime alliance which was directed against the French. It provided that 'a person of the French nation' at this court (either the French physician or a French officer on one of his vessels) should be dismissed, and agreed to the occupation of Gombroon by a force of seven to eight hundred sepoys of the East India Company.[19] A British physician shortly replaced his French counterpart in January 1800. In the same month, the treaty of 1798 was renewed with the added provision that an agent of the East India Company be appointed at Muscat.

The French were not quiescent in the face of these British diplomatic gains, but were not very successful in offsetting them. A French official mission under M. de Cavaignac, in 1803, failed to wean the Sultan from the British connection, as did attempts to renew the French friendship with the Sultan in 1804, owing to continued French privateering which affected Muscat shipping as well as that of the British and strained relations with the Sultan. And they remained strained. For a treaty with the French in June 1807 extending to each other 'most favoured nation privileges' in matters of commerce and navigation, and providing for the appointment of French commercial agents in Said's dominions, was restrictive on Omani commerce with British ports, and was resented and ignored by Said's shipping. French privateering also continued up to the surrender of Mauritius to General Abercromby in December 1810.[20] And when the threatened French invasion of India failed to take place following Napoleon's costly Spanish diversion the scales were tipped in Britain's favour. The arrival of a British mission in Muscat in January 1810 was well received.

Said was soon aware of the British desire in the matter of ending the slave trade. In early 1812, the Bombay government informed him of the prohibition of the slave trade in British India, furnished him with a copy of the Bengal regulations of 1811, and requested that he give it publicity throughout his dominions, so that his subjects, 'so much in the habit of frequenting the port of Calcutta', might not incur its penalties.[21] His attention was also drawn to the Arab slave trade in the matter of the Jawasmi pirates in the Persian Gulf. The Jawasmi, the tribes on the southern 'Pirate Coast' of the Persian Gulf (better known today as Trucial Oman), were strung out in a series of scraggy villages on the salt water inlets of the Gulf, unapproachable by British cruisers owing to their shallow waters. These maritime robbers had long preyed on and pirated Omani and British shipping and indulged in the somewhat unusual occupation of hijacking slave cargoes.[22] Various minor expeditions against them had kept them at bay, but their depredations took on new import when, in 1815, a vessel 'with a vast number of slaves on board from Zanzibar to Muscat' was taken by the Jawasmi, and every soul on board 'barbarously put to death'. Sir Evan Nepean, Governor of

Bombay, sent a personal letter to Said, urging him to take steps against the Jawasmi, and to align himself with civilized opinion in the world by interdicting the slave trade carried on by his subjects.[23] This pious exhortation against the slave trade brought no response from Said; he was, however, interested in pursuing joint cause with the British against the Jawasmi.

An effective drive was launched against them in 1819 and by the end of that year their power was broken. By a General Treaty of 1820, they pledged themselves to abstain from the Slave Trade,

> The carrying off of slaves, men, women, or children, from the coasts of Africa or elsewhere and the transporting them in vessels is plunder and piracy; and the Arabs who accept the Peace shall do nothing of this nature.[24]

But the treaty with the Jawasmi did not affect the Omani Arabs, Said's own subjects, who were the main culprits in carrying on the external slave trade from Said's dominions in East Africa. Ending this trade would not interfere with the internal slave trade. Farquhar sought a treaty with Muscat similar to that with Radama of Madagascar. But since the ruler of Oman was 'closely allied in commercial and territorial interests with the English East India Company'[25] it was through this avenue that a treaty might be attained. Thus Farquhar requested Lord Hastings, Governor-General of India, to approach Said to end the slave trade from his 'ports and subordinate dependencies of Zanzibar, Kilwa, and other petty factories on the East Coast of Africa' so that 'this hemisphere would for the future be cleared entirely of that pollution which has stained it from the earliest times'.[26] Hastings was sympathetic. The Governor of Bombay, would make strong representations to end 'this criminal and disgraceful traffic'.[27]

In the autumn of 1821 following further correspondence between Farquhar and Mountstuart Elphinstone (who had succeeded Nepean in 1819), as to the form of a draft treaty, a joint request was made by Mauritius and Bombay to Said for the 'immediate interference' in the operation of the 'external trade', and for the issue of 'peremptory orders' to prevent all dealings in slaves from being carried on by European agents.[28] Thus was instituted the first step in the long-drawn-out campaign which was to last for most of the nineteenth century.

This communication caused Said to ponder gravely. He would lose a substantial portion of his revenue if the external slave trade from his dominions were ended; but the 'legitmate' slave trade might be increased, and he needed British support in his struggle against

THE NORTHERN SLAVE TRADE 43

the Wahabi and the Jawasmi. He was aware that he was principally indebted to Britain for his political existence. There were solid advantages for himself and his subjects in their commerce with British possessions in the East. In December 1821 he had sent a letter to Farquhar requesting that the vessels of his subjects be placed on the same footing in Mauritius as in other British ports to the eastward, and intimated his desire to meet Farquhar as far as possible in his wish to abolish the external slave trade.[29]

Farquhar and Elphinstone congratulated Said on his enlightened attitude. His fame, humanity and generosity would be widely spread among the Nations of Europe, and his Nation would thus 'yield to none in the early adoption of those principles of honour, justice and humanity which have been recognized by the Sovereigns of Europe as the grounds of the annihilation of the Slave Trade'.[30] Captain William Bruce, British Resident in the Persian Gulf, visited him in February 1822. He was 'peculiarly distressed' in that, although he was most anxious to meet British wishes in the matter, he could not do so as freely as he wished, as it 'affected his subjects in a religious point of view'. However he had issued the 'most positive instructions to his lieutenants at Zanzibar and the other ports on the African coast hereafter not to allow slaves to be sold to French, Portuguese and American vessels or to any Christian people whatever.'[31] This prohibition cost him an annual loss in duty on slaves of forty to fifty thousand dollars.

These *pourparlers* and tentative agreements by Said were confirmed when, in the early summer of 1822, Farquhar instructed Captain Moresby to proceed to Muscat to conclude a convention with the Imam on the lines already drafted. The British government did not wish to

> innovate on religious practices or observances relative to Slavery, recognized and encouraged by the Mahometan faith, nor the practice of Slavery or the disposal of slaves in his own dominions. It is the slave traffic alone for exportation which it is our object to annihilate.[32]

The East India Company might possibly 'find a mode of remunerating the Imam, for the "considerable defalcation" in his revenues', but Farquhar warned Moresby on no account to commit the Government of Mauritius to any expenditure not previously sanctioned from home.[33]

Moresby was an enthusiastic emissary whose 'generous and indefatigable exertions for the suppression of the Slave Trade on the eastern side of Africa' won an encomium from the great liberator Wilberforce himself... 'When you return, I hope you will allow me the pleasure of paying my personal respects to you'.[34] And just as the treaty with Radama was the best preventative in that hitherto great mart for slaves, so also if he could succeed in the mission to Muscat, 'more will be effected than has been done since the existence of the Abolition Acts'.[35]

The treaty to which Said assented on 8 September 1822, along with supplementary articles a few days later, prohibited 'all external traffic in slaves' from his dominions and dependencies, and the sale of slaves by any of his subjects 'to Christians of every description'. Violation of these engagements by Omani Arabs would result in seizure and confiscation of their ships, and punishment of their owners and officers as pirates. Such ships might also be seized by British cruisers, if found south of Cape Delgado, 'His Highness' most southern possession in Africa', or to the east of a line drawn therefrom to a point sixty miles east of Socotra, and from thence to Diu Head at the western end of the Gulf of Cambay on the west coast of India 'even though bound for Madagascar', unless driven east of that line by stress of weather, or carrying satisfactory papers certifying point of departure and destination.[36] Provision was made in the treaty for appointment of a British agent in Said's dominions 'to have intelligence of sale of slaves to Christians'.

The Moresby Treaty fell far short of complete abolition, but it was a surprising achievement in the light of slow progress made later in the nineteenth century to end the East African slave trade, and in that it was a direct blow to Said's revenue, diminishing it, according to Hamerton, British consul at Zanzibar, by 100,000 crowns (about £11,250).[37] Said gained, however, in that his territorial claims to the East African coast were indirectly recognized by the treaty. It referred to his 'overlordship' in East Africa, his 'dependencies' as far south as Cape Delgado, and his Governors there. Omani merchant ships were now treated in the ports of British India on the same footing as British ships.

The Moresby Treaty initiated a campaign against the East African slave trade which, in its linear-like progress throughout the nineteenth century, is a classic example of that state of affairs, praised by positivist historians, wherein 'things got gradually better and better'. In channelling the slave trade within legally defined limits, much light was thrown on its wider dimensions and character. The scale of this was only now comprehended by the British government and concerned persons, official and unofficial. But paring down and cutting off the branches of the slave trade with Christians and British India left the main trunk, the slave trade with the Middle East, renewed and invigorated. For the banning of the slave trade with Christian nations, despite the resounding article in the Moresby Treaty, was not so important as might first appear, for it was already being slowly brought to an end.

Nevertheless, in curtailing the slave trade to India, by laying down a corridor the lines of which, as cartographically drawn, were placed far too generously to the eastward, and had subsequently to be redrawn, the Moresby Treaty was a grand gesture by the British Raj. It threw a three-thousand-mile line across the Indian Ocean, a tight rope across which slavers, Christian and Arab alike, were dared to step; it was self-confident in the extreme, although showing little comprehension of the immense task involved in policing it, and the burden thus cast on the small British anti-slave trade naval patrol. The Moresby Treaty was more likely to be honoured in the breach than in the observance.

Was Said sincere in his intentions to limit the slave trade? Commodore Nourse, Commander at the Cape Station, who visited Zanzibar in HMS *Andromache* in January 1822, remarked that

> the Imam of Muscat had issued the most positive orders forbidding the traffic in slaves with any Christians whatsoever; and from all the intelligence I could obtain those orders had been most strictly attended to by the Governor of Zanzibar.[38]

Lieutenant Boteler and Captain Owen, carrying out a hydrographical survey of the East African coast in 1823-5, found the inhabitants of Pate relying on the protection of the Imam of Muscat under the Moresby treaty; and the Governor of Lamu had published the Imam's orders authorizing seizure of vessels carrying slaves southward of Kilwa and Cape Delgado.[39] But Owen was not optimistic. The Sultan had exclaimed, when Owen visited Muscat in December 1823, that 'to put down the Slave Trade with Mahometans . . . was a stone too heavy for him to lift without some strong hand to help him'.[40] And the Sultan's 'power and purse' were upheld by this infamous commerce,

> his soldiers and his servants are supplied by it, and the Red Sea and Persia and some parts of North India pay him immense sums annually for slaves to be cut for the seraglios and other faithful services for which those from the East Coast are held in the highest esteem.[41]

The Moresby Treaty, by channelling the slave trade with the Middle East, intensified it, and gave its main nodal points, Zanzibar to the south and Muscat to the north, a new significance. Said's transference of his court to Zanzibar in 1833 brought a new dimension to that island. This move came indirectly as a result of his having to turn his attention to recalcitrant elements in his East

African dominions. Fitful protection from Oman had caused the inhabitants of the East African coast to look to their own defense and government. The Mazrui clan at Mombasa became so contumacious of Said's authority that he determined to bring them to heel. The Mazrui appealed for protection to the Bombay government in 1823, and then more[42] directly to Captain William Owen of HMS *Leven,* carrying out a survey of the East African coast. Owen looked favourably on this appeal. He was disappointed with the lack of Said's zeal in putting down the slave trade. Control of Mombasa might be able to effect this.

When Owen arrived there in February 1824, he found that its inhabitants had already raised a 'home-made jack'.[43] They now 'unanimously craved permission to place the whole country under the protection of the British nation'. They were informed by Owen that, provided they consented to the abolition of the slave trade, he would forward their proposal to his government for decision, and in the meantime he would hold Mombasa. 'To these conditions they readily assented, made formal cession of their island, Pemba, and the country from Melinda to Panghany'.[44] The British flag was hoisted over Fort Jesus, and Lieutenant Reitz left in charge as Commandant. Owen contemplated similar action at Pemba, Lamu, and Pate, but the hesitation of local chiefs at those places, owing to their fear of Said, deterred him from making this step.[45]

Owen's protectorate over Mombasa was short-lived. It was formally disavowed by the British government, and the British flag lowered there on 26 July 1826. Good relations with the ruler of Muscat were far more important than a little-known harbour on the East African coast. Owen's protectorate also violated the Moresby Treaty of 1822, and complicated Britain's diplomacy vis-a-vis the French in East Africa and the Persian Gulf. But it was a missed opportunity, for Mombasa would have provided a fine base on the East African coast from which to prosecute the anti-slave trade campaign, and a centre for British influence on the coast.[46]

Said moved in to re-assert his authority over Mombasa when the British flag was lowered there. Although resistance was not finally overcome until the 1830s, the episode had brought Said into contact with Zanzibar in 1828.

He was captivated by its charm, beauty of verdure, its serenity, and 'abundance of all good things', a direct contrast to the starkness of Oman. This lush tropical island, 640 square miles in area, 25 miles off the African mainland, with deep protected harbour on its western and leeward side, and lying in the path of the monsoons, giving easy and regular communication with India and countries of the Persian Gulf, was ideally suited to be the capital of an East African dominion. Contemporary accounts of Zanzibar by European visitors attest to Said's discernment.[47] With its soft sea breezes, palm-studded beaches, fresh water, green foliage, tropical fruits and spices, and exceedingly fertile soil, Zanzibar was a virtual Shangri-la, and Pemba, its sister island, some 25 miles to the northeast, half its size, and less well known than Zanzibar, was scarcely less attractive, as its Arab name *al-Hadhra* (Green Isle) would suggest. In addition to its physical attractions, political and commercial advantages also weighed heavily in Zanzibar's favour, as against Muscat. There was freedom from the fierce internecine squabbles which so often wracked dynastic families in Oman, and ended in the rule of the dagger. Commerce was rapidly developing at Zanzibar, American traders were resorting there, the number of Indians in the island was increasing, and with them came business acumen and trading connections. These could be utilized.

By 1832 Said appears to have resolved to fix his residence at Zanzibar, and began to build a palace there, and to lay out clove and rice plantations. And in 1833 he transferred his court to Zanzibar. Henceforth that island, apart from a few visits to Oman in the early years to attend to dynastic matters, was to be his home. Captain Hart, of HMS *Imogene*, visiting Zanzibar in January 1834, noted the brisk development consequent on Said's move to this island, and the Frenchman, M. Guillain, who visited there in 1838, described it as the commercial entrepot of the coast.

With its insular position and convenient distance from the mainland Zanzibar was an ideal holding depot for slaves. They had no avenue of escape here, and their maintenance was cheap. There was a continuing demand for slave labour in the island as well as for overseas export. Two-thirds of Zanzibar's population of 200,000 were slaves; the slave market operated daily, and was one of the sights of the town for visitors to the island. Said's move there had made it the 'Lagos of the East'. He and his family and most of the leading Arabs were soon involved in the slave trade. Their business dealings in it and the support for slavers had caused the latter to extend their transactions ever further inland, so that Arab merchants were established at Tabora some 600 miles from the coast by 1840, and were at Lake Tanganyika by the late 1840s. An Arab trader was at the court of Suna, ruler of Buganda, on the northwest side of Lake Victoria, by 1843. As the slave trade from the interior developed, Bagamoyo on the coast opposite Zanzibar became an outlet for it, thus augmenting the long-standing slave export from Kilwa.

The number of slaves shipped northwards from the Sultan's East African dominions in the nineteenth century is variously estimated. Captain Cogan, of the Indian Navy, who visited Zanzibar in 1838 put the number 'legally' shipped north at 20,000, but estimated that another 10,000 were illicitly run north (that is without paying tax at the Sultan's ports).[48] Hamerton, British consul at Zanzibar, estimated in 1841 that 40,000 slaves were annually imported into Zanzibar, and about 20,000 were shipped north from there. In 1844 he revised these figures, placing the import into Zanzibar at 15,000 to 20,000 annually (as based on customs returns) with an export northwards of about 10,000. But he admitted there were 'vast numbers' imported into Zanzibar on which no duty was paid. The Sultan and family brought over slaves 'as many as 3000 to 4000 at a time', and on these no tax was paid.[49] Hamerton's original estimate that 40,000 slaves were imported into Zanzibar agrees with that of Burton in 1856, and of Rigby in 1858. But since Customs returns can be adduced for the figure of 20,000, this is the number usually put forth as the import of slaves into Zanzibar. The figure of 8000 to 10,000 for slave exports from Zanzibar northwards, as estimated by contemporary observers in Zanzibar, is supported by the estimate of slave imports into the Arabian Sea and Persian Gulf by observers at that end,[50] with about 100 vessels involved in the carrying of slaves.[51]

The slave-importing coast of southern and eastern Arabia extended from the straits of Bab al-Mandab to the head of the Persian Gulf, an overall distance of 3000 miles, with many small ports, Mocha, Mukalla, and Sur,[52] involved in the trade. But it was Muscat, in Oman, on the northeast corner of the Arabian peninsula, which dominated the East African slave trade with Arabia and the Persian Gulf area. Trading in slaves came easily to the Omani Arabs. Forced by the desert character of their country, 'there is not on the face of the earth a more barren-looking coast than Arabia',[53] they had taken to the sea for a living. They were true rovers. They had ranged down the east coast of Africa for centuries. Their capital, Muscat, 'absolutely dependent on commerce for its daily bread',[54] was the nexus of an extensive re-export trade in slaves to points along the Makran coast, to India, and into the Persian Gulf. Through its slave market passed annually some 4000 East African slaves.[55] The social life of Oman was bound up with the institution of slavery. The Imam, Saif bin Sultan, at the end of the seventeenth century had 700 male slaves in his private retinue;[56] and Ahmad bin Said, ruler of Oman in the mid-eighteenth century, had as soldiery East African slaves, 'well-behaved and faithful'.[57] An

THE NORTHERN SLAVE TRADE   49

Italian physician at the royal court in Oman from 1809 to 1814 stated that its revenue of 75,000 dollars was almost entirely drawn from the capitation tax on slave imports.[58] And Brucks, about 1840, estimated that out of Oman's population of 800,000 one-third were black.[59]

During Portuguese times, Muscat had been their main stronghold in the Arabian world. Extensive ruins testified to this former importance. It possessed one of the best harbours in that part of the world. The American, Horace P. Putnam, visiting there in January 1851, with his eyes playing over the vessels of different nations in its harbour reflected

> I don't know of any place that I ever visited that would afford so fine a subject for a painting as the harbour of Muscat. It is almost entirely shut in from the sea. The entrance is very narrow, and the harbour not very large in extent though there could lay at anchor here the whole American navy with perfect security and ease, the water lying deep and the shore bold.[60]

It was the harbour and its strategic coign of vantage which gave Muscat its importance. The town itself, cut off from the interior by a ring of gaunt, red-brown mountains, and lying under a shimmering heat, was a desolate and forbidding scene. On the summit of hills on either side of the harbour cove, divided mid-way by a lookout tower, two lofty forts, *Halali* and *Morani,* connected lesser defence works with the sea. Within the town there were few buildings of architectural merit, apart from the Sultan's palace, El Jereza, a three-storeyed building dating from Portuguese times. The bazaar which occupied the area between the Sultan's palace and the harbour roadstead, was

> knee-deep in mud; and, as neither the sun or the wind can find admission, it remains in that state until the moisture is evaporated by the animal heat arising from the numerous passengers constantly in motion, or the mud carried away upon their feet in cumbrous masses.[61]

There was no organized slave market as at Zanzibar. The sale of slaves was dispersed throughout the bazaar in a series of small squalid squares.[62] It was here that George Keppel witnessed the sale of 'Some twenty or thirty fat little negresses from twelve to fourteen years of age ... giggling and chatting with the utmost nonchalance';[63] and Wellsted noted that the 'Women of Dongola, or Darfur, and the copper beauties of Abyssinia sell for about one hundred and fifty dollars each; the negresses from Zanzibar, or Central Africa, seldom for more than eighty dollars'.[64]

In addition to some 2000 slaves absorbed internally, Muscat was a great dispersal centre for the export of slaves to many parts of the Middle East world. They were sold at small fishing ports, Jask, Chabhar, Pasni, Ormara, along the Makran coast, and were taken into the interior blindfolded, so as to prevent their finding the way back.[65] In Baluchistan, no family of any consideration was without male and female slaves, and 'the greater number of Sidis, or negroes came from Muskat'.[66] This infusion of African blood is discernible today in the population of the Makran coast. A British traveller at the port of Chabhar in the mid-twentieth century remarked

> These people were quite different from the Persians inland; many of them had almost black skins and seemed to come of African stock, with thick lips and broad noses.[67]

Slaves were carried from Muscat to Karachi and Bombay. General Rigby, political agent at Kathiawar, had seen them imported there, and Burton, when in India,

> with that extraordinary linguistic facility for which he was so remarkable, mastered the language of these 'Ceedees', and reduced it to a kind of grammar as a literary curiosity, being ignorant at the time of the origin of these people. His astonishment was great when, on coming to Africa, he found the language to be Swahili.[68]

It was evident by the 1830s that the Moresby Treaty needed tightening up to check the slave trade to India. Another 'maritime truce' with the sheikhs of the Trucial Coast, in 1835, whereby they again bound themselves to refrain from 'piratical pursuits', was reconfirmed in July 1839. More important was the convention with Said, ruler of Oman, on 31 May 1839, renewing the Moresby Treaty; and binding more closely the checks on the slave trade to India by moving the northern terminus of the sea corridor as laid down by the Moresby Treaty and placing it 500 miles to the west, at Pasni on the Makran coast. By the same convention, enslavement of the Somali, they being Muslim and thus *hur* (free), was proclaimed piracy.[69]

These agreements, ambitious in their aims, had little effect. Captain Atkins Hamerton arrived in Zanzibar in May 1841 as British consul and was shocked at the extent of the slave trade prevailing there. The Moresby Treaty and subsequent legislation against the slave trade were openly flouted. Spanish slavers operated off the East African coast. They had recently seized the occupants of two of the Sultan's dhows at Kilwa, and Arab dhows smuggled slaves from the Sultan's dominions into Mozambique and Madagascar. At Zanzibar,

> In no part of the world is the misery and human suffering the

wretched slaves undergo while being brought here, and until they are sold, exceeded in any part of the Universe; they are in such a wretched state from starvation and disease that they are sometimes not considered worth, landing, and are allowed to expire in the boats to save the duty of the dollar a head, and eaten by the dogs, none are buried.[70]

Hamerton's reports coming at about the same time as those of Major W. C. Harris, who had visited Shoa in Ethiopia in 1841 and graphically described the horrors of the slave trade there,[71] made a deep impact on Palmerston's mind. As a result of his prodding, the Foreign Office, in June 1841, raised with the Indian government the question of obtaining a treaty from the Sultan of Zanzibar and Trucial sheikhs to enter into a treaty to abolish the slave trade carried on by their subjects at sea.[72] This would cut them off from the source of their slaves in Africa.

Thus, in his first year at Zanzibar, Hamerton approached Said in the matter. Britain would make him an annual payment of £2000 for three years as compensation for loss of revenue if the slave trade at sea were abolished. Said was affronted. The sum was but a fraction of what he stood to lose. He was also in high dudgeon at the time over seizure in Zanzibar harbour by a British brig of a slave ship owned by one of his subjects. The incident had taken place in sight of Said's palace. A rumour was also current that Hamerton had been sent out to Zanzibar by the British for the sole purpose of ending the slave trade.

Reluctant and difficult to deal with as he was in the matter, Said was shrewd enough to see what most of his subjects could not see, that the slave trade must eventually be curbed, if not ended. He would thus parley in the matter. He would consider a treaty to check the slave trade in return for British support in a venture dear to his heart, the acquisition of the coveted island of Bahrain in the Persian Gulf. In 1842 he sent a delegate to London to discuss the matter. The British were guarded in their response. They would give no promise of such support, and it would be unwise for the Sultan to send an expedition against Bahrein. According to Hamerton, 'His Highness was pleased with the advice', and the matter of Bahrein was dropped.[73]

Said next sought formal recognition from Britain for his claim to the Somali coast south of Guardafui, where the French, under Captain Guillain, were seeking concessions from the local chiefs at Lamu and Barawa.[74] But he was unable to substantiate his claims to that coast, and this too was dropped. When Palmerston continued to press for an end to the slave trade at sea, Said pleaded that if he acceded to British demands his subjects would withdraw their loyalty from him, and support another claimant to the throne.[75] And was he not looked up to by all Arabs generally 'as the person who should protect and guarantee for them their dearest interest—the right to carry on the slave trade?' He reminded Hamerton that Arabs were not 'like the English and other European people who were always reading and writing' and were unable to understand the anti-slavery viewpoint. The British obsession with it was quite inexplicable to them.[76]

However the Sultan would bend if he would not break, and a compromise was arrived at. He agreed to prohibit the export of slaves from his African dominions to Asia, while leaving the slave trade between the various parts of his African dominions unhindered. A treaty to this effect was signed on 2 October 1845, and came into effect on 1 January 1847. It authorized seizure and confiscation by the British of any vessel belonging to His Highness or his subjects carrying on the slave trade . . . 'excepting such only as are engaged in the transport of slaves from one part to another of his dominions in Africa' between the port of Lamu to the north and the port of Kilwa to the south—including the islands of Zanzibar, Pemba, and Mafia.[77] Agreements to similar effect were entered into with the Arabian sheikhs in the Persian Gulf and the Chief of Sohar in the Gulf of Oman, in 1847, and 1849.[78]

In the negotiations leading up to the treaty with Said, he sought immunity from search and seizure for vessels of his subjects bound from the Red Sea or Arabian Sea to his dominions in Africa or Asia. In this sought-for concession lies a veritable exposé of the Arab slave trade. For it was meant to ensure the supply of Abyssinian concubines and eunuchs for Said's dominions. So strongly did he feel in the matter that Said requested Hamerton to obtain the agreement of every nation to non-interference in this aspect of the East African slave trade. In return for this he was prepared to throw in a bonne bouche: a promise that henceforth all dead slaves in Zanzibar would be buried, instead of being left as Hamerton had seen them, 'dead Africans, men and women, lying on the beach and the dogs tearing them to pieces as one sees carrion eaten by the dogs in India'.[79]

Said obtained neither this additional article to the treaty, nor the £2000 annual payment for three years, as originally suggested. For there were to be no more concessions. Palmerston, now at the Foreign Office, was increasingly impatient with these intransigent Arabs; did they not realize that

Great Britain was the chief instrument in the hands of Providence for the accomplishment of this object; that it is useless for these Arabs to oppose what is written in the Book of Fate, that if they persisted in the continuance of this traffic it would involve them in trouble and losses; that they had better therefore submit to the will of Providence, and abandon this traffic, cultivate their soil, and engage in lawful commerce.[80]

Palmerson's adjuration failed to impress Hamerton. There is an increasing note of cynical resignation in his despatches.

> The Sultan has neither officers nor seamen, only five empty ships ... I do not believe he has one officer in his service who would do his duty and carry the Imam's orders fairly into effect if sent upon any service for the suppression of the Slave Trade.[81]
> I assure you for the information of government that no negotiation nor remonstrance of any kind nor on the part of anyone will succeed, with His Highness for the suppression of the Slave Trade in his dominions unless backed by force.[82]

Hamerton instanced the case of the master of a Persian Gulf vessel who openly sought Said's permission to take on slaves in Zanzibar; the applicant was a fool, said Said, for not managing his business without troubling His Highness on the subject.[83] The Sultan's objection to English merchants purchasing ivory and copal on the mainland coast arose from his fear lest they report on the 'immense slave trade carried on there.'[84] But even allowing for these derelictions on the Sultan's part, these agreements of the late 1840s were substantial gains, when it is remembered that they reduced his revenue by 6000 sovereigns annually, and that, as the largest slaveholder in Zanzibar, he had a vested interest in the continuance of the slave trade. When an emissary, a Turkish Arab, arrived in Zanzibar in 1850, claiming to have come from the Sherrif of Mecca to 'remonstrate with the Imam for the injury he had inflicted on the Moslem world' by acquiescence in the British campaign against the slave trade, the Imam, despite this personage being 'an inspired man, a most holy person', told him to go on his way, for he, Said, would do all in his power 'to meet the views of the British government as long as he lived.'[85]

The emissary need not have worried himself. Defects in the so-called 'Hamerton Treaty' were soon revealed. No provision had been made for adjudication of captured slave vessels nor mixed commission courts set up as in previous slave trade treaties. This was rectified by British statute on 15 September 1848,[86] but in the meantime vessels seized for slaving and taken to Bombay had to be released owing to lack of facilities there for adjudication. This omission left a most unfortunate impression with the Arab slavers that the 1845 treaty was impotent. There was confusion as to whether the treaty permitted trade by sea in Abyssinian slaves; Arabs and Said feigned to believe it did, until Palmerston's despatch of September 1848 disabused their minds in the matter.[87] Article II of the 1845 treaty, it was pointed out, clearly forbade Said's subjects to import slaves into his Asiatic dominions from *any part* of Africa.

The gravest weakness in the treaty was that under it slaves could be passed off as domestic servants, as wives of the master and crew (they in turn might be slaves), or decked out in finery and listed as passengers. The dumb passivity of slaves, and the language barrier, hampered efforts to get them to testify and openly declare that they were unwilling passengers.

There was a loophole in the Hamerton treaty in that the coast between Kilwa and Cape Delgado lay outside the limits within which British cruisers had right of search; slaves could be shipped from this section of the coast with impunity. Following a request from Commodore Wyvill, Commander-in-Chief at the Cape, in 1850, the Sultan granted permission to Her Majesty's ships-of-war to seize slave vessels on this section of the coast, and destroy slave barracoons there.[88] In May and June 1850, HMS *Castor* and *Dee* destroyed two large barracoons north of Lindi, each holding 1000 slaves.

The ineffectiveness of Hamerton's treaty was observed by the Reverend J. L. Krapf in 1850, when at Kilwa he saw 'slavers bound for the forbidden Arabia', and in 1861, witnessed 18 large Arab slave dhows leaving that same port, sailing direct for the Persian Gulf with full cargoes.[89] At Zanzibar stealing of slaves was rampant. They were inveigled into houses, or kidnapped on their way to and from the bazaar, and then secreted away. Canoes, lying inshore during daylight hours, silently slipped out to sea at night with slaves for a waiting dhow offshore. Profits were high and certain. A slave purchased at Zanzibar for five to ten dollars could be sold at Muscat for 25 dollars; at Bushire or Basra for 40 dollars; and at Kathiawar for as much as 100 dollars.

It was during this resurgence of the slave trade that there took place the death of both Said and Hamerton. Said's outward goodwill, whatever his inward feelings, had been a powerful asset for the anti-slave trade cause. His death, on 19 October 1856, en route from Oman to Zanzibar, followed by the death of Hamerton on 5 July 1857, marked the end of an era.[90] Hamerton had attained a position of real influence at Said's court . . . 'the Sultan actually trembles for fear of displeasing him lest he bring down the vengeance of the British Government on him'.[91]

The British consulate at Zanzibar remained closed for a year following Hamerton's death, until Colonel Rigby, his successor, arrived in 1858. Rigby had seen African slaves in the slave markets of Bahrain and Cairo, and at Aden and in the Persian Gulf, and he had been curious as to their origin. Now at Zanzibar, he was at the fountain-head of the trade. It permeated all levels of society there. Out of a total population of 250,000 in Zanzibar and Pemba, two-thirds were slaves. Most of the Arabs in Zanzibar, including the Sultan's relatives, appeared to be involved in the slave trade. Letters from Arabs in Muscat to relatives in Zanzibar, which were intercepted, set out details and numbers of slaves to be supplied. Rigby was shocked to discover that the 'old and trusted chief native official of the Consulate was himself a purchaser of slaves', and he states that on his arrival everyone tried to keep him ignorant of the slave trade. But it was soon the dominant issue with which he was faced.

In a long report of 1 July 1860,[92] he set out the position of the slave trade at Zanzibar. In 1859, 19,000 slaves were imported there. But this figure, based on custom house returns, did not include slaves smuggled in, nor those brought in by the Sultan and family duty free. The slave trade had increased almost threefold in the last twenty years. Whereas at the time of Smee's and Owen's visit, vessels took on only a few slaves in addition to normal cargo, they were now making it their sole business, and carrying 100 to 200 slaves at a time. Rigby put the number of vessels involved in the northern slave trade at 150—capable of transporting 10,000 slaves annually. The number of northern Arabs arriving at Zanzibar increased yearly, and their outrages grew bolder. When the Sultan attempted to purchase their forbearance by paying them sums of money, 15,000 to 20,000 dollars as a form of tribute, they used this to invest in additional slaves.[93] In the spring of 1861, they attacked the Sultan's guard, blockaded the American consulate, and went about the town brandishing their swords. Dhows openly loaded slaves in Zanzibar harbour, and rested there unmolested, awaiting winds to take them to Arabia. Arab slavers stole slaves when they could not purchase them, and even the Sultan's slaves were not safe from their depredations.

During the annual visit of the northern Arabs Zanzibar was under a reign of terror. The Sultan discontinued his daily baraza, retired to the upper story of his palace, and his soldiers were afraid to venture out after dark. The situation was temporarily relieved when HMS *Lyra* anchored in Zanzibar harbour; her presence had a wonderfully pacifying effect. 'Al-Shaitan', the Devil, as the Arabs termed her, forced a Somali vessel to unload 140 slaves, and with her guns menaced and deterred Arab dhows from loading slaves in Zanzibar harbour. Rigby was so impressed with this performance, that he requested the presence of a British cruiser at Zanzibar during the slave season every year. But Majid protested that this overstepped the concessions he had already conceded to the British. He himself would establish an effective naval presence in Zanzibar harbour. Great expectations were raised when, in October 1860, in conjunction with his closing the slave markets during the season of the northeast monsoon, he stationed his frigate, *Piedmontese*, at the north end of Zanzibar to prevent slave dhows from proceeding north. The *Piedmontese* later moved down to the narrow channel at the harbour entrance, but she achieved nothing. Meanwhile the slave market opened daily. It was not until the cruiser HMS *London* was assigned to the task in the 1870s that a similar effect to that achieved by the *Lyra* was attained.

Rigby attempted to restrict slave-holding by Indians. Nearly 6000 slaves were in their possession. By an act of 1861, fortunately approved retroactively by the British government, Rigby forbade British Indians, of whom there were 4000 in Zanzibar and Pemba, to possess slaves. These were now freed and given certificates of emancipation.[94] This high-handed action incurred for Rigby the hatred of many wealthy Indians,[95] it caused a glut in slaves in the Zanzibar market, and many of the slaves freed were promptly re-enslaved by the Arabs. Rigby's work was further undone when his successors, Pelly and Playfair, by making a distinction between British 'protected' and British 'subjects', opened the way for renewed slave-holding by Indians in Zanzibar, who were, under the new interpretation, freed from the restraints of British jurisdiction.

During his last few months in Zanzibar Rigby was in ill-health. The Sultan took advantage of this to equivocate and avoid action against the slave trade.[96] The last news to reach Rigby on his departure from Zanzibar on 6 September 1861 was that eighteen large slave dhows with full cargoes had sailed north from Kilwa in the current season. Rigby reckoned that not more than one per cent of the slaves taken north were captured by British cruisers.[97]

Rigby's successors, Lewis Pelly (1861-2) and Robert Playfair (1863-5), pursued a weak anti-slave trade policy. They failed to persuade Majid to take a strong line against the slave trade, and the Arabs were quick to note this lessening in vigour and oscillation in British policy. Dhows were coming down from the north in squadrons of 50 to 60 vessels, 40 to 200 tons each, bringing dried fish, cotton goods and dates, and returning with full cargoes of slaves. The slavers were in league with the local population in Zanzibar and Pemba. The British Consul's interpreter, when he possessed secret information, was perverse in imparting it. According to Commodore Hillyar, 'as a standing rule not an Arab in Zanzibar was to be trusted'.[98] Arab slavers were practically in possession of northern Pemba, the Sultan's governor there was implicated in the slave trade, and no one dared to inform on him.

In May 1865, Playfair reported that for many years past there had not been so many slaves exported from Zanzibar.[99] When Majid was pressed to adhere to the treaties made by his father with the British, he gave lip service to them, but privately accepted slavery as a natural institution, and was loath to act against the wishes of his subjects. At the time of the 'Canning Award' of 1861, the Sultan had nominally agreed to limit the number of slaves entering Zanzibar to agricultural labour requirements there. These were estimated at between 1700 and 4000 slaves annually, but the Sultan insisted that he alone was the judge of these requirements. When Pelly objected that the number of slaves entering Zanzibar was much in excess of agricultural needs, the Sultan claimed that to limit their import would ruin his subjects, and hinder the growing sugar industry in Zanzibar.[100]

Pressure from Pelly and Playfair brought spurts of activity from Majid. In March 1862, he had a number of northern Arabs flogged and imprisoned until the slave season was over. Householders in Zanzibar were forbidden to shelter northern Arabs suspected of kidnapping slaves.[101] In September 1864, his soldiery captured a dhow with 50 slaves in Zanzibar harbour, and the Arab crew were punished. In another encounter the northern Arabs were deprived of 250 slaves. Majid ordered that bona fide transport of slaves between ports in his dominions must be covered by a custom house manifest showing the number of slaves on board a vessel. In October 1863 he forbade the export of slaves from Kilwa during the period of the northeast monsoon, (1 January to 1 May), and on 1 January 1864 this was extended to all ports in his African dominions. Arab dhows violating this prohibition might be seized by British cruisers and taken to Zanzibar for adjudication.

This auspicious display of zeal by Majid was shortlived, and was followed by intransigency and non-co-operation on his part. There was a 'neat bit of Eastern Diplomacy' in his prohibitions. Slaves were not usually shipped from the mainland to Zanzibar during the period of the northeast monsoon, but in these months a great build-up of slaves could take place. The directive forbidding the sheltering of northern Arabs suspected of kidnapping slaves was to prevent the kidnapping of the Sultan's own slaves. As to ferreting out northern Arabs in Zanzibar, this was almost impossible in the warren-like teeming bazaar of the town. And northern Arabs during the slave season usually lived in their dhows beached to the immediate north of Zanzibar town.

Slave vessels in Zanzibar harbour could not be boarded without special permission from the Sultan's officials, and this was never given unless it served the Sultan's interests. Officers of the Royal Navy were reluctant to seize a dhow in the vicinity of Zanzibar and bring it into Zanzibar harbour, for they knew she would probably go free. Procedure on arrival there was that two of the Sultan's officers would be sent on board to investigate. The Arab crew would then swear by the Prophet that the dhow was an honest trader carrying only domestic slaves. She was then usually freed. There were a few exceptions, however, as in the case of a slave dhow brought in by HMS *Wasp* in 1866, where conviction followed largely because valuable lives had been lost by the *Wasp* in overcoming fierce resistance by the Arab crew, and her officers were in no mood to be thwarted.[102] Otherwise it would have been quietly represented as a dhow carrying slaves for domestic purposes.

The Sultan's decrees were personal concessions without force of treaty, and could be enforced or ignored as he chose. And they left open channels in which the slave trade could flourish if certan formalities were observed. During the so-called legal period of the slave trade it was only necessary to pay the requisite tax, obtain a licence giving exemption from detention and capture by British cruisers within the legal limits of the slave trade, and, provided with proper clearances from either Kilwa or Zanzibar for Lamu, the dhow would journey unmolested by British cruisers, except when it was discovered that old and out-dated passes from Zanzibar were used, or it had neither colours nor pass.[103] Slaves could be imported on one pass from Kilwa to Zanzibar, and then forwarded to Lamu on another pass. At Lamu her license ceased, and a dhow proceeded north at her own risk. But her captain, acting on the old proverb 'one may as well be hung for a sheep as a lamb', would take on as many slaves as possible and, ascertaining first by messengers sent north to the Juba river that the coast was clear of British cruisers, would sail northward keeping close to land, ready to run ashore if pursued. The dhow might touch at various points on her way north to obtain rice and water and to fill gaps in slave numbers caused by deaths, and also to ascertain from local intelligence at each stopping place that the coast was clear for the next step north. In 1865, 6000 slaves went under authority of pass to Lamu and other northern ports in the Sultan's East African dominions. But it was assumed that most of these went illegally north to Arabia.[104] And, similarly, south of Kilwa an illegal and active slave trade persisted. On obtaining the necessary pass at Kilwa and paying the tax at the custom house there, slave dhows would slip away to the Portuguese ports, Comoro Islands and Madagascar.

To avoid Majid's prohibitions and the closer watch kept on Zanzibar, slaves were shipped from remote points on the island, as Mkokotoni Bay on the northwest side, and from Pemba. When Playfair visited that island in 1863, he found its many creeks used as hideouts for slave dhows, and there were several barracoons each capable of holding up to 500 slaves. Reefs and shoals off Pemba gave protection against a man-of-war, and slaves were brought over from Zanzibar in small batches and loaded on to dhows lurking off the island, and thence conveyed north. During 1865 and 1866 the *Rapid* and *Wasp* attempted to ferret out the slave trade at Pemba, and approached the hideouts, but the slaves were then hurried into the bush. It was exceedingly difficult to make captures in Pemba waters. The Pemba Channel was hazardous and anchorage dangerous, owing to the strength and direction of the currents and a navigation chart '40 years out of date'.[105]

Henry Adrian Churchill, British Consul at Zanzibar, 1865-70, assumed office at a difficult time. There was renewed slave-holding by Indians and 1200 slaves were again in their possession, owing to the undoing of Rigby's legislation by Pelly and Playfair. Churchill's representations to the Bombay government in the matter brought a discouraging reply. Compensation must be paid to owners if these slaves were freed, and who would pay this—Zanzibar? The matter was quickly dropped.[106] Churchill was also faced with some of the worst brawls by the northern Arabs in Zanzibar town's history. An alarming incursion took place in April 1868, when they arrived in great numbers, armed and vengeful over recent hostile proceedings of British cruisers against Arab slavers in the Persian Gulf, and the escape of the Sultan's sister (who had married a German) from Zanzibar in an English man-of-war.[107] The swaggering Suris became involved in an old blood feud, and twenty persons were hacked to pieces. The people of Zanzibar henceforth were in dread of the annual visitation.

Churchill was faced with the entrenched position of the slave trade, and failing its abolition, he tried to limit its operation from the coast to one point only and then solely for the Sultan's requirements. On 2 September 1867, backed by Commodore Heath, he submitted to the Sultan a plan to make the slave trade the

Sultan's monopoly. It would be under strict inspection, confined to vessels of 'European build', painted a distinctive colour—possibly red—their sails marked with a large black cross. Export of slaves from the mainland would be confined to Dar es Salaam, and import to Zanzibar. Traffic in slaves at sea would be forbidden, and transference between points on the mainland and to Pemba would only be permitted at the Sultan's discretion.

Majid was interested in the plan, and agreed to adopt it on a trial basis for four months. He instructed owners of slave dhows that they should henceforth carry only half their usual number of slaves and that their dhows should carry a distinguishing mark, but he declined to confine their activities to the narrow channel suggested by Churchill. He said this would ruin his country.[108] The trial period scarcely ran the four months' course before the Sultan lost interest in it. He was now absorbed in a much more serious question. His brother, Thwain, in Oman, had been murdered, and Majid was brooding over the need to avenge his brother's death. It was a most inauspicious time to press Majid for further restrictions on the slave trade. Churchill's plan faded out.

In a long report to Lord Stanley from Zanzibar on 21 August 1868, Churchill set out the pattern of the slave trade as it revolved on Zanzibar.[109] About 30,000 slaves, mostly from the Nyasa area, arrived at Kilwa annually. This number represented only about half those originally enslaved, owing to the loss of life during the slave hunt and trek to the coast. At Kilwa slaves were subject to customs duties, the collection of which was in the hands of the Sultan's official, usually an Indian. As from 24 November 1864, the duty on slaves shipped to Zanzibar was raised from one dollar to two dollars a head, with a similar amount for slaves shipped directly to Mombasa, Pemba, and Lamu.[110] Port clearances and passes were given on payment of duty. About two-thirds of the slaves shipped from Kilwa went directly to Zanzibar. The remainder went to the Sultan's northern ports, or were smuggled directly north to the Persian Gulf or across the Mozambique Channel to the Comoro Islands and Madagascar.

The sea journey from the mainland to Zanzibar was the worst ordeal for the slaves. Up to three hundred at a time were crowded into small coastal dhows for the run across to Zanzibar. They were packed between two or three extemporized bamboo decks. 'Often 1000 slaves are stowed into a space hardly capable of receiving as many bags of rice'.[111] The run was usually made across at night when it was cool. But there could be delays; and if extended into the daytime, what was meant to be a short run of ten to twelve hours could be prolonged into an agony of twenty-four hours, owing to want of breeze or adverse currents. The fierce sun would take its toll. The slaves, already weakened by the trek to the coast, died like flies. Bagamoyo marked the last point of contact with the mainland for the slave embarking into an unknown world.

At Zanzibar there were no harbour or pilot dues, and no register kept of dhows. Slaves were discharged much in the manner of a load of sheep,

> the dead ones thrown overboard to drift down with the tide and if in their course they strike the beach and ground, the natives come with a pole and push them from the beach and thus their bodies drift on until another stoppage when they are served in a similar manner[112]

until they finally ended up as poor heaps of corruption. The sick and feeble were frequently left lying on the beach to avoid paying the two-dollar tax on passing them through the custom house for they might die before a sale was made. The living were put over the side in water up to their necks and made to wade ashore to the custom house, where they squatted in a circle, and were fed parched corn and water to their fill. They were then taken to their owner's house, and kept a few days before being taken to the market for sale. And to appear to best advantage there, they were greased with a large profusion of cocoanut oil from head to foot, and covered with a very showy robe.

The Zanzibar slave market, before it was moved to a new site at the end of 1873, occupied a large square, a mile or more from the harbour roadstead, and next to the densely packed bazaar area. On arrival in the market the slaves were made to form a line so the buyer could have a fair view of them.

> The purchaser walks up to one he likes the looks of and throws a stick at some distance and tells the slave to pick it up. By this he has a chance to see his gait or if there is any lameness. He is then taken apart from the rest of the group and examined from head to foot (every part of their body). If the slave is purchased the dress is taken from them and goes for the clothing of some other one. The next day they will appear in a dress like the other slaves of the place walking the streets with nothing but a small piece of cloth around their loins and if fortunate enough a piece over their shoulders. It has been said by some that the Arabs are very cruel to their slaves, but it is quite the reverse. Many of the slaves are sent to school and obtain as good an education as some of the head Arabs of the place.[113]

European visitors to Zanzibar usually made the slave market their first call. Smee, as we have seen, in 1811, described the auction of slaves held twice daily. Ephraim A. Emmerton, visiting Zanzibar in 1848, noted that the slave market was the favourite resort of all classes in Zanzibar: 85 to 100 slaves were on sale there, when he visited it.[114] They were examined as though they were livestock, and appeared to evince little emotion or interest in their fate. Prices were 15 to 20 dollars apiece, with somewhat more for comely females—25 dollars.

Most observers of the slave market experienced a deep shock at the display of human misery on view there, and noted its debasing effect on slave and buyer alike. According to Livingstone, writing on 11 June, 1866,

> This is now almost the only spot in the world where 100 to 300 slaves are daily exposed for sale in open market. This disgraceful scene I several times personally witnessed, and the purchasers were Arabs or Persians, whose dhows lay anchored in the harbour, and these men were daily at their occupation examining the teeth, gait and limbs of the slaves, as openly as horse dealers engage in their business in England.[115]

Colomb on his first visit to the Zanzibar slave market did not see 'violence or rudeness of any kind; neither did I see coarseness or indecency'.[116] Valuable females were kept aside. On his second visit he saw children—some very emaciated, probably the result of the land journey to Kilwa and the harrowing sea voyage across from the mainland to Zanzibar. According to Colomb the scene of human beings penned and sold like cattle created such nausea and disgust that it was dangerous to allow British seamen to land at Zanzibar, for 'the blue jacket is impelled to make a clearance of the place, which he has more than once done on the spur of the moment.'[117]

The most detailed description of the Zanzibar slave market came from Sir Bartle Frere in 1873.

> On entering the market we passed by wooden sheds under which sat, on the left some half-caste Arabs, on the right, some half-clothed negroes. The market was comparatively empty when we arrived at half-past four in the afternoon, so we had a good opportunity of seeing the slaves who were already there. They were seated, in rows round the square, each batch sitting packed close together, and herded by an Arab or Negro (for the Negro seems to forget the miseries he once underwent as a newly-captured slave, or like a schoolboy bullied as a youngster, bullies again when able), who forced into position the luckless wretch who stretched his stiffening limbs beyond the limits allowed him.
> We counted at that time ninety, of all ages, and of both sexes. Many wore a set and wearied look, many were fat and gay, while

two young men and a boy alone confirmed, by their skeleton frames and looks of misery, the sensational tales often written of these markets. The impression left upon the mind at this time, was that the process of sales was not more debasing to the Negro than were the statute-hiring fairs of recent English times to the servant class of England. Most of the slaves were naked, some a clout round the waist of the men and a cloth thrown loosely over the women. I may say 'naked' for one can hardly consider as clothing what some held to be full-dress, viz. the scars and slashes on their faces, and the rings in their ears and noses. Some, however, of the women, chosen probably for some attraction which great doubtless to Zanzibarite eyes were hardly appreciable by Europeans, were gaudily dressed in coloured robes, with short-clipped hair; eyes and eyebrows painted black, and henna-dyed foreheads, while the rings and armlets they wore were heavy and large.

About 5 o'clock the frequenters of the market—the lounge of the true Zanzibarite, strolled quietly in, Arabs and half-caste Persians of the Guard in their long caps, and all armed with matchlock and dagger. At once the salesmen woke up, and all was bustle. And now came a cruel time. With a cruel knowledge of business, the sickliest and most wretched slaves were trotted out first, led round by the hand among the crowd and their price called out.

The price of one boy was seven dollars: he was stripped and examined by a connoiseur, his arms felt, his teeth examined, his eyes looked at, and finally he was rejected.

The examination of the women was still more disgusting. Bloated and henna-dyed old debauches gloated over them, handled them from head to foot before a crowd of lookers-on, like a cowseller, or a horse-dealer, and finally when one was apparently satisfactory, buyer and seller and woman all retired behind the curtain of the shed to play out the final examination.

The prices we heard mentioned, varied from 67 dollars for a woman to 7 dollars for a boy whose case I mentioned. We saw no details actually effected, and were told that the presence of the Mission in Zanzibar had sensibly affected the commerce in slaves as well as in other ordinary articles of trade. This being the closing time, the market was not at its full height though there must have been at least 200 slaves there before we left.

No rudeness was shown to us by anyone, though I have been told that some officers of the squadron now here have been insulted and hissed by the Arabs.

The market place was a far more brutal and degrading sight than I ever saw in Egypt or Arabia, and no description could well do justice to its degradation.[118]

The business of buying and selling of slaves spread from the slave market throughout the town almost by a process of osmosis. It dominated daily transactions, was the subject of conversation, even among slaves themselves, and few classes in Zanzibar, apart from Europeans, were exempt from connection with it.

> For Zanzibar Arabs even of the highest class, the speculation in slaves seems to have the same sort of attraction, which horse-dealing has for an ordinary Yorkshireman. They [the Yorkshiremen] examine and discuss the points, bargain and bid, and, if they purchase an animal they like they keep it till tired and then exchange or sell it.[119]

The lower classes in Zanzibar saw in slaves a safe, easy, and profitable investment. They talked, even when slaves themselves, of investing a windfall of money in a slave or two, just as a native of India would of investing it in a pair of bullocks, or an English servant of putting it in a savings bank. If they could not afford to keep their slave at home, they sent him out to work, and his earnings in turn would be used to purchase another slave. When hired out a slave was paid about one and a half pence per day, of which the master usually took half. A servant receiving four or five dollars a month might possess one or more slaves whom he would hire out. The hiring out of slaves was a popular business with the indolent Arabs, who might then sit back and live on their slaves' earnings.

The passivity of slaves in the face of the tiny Arab minority which held them in thraldom was a cause of surprise to foreign observers. Frere thought the whole business 'exceedingly strange'. For slaves, both individually and collectively, were superior to the Arabs in physical strength, and if they had chosen to rebel might have sent the latter flying out of the land. But they seemed 'spell-bound', not knowing their strength, and also considered it dishonest to run away after being purchased, thus bringing pecuniary loss on their owners.[120]

Rigby, Churchill, Waller, Livingstone, Colomb, and many others, testify that the Arab was not a cruel master. He was less so than a negro master, and, although passionate and hot-tempered, was nothing like the French or Portuguese in their treatment of slaves. The inhuman callousness displayed in the Zanzibar slave market was only a preliminary to purchase; once that was accomplished, the lot of the slave was not unhappy. Smee observed that the Arabs were 'justly famed for the mild treatment of their slaves'. Slaves were not overworked, they were allowed to live on their master's estate, and to grow their own food. They seemed fairly happy and contented. The slaves Emmerton saw at Zanzibar were

> almost as much masters as their owners . . . many of them have slaves some three or four . . . Slaves are owned here because it is fashionable to have them.[121]

THE NORTHERN SLAVE TRADE

The invigorated slave trade on the East African coast and at Zanzibar in the mid-nineteenth century arose from various causes. Indians claimed that when they first arrived in the early nineteenth century, the whole country was densely populated up to the coast, but now it was eighteen days' journey inland (about 150 miles) before an African village of any consequence was reached. The opening up of the interior in the 1850s and 1860s by Arab traders in search of ivory presented new opportunities for acquiring slaves.

James Prior, surgeon on the *Nisus*, which visited Kilwa in 1811, remarked on the considerable depopulation in its vicinity, and conjectured that it was the result of the slave trade.[122] Rigby's statement that the older slaves in Zanzibar all recollected having been taken from near the coast supported this view. Baron von der Decken and Dr Roscher had seen miles and miles of ruined villages, the result of slavers' activity, on the way to Lake Nyasa in 1859-60. When Rigby took up his post in Zanzibar he noted that recent arrivals there were mainly from the Nyasa area. Mostly Manganya, Mnyasa, Minyana, Miganda, as he termed them, with a sprinkling of Yao. By the mid-fifties, freshly-purchased slaves no longer spoke Swahili, an indication of their inland origin. The Nyasa region especially was the main source of their supply. And it continued to be so well into the nineteenth century, after Bagamoyo, opposite Zanzibar, had become an active slave-exporting centre.

In the late eighteenth and early nineteenth century the French had been active at Zanzibar and along the coast. They enjoyed favourable terms under treaties with the Sultan, and could always outbid the Arabs in acquiring slaves, for they would pay as much as 30 to 40 dollars for a full-grown slave in Zanzibar. But the French had now withdrawn. The bidding was in the hands of the Arabs.

The security to be had under a British consul at Zanzibar had attracted many Indians to East Africa. They encouraged the slave trade by abetting it financially and by extending credit to Arab traders in the form of trade goods for slaving. The whole role of the Indian trader in the Indian Ocean, from Muscat, Aden and to Zanzibar, had been enhanced by the gradual diminution of the commercial monopoly of the East India Company, which had created more freedom of trade and commerce in the western Indian Ocean after the Royal Navy took over from the Indian Navy in mid-century. This aided the rise of the slave trade, in that many of the old pirate tribes, chiefly the Omani, were now actively involved in slave-trading; it was an alternative occupation to piracy. The wonder is that piratical proclivities did not stir them into hijacking slave dhows. This valuable and portable cargo was surely an unusual temptation for pirates.

The great increase in the production of cloves in the islands of Zanzibar and Pemba created a large demand for slave labour. The great hurricane of 1872 destroyed two-thirds of the clove and coconut plantations in Zanzibar, but left the island of Pemba comparatively untouched. The demand for slaves there, and for the replanting of clove trees in Zanzibar, continued unabated. The trade of Zanzibar increased by 50% during the years 1850 to 1870. In 1864 the customs farmed out to Messrs. Jairam Sewjee of Bombay amounted to 42,102 dollars; six years later the same firm was paying 65,263 dollars for farming the same customs.[123]

But allowing for and assessing the above causes, the main contributing factor to the stimulus in slave exports arose from the keen and expanding market for slaves in the Middle East. The task of intercepting the slave trade supplying this market reposed almost entirely on the small British naval anti-slave trade patrol operating off the east coast of Africa.

4
The Anti-Slave Trade Patrol on the East African coast in the Nineteenth Century

From October to April the northeast monsoon blows across from India down along the southern coast of Arabia and the East African coast, as far as the Mozambique Channel to about latitude 20°S. Here it is countered by the southeasterly airstream; a reverse process is set in motion and the southwest monsoon traverses the path of the northeast monsoon. The whole flux of winds and currents extends over a vast area in a massive and constant clockwise movement.

Sailing conditions are at their best for dhows[1] during the northeast monsoon and they embark on it almost as soon as it sets in, and run until it begins to break up. Dhows from Oman and the Persian Gulf average 30 to 40 days for the run to the East African coast. From India the journey can be done in 20 to 30 days. Dhows arrive in Zanzibar and Mombasa from late December onwards; the last stragglers come in about early March. Until recently the arrival of the annual fleet in Mombasa Old Harbour was a remarkable sight. Dhows entered the harbour with flags flying and crews dancing to the beating of drums.

The journey northwards on the southwest monsoon is risky and turbulent; sailing conditions are unpredictable owing to thunderstorms, lightning, rain, poor visibility and cloud. For the wooden-built dhow relying on one mainsail and primitive navigational aids the journey northwards can still be a harrowing experience. Dhow masters are never too happy when out of sight of land.[2] The worst weather is met near the islands terminating in Socotra—the area of the 'Bad Sea' and 'Enchanted breakers'. Light sailing craft despite their splendid sailing qualities find this bad patch, lying immediately in their path, a most difficult gauntlet to run.

The change of monsoon from northeast to southwest is not automatic nor simultaneous in all areas. During the middle of the southwest monsoon—the months of June and July—the wind practically ceases. Thus it is unwise for ocean-going dhows to leave

East Africa during this period. A voyage taken on the verge of the height of the monsoon is safe and speedy. An early start will not get one there any quicker. Dhows usually leave East Africa from early April onwards and normally cover the 2400 miles from Zanzibar to the northeastern corner of Arabia in from 17 to 20 days. With a favourable current of 50 to 90 miles a day north of Lamu, and accompanying winds of seven to eight miles an hour, the whole run can be done in as little as 10 to 12 days.

For the British naval officer on the anti-slave trade patrol in the nineteenth century the first glimpse of an Indian Ocean dhow riding at anchor in Zanzibar harbour must have been a startling sight. Here was probably the strangest craft his eyes had yet lighted on. With her bow sinking deeply in the water, her high stern, elaborately carved super-structure and jutting poop, floating lightly on the surface, she appeared to be constructed in reverse. Propped up on stilts on the Fungani spit off Zanzibar harbour, undergoing her annual repair, she looked for all the world like a praying mantis. Outlandish in appearance, almost grotesque in form, she was constructed contrariwise to all the accepted traditions of ship-building. The Arab dhow took some weighing up.

> If a pear be sharpened at the thin end, and then cut in half longitudinally, two models will have been made resembling in all essential respects the ordinary slave dhow.[3]

The dhow usually carried one mast—a heavy rough spar tapered to its head, and raked forward towards the bow.[4] On it was hoisted a long yard to which was secured the hypotenuse side of the enormous triangular-shaped spread of canvas, the right-angle of which was the lower aft corner, while the base ran almost parallel with the side of the dhow.

On the high seas, running before the full strength of the monsoon, with rudder lashed firm, and her full sail bleached to a glittering whiteness so that it seemed to 'shine like a star when first seen on the horizon', the dhow became a thing of beauty; she then revealed her marvellous sailing qualities. She could skim over the surface like a water gnat, and when overtaken by a cruiser, or forced to tack before the wind, she displayed her most amazing pas-de-deux. By shipping her one great sail round before the yard, and bringing it aft against the other side, the dhow could be caused to tack so quickly as to spin on her bottom like a top, and this amazing pirouette was followed by such a quick get-away that her pursuer was left behind, not quite realizing what had happened. The Arab dhow 'could sail like a witch.'[5]

The dhow-building industry of the Persian Gulf and Arabian seas is of great antiquity, dating back to Sabaean times.[6] The main centres in the nineteenth century for construction of the large, ocean-going dhow—the 'buggalow', or 'baghalah' ('she mule')—of 200 to 300 tons, were along the Hadhramaut coast, at Ma'ala and Mukalla, and in the Persian Gulf at Kuwait and Lingah. Dhows from the Persian Gulf were in a class of their own. They were more ornate, with high decorated poop and row of stern windows, and an enormous rudder.[7] With their massive bulwark they had a slight resemblance to an old wooden man-of-war. They were much better finished, with smoother planking, curled bowsprit, and carved adornments. They might range in length from 60 to 100 feet and were 14 to 25 feet across the beam.[8]

The dhow was simply constructed and furnished. The ribs were usually made from the branches of the large thorn bush growing on the Arabian coast, pieces being sought of natural shape and size. Hand-drawn planks of Malabar teak were laid on the inside and outside of these ribs, the interstices being filled with rope and tar. Sometimes there was an exterior and interior wall, with the space between filled with a mixture of lime and other materials which hardened and became water-tight. Sometimes only a covering of gypsum from Mukalla or Shihr, ground in a camel press and mixed with oil, was applied. Primitive iron nails and wooden plugs were used, although coastal dhows might be only warped together with coconut fibre rope. Stigand fancifully refers to the use of wooden pegs in the construction of dhows as a safeguard against the pull of the 'Mountains of the magnet' which old Arab geographers solemnly asserted to exist in the regions of Ras Hafun.

The dhow was seldom wholly decked. Partial planking was laid at intervals, and was used to reinforce the main mast mounted amidships. Over the connecting cross beams were laid strips of bamboo and matting for protection from the sun. Awning mounted at various places served the same purpose. The fittings throughout the dhow were of the rudest sort. The woodwork was bare or smeared with shark's oil, 'whose stench was like nothing earthly.' The ballast was usually sand and shingle. The dhows were generally leaky but this did not seem to affect their seaworthiness. The ropes were of coir from coconut fibre. The anchor was a primitive affair, a shank and several hooks. The dhow usually carried arms, long-stocked eastern firelock type, sometimes a small brass cannon, swords and daggers in plenty, and shields of boiled hippo hide.

The dhows from the Persian Gulf brought down carpets, cloth, coarse silk and woven garments, dried fish, usually shark's flesh, cooking pots, Arab furniture and dates—the date-ripening season coincided with the onset of the northeast monsoon. On the return journey, in addition to the main cargo of slaves, large dhows carried rice, mangrove poles, sesame oil seed, fish, coffee, and coconuts. Unlike the large well-founded vessels in the Atlantic slave trade which were specially fitted out with extra water tanks, extra cooking places, slave irons, and special decks, all proof of slaving, slave dhows captured off the East African coast had no special fittings to identify their trade, apart possibly from extra provisions and water. Slave irons were rarely found on Arab dhows. Water was usually stored in two or three large square wooden tanks holding 100 to 150 gallons each. The tanks were leaky, and evaporation was rapid. British cruisers, and modern liners when they began to run on the East African coast, were sometimes approached by dhows whose crews begged for water and food. Although the quantity of water carried on a dhow was no sure indication as to the nature of her trade, it is significant that in Zanzibar and Mombasa in the early twentieth century, as a safeguard against the slave trade, regulations decreed that a dhow must carry only a certain amount of water per man and that sand ballast must be examined carefully for hidden slaves.[9]

Living conditions on a dhow were crowded and primitive. From the large poop or canopied space at the stern which provided a dwelling for the captain, women, servants and upper class passengers, the turbaned old chief, the Nahodha, issued his commands. A certain decorum was observed, there were daily rounds of Yemen coffee and the hookah, and a semblance of civilized living was maintained.

This then, as described above, was the sea craft which plied the Arabian seas and conveyed thousands of slaves from the East African coast to the Middle East world, and the interception of which was the main task of the British naval anti-slave trade patrol.

The task of the naval anti-slave trade patrol on the East African coast was almost insuperable. There was perhaps no coastline in the world so suited to the activities of an Arab slave dhow, and quite so designed to make the task of a man-of-war difficult.

The vast littoral over which the British naval anti-slave trade patrol kept watch stretched from the coast of Mozambique in the south to the Gulf of Oman and the Makran coast in the north. In all, a total distance of 6000 miles, it comprised the coast extending north from the Tropic of Capricorn, with its many tortuosities, innumerable creeks, inlets, coves and bays, mangrove swamps and shallows, up to the Juba river, and then continuing along the 1500 miles of white sands of the Somaliland coast, as far as Cape Guardafui on the Horn; and from here across the Gulf of Aden and up the 2000 miles of barren wastes of the Arabian coast and along the sea run from India to the head of the Persian Gulf.

To patrol this vast semi-quadrilateral of coasts and adjacent waters, at a time when the East African slave trade was increasing in scale and intensity, the Royal Navy never had at its disposal more than six or seven vessels. And yet on the west coast of Africa, where the slave trade at sea had practically ceased, it was felt necessary as late as 1868 to maintain a force of eight cruisers in addition to the flagship, store ship, and two depot ships.[10] The Admiralty had apparently not yet taken the slave trade on the East African coast seriously.

The availability of vessels for the anti-slave trade patrol was very much determined by the limits of the Cape of Good Hope station and the East Indies station within which the East African coast was at one time or another assigned.[11] These limits tended to fluctuate according to the wide-ranging and changing global commitments of the Royal Navy.

The limits of the Cape of Good Hope station as established in 1810, following the acquisition of the Cape, extended northward on both sides of Africa to 3°S. On the west it included St. Helena, and on the east Madagascar, Zanzibar and the Seychelles. An adjustment in September 1812 placed the northern boundary at the latitude of the Tropic of Capricorn excluding the Seychelles, Zanzibar and Mauritius, but retaining the southern end of Madagascar in the Cape Command.

The patrol of the Indian Ocean to the north was left to the Indian Navy with headquarters at Bombay. In December 1816 when the task of guarding Napoleon at St. Helena was 'the first and most important object of the command', the eastern limit of the Cape Station was narrowed to 40°E. and its northern limit was raised to the Equator. In December 1819 the eastern limit was extended to 60°E., and in 1827 to 75°E., thus bringing Madagascar, Mauritius and the Seychelles again within its command. In 1844 the East Indies station now based on Hong Kong was given a subsidiary command at Bombay, to keep watch over the Indian Ocean between the Red Sea and Banda Atjch on the northwest corner of Sumatra.[12]

In 1864 following the replacement of the Indian Navy by the Royal

Navy, the East Indies Station's subsidiary command was united with the Cape Station but with headquarters retained at Bombay. Two years later they separated again, the dividing line being the Tropic of Capricorn, cutting the East African coast just north of Inhambane.

For the next ten years the East Indies Squadron based on Bombay was responsible for most of the East African, Arabian, Indian and Burma coasts. For this immense task there were usually never more than seven, and at the most eleven, ships with a total complement of about 1000 to 1500 men. Scarcely more than three were ever on active service at one time (the names of the few vessels on the anti-slave trade patrol on the East African coast at one time or another, which constantly recur in official reports, were the *Wasp, Lyra, Rapid, Pantaloon, Penguin, Forte* (Flagship), *Nymphe, Daphne, Columbine, Cossack, Bullfinch, Teazer, Wolverine* and *London*). In the autumn of 1864 when the *Penguin* was wrecked near Brava and the *Lyra* and *Wasp* went to her aid, the *Pantaloon* alone guarded the seaway against the slavers. The flagship was mostly on the coast of India, and came on to the East African coast only during the post-monsoon season. There were usually one or two vessels at Bombay undergoing repairs.

Bitter complaints, wearying in their repetition, came from British naval officers and consuls about the quality of the ships assigned to the East African patrol. Rigby complained of the *Sidon,* an old tub that any dhow on the coast could outsail, and the *Gorgon,* which took 40 days to do 800 miles. While dhows were improving in quality and increasing in size, up to as much as 250 tons burthen, and were of light draught, running marvellously well before the wind, and well-armed, ships on the anti-slave trade patrol seemed to be deteriorating in speed and efficiency. Cruisers were too large and cumbersome for inshore work, especially in the absence of an accurate and up-to-date survey of the East African coast. They had neither the speed, flexibility nor arms to cope with the dhows. Admiral Walker complained that his cruisers were too large and too slow, and that vessels of a gunboat class for river and inshore work were essential for the East African patrol.[13]

Rear-Admiral C. F. Hillyar, Commander-in-Chief of the Squadron on the East India Station from early 1866 to July 1867, and previously on the west coast of Africa and present at the capture of Lagos—'that death blow to the slave trade on the West Coast'—recommended that Britain should occupy Zanzibar and make it a naval base, and that the patrol force should be increased to twelve vessels of a superior type of corvette of 1000 to 1200 tons, carrying steam launches, and burning smokeless fuel. Better coaling facilities were necessary to avoid the practise of using sail to save coal on the run from Bombay to Muscat; dhows could escape a vessel under canvas with the greatest ease. A reliable supply of coal was essential. Consul Seward's suggestion that the island of Abd al-Kuri in the Socotra group might offer facilities for a coaling and provision depot for the anti-slave trade squadron should have been taken up.[14] But the Admiralty considered that the facilities offered by Abd al-Kuri were inferior to those already possessed by the British base at Aden.

Some modification of the vessels on the anti-slave trade patrol was necessary for the sake of the crew's health. Better ventilation especially was essential. More frequent victualling of fresh water and food was necessary. The maximum for a ship to be on a station was three years. It was the practice to send the crew north when the sun was in the south, and vice-versa, for the sake of their health. Thus the naval patrol on the East Indian Station took up its watch on the Indian coast during that part of the year when the slavers did not run, November to March. During the slave-running season, April-June, September-November, they returned to the East African coast. But for an effective watch against the slave traders the position should have been exactly reversed. In addition to its anti-slave trade duties the squadron was on call for other purposes. In 1852 most of the Indian Navy had been employed in the campaign against Burma.[15] In 1867 a revolution in Madagascar made it necessary to withdraw naval vessels from the East African coast, and during 1867-1868 they were employed in Annesley Bay when Lord Napier carried out his campaign against the Abyssinians. The slavers made the most of the opportunity afforded by the unguarded seaways.

The question of the quality of ship assigned to the anti-slave trade patrol, and the competing demands made on the squadron on the East African coast, raises the whole matter of naval policy as regards the slave trade. What priority did the Admiralty give to this work—was it merely a useful exercise to keep crew and officers on active patrol? The best ships always seemed to be in the North Atlantic or on the Far East Station.

The greatest number of vessels to converge on the East African coast was in 1873 when Sir Bartle Frere made a lordly entry into Zanzibar harbour with a man-of-war escorted by three cruisers. This prestige 'presence' was not sustained following his departure, and the patrol was again reduced to four vessels.

These few ships on the patrol were faced with periods of intense activity. In the early 1860s most of the captures were made on the African coast, but actual results in terms of slaves freed were meagre. In the spring of 1868, 400 dhows were boarded, but only eleven, carrying 1000 slaves, were seized. In the three years ending November 1863, only a hundred vessels were captured or destroyed on the East African coast, a mere fraction of those involved in the slave trade.

It was only gradually that naval officers divined the way of the slavers, their course at sea, the adroit tactics to evade capture and to elude pursuers. As the track of the dhow on the sea voyage northward became more clearly known, so also did strategy for interception. It was learned that the dhow usually put into shore two or three times for water on the way northward. Brava on the Somali coast was a favourite stopping place for dhows running north from Zanzibar and Lamu. Gallonsier Bay on the northwest corner of Socotra was a favourite watering place and so also the nearby island of Abd al-Kuri (Captain Benefield in 1866, lying in wait here, captured eight large dhows in one month). Ras Mahbar on the Arabian coast at 17°N. and the Kuria Muria Islands were the chief watering places for dhows on the last leg of their journey northwards. At Ras Mahber there was good anchorage during the southwest monsoon, and sheep of reasonable quality and price were obtainable. The *Penguin,* during a very successful year in 1866, made a grand scoop of 51 dhows on the way up from Zanzibar to Ras Mahbar, the majority taken near the latter place.

When Colomb was appointed to the command of the *Dryad* in 1868 and joined his ship at Aden, he noted that there had been little attempt to patrol the southern coast of Arabia, and that no one knew at what point the flock of dhows coming up from the south made their landfall on the Arabian coast.

> Whereabouts did the ordinary Zanzibar trader or the slave trader strike the coast of Arabia. Did both, or either, pass inside or outside Socotra?[16]

Dhows sailing north from Socotra were compressed into a narrow channel at Ras al-Madraka before making their landfall on the coast of Arabia. Thus, in the spring of 1869, for the first time since the Royal Navy took over the task, five ships, including the *Dryad*, 'spread a spider's web all along the northern shores of the Arabian Sea' to anticipate dhows heading for the Gulf of Oman.[17] Colomb obtained most of his prizes—six slavers during the period January 1869 to May 1870—while posted off Ras al-Madraka. He was thus confirmed in the belief that this was the area to watch, but he soon found that the dhows were making their landfall farther to the south.

Ras al-Hadd at the entrance to the Gulf of Oman was also a great concentration point for slave dhows heading for Oman and the Persian Gulf. Slaves were landed near here on the twenty-mile line of coast immediately below Muscat, or at Murraye 160 miles north of Muscat. They were then taken to Bandar Abbas and up the Persian Gulf.

Dhows coming from the Gulf of Aden and the Red Sea, under the treaty of 1847 between Great Britain and the Sultan of Muscat and Zanzibar, were free from seizure. Vessels from this area very often flew the Turkish flag and were thus immune from search and capture.

There was no agreement nor certainty on the part of naval commanders as to how best to position their few vessels to intercept the slave traders. The basic argument turned on whether the evil should be nipped on the East African coast or whether naval forces should be concentrated to the north at the receiving end, in the Arabian Sea and Persian Gulf. Admirals, Commanders-in-Chief, and naval officers had different views on the matter; even consular officers were not averse to trying their hand at naval strategy.

Hillyar tried placing one ship off Socotra, and one off the mouth of the Persian Gulf, and the three remaining serviceable vessels cruised between Zanzibar, Madagascar and the Seychelles. With this force, Hillyar estimated that he captured one dhow for every eight escaping.

Sir Leopold Heath, Commander-in-Chief of the East Indies squadron (1868–70), placed his eastern ship on the Arabian coast off Ras al-Hadd, his western vessel at Mukalla, and another ship between these two points, with the flagship cruising between all three. He also stationed one ship off Cape Guardafui, and two off Zanzibar. But positioning ships too far to the north left the southernmost coast unwatched, and slavers were quick to make the most of the absence of the cruisers here. In 1871 a new tactic of positioning the entire patrol off the Somaliland coast failed to achieve results. The slave dhows made the most of their opportunity on the unwatched southern coastline.

Pelly and Plaifair recommended blockading the ports of Arabia where there were fewer hideouts and no complicated treaties to hamper movements. Captain Bowden was of the same view, that a few key points only needed to be watched at certain times of the year. Their argument was based on the fact that the dhows commenced to run south about the beginning of November and stayed on the East African coast until the end of April, and, if not off by then, waited until August when there was good going until mid-October. Dhows going north usually passed between Cape Guardafui and the island of Socotra; if they went east of Socotra, so it was claimed, the current would take them to Malabar on the Indian coast. Thus a strict watch was only needed between Cape Guardafui and Socotra and 'a single gunboat there would have more effect than the whole Indian Squadron further south'. But, as it was discovered, dhows did run to the east of Socotra, and still managed to reach the Arabian coast. It was also argued that it was only necessary to place a vessel mid-channel between Cape Mussendam and Jask, another at Ras al-Hadd, and one at Socotra; craft from Africa must sight one of these points for water or to verify their position.

After much trial and error naval officers came around to the view that placing a cordon across the track of the dhows or cruising endlessly and aimlessly along the coasts was useless, and so also was placing their ships at a few points of vantage in the north. A better plan was to disperse them between Ras al-Madraka on the Arabian coast and Ras al-Hadd at the entrance to the Gulf of Oman, at Cape Guardafui or Socotra to guard the Gulf of Aden, between Mogadishu and Lamu on the Somali coast to close the inner passage up the coast from Kilwa, with two vessels in the neighbourhood of Zanzibar and Pemba.[18]

Of the fourteen dhows—all prizes of the *Ariel* under Commander Oldfield, condemned in the Vice-Admiralty Court at the Cape in February 1864— eight were captured off Pemba, five off the Comoro Islands, and one near Brava. During the period August to October 1861, the *Gorgon* under Captain Wilson captured 18 vessels between Zanzibar and the mainland. Out of 22 vessels captured in 1862, only six carried slaves; the remainder were seized because they were equipped for slaving. During the period 1866-9, 129 slave vessels were captured and 3380 slaves freed.

The Arabs were sharpening their tactics by the late sixties. In addition to carrying larger number of slaves than formerly in a dhow, in some cases as many as 500, they were more closely watching the winds to make a quick getaway. The southwest monsoon sets in sooner to the northwards than it does to the southward; thus dhows, by keeping in close to the shore and trusting to the land sea breezes, might make the Gulf of Aden in time to catch the early onset of the southwest monsoon in the north, and would thus gain a headstart over the main fleet arriving some weeks later. By keeping inshore and lowering their sails, ready to run ashore or seek safety behind a reef if a cruiser was sighted, Arab slavers might manage to get away from Zanzibar at the beginning of April or earlier, although the prevailing winds would get them no farther than Wasin or, at the most, Brava, where they would wait for the onset of the southwest monsoon in early May.

Dhow masters normally tended to follow the coastline up from Zanzibar. But to evade British cruisers, the dhow fleet would sometimes sail northwards in small fleets well out to sea, every eight to ten boats being provided with a person qualified to navigate out of sight of land. In 1866 five large dhows which were captured all carried nautical instruments, contrary to the belief that the Arab dhow master navigated solely by instinct and with natural aids.[19]

Rather than face capture slavers were prepared to run their dhows ashore into the mangrove swamps south of Lamu, or on to the sand beaches of the Somaliland coast, and the slaves might then be drowned, or, if surviving, run inland. Papers and flags were taken by the fleeing Arabs, presumably to be used again.[20]

The captain of the *Ariel* reported a typical case when, on 4 April 1862,

at daylight, a dhow was observed to the north of Brava, rounding to the northward. At 9 a.m. the *Ariel* stood for her, when she immediately bore up for the land, upon which the *Ariel* made chase. At 11 a.m. the dhow anchored on the edge of the surf, about 16 miles north of Brava, and the *Ariel* at 12:30 anchored about 800 yards off her. It was observed that she was full of slaves, and that the crew with their effects were escaping to the land. Captain Oldfield proceeded with two gigs of the *Ariel* and boarded the dhow, which was thoroughly equipped for the Slave Trade, and had from 80 to 100 slaves on board. When boarded the crew had to cut her cables, and she was fast drifting into the surf. Her position rendered it impossible to remove the slaves, one man excepted. The dhow drifted on to the beach, and the boats were in the most imminent peril; that commanded by Captain Oldfield, being swamped, and the crew with difficulty saved, while the shore was lined with armed men, who with muskets and spears attacked the boats and such of the slaves as attempted to make for them. Captain Oldfield thereupon declared the dhow seized as a slaver, and she soon afterwards became a total wreck, the slaves escaped to the shore, where they were seized by armed men, apparently Somali Arabs, and the dhow being deserted, her destruction was completed by shelling her. She appeared to be from 150 to 175 tons burthen.[21]

The cost of a dhow so lost could easily be recouped from the profits of the trade; a dhow worth 900 dollars could carry 150 slaves, which, at 12 dollars per head, meant a total of 1800 dollars. Thus a dhow would pay for herself twice over in one trip.

Colomb argued that Arab captains were afraid to run their dhows ashore north of Mogadishu because of the fierce Somalis, but there are numerous cases to show that Colomb was mistaken in this belief. Neither the risk of murder by the Somali nor fear of the dread Siu Siu (perhaps from 'wasiu'—old Swahili for 'bad people' from the Arabic 'siywi') near Pate, who cut off the 'prime members' of their captives—'a terrible stroke of destiny' to the Arab—deterred the slavers from running their slaves ashore to avoid capture.

It was also the practice of the northern Arabs to send forward one or two vessels full of slaves with the intention that they should be captured by the cruiser stationed in the Straits of Socotra. The Straits were no sooner left unguarded than the whole Arab fleet with their living cargoes would sail through inviolate. There was not much concern for the capture of their fellow Arabs. There were no specific instructions for dealing with the crews of captured vessels, and these were usually put ashore at the most convenient point or taken to the port of adjudication. It was not until 1871 that regulations specifically instructed that the crew of captured dhows must be forwarded along with the vessel to the port of adjudication.[22]

Vessels from Zanzibar often touched at Lamu for food and water, as they could not lay in supplies on an extensive scale at Zanzibar for fear of exciting suspicion. Naval officers aware of this fact would lie in wait north of Brava. Captain Paisley in 1870 tried this expedient and made a good number of hauls near Ras Hafun, capturing seven dhows out of 40 which had awaited his departure from Zanzibar before venturing out. Paisley estimated that the fleet of 40 dhows must have carried 4000 slaves. Similarly, Captain Blomfield cruising off Brava and Merka overhauled 60 dhows, and captured and destroyed three, one of which belonged to an Indian.

Among the tactics employed to evade capture there was already appearing in the 1860s the use of the French flag. This was to become a major problem for the Royal Navy later in the century. Playfair noted in 1863 that

'The Arabs are well aware that under it [the French flag] the right of search is denied to us, and it has now become the great object of their desire to obtain a French register.'[23]

But the main problem for naval officers, apart from the larger question of naval strategy, was that of identifying genuine slaves among the many passengers and crew to be found on an Arab dhow. The Sultan's clearance certificate in Arabic granting safe passage to crew and passengers was used as cover for the transport of slaves.[24]

Captain Sulivan claimed that one of the greatest difficulties met with by officers when taking up duty on the East African anti-slave trade patrol was the absence of any record or document of the previous personal experiences of officers, the knowledge they had gained about the secrets of the slave trade, the places from which slaves were shipped, the distinction between illegal and legitimate trade, the reliance to be placed on interpreters etc.

There was no handbook specifically for the East African anti-slave trade patrol until 1869, when the Admiralty issued 'Slave Trade Instructions to Officers employed on Detached Boat Service: East African Slave Trade'. This contained instructions for boarding, ascertaining cargoes, distinguishing French papers if genuine, and interrogation in the Swahili tongue with useful phrases.

But until this manual appeared, naval officers on taking up command in East African waters received an octavo volume based on West Coast practice, 'Instructions for the Suppression of the Slave Trade', which dealt mainly with treaties and mutual rights of search etc.[25] Under the heading 'France', it was stated:

> There is no treaty in force between Great Britain and France for the suppression of the slave trade. None of the general instructions therefore are applicable to French vessels. Your conduct towards vessels hoisting French colours shall be regulated exclusively by the confidential instructions with which you have been furnished by the Admiralty.

Turkey and Egypt were not even mentioned in the handbook. There were however, many treaties with minor countries—even the Comoro Islands.

The conditions and general instructions in the handbook related wholly to a condition of things which did not exist on the East India Station. There was confusion over 'territorial waters'; in essence this meant waters over which Powers possessing the coast could throw shot, but international lawyers gave it an arbitrary range of three miles. But the great problem in East African waters was the question 'Who claims the coast?' The Sultan of Zanzibar's territory supposedly began at Kilwa and ended at Lamu, but north of this, suzerainty over the coast was undefined. Similarly on the Arabian coast between Aden and Muscat, and between Oman and Karachi along the Baluchistan coast, it was not clear who exercised territorial claims. And the matter was not made any easier by the fact that waters 'naturally territorial' could be made 'high seas' by treaty, and this a naval commander must ascertain by reference to his handbook or instructions. For example, the Sultan of Zanzibar had voluntarily rendered his territorial waters 'high seas' in respect of the slave trade during the months of January to April inclusive each year, but he retained his claim over them as 'territorial waters' for the remaining months; and in 1873 he appealed against a decision condemning slave vessels in the closed season on the grounds that they were captured in his territorial waters.

The Sultan of Oman by a treaty of 1845 surrendered his rights over Oman waters as far as the slave trade was concerned, and a slave vessel might be captured under the windows of his palace at Muscat without remonstrance from him. In Persian Gulf waters Persian vessels were subject to search and capture but only if a Persian officer accompanied the vessel making the capture.

But all these refinements were no great help to the naval officer in what concerned him most of all—the ship styled 'no name or nation'. For the ordinary slave-trader on the East African coast flew no flag, carried no papers, belonged to nowhere, and claimed nobody's protection, and, as Captain Colomb maintained, all the instructions and twenty-one clauses prescribing formalities proper to first visit and the twelve clauses directing search were scarcely applicable to 'the crazy old Arab dhow often guiltless of name, papers, books or flag, which carries on both the lawful and unlawful trade in East African waters'.[26]

The fact that Arab dhows usually flew a plain red flag denoted their nationality 'no more closely' than the word 'Arab' expressed it. British officers faced with lack of guidance and want of experience made up their own rules. Colomb for example, on overhauling a dhow and finding no slaves on her, issued a pass to her master which exonerated him from further search on his way north. Colomb admits that although it was *his* practice to give such passes, it was not regular usage.[27] He seems to have overlooked the possible use of this pass on the way north to pick up slaves and carry them under safe conduct.

Prima facie evidence of slave-trading, detailed in the Slave Trade Consolidation Act 1873, was largely based on West African experience, and had little relevance to East African conditions, apart from the larger quantity of provisions and water than usual that might be found on slave dhows.[28]

THE ANTI-SLAVE TRADE PATROL 81

Arab slave dhows carried few fittings. If they carried cargo, slaves sat on it; and if no cargo, slaves sat on the sand ballast. Grain, oranges, betel-nut, cocoanuts, rice and dates provided food for the slaves but this was also ordinary cargo. As for the quantity of water carried by a dhow, this, if unusually large, might be taken as evidence of slaving; for example, a dhow of 198 tons captured off Malindi in March 1863 was equipped with three large water tanks holding three tons of water more than necessary for her crew and it was later ascertained she was heading for Tola to take on 500 slaves. But the amount of water on board a dhow was not always a sure guide as to whether she was a slaver. Water could be obtained at a number of stopping places on the way north, and the southwest monsoon winds, on which the slave dhows sailed north, were the rain-bringing winds, providing much needed drinking water for crew and slaves.

The crew of a British cruiser on the anti-slave trade patrol were an eager lively lot. There were the young officers, dedicated to a career in the Service, and the ordinary seamen from port towns in Britain, plus a sprinkling of Kroomen from West Africa. Despite the climate, ill-health, frustration and delay in achieving results, the great expenditure of time and energy for naval prizes—e.g. the long arduous chase of a dhow four days out from Kilwa, and the ensuing prize of one slave boy choked with flour to stifle his cries—despite all this, it was an adventurous life. It was made up of

'Incessant boardings of dhows; constant and prolonged examinations generally resulting in acquittal. Perpetual rushing to sea at all hours of day and night; and eternal weighing and anchoring. Changing a dry boat's crew for a wet and exhausted one; substituting a fresh boat for one damaged under a rolling dhow. Noting a wind every day increasing, and a coal supply every day decreasing.'[29]

Colomb gives an instance of the excitement of the chase when he pursued a dhow, and after overtaking her and capturing the 20 Arabs on board and the 113 'plump, well-fed healthy looking negroes', shot holes in the dhow and sank her. The Arabs captured were cool customers—they complained of the food and asked for curry.

Arab slavers could be aggressive on the high seas. Commodore Hillyar after a number of engagements expressed high respect for their courage, 'the dhows will fight, a very plucky set indeed'. In 1865, the *Wasp* captured a large dhow of 200 tons carrying 300 slaves from the east side of the island of Zanzibar. The *Wasp* expected trouble and had on board a force of 46 fighting men. The dhow was caught by the pinnace and cutter of the *Wasp*; a desperate resistance followed in which the coxswain of the pinnace was killed and several of the crew injured, including Lieutenant Rising.[30]

Much of the verve and dash on the part of the British sailors arose from bounties payable for the successful conviction of a slaver. Bounties payable by the British Treasury dated from the reign of George IV; they were derived from West African experience, and emanated from the right of government to sell vessels condemned as slavers and to give the proceeds to the captors. Captured slave ships were much in demand for their sailing qualities and speed. They were sold and recaptured—sometimes as much as five or six times. To end this state of affairs, slave ships were broken up, and, in lieu of proceeds of sale, a bounty of £1-10-0 per ton on every vessel condemned was given to the captors. In addition there was a bounty of £5 per head on every slave landed alive at an appointed place. There was also a bounty £4-4-0 per ton for every slaver without slaves on capture, or containing so few slaves that the captors surrendered their claim for head money. Admiralty instructions of November 1869 prohibited the destruction of vessels prior to condemnation at a port of adjudication unless circumstances justified the destruction of the vessel.

The unusual shape of the Arab dhow made it most difficult to obtain accurate measurements, and in their zeal to collect bounties her captors tended to exaggerate these measurements. The Treasury in calculating the final award usually made allowance for such exaggeration. Thus the resulting figures were likely to be a close approximation to the real tonnage of the captured vessel.[31]

Some captains claimed that it was difficult to keep their crews within the limit of justice and yet not dissatisfy them. Churchill, from his windows in Zanzibar, had to go out and restrain the *Penguin* which had just overhauled a dhow coming in, and with the 'greatest difficulty' persuade her crew that they had seized a wrong dhow. Churchill claimed that because of bounties, investigations to ascertain whether a dhow was really engaged in the illicit slave trade were not always very minutely carried out, and frequently a dhow engaged in legitimate trade was destroyed. There were many complaints of such practice forwarded to HMG.[32]

The difficulty in bringing a captured dhow into port also led to illegal actions on the part of the British crew. If possible the dhow might be towed, but they could rarely stand up to this, and it also meant the naval vessel deserting her station for a long period of time. The common practice of destroying a vessel immediately on capture if there was suspicion of her complicity in slave-trading was a grave and serious act, justified only in extreme emergency, but it was frequently carried out on little or no evidence of guilt, and even when she was engaged in lawful commerce. Captured slaves had to be produced to obtain the bounty per head, but they might have smallpox or cholera, or, as in the case of a capture made by the *Daphne* in March 1874, dysentery might break out among them.

There was an illegal but fairly common practice of landing crew and passengers of any vessel captured or destroyed at some out-of-the-way place, or placing the crew on a legal trader going to Arabia, and taking the freed slaves to a freed slave settlement, and then obtaining the condemnation of the vessel on a purely ex parte statement. These acts were little short of piracy. Bounties were meant to be payable only when the slaves were produced and the vessel was legally condemned at the port of adjudication, or when circumstances justified the destruction of the vessel.

The procedure of adjudication at a Prize Court of a captured slave dhow was simple and informal. The main evidence was the physical presence of the captured slaves.

> The Resident (civil governor) is ex-officio the judge of the Court, and practically he is the whole Court, vice-Admiral, Judge, and Registrar. The Court is held generally in one of the rooms of the Residency, or other convenient place. The form is very simple. The Court is prayed to exercise its jurisdiction; and the captain of the capturing vessel, or other officer deputed by him, together with the necessary witnesses, attend on a given day with certificates of the number of slaves taken out of the vessels, the measurements of the latter, and a certificate of their destination. The witnesses—one or two—then state, on oath, the circustances of the capture; and if the case is clear, a decree of condemnation of the vessel as lawful prize to the capturing ship, follows immediately . . . In the six cases of capture, or destruction, which we offered for adjudication, it was necessary only to take formal evidence, the whole thing was over in an hour and a half, and we returned to ship, happy, in the possession of documents equivalent to a demand on the English Treasury for about £2200.[33]

The long sea-voyage endured by the slaves shipped north to Arabia and the Persian Gulf had not the horrors of the Atlantic 'middle passage'. Severe hardship often resulted from overcrowding and ill-feeding. But it was not calculated brutality, despite Churchill's surmise that the slaves were ill-fed on the northern journey to weaken them, otherwise they might overpower the crew.

Everyone in a slave dhow, Arab and slave alike, lived under cramped conditions. Colomb said he never saw slaves bound, nor force used against them, and the British Resident in the Persian Gulf in 1844 remarked

> The treatment of African slaves is at no time either severe or cruel. During the sea voyage they are not bound, or kept under particular restraint. Rice, dates and fish, in sufficient quantities form their food, and a coarse cloth around the middle of the body, constitutes their only clothing.[34]

Sulivan had never seen a fettered negro in any of the dhows on the East African coast, and he doubted if anyone else had.

According to Colomb, conditions for slaves on an Arab dhow were no worse than those of an Irish peasant in his cabin. As for the effluvium, one could simply play the hose on the slaves—they would get to like it; Commander Cutfield of the *Undine* in the Mozambique Channel in July 1883, speaking of the 103 slaves they took on board—'Every morning all are stripped, and the fire hose played on them indiscriminately, and don't they need it too!'[35]

Females were well cared for, Galla females especially being treated with marked tenderness. According to Captain Bowden, in command of the *Wasp*:

> Those who are young, especially the women and girls, by no means dislike the idea of going as slaves to Muscat—many of those we emancipated at Mahé regretted being taken there, dreading the idea of having to work as they had never been accustomed to it.[36]

Colomb marvelled at the sheer passivity of the slave who showed no delight at being rescued—'What I saw in the faces of these creatures was not suffering, but want of idea'.

> To spend weeks sitting, crouching, or lying on the sunny deck of a man-of-war, without employment for mind or body, would be horribly irksome to Western races. I should say they are the happiest hours the negro ever passes in his unhappy life.[37]

The worst lot that could befall the slaves was when the slaver was overhauled by a British cruiser, and they then might be flung overboard so as to dispose of all evidence. Devereux mentions a case where the Arabs, when pursued by an English cruiser, cut the throats of 240 slaves and threw them overboard.[38] Colomb also stated that the Arabs would not hesitate to knock slaves on the head and throw them overboard to avoid capture.

Suffering among slaves arose when dhows put off their departure for the north to the last moment, or if the northern winds set in earlier and they then had to beat northwards against a headwind. In such cases the prolonged journey might bring frightful suffering. The ill-effects of delayed departure were well illustrated in two captures by HMS *Lyra* and *Thetis*. In the one case there were 112 girls on board the captured dhow. They had been carefully selected, and were to be sold at a high price for the harems of Arabia and Persia. The dhow was taken alongside the *Lyra* and the slaves were taken out. A fatigue party from the *Lyra* went on board the dhow and as each man entered the hold he 'fainted straight away'. On the doctor's orders the dhow was towed and scuttled. Rigby thought that most of these slaves would have died on the northward journey. In the other case, a capture made by the *Thetis*, there were 250 slaves, 53 Arabs and the crew; the slaves were stowed on two decks, squatting side by side, with no room to stand up, or to move, and were compelled to squat in their own excrement. Both the slaves and the Arabs had loathsome disease and the itch.

The question of the disposal of freed slaves taken from captured slave dhows was a long-standing and vexatious problem for the British naval anti-slave trade patrol. During the early years of the century freed slaves were landed at the Cape. But for naval vessels on the East African coast far to the north this meant a long journey southwards and deserting their stations for weeks on end. During the brief period of Owen's protectorate over Mombasa, 1824–6, a few slaves from a captured dhow were settled on what is now English Point; each freed slave was given a plot of ground. But proper freed slave settlements did not exist on the East African coast until well into the second half of the nineteenth century.

African slaves were not an unfamiliar sight at Bombay and Madras where small numbers of Abyssinian females were imported in the eighteenth century. A number of freed slaves were landed at Bombay by British cruisers in the 1830s and 1840s, and it became the practice to hand them over to the chief of police at Bombay, and he had the duty of finding employment for them. But the problem was more than he could handle; employment was scarce, some of the children were kidnapped, and some of the females ended up as prostitutes in the bazaars. Owing to lack of care, there were 754 deaths and only 37 births among a thousand freed slaves landed at Bombay in five years.

Christian missionaries gradually took over the care of the freed slaves landed at Bombay, and, at the suggestion of the government, the system became regularized. There grew up at Nassick some 117 miles north-east of Bombay what became known as the 'African Asylum' which was run by the Church Missionary Society.[39] Here freed slaves were taught useful skills such as bricklaying and carpentry. Nassick eventually became entirely maintained by the Bombay government, and between 1860 and 1870 about 200 slaves were received there. It was from this institution that Livingstone took nine boys back to Africa. One lad who accompanied him into the interior met up with his uncle who, finding that the boy had been taught useful skills at Nassick, wished to retain him, but the boy preferred to stay with Livingstone.

But the opinion of British officials in India, on the whole, was against freed slaves being sent to Bombay. It was felt that they should be returned to their own natural environment in East Africa, and after 1870 no more were sent to Bombay. In 1875 the African Asylum was closed.

The crowded, barren, desolate, volcanic rock peninsula of Aden was still less suitable for a home for freed slaves than Nassick. Freed slaves were at first confined to a small rock island, 'Slave Island', in the harbour at Aden. It formed a kind of labour compound, with a few large open sheds, and food supplied by contract. Slaves led a useless life here unless they found employment or could be hired out to someone interested in their services, or could be shipped to Bombay. Many were found in the employ of Parsees, while some were spirited away to the Hadhramaut coast. Others, after an apprenticeship to residents in Aden, ended up in domestic slavery in the Arabian interior.

Sir Bartle Frere travelling out to Zanzibar in 1872 found Aden teeming with freed slaves. Such was the convenience of Aden for British cruisers in nearby waters that slaves continued to be sent here up to the 1870s. Aden was extremely convenient for those ships operating off the Gulf of Aden and Arabian coast, and especially those in the neighbourhood of Cape Guardafui; a letter from a naval officer at the latter place, in September 1867, speaks of a quick run to Aden with captured slaves to escape the dread smallpox. Cruisers could land freed slaves at Aden and be back at their stations in a matter of days, as was noted by Captain Sulivan of HMS *Star* after landing 300 liberated Africans in one batch at Aden in 1868.[40] Thirteen dhows were destroyed and 967 slaves were released in less than one month and handed over to the civil authorities at Aden in the following year. But even Aden was not sufficiently convenient for some cruisers. Captain Bowden in June 1865 stated that the *Penguin* made four prizes in the early 1865 season, and would have made more, but had to desert her station to land slaves at Aden.

And it was a costly business—the imperial exchequer had to pay out £16,000 for the care of the 2197 freed slaves landed at Aden in the five years ending in 1870. Some of the freed slaves were handed over to the Roman Catholic Sisters of Mercy and the Church of Scotland Mission at Aden. Others were employed as dock workers in the harbour department, and for coaling.

Sir William Coghlan, after nine years as Political Resident and Commandant at Aden and Judge of the Admiralty Court, and after seeing the efforts to make Aden a home for the freed slaves—trying to turn them into freed labourers, apportioning the women among respectable families, and sending the children to Bombay—came round to the view that, on the whole, Aden was not the proper place for a freed slave settlement.

Admiral Sir Leopold Heath's plan put before the Select Committee of 1870/1, which provided for the concentration of patrol ships on the Arabian coast, was based on the assumption that Aden would still be used as a freed slave depot. Sir Bartle Frere held the view that it was definitely unsuitable, and his opinion was influential in the search for an alternative home for freed slaves.

Rigby had recommended the Seychelles as a home for freed slaves shortly after his arrival in 1858. Sporadic numbers had been landed there unofficially since the 1830s. In 1861 a batch of freed slaves was officially directed to the Seychelles, and in the six years ending May 1860 over 2000 slaves were landed there.

The journey to the Seychelles from Zanzibar with freed slaves is described in a letter by Captain Cornish-Bowden of HMS *Wasp* to his wife in May 1865.

> As soon as they are safe to stand a little racket I shall go across to the Seychelles with my slaves. This rainy weather puzzles me how to stow them. I had 180 on board today, chiefly the small children and weakly ones. As they came on board they were all put in tubs, and well washed by the crew men with soft soap. While the tubbing was going on I found many had small wounds . . . They are all greatly pleased at being told they will never again be slaves . . . You may fancy the state we are in. From the mizen mast aft is a hospital, the rest of the ship a slave yard. On the whole they behave very well, but now they have got over their awe and sea sickness they made a great noise. We have had four die, poor creatures. I cannot have them below, they smell too strong. Most of them, 19 out of 20 are fat and jolly. Every morning they are washed in large tubs, with the hose playing over them. I think they never had so much cleaning before. Many of them are covered with craw, or African itch—I think all have it more or less.[41]

There was heavy mortality among these slaves on immediate arrival, but the sickly slaves who survived usually recovered rapidly in the Seychelles. Landings of freed slaves continued over the next few years. The Seychelles lay athwart the sea lanes between the East African coast, Zanzibar, and the Arabian Sea, and were not overcrowded. In fact the suggestion had been made in 1850 that they might offer a home for famine-stricken Irishmen. An archipelago of some forty-five islands, of great fertility, with a healthy and equable climate, and sparsely populated, the Seychelles were a veritable Garden of Eden, and for long a favoured spot for British sailors on shore leave. Sick missionaries in Zanzibar were sent to the Seychelles as 'the natural sanitorium of that part of the world'. There was also, according to the Church Missionary Society, less immorality in the Seychelles, especially on the island of Mahé, where most of the freed slaves were landed. The Seychelles, in their own way, offered something comparable to the slave depot at St. Helena on the west coast of Africa, where 3000 slaves a year were landed in the 1840s.

It was thought that Mauritius also offered possibilities as a freed slave settlement. In 1840 the sloop of war *Lily* had landed 260 slaves there, taken from a Portuguese slaver, the *José*.[42] However the great cholera epidemic which hit Mauritius in 1855, and the wave of malarial fever which carried off thousands in 1867, acted as a deterrent to making it a settlement for freed slaves, but occasional cargoes of captured slaves continued to be landed there throughout the 1860s.[43] The 500 slaves rescued from the captured brigantine *Immanuela* in 1861, and 140 slaves in a capture referred to by Colomb, were landed at Mauritius. Planters in Mauritius were ready to pay premiums to obtain freed slaves as labourers, and witnesses before the Select Committee of 1870/1 thought Mauritius a 'good happy place' for freed slaves. The island was almost like one vast sugar factory, and labour was in keen demand. But there was a high mortality rate, and the climate of Mauritius seemed to be peculiarly unsuitable for freed slaves from Africa. Naval officers might maintain that Mauritius was the 'pleasantest spot on the East Indian Station', but it was not an ideal freed slave settlement, and very few slaves were sent there after 1870, except those captured in not too distant waters.

There were various suggestions for the establishment of other freed slave settlements in the 1860s and 1870s. Churchill thought that the island of Mafia had possibilities, and Kirk recommended Lamu as a healthy, suitable place, where watch could be kept over freed slaves. The Select Committee of 1870/71 recommended the establishment of a freed slaves base on the mainland—Dar es Salaam was a likely site. Lieutenant Fellowes in 1872, in command of the *Briton*, was sent from Aden to Socotra to see if that island and nearby Abd-al-Kuri were suitable for liberated slaves. But Fellowes decided against both. Socotra was short of food and water, and practically dependent on Muscat; freed slaves landed here would run the risk of being starved or stolen again by the northern Arabs. Abd-al-Kuri was destitute of cultivation and water; its 300 inhabitants were reduced to a miserable level of subsistance, and obtained only a few drops of water by digging in the sand.

Of all places considered, the Seychelles appeared to be most suitable as a home for freed slaves. Employment was available here. Coffee plantations in the Seychelles, deserted when the institution of slavery was abolished, would thrive again if labour were available. Slaves on arrival in the Seychelles were usually hired out, if adults, on a three- to five-year contract under the supervision of the British civil commissioner. The 400 slaves captured in two prizes by the *Orestes* and *Rapid* in 1865, which were condemned at the Vice-Admiralty Court at the Cape, were landed at the Seychelles, and the two Captains commented favourably on conditions there.[44]

In March 1866, when the Admiralty was considering moving the naval depot from Zanzibar to Mahé in the Seychelles, there was added argument for a freed slave settlement there. The Church Missionary Society offered to supervise the settlement. The Seychelles might have become the Sierra Leone of the East African coast. But there were second thoughts by 1870. Employment prospects were not as high as originally assumed, and much supervision was necessary if the freed slaves were to be hired out to carefully selected masters. Labourers from India were increasingly preferred, and there was an organized immigration from this source into the Seychelles. Nevertheless, in the ten years 1862-72, 2500 slaves were landed at Mahé by the British anti-slave trade patrol.[45]

The Clarendon Committee of 1869 considered the possibilities offered by Zanzibar as a freed slaves' home, perhaps making it the chief depot for liberated slaves on the East African coast. There was an increasing demand for labour here on the clove estates, and no charge would be incurred by the imperial government for their upkeep. A close control could be exercised, a register could be kept of freed slaves by the British consulate, and they would be provided with printed certificates of freedom. By 1869, there were over 2000 freed slaves in Zanzibar, some in the care of the Roman Catholic Mission, and Dr Christie, the medical officer, was looking after others. A few slaves had been sent to the Church Missionary Society schools in the Seychelles for their education but this could be done equally well in Zanzibar. An Englishman, Captain Fraser, employed 500 freed slaves on his sugar estate in Zanzibar, and there were opportunities for more work of this kind.

The Clarendon Committee also considered the request of the French planters in Réunion for freed slaves, but the Committee, although not averse to some experimentation with this proposition, thought it should be approached with caution; it was a possible step to re-enslavement. Socotra was ruled out by the Clarendon Commission; it could only be a temporary slave depot pending transport to either Zanzibar or Bombay.

The whole question of the disposal of freed slaves came to the fore following Sir Bartle Frere's visit to East Africa in 1873. Frere urged that definite action be taken in the matter, and suggested the possibility of Port Durnford on the East African coast, about 120 miles north of Lamu, as a site; it was a healthy place, and not too far from the slaving ground. Captain Elton, at about the same time, suggested Natal as an ideal place for freed slaves. Elton also suggested Mozambique as an alternative, and visited Mozambique to discuss the matter with its governor.[46] Lord Granville, the Foreign Secretary, inquired into the feasibility of making the island of Johanna, in the Comoro Islands, a depot for captured slaves.

A final solution to the problem came when Christian missions in East Africa offered to take over the task. The Universities Mission to Central Africa, after the transference of its headquarters to Zanzibar in 1864 and the establishment of branches at Kiungani and Mbweni, and later at Pemba, took on the care of freed slaves. In 1867 they established a station on the mainland at Magila, in the hill country behind Tanga, and in 1875 at Masasi, inland from Lindi. Freed slaves were cared for by these Missions.

The Holy Ghost Fathers Mission at Bagamoyo, founded in 1868, was quickly turned to this purpose, and its example was followed shortly by the Church Missionary Society missions at Freretown and Rabai, near Mombasa. The CMS station at Freetown, under the Reverend Salter Price, received its first freed slaves in 1874, and by the end of 1888 there were over 3000 settled there, and it continued to receive freed slaves until the end of the nineteenth century. By 1888 over 900 runaway slaves had been harboured at Rabai.[47] During the early 1890s, the Imperial British East Africa Company handed over freed slaves to the missions' care, and from July 1884 the British government made a contribution of £5 to mission stations, Catholic and Protestant, for each freed slave placed in their care; this figure was based on Père Horner's reckoning that it would pay for the training to make an ex-slave self-supporting.

After 1890 the majority of freed slaves seem to have been handed over to the Roman Catholic missions, although the Protestant missions at Rabai and Freretown continued to be a refuge for runaway slaves from Arab masters along the coast. The harbouring of such slaves by the missions was the cause of much acrimony between government and missions during the mid-1890s.[48]

Perhaps unique of its kind was the runaway slave settlement on the Juba River. Here freed slaves had themselves settled the problem of finding a home of their own. They congregated in great numbers on the bank of the lower Juba, and by their own unaided efforts established a reputation for industry and skill in managing their own affairs. They irrigated the land on either side of the Juba for a distance of 100 miles, and by the latter part of the nineteenth century were a thriving community of 30,000 to 40,000 freed slaves, their numbers continually augmented by newcomers.[49]

Similarly, on the Sabaki river, freed slaves set up their own communities. Lugard, in the employ of the IBEAC, during his first few months on the coast in 1889 worked with colonies of runaway slaves on the Sabaki, where, for self-protection, they had banded together in communities, carrying on cultivation to a high degree, and resisting successfully attempts by the Arabs to re-enslave them.[50] The Company was in a dilemma as to how best meet this situation. It could ransom the slaves as the missions had done; but this was unwise—the practice could give rise to abuses. It encouraged slaves to run away. Cases were recorded by Lugard where slaves, after being redeemed, returned voluntarily to their former masters. A liberated slave would sell his freedom paper to another man. This was fairly easy in a country 'where you can find twenty men of the same name in a square mile' and names changed daily; and a redeemed slave might sell himself twice over and 'get double value for his paper'. The whole mess was inextricable. 'Owners will co-operate in this swindle, and arranging that their slaves shall return to them, will get the price of their liberation and their slave as well'. The law courts at Mombasa and Zanzibar daily recognized the validity of these claims of ownership. Faced with this problem, the British East Africa Company entered into an arrangement with slave owners near Fuladoyo and Rabai whereby their slaves who sought refuge with the British were allowed to work out their freedom, at the rate of £2 per slave, equivalent to three months' pay; in the meantime, owners agreed not to seize the slaves or molest them. In all about 300 fugitive slaves were redeemed in this fashion.

These self-liberated slaves provided a labour force for the British East Africa Company's plantations at Malindi, and along the Sabaki river, and stockades which Lugard built around these fugitive slave colonies were meant to protect them from fresh enslavement. Lugard favoured the industrial type of mission, such as he had admired at the Catholic Mission at Bagamoyo, and like that of the Scottish Missionaries at Kibwezi, 200 miles inland from the coast. He would liked to have seen similar institutions established inland, and he had worked out plans for such a colony of liberated slaves in Uganda, when his departure for England in 1892 resulted in the project being dropped.

The Arabs resented freed slave homes, and the militant attitude of missions in appropriating their slaves. Lugard cites a case where missionary caravans broke up and dispersed slave caravans by force; and when the Arabs declared their intention of attacking a Church Missionary Society station, the latter raised a flag of war inscribed 'Ungwana' (freedom).[51] Kirk took the official view that Arabs were entitled under Islamic law to recover their slaves in the Sultan's dominions, and he only managed to restrain them from wreaking vengeance on the missionaries with the promise that the latter would harbour no more escaped slaves. This compromise lasted only a few years. The missionaries were again harbouring refugee slaves by the early 1890s.

During the Anglo-German blockade of the East African coast in 1888-9, when the import of arms and power was restricted, the missionaries at Rabai and Freretown were in a precarious position. The Arabs were in angry mood, and demanded the return of their slaves who had sought refuge at the missions. The Arabs were only assuaged when the Imperial British East Africa Company, the missions, and the British government between them advanced £3500 for the redemption of these slaves.[52] However, fugitive slaves continued to come to the missions in small numbers well into the late 1890s. Lugard and other British officials were never happy in the matter of missionaries freeing slaves. In Uganda Lugard saw the result of handing over freed women to the French Catholic missions, for these women were subsequently placed in the care of Roman Catholic chiefs. And Lugard opposed the purchase of children by the missions for religious education; it was an illegal business, and smacked of proselytizing on the cheap! It was forcible detention and instruction,[53] and these purchases were likely to be looked upon as mission property. According to the letter of the law, these missions were guilty of trafficking in slaves, even though they were ransomed or purchased with the intention of granting them freedom later.

The solution to the problem of the disposal of freed slaves came as a welcome relief to the hard-pressed naval anti-slave trade patrol, faced with the new and increasing challenge of Arab slavers running under the protection of the French flag. This was to be the major obstacle to an effective anti-slave trade patrol for the remainder of the century.

5
The Clarendon Committee 1869
Select Committee 1870/71
the 1873 Treaty

By the 1860s, the anti-slave trade crusade on the west coast of Africa was drawing to a close. In England there was a relaxation of the fine fervour which had existed in Lord Palmerston's time; there seemed hardly enough enthusiasm to generate and sustain a campaign against the East African trade. The press and officialdom appeared to be ignorant of the subject. Along the whole east African littoral, from Cape Guardafui to Port Natal, there was no official British representative to keep the home government informed as to the state of the slave trade; a motion in the House of Lords in 1866, to appoint a consul at Mozambique, was never acted on. A legal adviser to the Treasury stated before the Select Committee of 1870 that notice of the East African slave trade only came to his attention in 1864, in the matter of a slave vessel captured in East African waters and dealt with by his department.

But in many ways the 1860s were propitious for an East African campaign. Attention was directed to that coast by a number of factors. The loss of the British vessel, *St Abbs*, on the Somali coast in 1858, the disappearance of her crew, and subsequent rumours of a small band of white men lost in the interior, followed shortly after by the massacre of Sub-Lieutenant Fountaine and fourteen men from the gunboat *Penguin* by the Somalis near Cape Guardafui; the story, which spread in 1867, that Livingstone was dead, the sadness, and then glad relief when it was learned that he was still alive; and finally, the prospects opened up by the Suez Canal, now nearing completion, which would link more closely the Indian Ocean to Europe: all attracted attention to East Africa and to the slave trade in that part of the world. Evidence of this concern over the East African slave trade was reflected in the treaty made by Britain on 27 June 1865 with the Queen of Madagascar, whereby she forbade her subjects to engage in the slave trade, prohibiting the landing of slaves at Madagascar, and gave to Her Majesty's cruisers full power of search over Malagasy or Arab vessels 'suspected of being engaged in the slave trade whether under sail or at anchor in the waters of Madagascar'. A treaty between the United States and Britain on 7 April 1862, for the suppression of the African slave trade, was revised in June 1870, because it had underestimated the dimensions of the East African slave trade.

Livingstone was the great beacon of the abolitionists. His reports, written in simple prose and with graphic detail, compelled attention. His accounts of the East African slave trade—although perhaps overdrawn in some cases—nevertheless went unchallenged. In his *Narrative of an Expedition to the Zambezi and its Tributaries* (1865) he described the desolation and horror caused by the slavers in the Nyasa region, where he met 'a long line of manacled men, women, and children', with the black drivers 'armed with muskets, and bedecked with various articles of finery,' marching jauntily in front, middle, and rear of the line . . . 'some of them blowing exulting notes out of long tin horns' as if they were doing 'a very noble thing'.

When the caravan leaders fled, and Livingstone liberated the captives, they knelt down, and

> in their way of expressing thanks, clapped their hands with great energy . . . each adult had his neck in the fork of a stout stick, six or seven feet long, and kept in by an iron rod, riveted at both ends across the throat . . . one by one the men were sawn out into freedom. The women, on being told to take the meal they were carrying, and cook breakfast for themselves and the children, seemed to consider the news too good to be true; but, after a little coaxing, went at it with alacrity, and made a capital fire by which to boil their pots, with the slave sticks and bonds, their old acquaintances through many a sad night and weary day. Many were mere children, about five years of age and under. One little boy, with the simplicity of childhood, said to our men, 'The others tied and starved us; you cut our ropes and tell us to eat. What sort of people are you? Where did you come from?' Two of the women had been shot the day before, for attempting to untie the thongs. This, the rest were told, was to prevent them attempting to escape. One woman had her infant's brains knocked out because she could not carry her load and it; and a man was despatched with an axe, because he had broken down with fatigue.
>
> It is our deliberate opinion, from what we know and have seen, that not one-fifth of the victims of the slave-trade ever become slaves. Taking the Shire valley as an average, we should say, not even one-tenth arrive at their destination.[1]

This was the very stuff to wring the hearts of the Victorian reading public.

In 1865, Livingstone entered on his last great expedition—'the first that ever saw slavery at its fountainhead'. His object was to explore that part of Africa lying between the 5th degrees of north and south latitude, to encourage lawful trade, and discourage the export of slaves. The British government expressed a deep and 'lively' interest in the objects of Livingstone's expedition.

While provisioning for it at Zanzibar, Livingstone noted that that island was 'the only spot in the world where from 100 to 300 slaves are daily exposed for sale in open market'. The northern Arabs were entirely to blame for this. The Sultan of Zanzibar, although willing to co-operate with the British, was unable to coerce the Omani Arabs, for to abolish the slave trade in 'his dominions would start a revolution which might end in his own expulsion or even death'. Livingstone estimated that 3000 slaves annually were imported into Zanzibar by the reigning family and another 12,000 by the other inhabitants. There were 100,000 slaves in Zanzibar, and the institution of slavery permeated the whole life of the island. As to abolishing it,

> there is a sort of charm in the prospect of gradual amelioration of the state of slavery by the steady advance of trade and civilization, yet all experience proved the prospect to be delusive.[2]

The scale of the slave trade as witnessed at Zanzibar continued to trouble Livingstone's mind, long after he left that island. Writing from Lake Nyasa in August 1866, he was still pondering as to how the slave trade based on Zanzibar might be demolished; this was 'the most important crisis of action'.

In late 1866, while up the Ruvuma river, and during the months which followed, Livingstone sent out accounts of the slave trade in the interior. In a report to Lord Clarendon, 20 August 1866, he described a tract of very fine, well-watered, but depopulated country which took eight days' hard marching to cross:

> It was about 100 miles broad, and so long, there was no possibility of going round either end. It bore all the marks of having been densely populated at some former period . . . The process of depopulation to which I have adverted goes on annually.

In a letter dated 1 February 1867, when near the southern end of Lake Tanganyika, Livingstone described the methods of the slave hunters in the interior. The Arabs were provided by their agents in Zanzibar with needful articles for barter—beads, common cotton cloth, muskets and ammunition. The beads and cloth were used for paying their way during the early part of the journey and for the purchase of ivory, and this mercantile character was preserved for a large portion of the trip. The Arabs would then settle down with some chieftain and cultivate the soil, and would assist him in raids against neighbouring tribes; and the captives from these raids fell into their hands. It was a simple pattern to be duplicated time and again throughout East/Central Africa.

Livingstone's reports coming in during the summer of 1867 were especially propitious for the anti-slave trade cause. The British and Foreign Anti-Slavery Society had taken advantage of the Great Exhibition in Paris in August 1867, where many important friends of the anti-slavery cause would be present, to convene an Anti-Slavery Conference there. The time was ripe for action. The American Civil War was ended. Everyone was aware of Livingstone. The Suez Canal was in its final stage of completion. The Anti-Slavery Conference in Paris saw East Africa as the last great region of the world where an active slave trade still existed. Thus it saw the need for

> a new and earnest appeal to the justice of sovereigns and the opinion of peoples in favour of the radical and immediate abolition of the slave trade.

Memorials were sent to the Sultan of Turkey, the Khedive of Egypt, the Pope, and the Sultan of Zanzibar, seeking their aid in putting down the slave trade in Africa and the Middle East. A deputation from the Comité Francaise d'Emancipation and the British and Foreign Anti-Slavery Society had an audience with the Khedive of Egypt, then in Paris, in the summer of 1867, and raised with him the question of slavery in his dominions. They got small satisfaction. Ismail claimed that boats engaged in the slavery on the Nile generally hoisted 'European colours', and that so-called slaves were often crew members. Female slaves were wives or concubines, and young slaves were usually their children. Ismail was not enthused over the anti-slave trade cause, and could not promise quick results.

> Slavery had existed in the country for 1283 years, and was mixed up with religion. It was a horrible institution, and he desired to see it extinguished, but it was not to be done in a day.

There were resolutions and exchange of information at the Conference. Horace Waller, Lay Superintendent of the Universities Mission to Central Africa and, later, editor of Livingstone's *Last Journals,* was a vocal and influential delegate. He drew attention to the slave trade from Central and East Africa which supplied 'not the Brazils nor Cuba, but the Persian Gulf, the Red Sea and the Comoro

Islands and Madagascar'. The Zanzibar market

> year by year receives into its pens, and hands over to the miserable Arabs, from 20,000 to 25,000 human beings, who have been in many cases purchased in the interior of Africa for two yards of calico a piece.[3]

According to Waller thirty thousand slaves were taken from the mainland annually and, since he added that 'for each marketable slave that reaches the seaboard, ten lives are lost in the interior of the country', it could be assumed there was an overall drain of 300,000 human beings from East/Central Africa.

Delegates at the Conference drew attention to the connection between Islam and the East African slave trade—'So long as Islamism encourages polygamy and Slavery in Africa that continent will be a dishonoured land'. Thus a proposal was made to approach the Sultan of Turkey and Pasha of Egypt 'to diminish the female slavery which still exists in Africa and Asia'.

The Sultan of Zanzibar, in response to an appeal from the Conference for co-operation, sent two Commissioners to London to affirm his good intentions in the matter. The British Anti-Slavery Society took the opportunity to press on these commissioners another copy of the memorial from the recent Anti-Slavery Conference in Paris. The Commissioners affirmed their master's good intentions and that was about all. Little of a concrete nature resulted from the Paris Conference.

But events were still moving in favour of the abolitionists. The year 1869 marked the beginning of a new era in British interest in East Africa. In that year the Suez Canal was opened and the greater volume of traffic passing through it was British, an increasing portion of which was directed to the East African coast. Quicker journeys brought more contact and more frequent capital turnover and development of commerce with East Africa. Passengers on the first ships passing through the newly-opened canal became aware of slaves at Port Said, Suez, and Aden, and the freed slave home at the latter place. There was a desire for more up-to-date information on the East African coast-line. Nothing had been added since Owen's survey of 1823-4. Information about the interior was coming in from explorers—notably from Livingstone now journeying in the region of Lake Tanganyika.

At the same time reports from officers on the British anti-slave trade patrol in 1868-9 showed an increase in the slave trade. But their zeal in attempting to check it brought complaints from the French of serious irregularities and mistakes committed by officers commanding HM's ships employed in the suppression of the slave trade on the East Coast of Africa.

Special instructions issued in 1869, warning naval officers of the need for prudence in the exercise of their duties, came at the same time as Consul Churchill, at Zanzibar, and Commodore Heath, in charge of the naval squadron, were urging a new approach in the suppression of the East African slave trade. The conjoint effect was that Lord Clarendon, in 1869, addressed a circular letter to British consular agents in the Near and Middle East, asking for up-to-date information on the slave trade in that part of the world.

In the same year, Clarendon appointed a Committee to inquire into the East African slave trade and recommend measures for its suppression. This Committee submitted their report to Lord Clarendon on 25 January 1870.[4] The Committee found the slave trade almost exclusively confined to the East Coast of Africa, especially the territories of the Sultan of Zanzibar, where a domestic legal slave trade was a disguise for a foreign and illegal traffic. The Sultan had a vested interest in the continuance of this slave trade. He obtained a large revenue from it, and members of his family were involved in it. The support of his own Arab subjects largely rested on his not disturbing the institution. The difficulties faced by the anti-slave trade patrol in its watch against this slave trade along a vast stretch of coast, extending from Mozambique to the Persian Gulf, engrossed the attention of the Committee. A better strategic positioning of cruisers was suggested, and a stricter watch during the period of the south-west monsoon. A depot ship at Zanzibar, with a decked steam launch attached, would help. Boats on inshore service should be lightly armed, sufficiently manned, and swift, to prevent dhows hugging the coast. The Committee deprecated too frequent change of officers. Better and more reliable interpreters were needed. An increase in pay and allowances rather than a bounty system—unequal in its operation and leading to abuse— was necessary to encourage zeal in the service. The Committee recommended an improvement in the conditions for officers and men on the anti-slave trade patrol (and this was reflected in the new Admiralty handbook that came out the same year). The Committee would limit adjudication over captured slave vessels to three Vice-Admiralty Courts—Aden, Zanzibar and Muscat, they being more nearly within the perimeter of the activities of the naval anti-slave patrol.[5]

The Committee did not advocate immediate prohibition of the

slave trade. This might ruin the commerce of Zanzibar, and 'where there is commerce there is most slaves'. Prohibition would also drastically reduce the Sultan's revenue, weaken his power, and possibly lead to the loss of his throne—even his life. But the Committee advocated control over the supply of slaves going to Zanzibar by making Dar es Salaam the sole point on the mainland for their export to Zanzibar, from whence they could be re-exported to Pemba and Mombasa to meet the requirements of those places, as determined annually by the Sultan and British Agent at Zanzibar. The number of slaves thus imported into Zanzibar would be gradually decreased so as to cease altogether within a time to be decided on later. Dar es Salaam, nearly opposite Zanzibar, had a good harbour: Sultan Majid had commenced building a palace, shops and gardens there, with a view to making it his mainland entrepot and royal residence. The ivory trade at Bagamoyo could be diverted to Dar es Salaam, which had all the makings of a prominent seaport. From here a watch could be kept on the slave trade, especially during the south-west monsoon when slavers had to pass between Zanzibar and the mainland. A legal slave trade would be carried on by vessels provided with a pass from the Sultan and with a large distinctive mark on their hull or sails. Closer regulation of the slave trade would also be secured by closing the public slave market at Zanzibar and adjusting the period of prohibition of the slave trade, as it presently stood, 1 January to 30 April, to more nearly coincide with the period of the monsoon. Severe penalties for persons involved in an illegal slave trade or interfering with liberated slaves, and prohibiting natives of Indian states under British protection from possessing slaves after a date to be fixed and in the meantime from acquiring fresh slaves, were also recommended by the Committee.

The slave trade could not be discussed without touching on Britain's relations with other states. Her Majesty's Government had treaties with Persia, Madagascar, Muscat, and states on the coast of Arabia, for the suppression of the slave trade. But these treaties were systematically violated. A most contentious question was that of Arab slavers sheltering under the French flag. This practice was increasing and posed a most serious problem for the anti-slave trade patrol. Her Majesty's Government had called the attention of the French Government to this abuse a number of times, and had met the latter's wishes in directing her naval officers to take special care lest they violate the French flag, as witnessed in recent Admiralty instructions to naval officers. It was now hoped that French authorities at Nossi-Bé and Mayotta would take strict precautions in issuing French papers to Arab vessels.

Finally, to secure a new approach to the problem of the East African slave trade, the Committee urged a treaty with the Sultan of Zanzibar providing for the eventual entire prohibition of the export of slaves from his East African dominions.

The Clarendon Committee's recommendations were challenged by Rigby, former consul at Zanzibar, who maintained that a regularized slave trade, narrowly channelled along certain routes, would worsen the lot of the slaves. As for confining the slave trade to certain months of the year, by whose calendar would this be reckoned, Arab lunar month or Christian calendar? The Arabs were unfamiliar with the latter. Rigby also wanted more attention directed to the Middle East—demand for slaves there would always generate a slave trade to meet it. The Committee's proposed subsidy for an East African steamship line as a means of encouraging legitimate commerce with East Africa was objected to by the British Treasury. Trade should develop on its own initiative, not be propped up by British taxpayers' money.

The Clarendon Committee completed its report at a time when the last replies to Lord Clarendon's circular were coming in. It was evident from these that the Committee in its inquiries had overlooked many issues, and had not faced the real complexity of the problem in suppressing the slave trade. Livingstone's descriptions of the horrors of the slave trade in the interior were still coming in, and making a deep impression. Abolitionists were urging action. Parliament was now awakened to the fact that the East African slave trade existed on a scale hitherto unimagined. It presented as grave a problem as that previously faced on the west coast of Africa. The Clarendon Committee's enquiries and replies to Clarendon's circular merely pointed to the need for a full-scale inquiry into the East African slave trade.

On 6 July 1870, the Government announced the appointment of a Select Committee of the House of Commons

> to inquire into the whole question of the Slave Trade on the East Coast of Africa, into the increased and increasing amount of that traffic, the particulars of existing treaties and agreements with the Sultan of Zanzibar upon the subject and the possibility of putting an end entirely to the traffic in slaves by sea.[6]

In the meantime, there had been a change in the main personalities involved in the scene. On 27 June 1870, the Foreign Secretary, Lord Clarendon, died and was succeeded by Lord Granville; on 7 October

1870, Majid, Sultan of Zanzibar, died. His successor, half-brother and former rival, Barghash, had previously lived in exile in Bombay. He was more a man of the world than his predecessor; he had lived abroad and had greater awareness of social and political questions than the Arab coterie which surrounded him in Zanzibar. But, like his predecessors, Barghash found it most difficult to go against their wishes.

Prior to accession to the Sultanate, he had given promises of good faith to H. A. Churchill, the British consul, stating that he would honour the treaties entered into by his predecessors for the suppression of the slave trade. But once on the throne, Barghash disavowed promises made to Churchill. Expectation of French support may have caused this change of attitude. French influence at Zanzibar at the time is difficult to asses. The construction of a large French barracks in Zanzibar in 1861 had caused British apprehension; it seemed a prelude to French occupation, but this never came. French influence in Zanzibar always remained a threat insofar as the Sultan could invoke it when making a stand against the British. On the question of the slave trade, however, it was more likely the resistance of the Arabs that shored up Barghash in his stand against its abolition.

Churchill spoke of an increasing lack of courtesy on Barghash's part, possibly adopted to impress his wealthy Arab subjects. Barghash protested against the activities of the anti-slave trade patrol and would have nothing to do with a controlled slave export from Dar es Salaam. Dar es Salaam was the creation of his predecessor, Majid, for whom, together with everything associated with his name, he had a hearty dislike. The recommendation of the Clarendon Committee and Churchill that, in return for a treaty to suppress the trade, the Sultan should be released from the obligation to pay the annual subsidy of 40,000 Maria Theresa dollars (£8,500) to the ruler of Muscat (Majid always argued that the slave tax was necessary to pay this) and that henceforth it would be paid jointly by the India Office and the Foreign Office,[7] was a most tempting bait, but it was insufficient to sway the new sultan. He was opposed to any new anti-slave trade treaty.

In the face of this obduracy, Churchill wrote to Barghash on 10 November 1870

> It was your own father who solicited of the British Government the presence of a British Agent at his Court

and reminded him of past British friendship, that he was dependent on British goodwill, and that a new slave trade treaty was inevitable. There was increasing estrangement between the British consul and the Sultan. Ill health forced Churchill to leave Zanzibar within two months of Barghash's succession to the throne. Dr Kirk, the agency surgeon, took over as acting consul, and achieved a more friendly rapport with the Sultan. The latter, apparently alarmed over rumours that his half-brother, Turki, who had recently seized the throne of Oman, had eyes on Zanzibar, turned to the British for support, and Kirk was soon able to report a change in Barghash's attitude. But the Select Committee was now in the midst of its sittings and, pending the result of its inquiries, nothing more was done about a treaty.

The Select Committee of 1870/71,[8] under the Chairmanship of Russell Gurney, a prominent Quaker, sat from July 1870 to August 1871. It had before it the report of the Committee of 1869/70, and it heard a variety of witnesses: Sir Bartle Frere, late Governor of Bombay; officials of the Slave Trade Department at the Foreign Office; former Consuls Rigby and Churchill; admirals formerly in command of the East Indies Squadron; Captains of cruisers, Colomb and Sulivan; and missionaries, friends of Livingstone, notably Horace Waller, shortly to publish the *Last Journals* of the great explorer. Whenever the Committee tended to stray away from the humane to the more technical aspect of the problem, the latest accounts from Livingstone always brought it back to its task with a jolt.

There were self-evident facts facing the Select Committee. The predominant branch of the slave trade was that from the African dominions of the Sultan of Zanzibar to the Arabian and Persian Gulf world, and the naval anti-slave trade patrol faced exceedingly great difficulties in suppressing this slave trade. The most pernicious aspect of it was the so-called 'domestic' slave trade, which acted as a cloak for the foreign and illegal slave trade. Slaves were increasingly passed off as crew necessary for working the ship, they frequently made up half the crew,[9] and letters found on captured dhows showed that 'domestic slaves' were often destined for sale overseas. The difference between 'domestic' and 'raw' slaves might sometimes be detected by their physical condition; otherwise it usually took two or three days to ferret out their real status. The slavers had instilled in the slave's mind a dislike and fear of Europeans, spreading the report that they were cannibals or wished to steal the slaves for themselves. Sulivan stated that it was almost impossible to ascertain whether slaves were 'domestic' or not.

The Select Committee examined the strategy employed by HM's

Navy on its East India Station. During the years 1867-9, over 800 dhows had been boarded, but only 116, carrying 2645 slaves, had been captured; yet it was estimated that 37,000 slaves had been exported northwards during this period. The naval squadron was handicapped by too few ships, the guise of domestic slaves used to camouflage the real slave trade, existing treaties with the Sultan which prohibited the seizure of dhows south of Lamu, difficulty in intercepting dhows hugging the coast, want of information as to their movements, too frequent change of naval officers and lack of recorded information by officers who had preceded them, untrustworthy interpreters who were often in league with slavers and who misled the commander of the squadron. One interpeter, a half-caste Arab, was himself a former slaver. The disposal of unseaworthy captured dhows posed a problem. The latest official instructions ruled out the longstanding practice of scuttling them except as an extreme measure.

> Nothing will excuse the officer in not sending the vessel to a court of adjudication except the facts showing satisfactorily that doing so would have involved serious danger to the lives of the prize crew.

If a captured vessel could not be taken to a port of adjudication she must be left at some secure point under the Sultan's governors along the coast, or with authorities at Socotra, Johanna, or neighbouring islands, until an order was sent for her disposal. But only if this were not possible, or if the vessel were not in a condition to be taken to the port of adjudication, might she be destroyed.

A clearer definition of the areas of jurisdiction of the Admiralty Courts was essential. That at Zanzibar should have jurisdiction between the latitudes of Cape Guardafui and Delagoa Bay; that at Aden over the Red Sea, Gulf of Aden, and sector north of the equator; and the court at Muscat would serve the Persian Gulf, Gulf of Oman and the area east of Cape Guardafui. Some overlapping of jurisdiction was permissible, for it would depend on the season of the year and prevailing wind whether a prize should be taken to one Court rather than another. The master and crew of captured vessels must in all cases have the opportunity of establishing their innocence. In addition, a supply depot ship based on Zanzibar might, as on the west coast of Africa, facilitate the operation of light scouting craft.

Admirals Heath and Hillyar, and Captain Colomb, all with first-hand experience, were alarmed by what they considered to be the temporizing of the Select Committee, and the ineffective measures which it proposed. They were for drastic solutions. Why not purchase Zanzibar, acquire it lock, stock and barrel as was done in the case of Lagos on the West Coast of Africa? This would end the problem once and for all. Rigby was for a drastic strengthening of the naval patrol; more captures would destroy the slave trade. He had no faith in paper promises—'Treaties with Arabs are mere waste paper'. Vivian favoured a 'complete paper blockade' of the whole coast of East Africa and strict enforcement of the anti-slave trade treaties. More international co-operation was necessary: the United States and other powers had taken no active part in suppressing the slave trade in East Africa. They could put pressure on the Sultan through their various commercial treaties with him; these, if revoked, would deprive him of much revenue. Admiral Cockburn suggested that the Sultan receive an annual subsidy equal to the present tax revenue from the slave trade in return for abolishing it. Britain would more than save this sum in bounties and the cost of the anti-slave trade patrol,[10] and thereafter a British man-of-war and an officer stationed at Zanzibar would suffice to counter the small scale smuggling of slaves. Sir Bartle Frere argued for the closing of ports of reception for slaves in the Middle East: the Persian Gulf should be blockaded rather than the East African coast. Frere also recommended more use of telegraphic advice for warning of slave dhow movements.

There were what might be termed fringe problems which engaged the Select Committee's attention. Slave-holding by British Indians (natives of British protected Indian states) had continued despite Rigby's attempt to deal with the problem, and despite a proclamation of the Rao of Kutch making over to Britain protection of his subjects abroad. But there were other Indians—British subjects in East Africa—not affected by this proclamation, whose slave-holding in Zanzibar dominions had to be ended. Divided superintendence and the dual nature of the British political agent and consul at Zanzibar led to confusion and recrimination between the India Office and Foreign Office. As political agent, he represented the Bombay government but he was also, ex-officio, consul for the British government. This led to dual correspondence, copies to the India Office and to the Foreign Office, and from both he received instructions. The consul was increasingly devoting most of his time to slave trade matters under the direction of the Foreign Office, and these had become particularly onerous following the establishment of the Vice-Admiralty Court at Zanzibar in 1866. The Indian government argued that their agent was devoting too much of his time to slave trade matters, and the Foreign Office should bear the major cost of the Zanzibar agency, and should open negotiations with the British India Steamship Navigation Company for a subsidized mail service to Zanzibar.[11] In return, the India office would share the cost of the Zanzibar subsidy to Muscat. But the Treasury, with characteristic parsimony, and ill-disposed towards the anti-slave trade campaign—'the game was not worth the candle'—had refused funds to the Foreign Office for the purpose. But the point had been made and the Select Committee recognized the need for a separate officer at Zanzibar to deal with slave trade matters.

What were the Select Committee's conclusions? It recommended the appointment of an Assistant Political Agent and Vice-Consul at Zanzibar to assist in matters pertaining to the slave trade. Kirk would be ideal for the post, and the Imperial Exchequer should bear the charge. There should also be consular officers at Kilwa, Dar es Salaam and Lamu. But the main need was to prohibit the foreign slave trade from the Zanzibar dominions and, in focusing on this question, the Committee set aside the suggestion that Zanzibar should be purchased; this was quite unrealistic. A new treaty was required, as recommended by the Clarendon Committee, and it should contain provisions for ending the foreign slave trade and closing the Zanzibar and Kilwa slave markets. The Committee seemed to think that difficulty in getting the Sultan to accede to such a treaty would be overcome by the argument that he would benefit from the increased legitimate commerce at Zanzibar which would result from abolition of the slave trade. Hence, there was no mention of compensation for the Sultan to cover the financial loss he would incur from the abolition of the slave trade and the cessation of the tax on slave imports and exports. As a last resort, if the Sultan refused to sign a new treaty, Her Majesty's Government must take measures to end the slave trade.

To ensure the prohibition of the slave trade as provided for under the proposed treaty, the Committee recommended increased and regular naval patrols, a strengthened naval squadron, provision of steam launches for inshore duty, recorded information on the slave trade to be made available to officers on the anti-slave trade patrol, efficient and trustworthy interpreters, and that Zanzibar be made a depot for freed slaves with the Seychelles as an alternative. The establishment of regular steamship communication with Zanzibar linking up with the Seychelles some 800 miles to the east was recommended to offset French competition in that part of the world. The aid of other powers, France, USA, Portugal, and Germany, should be sought in suppressing the East African slave trade; Germany, especially, in view of her preponderant trade at Zanzibar, had a responsibility in the matter. Persia should offer greater facilities and co-operation for the anti-slave trade patrol in the Persian Gulf. A proposal that savings from the reduced patrol on the West Coast of Africa should be diverted to the East African campaign was dropped; this would have meant a running battle with the Treasury.[12]

The Select Committee had completed its task. And, although it had spent much longer on it and had much more information available to it than had the Clarendon Committee, it came to the same main conclusion as had the latter. The East African slave trade could only be brought to an end through the auspices of the Sultan of Zanzibar. And to this end a new treaty must be made with him.

Even while the Select Committee was sitting there was a pronounced increase in the slave trade. The great cholera epidemic of 1869-70 which had ravaged the western Indian Ocean world had heightened the demand for slaves in the Arabian seas and Persian Gulf regions, while at Zanzibar it caused a glut of slaves. Kirk reported from there early in 1870 that

> There died here in this town alone upwards of 10,000 in one month and a half, and 30,000 in the whole island: now it rages up and down the coast. At Quiloa—by the last account, there were 200 deaths a day among the slaves. When offered at one dollar a head they found no purchasers, so very worthless had slave property become from the disease.[13]

Large numbers of slaves were assembled at Zanzibar for shipment northwards:

> Never since coming to Zanzibar have I seen so many large dhows come in crowded with slaves: and seldom have the slaves been landed in a worse state.[14]

But the market fluctuated again in 1872, when a disastrous hurricane ruined Arab plantations in Zanzibar, lessening enormously the demand for labour there.

> Less than one-quarter of the usual crop of cloves were expected. Slaves are now in fact a burden on the large estates, and expense to the owner.

The northern Arabs had a buyer's market and made the most of the opportunity.

As mentioned, the Select Committee's report appeared when the last letters from Livingstone were coming in, and information from Sir Samuel Baker, on his second expedition to Equatoria, showed that the slave traders had penetrated the farthest reaches of the upper Nile. The Anti-Slavery Society retailed at length details of the slave trade in East Africa. At a large meeting of the Society in July 1872, the French historian, M. Berlioux, was cited as asserting that in the eyes of other powers Britain condoned the slave trade in East Africa.[15] In a debate on the East African slave trade in the House of Lords, a motion was supported for an increase in British naval power on the East African coast.[16] In Zanzibar, Kirk pressed for action. Barghash had renewed the 'open season' which his predecessor had prohibited. There was urgent need to obtain a treaty from the Sultan of Zanzibar as recommended by the Select Committee.

But this was a task which would require finesse, patience, and an understanding of the oriental mind. Kirk, whose knowledge and ability were increasingly recognized, should have been given the task of obtaining this treaty, but he was passed over in favour of Sir Bartle Frere, a former governor of Bombay and member of the Council of India, whose high abilities, great experience, and distinguished service in the East were thought to pre-eminently qualify him for this diplomatic challenge. Frere, a strong opponent of slavery in India, had made a strong impression with his evidence before the Select Committee of 1871. He had consistently pressed for action against the East African slave trade and had suggested a special mission to East Africa for this purpose in December 1869. This suggestion was now taken up by Lord Argyle in April 1871, in a proposal to Lord Mayo of the India Council that advantage might be taken of the recent accession of Barghash and Turki, at Zanzibar and Muscat respectively, to obtain concessions towards ending the slave trade.[17] In return for these, Frere was empowered to offer as inducement to Barghash that he would be relieved of the obligation of paying the annual subsidy to Muscat and, in turn, Turki would be assured of its payment by the Government of Bombay, the cost to be shared by the Imperial and Indian Treasuries.[18] Whether Frere was the best choice for the assignment is debatable.[19] He was high-handed in his approach and conspicuously, and surprisingly in view of his long experience in the East, lacking in tact in dealing with an Arab prince with long and honourable relationship with Britain. But there was urgent need for a treaty, and Frere was the man to obtain it.

Frere and his mission left England on 21 November 1872.[20] Following an audience with Pope Pius IX, there was a meeting with the Khedive of Egypt, who professed sympathy for the anti-slave trade cause; he was pleased to point out that he had incurred much expense in sending Samuel Baker up the White Nile to check the slave trade, and instanced his attempt to establish a school in Cairo to train freed slave girls for domestic work. Frere was sceptical of Ismail's promises. The Khedive's mother, at the time of Frere's visit, was recruiting slaves for her granddaughter's trousseau.

On 12 January, Frere made an imposing entry into Zanzibar on board a man-of-war and supported by three cruisers. He came as a great pro-consul of Britain, bearing a letter and many valuable presents from Her Majesty the Queen. He was received with much fanfare. Zanzibar was agog with arrangements for the Livingstone Search Expedition. Zanzibar was a scene of activity. Granville's desire for publicity for Frere's altruistic mission was fully met. Advance notice had been circulated as far away as the Persian Gulf and Arabian Seas as to the significance of Frere's mission. The Queen's letter to the Sultan, couched in respectful terms, invited him to join in framing measures for the complete suppression of 'this cruel and destructive traffic'. This great work of civilization had already been achieved on the west coast of Africa. To achieve the same result on the east coast of Africa was the object of Her Majesty's Government, and it was their wish that the Sultan should share in this civilizing and beneficent task. But if the Sultan showed reluctance, Frere was instructed to use 'firm but conciliatory language': he could promise the Sultan relief from the payment of the subsidy of £8,500 to Muscat in return for engagements to suppress the slave trade.

The terms of the Draft Treaty which Frere was to place before the Sultans of Zanzibar and Muscat, in summary, were as follows:

> After a date to be fixed, all export of slaves from the mainland of Africa, would cease: all public slave markets in his dominions would be closed: liberated slaves to be protected and any molestation or attempt to re-enslave them would be punished: natives of Indian states under British protection after a date to be fixed, to be prohibited from possessing slaves and meanwhile from acquiring fresh ones.

The treaty would be ratified as soon as possible. There was urgent need for it. Even while Frere was at Zanzibar, he witnessed the capture of four slave dhows in Zanzibar harbour, one of which carried 80 slaves, and he saw slaves left to die on the beach at Zanzibar, to avoid the payment of customs duty on their entry into the island.

Not one moment too soon, not one whit too strongly, has England interfered to abolish forever the curse of Africa.²¹

But Frere's month's stay at Zanzibar was singularly fruitless. Barghash was reluctant to face up to the required treaty. Frere's tone grew increasingly imperious, and Barghash used all the 'exasperating arts of the East' to delay.

The Reverend G. Badger took over the negotiations. He reminded the Sultan of the slave trade in the interior, in territory over which the Sultan claimed sovereignty, as at Unyamwezi. But the Sultan claimed that these purported slaves were probably 'beggars'. At one stage in an interview with Badger, 'The Sultan was moved to tears over the consequences which would result from the treaty'. When pressed to take courage and sign it, he cried that he was unable to lift the pen.²² Final interviews on 21 January and 1 February resulted in Frere warning the Sultan of the severe measures that would follow unless a new treaty were signed. But the Sultan pointed to the many years of grace given to Portugal—15 years to end slavery. And God only knows, if he granted this concession to Britain, 'what the fifth demand may be'. Frere's last interview with the Sultan was decidedly cold. There was a 'cessation of the little civilities, in the shape of presents of fruit, ice, etc., which had been sent by His Highness to persons connected with the Mission on shore'.

Who was to blame for the impasse? Frere was not noted for sweet temper. His final word of warning that Britain would use naval means to bring about forcibly what could not be attained diplomatically caused the Sultan to break off any further discussion. Frere, on his part, no longer wished to meet the Sultan. Kirk intervened on 4 February, and the Sultan withdrew his refusal to consider a treaty, implying that he would gladly sign if its operation could be deferred for some years. But this Kirk could not promise. It would never be accepted by HMG nor the abolitionists. Customary presents and little courtesies now ceased.

On 13 February 1873, Frere left Zanzibar on a tour of inspection of the southern slave ports, hoping that by the time he returned the Sultan might have reconsidered his position. Frere blamed his failure to obtain a treaty on 'the action of some secret advice',²³ presumably from the French, for he had noted the hostility of the French Consul and naval officers in Zanzibar and there was a rumour that a French vessel was on its way to Zanzibar to support the Sultan in his stand against English pressure. Frere's tour of the southern ports was meant to take in Kilwa Kivinja, 'the real hotbed of the slave trade on the coast', but Indian residents there ran away on his approach and he was hindered in his attempt to interview slaves. As for Lindi, the town was beseiged by a hostile tribe, the population had sought refuge on an island, and the Indians were disembarking with their goods. At Mozambique, where he expected to see the much reputed Portuguese involvement in the slave trade, he met a Portuguese governor who admitted the existence of a considerable slave trade. But the Portuguese were showing signs of a new approach and vigour in administering their colony, and foreigners were no longer debarred from settling in the country. On his return journey northwards, Frere had his long-wished-for look at Kilwa Kivinja.

It turned out to be a very large town, even more thriving than Zanzibar, not marked on our charts, and placed out of sight of cruisers, among unsurveyed reefs, difficult of access to any but Arab dhows.

He met the greatest insolence from Arab governors and the 'usually mild obsequious Indians', and the local Wali was most uncooperative; all fearful that Frere would ascertain the large slave trade carried on at Kilwa Kivinja. Frere's tour along the coast convinced him that the Sultan's control over the coast was very superficial, and he appeared to have had little contact with it. Possibly the greatest impact that this tour along the coast made on Frere was the realization of the extensive control of commerce exercised by the Indians; they managed all the commercial enterprise and customs houses along the coast.

Back at Zanzibar on 15 March 1873, Frere again pressed the Sultan for a treaty. No response being forthcoming, Frere departed from Zanzibar on 17 March, leaving Kirk the unenviable task of extracting the treaty. On his return northward, Frere stopped at Bagamoyo where he noted the good work of the French Mission in caring for freed slaves, and was so impressed that he contributed £200 to the Mission, and recommended to the British government that £5 be henceforth given to all the Missions for every liberated slave placed in their care. Before leaving Mombasa, his next stop, Frere had instructed Kirk to enforce strictly previous treaties, to institute a naval blockade of Kilwa and Pemba, and to seize all slaves exported outside the legal season. This was high-handed action. It was meant to intimidate the Sultan and demonstrate the effect of what a blockade of Zanzibar would do, for it caused a drop in slave prices at Kilwa of as much as fifty per cent. Among dhows captured while running the blockade was one owned by the Sultan's sister and carrying 400 slaves. Frere would have taken even a firmer line than this. He would have closed the Zanzibar slave market and imposed an embargo on the custom house, but the Foreign Office overruled him.

At Mukalla, on the Arabian coast, he renewed an agreement of 14 May 1868 with its Naqib (Governor) for the suppression of the slave trade; and at Muscat, on 12 April, a similar treaty was made with its ruler, Sultan Sayyid Turki bin Said. From Muscat Frere issued a strong dispatch to Kirk, enjoining him to extract the treaty which he himself had failed to obtain,[24] for

> the Sultan of Zanzibar is left alone in his determination to resist the wishes of the civilized world and to maintain the horrors of the Slave Trade.

There was disappointment in the Foreign Office over Frere's failure to obtain a treaty and perturbation at his high-handed instructions to Kirk. The Law Officers advised that the blockade of Pemba and Kilwa was an act of war. Granville directed Kirk, on 9 May, to cease these measures. Nevertheless, Her Majesty's Government were not prepared to acquiesce in the Sultan's refusal to sign a treaty, and Kirk was instructed by telegram on 15 May 1873 to inform the Sultan that Her Majesty's Government was adamant in its demand for a treaty, and that if it were not

> accepted and signed by him before the arrival of Admiral Cumming, who is ordered to proceed at once to Zanzibar, the British naval forces will blockade the Island of Zanzibar.[25]

Fortified by these instructions, Kirk approached the Sultan. There is a story, possibly apocryphal, that he persuaded the Sultan's most trusted counsellor and Chief Astrologer, Sheikh Abd al-Aziz, to impress on him that continued obstinancy would lead him to disaster. The astrologer advised the Sultan that it was written in the stars that he should sign. The Sultan in great fright sent at once for Kirk, and on 5 June 1873, the Treaty was signed.[26] It was more likely the fact that Kirk had established good relations with the leading Arabs in Zanzibar and that he played on the Sultan's imagination as to the dire effects of the threatened blockade which caused the Sultan to sign. The blighting of the economic life of Zanzibar, the drastic reduction in the Sultan's revenue, the cordon thrown around Zanzibar which would prevent even one foreign vessel from penetrating it (an indirect reference to the hint that the Sultan was relying on the arrival of a French vessel to get him out of the predicament), had caused Barghash to exclaim, 'I will come and live with you'.[27] The signed treaty was delivered to Frere at Aden, on his way home.

We have got the Treaty, thanks to the orders you gave at Mombasa, which I carried out with rather an iron hand, more in the spirit of total prohibition than anything else.

The obtaining of the Treaty was a diplomatic achievement for Kirk; he had been relegated to a secondary position during Frere's visit to Zanzibar.

The substance of the Treaty is contained in Barghash's proclamation of 8 June 1873.

To all our subjects who may see this, and also to others, May God save you. Now that we have prohibited the transport of raw slaves by sea in all our harbours and have closed the markets which are for the sale of slaves throughout all our dominions. Whosoever, therefore, shall ship a raw slave after this date, will render himself liable to punishment, and this he will bring upon himself. Be this known.

The treaty of 5 June 1873 prohibited the holding of slaves by Indians who were natives of Indian states under British possession. It also provided for the establishment of regular mail steamer communication with Zanzibar. The Indian government assumed responsibility for the Muscat subsidy. The treaty appeared to have accomplished all that its architects had set out to do, and when, on 20 June 1873, Rear-Admiral Cumming arrived at Zanzibar with a force of five warships, the Sultan was convinced that it had been no idle threat on the part of the British to blockade Zanzibar.

Although the most glaring crudities of the slave trade, the open misery of the slave markets, and the short but cruel sea voyage from the mainland to Zanzibar and Pemba were removed by the treaty of 1873,[28] the old problem of 'raw' slaves carried under the guise of domestic slaves remained. To constitute a slaver, slaves must form the cargo, or part of it. The problem of how to distinguish domestic slaves, passengers, and crew from 'raw' slaves continued to be one of the main obstacles in the work of the anti-slave trade patrol. And the 1873 treaty never received sufficient publicity. O'Sullivan, Vice-Consul for Pemba, claimed some years later that 'it is probable that many slave-holders have never heard of the Treaty'. It was also increasingly evident that the committee of 1871 had been merely a sop to humanitarians and public opinion. Public interest, temporarily aroused by an appeal for aid in erecting a cathedral, schools, and a public dispensary on the site of the late slave market at Zanzibar as living testimony to the work of the abolitionists, soon flagged, although one would not gather this from the columns of the *Anti-Slavery Reporter.* So little interest did Mr Gladstone evince in the matter that, entering into conversation with Frere shortly after the latter's return to England, he never so much as alluded to the subject.[29] Thus, Sir George Clerk, writing to Frere, on 26 June 1873,

> Bear in mind that you must not expect that this Government cares, or that the next will care 'tuppence' for slavery out there—except for party purposes. The more need therefore that local functions should be in operation that no ministry here could restrain or treat with supineness, without affording Opposition a chance of tripping them up.[30]

But in the Middle East immediate results of the 1873 treaty were favourable. From Muscat, Major Miles reported in October 1874 that since the recent treaties with Zanzibar and Muscat there had been few imports of slaves; and HM's cruisers *Rifleman, Philomel* and *Daphne* had made no captures.[31] Exports of slaves from Kilwa were halted, and there was such a glut of slaves there that prices dropped to a low of one dollar per slave, and this curtailment was reflected in the Middle East.

But this was only a temporary lull. A coastwise land trade, from Kilwa northwards to Lamu, quickly sprang up and Kilwa, that 'old plague spot', was soon as active as ever. Sales picked up. In August 1873, six large caravans arrived from the interior and prices rose to $6 to $10 for a strong, able-bodied slave, if able to endure the rigours of the land journey north. The price for the weak and old remained at half-a-dollar. Kirk, Captain Wharton, and Captain Elton, who visited the mainland to implement the clause forbidding Indians to hold slaves,[32] observed the extent of the new slave trade by land. During the five days Elton was at Dar es Salaam, five slave caravans, with 350 slaves, passed up the Kisiju road. On his way south from Dar es Salaam, Elton met gangs of slaves, 250 to 400 at a time chained together and heading northwards.

> One gang of lads and women chained together with iron neck rings was in a horrible state, their lower extremities coated with dry mud and their own excrement and torn with thorns, their bodies mere frameworks, and their skeleton limbs tightly stretched over with wrinkled parchment-like skin. One wretched woman had been flung against a tree for slipping her rope, and came screaming up to us for protection, with one eye half out, and the side of her face and bosom streaming with blood.[33]

Many of the slaves had come from the Nyasa area, and had been a year and a half in slave gangs, moving very slowly. Arab caravan leaders fled at the sight of Elton, or tried to drive their slaves into the long grass. Others were belligerent. They refused to believe that the

Sultan of Zanzibar had outlawed the slave trade. In December 1873, Elton met 15 slave caravans, one with over 1000 slaves—the caravan leader was not quite sure of the exact number.[34] Elton estimated that 4076 slaves passed northward by the land route between Kilwa and Dar es Salaam during the period December 1873 to January 1874.

At Kisiju, at the mouth of the Magassi River in Kiwale district, a garden area supplying millet and rice for Kilwa, Elton observed that the area in the centre of the town was set apart for the accommodation of caravans. There were cooking places, huts for shelter, spare rings and chains in readiness, and an old Arab 'who's task it was to apprehend runaways'. The inhabitants of Kisiju did a large business buying up half-dead slaves, fattening them up and selling them to the next caravan. The place was full of walking skeletons. The slave road between Kisiju and Kilwa avoided the malarious creeks of Samanga, the mangrove swamps and muddy deltas of the River Rufiji. Elton met slave caravans almost daily, and the ubiquitous Indians along the coast were abetting the slave trade.

By mid-February 1874, Elton gazed over the 'broad sands and mud flats of Kilwa'; 'its enervating climate, bad water, and severe fevers' were not to his liking. It was a nondescript town: native huts, a few stone houses with slave enclosures, a custom house, a so-called fort, scattered coconut trees fringing a 'fetid' beach, with grass flats stretching away into the background to a wooded and prominent range of sandstone hills. A dreary place for a sordid business. The 'Place of Skulls' marked a spot where slave trails branched, and skeletons lay in the bush. The market and nearby custom house served a motley crowd gathered to do slave business. A dozen Arabs, newly arrived by sea from Lamu, were purchasing slaves to be sent north by the Kisiju road; in less than a month 4000 slaves had passed through their hands and replenishments were at hand from the interior.

The whole tone of commerce at Kilwa was set by the slave trade. The town was "the headquarters of ruffianly adventurers who were guided by keen Shylocks'. There was daily departure of slaves north. They were kept on plantations near the town until ready for the march. The Sultan's tax-collecting machinery still operated, for the recent treaty had decreed only against the slave trade at sea. A tax of one to two dollars was now levied by the local governor on slaves crossing the Mgungara River on the land route to the north, a few miles outside the town. The land route for slaves was easier and cheaper than that by sea; duties could be evaded, food and water were available, strong hearty slaves were no worse for the long march, and mortality on the journey ran at about ten per cent—much less than on the sea journey from Kilwa.

Within a year of the treaty of 1873, 4000 slaves a month, in the peak period, were travelling north by the coast road.[35] Kirk placed the figure at 12,000 a year; Consul Holmwood, after visiting the northern part of the coast in the autumn of 1874, placed it at 32,000 a year; and Vice-Admiral Macdonald estimated the number at 10,000 to 12,000.

The land trade was well organized. Pemba, which had escaped the worst effects of the hurricane of 1872, provided a lucrative market, with a ring of landowners who, when the clove harvest was over, had cash in hand, and sent agents down to Kilwa to purchase slaves at $30 to $40 per head. These slaves were delivered at points designated by the purchaser, at Bagamoyo, Saadani, Pangani, Wasin, or Mombasa. The slaves were paid for on delivery and smuggled by the purchaser across to Pemba. The active slave route by land also encouraged slaving along the line of march. The Reverend J. R. Farler, writing from Magila, Usambara, in February 1878, noted that a slave trade had recently sprung up in the Usambara mountains, and a Chief, Semboja, was sending slaves northward by way of Pangani and Tanga.[36] From these points they were shipped across to Pemba, or sent farther north by land to Kisimayu on the Ozi River, where Somali agents purchased them.

Thus, the hope of the abolitionists that the 1873 treaty had dealt a blow to the slave trade was illusory.

> The plain truth is, and there can be no disputing facts, that a brisker Slave trade has seldom been known than the one from Kilwa via the Kisiju Road.

Arab slavers, flushed with success, were sensitive to any attempt by Europeans to pry into the nature of the land traffic in slaves, and Lieutenant McCausland of the cruiser *Daphne* was murdered at their instigation when he attempted to investigate it.[37] Kirk, who first believed that Elton had exaggerated the extent of the land slave trade, found on investigating it that Elton had underrated its magnitude. And when Kirk brought the matter to the attention of the Sultan of Zanzibar, the latter claimed there had been no reference to land traffic in slaves in the 1873 Treaty. However, on Kirk's advice, he issued a proclamation on 18 April 1876, making transport of slaves by land illegal and interdicting the fitting out and dispatch of slave caravans for the interior. Copies of this proclamation were sent to his governors on the coast. These edicts were outlandish, for the Sultan had small power to enforce them despite a land force formed in 1877 under the command of naval Lieutenant Lloyd Mathews which, by 1880, numbered 1300 men.

The slave trade by land was also encouraged by the extensive plantation culture which was developing along the coast in the 1870s; at Malindi alone, 4000 to 5000 were employed, and 1000 slaves a year were needed to sustain the labour supply. Slaves employed along the coast were well off. They had their own gardens, were able to fish, and collect salt from sea preserves. The Sultan's governor at Bagamoyo connived at supplying this local market.[38]

Abolitionists were quick to note the new development of the slave trade in East Africa. A large meeting was convened in London in May 1874 by the Anti-Slavery Society. Frere was in the Chair. H. M. Stanley was there. But there was little in the way of practical suggestions for counteracting the land trade in slaves. Stanley's suggestions for establishing trading 'depots' on the inland lakes and basing steamers thereon were vague. However, the meeting presented a memorial to the Earl of Derby in June 1874, praying for action against the slavers.[39]

In 1875, when Barghash visited England, a deputation from the British and Foreign Anti-Slavery Society urged him to abolish slavery outright in his dominions.[40] In response to this appeal, Barghash made an impressive gesture. In the autumn of 1876, the Khedive of Egypt's naval force had seized ports on the northern section of the Sultan's mainland coastal strip. In return for Her Majesty's Government inducing the Egyptians to withdraw from these points, Sultan Barghash voluntarily decreed the entire abolition of slavery there. This proclamation, meant to impress the abolitionists, was never enforced at Kismayu until the declaration of the British East Africa Protectorate in July 1895. But the gesture was impressive. Bismark was

> very impressed when told of this Edict of the Sultan abolishing slavery in five northern ports in consequence of our inducing Egypt to evacuate these ports.[41]

The ineffectiveness of the 1873 treaty in checking the slave trade at sea was further revealed when, following complaints from the Sultan's subjects that their personal slaves were seized by the British naval anti-slave trade patrol, a supplementary treaty, 14 July 1875, stipulated that:

> the presence on board a vessel of domestic slaves in attendance with their masters, or of slaves, bona fide employed in the

navigation of the vessel, is permitted provided that such slaves are not detained on board against their will.

This supplementary treaty of July 1875 opened the door to wholesale abuse. Slaves were still carried under the guise of passengers, domestic servants, wives, and personal slaves. An Arab would marry his female slaves prior to departure and, arriving at Muscat or Bushire, would divorce and sell them. This was no easy problem for the naval patrol, already weakened as a result of the combination of the Cape and West African stations and the creation of the China and Australian stations, which left the East Indies station responsible for a vast area, with too few ships at its disposal. At one stage, as a result of other commitments, there were only two ships to watch over a two thousand-mile length of coast.

The blockade of Pemba by a 'Mosquito fleet' of steam pinnaces and small craft, capable of entering the shoal waters or creeks, was a farce. The steam pinnaces were practically useless owing to the use of salt water in their boilers and a speed of only two knots. Between Kilifi and Mombasa, slaves, hidden in large coral caves or grottos, awaited shipment to Zanzibar and Pemba, and were then transhipped northward from lonely points such as the slave pits on the beach at Mangapwani and the Mkokotoni Channel, a favourite haunt of slave runners. Not more than five per cent of the slaves run north were intercepted and liberated at sea, owing to their being shipped under the guise of domestic slaves or under the French flag.[42] Arabs, Comoro Islanders and Sakalavas from Madagascar were resorting to the use of the French flag. They obtained with facility the 'Acte de Francisation' and 'Congé', and, under the French flag, they could sail to the African coast with a legal cargo, and there take on slaves and carry them north.

Following British complaints, the subject of the French flag was raised in the French National Assembly in December 1872. The Minister of Marine announced new and precise instructions to naval officers for stricter surveillance of the use of the French flag. This availed little. Rear-Admiral Cumming in his report of 1873,[43] and the British ambassador in Paris in February 1875, drew the attention of the French government to this increasing abuse of the French flag by Arab slavers. In reply, the French government asserted that its consuls exercised due care in the matter. But the abuse continued.

The achievement of the British naval anti-slave trade patrol, in the face of these obstacles, was meagre reckoned in terms of slaves freed, and was purchased at high cost. The heavy drain, physical and mental, in keeping the squadron on the East African coast was reflected in the loss of 282 officers and men in the ten years 1875–85; and this did not include those invalided home. Naval personnel, wracked by fever, sunstroke and dysentery, were forced to retire prematurely and live on a small pittance. The cost of the upkeep of the squadron over the twenty years prior to 1890 was estimated at four millions sterling, and this did not take into account the large amount of work imposed on consular and judicial staff at Zanzibar in trying cases and dealing with reports, etc.

The most tangible result of the blockade of Pemba was the stationing of HMS *London,* a huge, old, wooden two-decker of 900 tons with a complement of 850 men, at Zanzibar in 1874.[44] For nine years, until paid out of commission in 1883, she fulfilled the duties of hospital ship, prison, factory, victualling station, depot and man-of-war. She was provided with a dozen smaller craft, including five pinnaces, for detached service along the coast and nearby islands. These, up to 45 feet in length, and carrying a crew of six to twelve men, well armed with pistols, rifles and swords and, in some cases, with a seven-pounder gun, with 42 days' provision, and coaling at small depots established in their cruising ground, provided a most effective 'mosquito fleet' to ferret out slavers. In one year, 1880, five hundred slaves were liberated and twenty dhows destroyed by the boats of the *London*. The most dramatic incident came in December 1881, when her Captain, C. I. Brownrigg, was killed in a clash with an Arab dhow flying French colours. This sad news, reported in the British press, drew attention to the problems faced by HM's anti-slave trade patrol in East African waters. The 'great hull' of the *London* in Zanzibar harbour was 'a demonstration of British power', and her withdrawal was interpreted by the slave traders as an indication of waning British interest, and was followed by a marked recrudescence of the slave trade.

Statistics of slave captures continued to belie the supposed effectiveness of the 1873 treaty. During the period from the middle of 1885 to the end of 1888, 100 vessels were condemned, 80 at the Vice-Admiralty Court at Zanzibar, and the remainder at the Courts of Aden and Muscat. These captures resulted in 1200 slaves being freed. On the basis that this represented only five per cent of slaves run north, the total number involved probably amounted to at least 24,000. The slavers were increasingly wary in their tactics, and kept a close watch on the movements of cruisers. During the 1886 season, having shipped their cargo near Zanzibar on the way north, and hearing rumours that the 'Christians' ' ships awaited them, they landed their slaves at Mukalla and al-Shihr on the Arabian coast.

HMS *Kingfisher,* in pursuit of them, discovered an extensive and well-concealed creek, behind a huge black rock some miles south of Ras al-Hadd, which was naviagable by dhows and which led into a lagoon several miles in circumference, and hitherto unsuspected. It was apparently a constant rendezvous for slavers. The survey of this part of the coast had been the last segment undertaken by the Indian Navy, executed under great difficulties and carried out with the assistance of two local pilots. The survey party, however, had failed to reveal this secret hide-away, perhaps intentionally diverted from doing so by the native pilots.

The slave trade to the Middle East remained vigorous and buoyant. A great market for slaves still existed in that part of the world.

6
Egypt and the Sudan

Within Egypt's own boundaries the institution of domestic slavery was deeply rooted, and largely sustained by slave-raiding in the Sudan. The practice of raiding for slaves in the Sudan was of ancient origin, going back to the early fourth millenium BC, when King Seneferu penetrated Nubia to the Fourth Cataract and collected slaves from the region between Abu Hamad and Khartoum.[1] Similar raids continued throughout subsequent millenia of dynastic Egypt, down through the Greek, Roman, and Byzantine periods. The establishment of Egypt's southern frontier at the First Cataract of the Nile, in the mid-seventh century AD, and a treaty between Egypt and Nubia providing for the supply to Egypt of 360 slaves a year, had little effect in curtailing the flow of slaves northwards, for the treaty permitted free movement of Egyptian traders in the lands to the south. Throughout the succeeding centuries slaves from the Sudan, along with Turkish slaves from Asia Minor, filled the ranks of the army in Egypt, and continued to do so during the dynasties of the Fatimids in Egypt, 969-1171, under Abbasid Caliphates and down to the Turkish conquest of Egypt in 1517.

The Mamelukes, an aristocracy of slaves, originally from and constantly renewed by recruits from Asia Minor, were a dynamic force in Egyptian society until Napoleon sorely weakened their power at the Battle of the Pyramids in 1798, and Mohammed Ali nearly annihilated them in a great massacre in March 1811. Only a remnant of the Mamelukes survived in Darfur, whither they had fled. Their numbers dwindled to a mere 2000 by the mid-nineteenth century, and these were mostly attached to leading Turkish families, 500 being in the employ of Abbas, 1848-54. A few rose to the status of governors of provinces. The institution of slavery, an established feature in Egyptian social life by the nineteenth century, owed much to Mameluke rule. Although rising to high position, they encouraged the institution from which they had sprung.

The Turkish race did not flourish in Egypt, largely owing to a high infant mortality: thus, the long-standing import of white female slaves from Circassia and Georgia. Ibrahim's Morean campaign of 1825-8 brought into Egypt 6000 Greek slaves, mostly women and children. The few males were employed on public works and as government functionaries; the females were taken into the harems and domestic service, and many became Muslims. This windfall was quickly absorbed, and there was increasing resort to black slaves, as they were plentiful and cheap—£4 to £6 each.

By 1838, there were reputed to be 12,000 female black slaves and 2000 males in Cairo,[2] and over 80 dealers in the caravanserais were specializing in the sale of these slaves and had associated themselves into guilds. Kinglake, when in Cairo in 1835, saw in the open slave market there about 50 girls exposed for sale, 'all of them black', or 'invisible brown': he was also offered the opportunity of viewing some white females kept in rooms on the upper floor, fattened up to enhance their appearance, and reserved for exclusive buyers only.[3] In 1855, Consul-General Bruce, at Cairo, stated

> Black slaves and black eunuchs form an essential part of the establishment of every rich Turk; and as they are supplied exclusively from the regions that border the Upper Nile, every attempt will be made to render inoperative the measures taken by Said Pasha for the abolition of the traffic.[4]

During the earlier part of the nineteenth century, black slaves came into Egypt by way of the ancient slave route from the districts of Kordofan, Sennar, and Darfur, on the fringes of the Muslim territories of the northern Sudan.[5] Slaves were collected at oases such as El Fasher and En Nahud, from whence they travelled by way of the Arbain (Forty Days) road to Es Siout, the great slave market for Egypt, on the Nile, about 250 miles south of Cairo.

These annual caravans brought into Egypt some 5000 to 6000 slaves, mostly females, along with camels, ostrich feathers, gums and ivory. A caravan arriving at Es Siout in July 1827 consisted of 3566 camels and 2820 slaves. It was a cruel and harrowing journey. The slaves were fed on camel flesh and blood en route, and there was little compassion shown for the weak and needy. During the long march the female slaves were the victims of the libidinous passions of the slave-hunters. On entering Egypt, a duty of about 21 shillings was payable on each slave, the collection of this duty being farmed out at a commission of 3 shillings per slave.[6] The caravan, on arriving at Es Siout, would remain for one to five months, disposing of its slaves, camels and produce and, in turn, loading up for the return journey.

By 1820, new sources of slaves were opening up, for following the conquest of the northern Sudan by Mohammed Ali, the Egyptians moved farther south. Khartoum, a small fishing village at the junction of the White and Blue Nile, had become by 1822 the permanent camp of the Egyptians, and in 1830 it was chosen as the commercial and political capital of the Egyptian possessions in the Sudan. It became the entrepot for caravan routes branching out to Korodofan, Sennar, the Red Sea and north to the Bayuda steppe and Nubian desert. Its heterogeneous population was estimated at 30,000 by 1863. Thousands of Dangla and Ja'liyin from the cultivated riverrain areas south of the Wadi Halfa, armed traders from Korodofan, Sennar, and the lands to the south, congregated at Khartoum. There was also a motley collection of other nationalities—Maltese, Greek traders, Levantines, Italians, an occasional Indian, a few Austrian missionaries, and American tourists.

The Sudan became the recruiting ground for the Viceroy's bodyguard and armies, and since the mortality of Nubians in Egypt was notoriously high—'they feel sensibly the change from their own climate near the Equator to the damp mild one of Egypt'—and there was general repugnance to military service, continual augmentation was necessary, and this resulted in raids penetrating ever farther south for slave recruits. Up to 5000 captives were taken in one foray.[7] It was Ismail's demand for 1000 slave recruits from Nair Mimr, Mek of Shendi (150 miles north of Khartoum), in October 1822, which stirred up a local rebellion. In 1838, military officers from as far away as the Hedjaz came to recruit 3000 blacks at Khartoum. The wages of the Pasha's troops on the frontier of Egypt were frequently paid in slaves, calculated at inflated prices. Captured slaves were shared out, half to the government and half to the military. The females, 'the refuse of their sex', were given to the soldiery, and the more select taken into the harems of the officers. The military, in turn, frequently disposed of their share to slave dealers. By 1838, it was estimated that 10,000 to 12,000 slaves annually were imported into Egypt. The males went into the soldiery, and females into domestic service. Mohammed Ali, though a hardened adventurer, was shocked at the methods of the slave-raiders and, following a visit to the Sudan in 1838, forbade further slave-hunts by his troops and freed 500 slaves captured in recent raids. But his injunctions were ignored and raids continued with increased vigour, especially after a Turkish frigate captain, Qapudan Salim, penetrated as far south as the region of Gondokoro on the White Nile at about 5°N. And the ivory trade, extending into the equatorial region, also brought a developing slave trade in its train into these upper regions of the Nile.

The southern Sudan is a vast expanse of land, extending approximately from latitude 4°N to 15°N. In its northern reaches it is a great alluvial plain stretching from the spur of the Abyssinian highlands on the east, to the hilly districts of Korodofan on the west. At about 13°N, the northern limit of the Nile sudd appears. South of this is a wide and desolate stretch of country, intersected by numerous secondary channels of the Nile, and flooded for many miles in the rainy season. In the dry season it is an arid, baked and cracked plain; animal and human life tends to concentrate near water courses. The great accumulation of sudd, masses of floating vegetation, obstructs navigation, and its removal is a herculean task, even for powerful dredgers and sudd-cutting machinery in the twentieth century. It is today a monotonous and depressing region. On all sides stretch reaches of the reed um suf (mother-of-wool). ambach, bus and papyrus. Tall grasses rise up from 15 to 20 feet, obstructing the view. The vast expanse is broken at intervals by heaps and clumps of brushwood and trees. The moisture in the air during the rainy season is excessive, and myriads of mosquitoes and swamp insects swarm so as to cloud the vision. But there are strange touches of exotic beauty. Water-lilies, white, blue and crimson, linger on the water surface. Rare birds, including the whale-headed stork, are occasionally seen among the tall reeds, and at night the whole scene is lit up with a magic lantern effect by a myriad of fireflies.

The Nilotes, the peoples of this southern region to the immediate east of the Upper Nile, between 5°N and 12°N, comprise a cluster of tribes basically negroid with Cushitic influences.[8] Their lack of broad internal cohesion and cephalic authority made them an easy prey for the slavers. To the west of the Upper Nile, ranging across the tributaries of the Bahr el Ghazal and extending south to the Congo-Nile watershed, the Azande and Niam-Niam group of peoples, frequently rent by dynastic rivalries in the nineteenth century, were also easy prey for the slavers. Still farther south and west, across the Wele River, the Mangbetu, well known for the beauty of their women, were contacted by slavers from the north in about the middle of the nineteenth century.

Thus this whole vast area, including what later became the Anglo-Egyptian Sudan, and to the south-west of it, well over a million square miles in all, became the slave hunting-ground for the Egyptians (more commonly known as the Turks) and their underlings, throughout most of the nineteenth century. The total number of slaves extracted from this part of Africa in the nineteenth century can only be hazarded; it would appear to have been substantial.

By the 1850s, Sudanese-Arab traders, their families, hangers-on, and refugees from the government, had settled in small colonies among the Shilluk people, and had contacted the Dinka, Nuer, and Bari farther south. From collecting points—zeribas—they ranged over the surrounding countryside, at first in search of ivory, and then slaves. A few Europeans were also pushing into the Upper Nile region. Knoblecher, an Austrian missionary, reached Rejaf in the Bari country, south of 5°North, in 1850, and Angelo Vince was settled among the Bari by 1852. European ivory traders, de Malzac, Vayssière and Franz Binder, were at Gondokoro in 1850, and by 1853-4, Vaudey, Sardinian Vice-Consul, and his two nephews were actively trading among the Bari.

Petherick, British Consul and ivory trader, who was officially based on Khartoum, a figure somewhat neglected by historians and maligned by official contemporaries, was assiduous in providing information on the slave trade in the Upper Nile region during the late 1850s and early 1860s. On his first journey to the southern Sudan he had seen the great slave market at El Obeid in Kordofan, where thousands of slaves were sold—'They ranged in colour from the black of the southern Sudan to the muddy white of the Egyptian fellah girl'—and had observed that Khartoum was the main collecting and distributing centre of a vast area stretching some 1200 miles up the Nile. It was the market for slaves from the mountain district of Denha, south of Sennar, Tahaly, south of Kordofan, and Gallabat (Mtemma) on the Abyssinian frontier. By the 1860s, Khartoum had a population of over 30,000, including a few dozen Europeans. It was the military centre for 8000 troops stationed in the Sudan province. Captains and crews of river steamers made it their rendezvous, and from here large numbers of boats went up the Nile during the annual season. In November 1864, 12 boats, each with 50 to 60 armed men paid five months' salary in advance, went south. The pay was poor; the inducement lay in the slaves they could bring back by boat. These first expeditions sought ivory and hides, and in exchange traded iron, copper bars, and glass beads. But as the ivory trade dwindled, recourse was had to slaves. By the time of his death in 1860, the ivory trader, de Malzac, had turned to the slave trade, and was giving his men slaves in lieu of pay. When Baker, on his first journey down the Nile, refused to allow 45 hands taken on at Khartoum to bring back slaves, the majority deserted. According to Petherick, by 1860, 50 to 60 boats, each containing about 50 men, mostly Berbers from distant parts of Dongola, were passing up the Nile to Khartoum annually. Many of these boats were owned and equipped by Copts and Arabs, some by Europeans. The Austrian missionaries at their Holy Cross Mission on the Nile, 150 miles north of Gondokoro, well placed to observe the slave trade on the river, noted 25 boats passing the Mission between 6 April and 23 May 1861, all carrying slaves, all destined for Khartoum; and the slavers were raiding for cattle and trading these for slaves.

Unlike other parts of East and North Africa where Arabs and Africans were the chief culprits, Europeans were involved in the slave trade. The Frenchman, Dolphin Bartholemy, ran a fleet of slave boats. Michael Luftolla, an Austrian, sometime British consular agent, hoisted the British flag on two large river boats capable of carrying 850 slaves, 'often in dreadful condition from over-crowding, so that one-third might be lost on the way down to Egypt'.[9] Ambroise and Jule Poncet, prior to selling their establishments on the river Rohl to the Egyptian government in 1867, employed over 300 persons, some of whom were suspected slave-dealers. The Maltese, Andrea de Bono, and his nephew, Amabile, in partnership with a merchant prince, Sheikh Ahmad al-Aqqad, government recruiting officer at Gondokoro,[10] operated among the Zande people. They owned several large river craft, each capable of carrying 500 slaves. On one journey, in 1860, over half their slaves died, and those surviving were sold at Khartoum at £2.5.0 apiece.[11] De Bono's trading activities extended as far south as Faloro, in what is now northern Uganda.

By the 1860s there was a noticeable shifting of this slave trade westward to the Bahr el Ghazal area, and from here some slaves were taken to the Shilluk country and bartered to the slave merchants, who took them to Aswan and thence down the river to Toora, about 12 miles south of Cairo, and then smuggled them into the city by night.

The slave routes from the Bahr el Ghazal did not follow the Nile, nor necessarily pass through Khartoum. When Arab slavers from Darfur moved south to the Bahr el Ghazal region, making it a 'slave preserve', they continued to sell slaves to the merchants of Darfur who, in turn, shipped them to Egypt by the Arbain road, the caravans striking the Nile as low down as Es-Siout. El Obeid in Kordofan continued to be a great clearing-house for slaves from the Bahr el Ghazal.

In all, by the late 1860s, about 3000 to 4000 slaves from the Bahr el Ghazal region were imported into Egypt annually. In the region between the Rohl and Lol Rivers, a dozen or more wealthy Khartoum merchants controlled 80 palisaded zeribas at intervals of 15 to 20 miles. Vast areas were thus farmed for slaves. By 1870, slaves were arriving from the Mangbetu country, south of the Wele River. Mangbetu women, much admired by the Arabs, were eagerly sought after. Schweinfurth estimated that 12,000 to 15,000 slaves were annually exported overland from the Azande and Mangbetu country.[12]

British efforts to check the slave trade in the southern Sudan followed reports from Petherick and missionaries as to the depredations of the Egyptian slave traders on the Upper Nile, and evidence of a great slave market flourishing at Ketkas, in the Shilluk country. Lord John Russell instructed the British Consul-General at Alexandria to press the Egyptian government for action against the slave trade, and to prohibit boats carrying slaves down the White Nile. Petherick was instructed to use the 'utmost influence to stop these "Razzias" (raids)'. Said, Viceroy of Egypt, in December 1854, under British pressure, instructed his governors in the southern provinces to stop the slave trade from Abyssinia and Dongola into Egypt. In 1855, a control post was established at Fashoda, and in 1856-7, the Viceroy himself visited the Sudan and proclaimed the slave trade there abolished, and in February 1858 and November 1861, instructed his governors in the Sudan province and Sennar to uphold this proclamation. But this did not accord with Said placing an order in 1860 with the slave-trading firm of Aqqad brothers for a bodyguard of 500 black soldiers; and when the Egyptian government placed boat patrols at strategic points on the Nile and set up inspection posts, the complicity of officials rendered these measures a dead letter. Tribute was exacted from slave runners by Egyptian officials at posts along the Nile, and at check points on the desert route to Karusco, frequently used by slave caravans. Petherick clashed with the slave dealers; he put his agent, Abd el Majid, in irons for bringing back 300 slaves from Gondokoro, and sent de Bono and Amabile down to Cairo for trial in April 1862 for slave-dealing, but the latter were released on grounds of insufficient evidence. Petherick claimed that given time he could produce more than ample evidence to convict them.[13] But Petherick himself was soon on his way out. His last few years at Khartoum were made miserable by ill health, carping criticism from British officials at home, and charges of dereliction of duty. The final blow came in January 1864, when his consulship at Khartoum was abolished. Petherick's last report before he left Khartoum was disheartening: the traffic in slaves was 'ostensibly increasing', and the slave traders' activities caused him almost to despair. Petherick's departure meant the cessation of intelligence on the slave trade from Khartoum. Britain did not even trouble to fill the consulate left vacant at Khartoum on his departure. Stanton, British consular agent at Alexandria, contented himself with instructing Samuel Baker, about to embark on his second journey up the Nile, to make enquiries about the slave trade.

Following Petherick's departure, widespread evasion of anti-slave trade legislation continued, and the immense distance that separates Cairo from the farther reaches of the Upper Nile permitted the slave raiders to continue their traffic despite every prohibition. The traffic was diverted into secret channels to avoid prying eyes of Europeans. A host of persons were directly or indirectly involved in the trade, and were out to circumvent anti-slave trade measures. The *mudir* (governor) and his chief military officer were usually in on the transactions and received a percentage, usually one-fifth of the sale price. Ahmed Bey, *mudir* in Sennar, and Mohammed Taha, *mudir* of Latuka, both backed forays for slaves in the Bahr el Ghazal and on the Upper Nile; and the *mudir* of Fashoda, in return for granting a through ticket to Egypt, exacted two thalers per head for all slaves shipped from his territory. Ibrahim Bey Foussi, Governor of the Equatorial Province, obtained slaves as *baksheesh* from his under-officers. The Egyptian government maintained at several places large barracoons for collecting slaves, the males for the army, the women and children as house-servants or to stock the harems. These barracoons were in a wretched state, and slaves often died like flies from smallpox; for every ten slaves reaching Cairo, fifty perished in transit.[14]

The Nile slavers ravaged the territory of the Shilluk and Dinka on both sides of the river about 11°N. Mohammed Kheir, an Ottoman subject, induced strong parties of horsemen, nomadic Arabs, to join him against the Shilluk. By ruthless methods they acquired large numbers of cattle and slaves, and forced the Shilluk and Dinka to pay taxes in slaves. But not all officials were corrupt. Musa Pasha Hamdi, Governor-General of the Egyptian Sudan in the 1860s, who prohibited the slave trade, and also his Wakeel, were shining beacons in a sea of general corruption. But after Musa Pasha Hamdi's death in 1865, their good work was undone.

The accounts of the British explorers, Speke and Grant, on their way home from Uganda in 1863 by way of the Nile, and those of Samuel Baker, who passed up the Nile in the same year, revealed the extent of the Nile slave trade. Even allowing for Baker dramatizing—he estimated that 50,000 slaves went down the white

Nile yearly—it is evident that the slave trade was increasing on the Upper Nile in the 1860s. Baker, on reaching Gondokoro on his first journey in 1863, found a populous region with vast herds of cattle. On his second journey in 1872, he found the area denuded of people. The slave trade had penetrated in the heart of Africa. Baker's book, *The Albert Nyanza: Great Basin of the Nile, and Exploration of the Nile Sources,* published in 1866[15] was read by a public in England already awakened to the horrors of the East African slave trade by Livingstone. But to check the slave trade, Baker had little to suggest apart from stating that cruisers should be placed on the Red Sea to stop the export of slaves from Africa across to Arabia. This would have required two or three hundred sloops.

In Ismail, who became Viceroy of Egypt in 1863, the humanitarians thought they had found their man. European educated and familiar with humanitarian aspirations, he presented himself as an enlightened devotee of the anti-slave trade cause. His early utterances and actions promised well. With a view to the suppression of the slave trade at Suakin and Massawa on the Red Sea, he obtained the lease of these ports from the Porte in 1865, and planned a railway linking Suakin with Berber on the Nile.[16] He reorganized the Sudan into provinces, Taka, Khartoum, Upper Nile, Berber and Fazogli, and made their governments directly responsible to himself. In June 1864, Ismail renewed and strengthened legislation whereby river boats on the Nile were allowed to proceed to the south only for trade in ivory. A capitation tax, equivalent to one month's pay, was placed on all personnel taking part in trading voyages; and the headquarters of the river police at Fashoda, in the Shilluk country, most southerly of Egyptian points, was strengthened.

But despite this anti-slave trade legislation and the sporadic cooperation of Egyptian officials, which resulted in the seizure of 3538 slaves in 1866, the slavers still ran many more thousands north. Reports of this state of affairs were coming in to the Anti-Slavery Society. And on 25 June 1867, a deputation from the Comité Français d'Emancipation and the British and Foreign Anti-Slave Society had an audience with Ismail, who was then in Paris. His bland assertions of support for the anti-slave trade cause were not convincing; they came at a time when Sheikh il Agad, with the Viceroy's money, was buying up slave trading stations on the White Nile. And it was well known that 'Ismail Pasha is master and Agad the tenant who pays the Viceroy an annual rental for the ivory trade'.[17] The Prussian Consular agent at Khartoum, Herr Caggenmacher, also reported that Ismail's vessels on the Nile were arriving at Cairo full of slaves, and that Ismail was not happy about Europeans travelling in the Sudan, for this inhibited the actions of his officials, most of whom were involved in the slave trade.[18] In many ways, Ismail's attitude was similar to that of the Sultan of Zanzibar, expressing outward sympathy with European aims, but privately averse to acting against the wishes of his subjects. His own mother had 300 Circassian slaves. Ismalia, his favoured Circassian concubine, had 50 Circassian and 30 Abyssinian slaves;[19] and his Finance Minister possessed 144 female slaves.[20] Even the lowly *fellahin*, during the cotton boom of the 1860s, aspired to the ownership of a Circassian concubine—a prestige symbol.

In his favour, the Khedive would concede to European pressure

> I believe I am safe in saying that none of our Consular officers ever brought a case, connected with slavery or the slave trade, to His Highness' notice without securing his hearty co-operation.[21]

But the simple test of his sincerity, as in the case of the Sultan of Zanzibar, would have been his readiness to free his own slaves.

Ismail was soon caught up in grand plans for territorial expansion, however, and he had little time for an anti-slave trade campaign. In 1868, the death of Theodore, Emperor of Abyssinia, removed a power long opposed to Egyptian expansion southwards, and which had threatened the security of the Sudan. The appointment by Ismail of Werner Munzinger, a Swiss administrator and explorer, as Governor of Massawa in 1871, inaugurated a policy of aggressive Egyptian expansion in north-east Africa. Ismail endeavoured to extend his sway over the whole East African coast from Suez to Cape Guardafui. He garrisoned the towns of Berbera and Zeila in the Gulf of Aden and, in 1874, seized the important towns of Harrar and Bogos in the hinterland of Massawa and claimed by Abyssinia.

Britain, at first, was not averse to the extension of Egyptian sovereignty from Suakin to Cape Guardafui; this would check Italian and French designs in the area. But when an Egyptian naval expedition under the Scotsman, McKillop, landed troops at the mouth of the Juba River on the East African coast in November 1875, and an invasion of the Sultan of Zanzibar's sphere over which Britain had a watching brief seemed imminent, strong protests from John Kirk, British consular agent at Zanzibar, resulted in the recall of the expedition.[22]

However, the British government was inclined to look benignly on Egyptian expansion into the regions of the Upper Nile especially if spearheaded by an Englishman. But humanitarians in England were concerned lest Egyptian expansion southwards encourage the slave trade.

> No one would object to see His Highness's power extended to the Lake Regions: but it would not be so if his new acquisitions were all turned into slave-hunting ground.[23]

In a memorial submitted to the Foreign Secretary on 31 October 1873, Sir Bartle Frere, Horace Waller, and several Members of Parliament maintained that the conditions of such extension must be the extinction of the slave trade; and in June 1874, Lord Derby was urged 'to withhold his sanction to the annexation of the territories of the Upper Nile till slavery had been abolished'. The humanitarians were influenced by the reports on the slave trade in Egypt by Sir Bartle Frere who visited there in early 1873, and who urged caution in supporting Egyptian expansion southwards.

Frere, in a sense, was making comparisons with what he had seen in Egypt in a visit there back in 1834. The slave market in Cairo had then been 'one of the sights for strangers', and many slave boats plied the Nile. Now, in 1873, Frere found the situation worsened. The institution of slavery permeated the whole life of Egypt. Increased wealth and luxury had trebled the number of well-to-do families and also their entourage of slaves. The Viceroy and family set the pattern; by 1869, they possessed 2000 Circassian, Abyssinian, and Nubian slaves. His Highness had, in addition, many hundreds on his sugar plantations in Upper Egypt. 'When His Highness's daughter married in April 1869, 50 to 100 slaves were presented to her'.[24] A well-to-do man in Egypt would have several wives, Circassian, Georgian and Arab; and these ladies in turn would each have one to four black slaves, and 'a few negresses as wet nurses'. In an average, better off family, there might be six or seven slaves. Coptic Christians also held slaves. The Patriarch, returning from a visit to Abyssinia, brought back nineteen slaves, and gave two to his sister.[25] In the cities and larger centres, among the lower class, there was aversion to domestic work—it was equated with slavery. Government employees in Cairo, a class on the increase, and on low salaries of a few dollars per month, employed domestic slaves. Egypt was one of the few Muslim countries where large numbers of out-of-door slaves were employed. The *fellahin*, or small farmer, sought to evade the corveé by sending slaves as substitutes, when summoned by the government. Large numbers of slaves were employed on coastal vessels and on irrigation works; by 1884, nine-tenths of the men working the water pumps in Isna Province were slaves. In Upper Egypt, Nubia and the Sudan, agricultural slavery was common. There was a practise, instituted in Mohammed Ali's reign and continued into the 1870s, whereby border regions contributed their taxes in the form of slaves.

It is difficult to estimate the total number of slaves entering Egypt annually. Frere placed the number entering Cairo at 1000 a year, but for Egypt as a whole he estimated a total import of 10,000. But this might be an underestimate, for Frere obtained much of his information from Europeans who tended to travel on the Nile during the cool season when there was not much slave trade on the river; they ignored the fact that slave traders used land routes at this time of year. How otherwise could one explain the presence of hundreds of slaves for sale the year round?

Frere had little to offer in the way of concrete suggestions for ending the slave trade in Egypt, apart from more consular agents, a watch at points in the Red Sea, and negotiations with Turkey to prevent misuse of the Turkish flag.

> Almost everyone thinks the Turkish flag is used as cover in the Red Sea, Arabian Seas and Persian Gulf and the practise is increasing.

He had a 'wild idea' of making Egypt 'free soil'.

> The real thing to do would be to abolish slavery in Egypt and so cut off the demand—I do not think it at all impossible he [the Viceroy] might take steps in that direction. It would put him clearly among the civilizing powers and in advance of Turkey, and not be so difficult as it will be ten years hence. With Egypt free soil no one would object to see His Highness' power extended to the Lake Regions: but it would not be so if his new acquisitions were all turned into slave-hunting ground.[26]

Frere was made acquainted with the ravages in the farther regions of the Upper Nile when he spoke to eyewitnesses of wholesale massacres and slave raids in these remote districts. And first-hand information from there was now coming in from Samuel Baker.

Baker, Governor of Equatoria, on his second journey up the Nile in 1870, observed that all the human flotsam in Khartoum was in one way or another conniving at the trade in human flesh. Shilluk society had disintegrated under the impact of the slave raids by the Egyptian garrison at Kaka. At Fashoda, the Mudir himself was raiding for slaves and ivory. Baker found that the slave traders were also active among the Acholi, in what is now Uganda. Egyptian stations were under the nominal control of a Khartoum firm, the Aqqad brothers, and for the past ten years their predatory agents had been scouring the countryside for ivory and slaves. The Acholi and Shilluk females were not so desirable as slaves as were the Mangbetu women, but their males suffered grieviously. At Masindi, capital of Bunyoro, where Baker arrived on 25 April 1872, he found many slaves at the court of its ruler, Kabarega, and there was widespread slaving throughout the country generally. Although there was not, as yet, a large organized slave export from Bunyoro, the explorer Cameron, journeying to the west of Lake Tanganyika far to the south at about this time, observed that Arab slavers there were 'already conscious of Egyptians to the north and do not want to close with them'. Baker was over-optimistic as to the results of his sojourn in Equatoria. 'The slave trade has been suppressed—and the country annexed so that Egypt extends to the equator'. Baker, in fact, had merely stirred up the slave traders without effecting concrete results. But his second journey and accounts of slave trade had caught the imagination of a large section of the British people, for his progress up the Nile had been closely reported by the British press.

Charles Gordon, Baker's successor as Governor of the Equatorial Province (1873-7), was faced with a slave trade of such magnitude in the territories under his administration that he was filled with a sense of futility and despair. He increasingly expressed grave doubts as to whether any good would ever come from Egyptian rule in Equatoria. On his arrival there in early 1874, he found few signs of orderly Egyptian administration. There were so-called 'forts' at Gondokoro and Fatiko. But the few Egyptian regular soldiers were deeply dependant on hundreds of supporting Danaqli, northern Arabs who had become thoroughly acclimatized and familiar with the country of the Upper Nile, and were lording it over a large area. The eleven Egyptian stations between the Sobat and Foweira spread demoralization among the Bari and the Shilluk, by the constant raiding for cattle and women. And when, during his first two years in Equatoria, Gordon established a chain of stations from Lado to Uganda, and opened up routes to Dufile to the south, he observed that at each of his stations there grew up 'a semi-native, semi-Arab by contact, population of lads and women'. Wherever his soldiery and the Danaqli went, they were accompanied by large numbers of Acholi, Bari, and Madi women slaves.

It was evident to Gordon, however, that the Bahr el Ghazal was the main source of slaves and that the White Nile region played a minor role in the trade. From zeriba settlements on the Bahr el Ghazal, the tentacles of the slave traders penetrated deep southwest into the basins of the Wele and Ubanghi Rivers; and caravan routes from this region ran northwards through Darfur and Kordofan to the great slave markets of upper Egypt. Arab and half-breed slave raiders in the Bahr el Ghazal were nominal subjects of the Khedive when it suited their interests, but at other times they threw off all control and were unmitigated freebooters. The main slave trader in the Bahr el Ghazal was Zubeir Pasha,[27] who exploited tribal rivalries among the Azande people, forcing the males into porterage and exporting the women.

By 1873, Zubeir had become such a dominant power in the land that Ismail recognized him as governor, with the rank of *Bey*, and supplied him with a small garrison. In return, Zubeir paid tribute in ivory equal to £15,000 per annum. It was an uneasy arrangement. On his own initiative, Zubeir challenged and defeated the Sultan of Darfur, and el Fasher fell to him in November 1874. Zubeir soon overreached himself and Ismail was determined to reduce his overmighty subject. Lured to Cairo in June 1876, under the assumption that his claims to high office would be discussed, Zubeir was retained in honourable but impotent captivity.

In 1877, Gordon was raised from Governor to Governor-General of the Sudan. He was determined to check the slave trade in all its wider ramifications, and had the support of Ismail.

> I am astonished at the power he has placed in my hands . . . it will be my fault if slavery does not cease, and if those countries are not opened to the world.

Gordon entered with zeal into the campaign against the slavers. In Darfur and Kordofan, 63 caravans with 2000 slaves were captured between June 1878 and March 1879. Hundreds of Jellaba were cleared out of Taweisha and a thousand slaves freed. In the Bahr el Ghazal, where the Azande were in the clutches of the slave raiders, Gordon faced his greatest challenge. At one stage, he was almost ready to abandon the task, and blockade the Bahr el Ghazal against further Egyptian penetration. But his aide, Romolo Gessi, had a more positive approach. He advocated permanent occupation of the Bahr el Ghazal, and strong measures against the slave traders. He defeated the slaver, Sulaiman, in 1879, captured Deim Zubeir in the same year, and scattered the slave raiders, some being diverted into procuring ivory for the government,[28] others joining the Dervishes who promised resumption of the slave trade.

Although Gessi was only partly successful in dispersing the slavers and in encouraging cotton cultivation as a peaceful and alternative pursuit to slave-raiding, the anti-slave trade cause lost one of its most redoubtable champions in his death at Suez on 30 April 1881.

By 1878, although the slave trade had been temporarily checked in Equatoria, Gordon was losing heart. He never managed to suppress the Dongola slavers, the cleverest and most determined in the Sudan, and he was increasingly despondent over the involvement of Egyptian officials in the slave trade, most of whom were obtaining 'hush money', two to five dollars per head, for slaves they allowed to pass through their districts. Gordon estimated that between 1875 and 1879, 80,000 to 100,000 slaves were exported northwards from the Bahr el Ghazal area.[29] The scale of the slave trade baffled Gordon.

> When one thinks of the enormous number of slaves which have passed into Egypt from these parts in the last few years, one can scarcely conceive what has become of them and then again, where do they come from? For the lands of the natives which I have seen are densely populated. We must have caught 2,000 in less than nine months and I expect we did not catch one-fifth of the caravans. Again how many died en route? The slaves are most undemonstrable. I suppose the long marches have taken all life out of them.[30]

Gordon's sympathies were all with the African. He was contemptuous of Egyptian slavers, a cowardly lot—'No Arab would go out among the blacks alone'. Gordon's disillusionment with Egyptian rule in Equatoria was complete by the end of 1878: 'As long as the Khedive and Pashas keep eunuchs and slaves, so long one must doubt their sincerity'. He decided to evacuate all stations on the Victoria Nile, in what is now Uganda, retaining only those flanking the river as far south as Lake Albert.

Meanwhile, the slave raiders, dispersed by Gessi in the Bahr el Ghazal, moved southeastward into the Madi county, in the upper basin of the Wele River. When Emin Pasha was placed in charge of the district in 1881, local chiefs complained that the Danaqli were enslaving their women and children. A slave-raiding expedition of over 1000 men had nearly wiped out the Kakika, a subtribe of the Madi.

But all this was soon overshadowed by the rise of the Mahdi, seismic in its effect on the Sudan and the pattern of the slave trade. The capture of El Obeid by the Mahdi's forces in January 1883, followed by the annihilation, in November 1883, of a large army under General Hicks, saw the arrival in January 1884 of a large force under a Dongolawi, Karam Allah, to take possession of the Bahr el Ghazal in the name of the Mahdi. In the face of this approaching danger, Emin Pasha withdrew to Lado, farther up the Nile and, by January 1885, his garrisons held only the narrow strip linking Lado and Dufile. Emin made regular tours of inspection along the beaten paths between the riverain posts of Lado and Dufile, but had little contact with the country away from the river. Emin exploited the rivalry between the native rulers, Kabarega and Rionga, in Bunyoro, and allowed his soldiery to ravage the countryside outside the riverain posts. Boat-loads of Bari slaves were shipped down the Nile. Bari chiefs who strenuously opposed Emin Pasha, when he took over administration of the Equatorial Province, were ordered to be brought in dead or alive. Punitive expeditions under native officers worked their will on the unfortunate people. They levied taxes and enslaved the recalcitrant taxpayers. Tales of the evil doings under Emin's regime only came to light in the early twentieth century.

In the face of the Dervish advance, Emin was finally forced to retire to Wadelai to the immediate north of Lake Albert. In the wake of his withdrawal, the Dervishes overran the whole country. They wiped out entire villages, killing the men and enslaving the women and children. They established posts all over the country; the remains of their stone zeribas were still to be seen in the twentieth century. Following the death of the Mahdi in June 1885, his successor, the Khalifa, maintained a base at Rejaf, and from here his underlings raided the surrounding country until dislodged by the Belgians in 1897. By the end of the nineteenth century, the Bari, Latuko and Madi, once powerful and warlike tribes, had been almost wiped out by the onslaught of the Egyptian regime, that of Emin Pasha and, finally, the Dervishes.[31]

But far to the north, at the other end of the Nile in Egypt, anti-slave trade legislation, as the result of unremitting pressure from abolitionists and humanitarians in Britain, was being introduced and implemented. Success in forcing the Sultan of Zanzibar to enact an anti-slave trade decree encouraged them to press for similar concessions in Egypt. When Ismail visited Constantinople in July 1873, the British ambassador used the opportunity to urge an Anglo-Egyptian agreement for the suppression of the slave trade.[32] The Anti-Slavery Society kept the issue alive by articles in the *Anti-Slavery Reporter,* letters to *The Times,* deputations to the Foreign Secretary, and the stirring up of Members of Parliament.

In December 1875, Lord Tenterden, Under-Secretary of State at the Foreign Office, spoke of the need for an Anglo-Egyptian agreement which 'would have a good effect on public opinion'.[33] But Ismail felt that in return for his commitment to the suppression of the slave trade there should be a *quid pro quo*: support for his claim to the mouth of the Juba and Upper Nile regions. Kirk, at Zanzibar, a staunch supporter of the Sultan's interests, was strenuously opposed to this. It seemed there might be an impasse. But Vivian, British Consul-General in Egypt, continued to press Ismail for an anti-slave trade convention, and he finally yielded to British pressure.

The Anglo-Egyptian Convention, signed at Alexandria on 4 August 1877, prohibited the import and export of Sudanese and Abyssinian slaves. The prohibition of selling slaves from family to family would come into force in Egypt after seven years, and in the Sudan after twelve years. The trade in white slaves was to be prohibited after 3 August 1885. British vessels in the Red Sea, Gulf of Aden and Egyptian maritime waters were empowered to search and arrest Egyptian ships transporting slaves and to set these slaves free.[34] Slave dealers were to be severely punished, and their slaves freed. Any person convicted of the mutilation of children was to be held guilty of the crime of murder. Under the Convention, every slave could secure his freedom by applying for letters of manumission. Any person depriving a slave of his liberty or manumission certificate was to be punished as a slave dealer. A special Khedival decree of the same date fixed the punishment for slave-dealing at from five months' to five years' hard labour. To implement the Convention (register manumissions, find work for freed slaves, and provide schools for slave children), a special Slave Trade Department was to be formed, with four special 'Bureaux', in Cairo, Alexandria, the Delta, and Upper Egypt. Captain George Malcolm RN was placed by the British government at the disposal of the Khedive to command the squadron in the Red Sea. But much of the Red Sea coast was under the domination of Turkey, which was under no obligation to respect the Convention.[35] The Red Sea Service was thus suppressed after a short time, owing also to the apathy of Egyptian officials.

The Convention was a grand gesture, but little of a concrete nature resulted from it. So long as the institution of slavery was permitted to exist, a slave trade would continue. Gordon's suggestion that all slaves be registered, and all children born to slaves after a stated date should be freed, received no support. The Convention caused a brief spurt of activity in Cairo, where the Bureau was more directly under the eyes of the government. In one quarter of Cairo, in three months in 1879, 358 slaves were manumitted. But in Egypt as a whole, during the period 1877 to 1879, only 1490 slaves were freed.

A far wider and more active patrol was necessary to halt the traffic. In June 1880, the Service for the Abolition of Slavery was established under an Italian, Count della Sala, a seasoned soldier who had served under Maximilian in Mexico. He was a man of force and character and, most important, had private means and was less likely to succumb to bribery. With the title 'Chief of the Service for the Abolition of the Slave Trade', the rank of Colonel, and a salary of £1200 per annum, della Sala was responsible for an area extending from Alexandria to Aswan, with headquarters at el Assiout, which was the hub of the slave traffic and the point of entry for slaves into Egypt. Count della Sala, on taking up his appointment, dismissed the governor and sub-governor of Es-Siout, the chief of the Slave Bureau for Upper Egypt, and court-martialled them for neglecting to seize a caravan of 1000 slaves.[36] Della Sala found that most of the villages near Daraw, about 25 miles north of Aswan, were involved in the slave trade. So long as 'A Pasha will pay as high as £100 for an Abyssinian girl of great beauty',[37] endeavours would be made to cater to his taste.

British occupation of Egypt in 1883 marked a turning point. There was now tighter control over anti-slave trade legislation. The 'Service' aforementioned, was merged into the gendarmie under a British officer and inspectors. The new verve was quickly felt. The number of slave dealers in Cairo was reduced from the thirty-two who had openly pursued their trade in 1883, to three by 1886. In 1885, the 'Service' was placed under a Colonel Schaefer, Head of the Police, and in 1888, it was set up as an independent department under the Minister of the Interior. In 1887, registration of slaves was made compulsory for any pilgrim leaving Egypt. By 1889, 18,000 slaves had been manumitted by the Bureaux, and a report for that year stated that slave imports and sales in Egypt no longer existed.[38]

Legislation affecting the slave trade in Egypt left the situation in the Sudan practically untouched. Before Gordon left the Sudan, he settled many captured slaves in fertile parts of the country. His successor gave up these colonies, and their occupants were promptly re-enslaved. Gordon, on his return to England in 1880, urged the appointment of a roving consul, based on Khartoum, to keep watch on the slave trade in the Sudan. The Church Missionary Society and prominent humanitarians, including Lord Shaftesbury and Cardinal Manning, supported the idea, and a memorial was sent to Gladstone to this effect. But the Mahdists overran the Sudan before anything could be done.

Meanwhile, there had been a brief flurry in the Sudan, following the Khedive's instructions to Raouf Pasha, Gordon's successor as Governor-General, to suppress the slave trade. In 1881, a number of Khartoum slave dealers were convicted, a few slaves were freed, and a company of Sudanese soldiers were quartered at Delen to suppress the slave trade.[39] But it was impossible to suppress it in all its wider ramifications. Gordon, in checking the slave trade on the main trunk line, the Nile, had merely diverted it into other channels, to overland routes on the east and west sides of the Nile. By April 1882, plans were drawn up for a more complete system of slave inspection in the Sudan. But Europeans, familiar with the entrenchment of slavery in Egypt and the Sudan, were not optimistic.

> Egypt, the old house of bondage, is now as ever, the prop of the Slave Trade in Africa, and the people are far from seeing any crime in slave capture, and shame in Slave Trade or any injustice in slave-owning.[40]

Gordon, on arrival at Khartoum in 1884, seems to have expected a revolt when the liberation of slaves would take place in the Sudan in 1889, as provided for under the Anglo-Egyptian Convention of 1877. A high proportion of the population of the Sudan were slaves, and the effect of sudden emancipation on the social and economic life of the country would be drastic. Gordon held that either compensation (impossible for lack of money), or compulsory registration of slaves by a certain date, after which all not registered might leave their masters, was the more cautious and suitable approach to end slavery and the slave trade in the Sudan. He would enforce a law compelling runaway slaves to return to their masters, if registered, except when cruelly treated. The only way to stop the slave trade in its entirety, however, was to extend the frontier of Egypt up to the 'negro frontier'. Gordon's attempt to do so broke his spirit, however, and left him completely disillusioned with the character of Egyptian officials and their hangers-on.

The slave trade in the Sudan received enormous impetus following the capture of the Bahr el Ghazal by the Mahdists. Slave-dealers, who after Gessi's victory over Sulaiman had fled into the interior, now reappeared under the Mahdi's banner at Gedaref, near the Abyssinian frontier. Slaves flocked to join the Mahdi along with their masters, or were sent by their masters while the latter stayed at home. At first, the Mahdi's pronouncements seemed to favour the lot of slaves: indicting cruel masters and enjoining kindness to slaves was a fine augury. But it lasted only a short time after the defeat of General Hicks. With every success, the Mahdi became more vainglorious and cruel. When tribes of blacks and Arabs were accused of revolting and disobeying, he declared war on them and enslaved them.

Matters did not improve under his successor, the Khalifa. The latter, during the last ten years of his life, scarcely moved out of Omdurman, but his levys raided far afield. Slaves again travelled across the dunes and flats on the road to Omdurman. Mahdism and the Khalifa re-established the slave trade in all its old vigour in the Sudan, and many slaves previously liberated were re-enslaved. Slave caravans from Dervish territory in the Nile valley converged on the Red Sea coast south of Ras Banas, where petty Bedouin sheikhs connived with dealers to ship slaves across to Arabia. The coral reefs on the African side provided ideal hide-outs for slavers who operated under the guise of pearl fishermen. The Khalifa kept forts in this wild district, and the brigands who guarded them, and the Dervish Emir in the neighbourhood, entered into the business of slave-dealing with gusto.

A. B. Wylde, sometime British consul at Jedda, stated in 1887 that slaves—male, female, and eunuchs—were never so cheap or so numerous in the Red Sea area. He attributed this to the 'want of proper government in the Sudan', the great numbers of prisoners of war taken by the followers of the Mahdi who were sold into slavery, and the wholesale connivance of officials at Suakin, allied to the effete nature of Turkish rule in the Red Sea. When Wylde travelled on a steamer from Jedda to Suez, pilgrims on board from Mecca openly flaunted slaves purchased there, including a number of eunuchs. The head slave dealer at Jedda, a prominent personage, flourished in this new and buoyant market.[41]

The people inhabiting the banks of the Nile near Berber were subject to the savage raids of the Baggara of Kordofan, let loose on them by the Khalifa. Campaigns of the Khalifa in the mountains of Dar-Nuba, the Blue Nile district near Fazogli, and on the Abyssinian borders, brought in thousands of captives. Black soldiers had their retinue of female slaves, and the Khalifa himself was reputed to have 500 wives.[42]

The Khalifa permitted the notorious slave-dealer, Ismail Wad el Andok of Haboba, with a force of 1600 men, to raid for slaves on the outskirts of Khartoum. On the caravan route to El Obeid, slaves from collecting points at Beni, Shangul, El Fasher, Dar Fazogli and Abour Rosah in the Bahr el Ghazal were again on the march, and the garrisons at Fashoda, Rejaf and Lado preyed on surrounding natives. The Khalifa's Abyssinian campaign, 1887-9, brought in thousands of slaves, including the wife and daughter of the Abyssinian general, Ras Adal. Gallabat, on the northwest frontier of Abyssinia, long an important collecting point for Galla slaves, took on renewed activity. The Khalifa's rule stimulated the slave traffic in some areas, and checked it in others. The Jaalin and Danaqla slave-hunters had a field day, preying on tribes greatly weakened and reduced in numbers by war and famine. In other areas, the blacks grew in strength and independence and were able to hold their own against their erstwhile tormentors; the Dervishes at Fashoda were almost beleaguered by surrounding tribes whom they had tried to enslave.

Great numbers of slaves were brought to Omdurman where they were forced to dig wells for the growing city, the centre of the Mahdi's cause. They were employed in mixing mortar, digging clay, and as water carriers, and in the tedious daily round of grinding grain for food. Male slaves sometimes gained their liberty by serving in the army. There was no such avenue of semi-freedom open to females. In Omdurman the market for female slaves flourished. It stood close to the beit et mal, and there were generally close to 100 women of various ages on sale at any one time. They were shown off to their best advantage, well oiled, and veiled. The more choice were decked in finery, and usually exposed to a more personal examination by buyers prior to purchase. With such a plethora of slaves on hand, the poorest house could afford a female Abyssinian slave. However, it was soon found that they were little fitted for rugged work and the Sudanese climate, and were always ailing.[43] Blacks, with their greater stamina, were increasingly preferred to copper-coloured slaves, and the whole role of menial duties, carrying corn and water, cultivation and heavier domestic chores, fell to their lot. As a result of the surfeit of Abyssinians following the Abyssinian wars, black slaves commanded higher prices. The price of slaves in Omdurman during the Khalifa's period ranged from a low of ten shillings to three pounds for a young boy to a high of six to twelve pounds for a young and pretty girl, with ordinary adult slaves running at prices in between.[44] The farther away from Omdurman, the lower prices dropped, so that in remote parts of the Sudan these figures might be halved.

During the latter years of the Khalifa's rule there was some moderation in the ferocity of the slavers, and some effect given to the injunction of Islamic law as regards treatment of slaves. It was permissible to grant male and female slaves papers of freedom, although the custom was rarely practised. If a female slave bore a child to her master, she could not be sold, and after her master's death she became a free woman.⁴⁵ When a slave was sold, the seller was obliged to produce a certificate showing the tribe, description, and legal authority conferring ownership, and a certificate of purchase had to be given.

The Khalifa was also increasingly careful not to send out large raiding expeditions for slaves, for they might become too independent and turn on him. Private individuals were no longer allowed to own firearms, and the export of slaves to Egypt and the Red Sea was forbidden because the Khalifa feared that the English might intercept them and make soldiers of them, but prisoners of war taken by the Khalifa's followers were sold into slavery, and numbers of females were always enslaved.

Although the Mahdist regime, followed by that of the Khalifa, stopped the great regularized slave trade from the southern Sudan northwards into Egypt, slaves continued to infiltrate from there into Egypt, often in the guise of refugees. Sudanese who escaped northwards and found safety at the Austrian Mission 'Agricultural Home' for escaped slaves on the Nile near Cairo related harrowing details of events in the Sudan. Pathetic stories were told by slave girls destined for sale in Egypt, and taken into custody by Colonel Schaefer Bey in the shadow of the Great Pyramid at Ghizeh in November 1889, and lodged in the Cairo Home for Freed Women slaves. During the first ten years of its existence, 1884–94, over a thousand women and girls passed through the portals of this institution, many being recent captures from the Sudan. The most sensational case was that of six slave girls in the purchase of which Ali Pasha Sherif, President of the Legislative Council, was involved. A few months previously, the same official had recommended to Council that the Slave Trade Department be abolished on the ground that 'no slave trade now existed in Egypt'.⁴⁶ As Sir John Scott, late Judicial Adviser to His Highness the Khedive, stated in 1900, slavery was sanctioned by law and custom and had become 'engrained in the bones of these people'.⁴⁷

The occupation of Tokar by Egyptian forces in February 1891, which closed the Red Sea route to Dervish slavers and directed the flow of slaves northwards to Egypt, drew attention to the need to end the slave trade in Egypt. The final attack on the institution in Egypt came on 21 November 1895, when a Convention was signed between England and Egypt for the Suppression of Slavery and the Slave Trade. Import and export of slaves was prohibited, and

> every slave on Egyptian territory is entitled to his full and

complete freedom, and may demand letters of enfranchisment whenever he desires to do so . . . the Egyptian Government shall use all the influence it may possess among the tribes of Central Africa with a view to prevent the wars which they are in the habit of making upon one another to procure and to sell slaves.[48]

The Slavery Department was to be continued, with control over manumission offices in each province and district. And the Egyptian government would pay £300 toward the Home for Freed Women Slaves in Cairo. Two Khedival decrees of January 1896 further amplified the Convention: laws were passed setting out detailed penalties for buyers and sellers of slaves, and owners of slave ships. Jurisdiction under the 1877 Convention, exercised by court martial, was now extended to native courts, except in the Red Sea area where courts martial were retained. A detailed reglément for Red Sea shipping provided for right of search and detention of Egyptian vessels by a British naval patrol.

These laws were half-heartedly enforced, and there was much evasion. Muslims bitterly resented them, and used the secrecy of the harem and family life to frustrate them. Certificates of manumission obtained from religious courts gave freed slaves immunity from seizure. They had only to take the initiative, take out letters of manumission, but until this was done they remained, legally and in fact, slaves. But manumissions were few in number: 363 in 1894, 891 in 1896, and 334 in 1898. The Cairo Home for Freed Women took in about 200 females a year, but this made little impact on the large number of female slaves remaining in the harems. In outlying oases, away from the prying eyes of British officials, slaves were held in considerable numbers and surreptitiously changed hands. This was chiefly because domestic slaves did not avail themselves of the freedom which they were now entitled to. The oasis of Siwa, 300 miles west of Cairo, was a notable centre for this slave traffic, and prying Christian visitors were generally thwarted when seeking admittance there.[49]

However, as a gradual realization of the potential status of freed slaves began to dawn, there was a drop in the price of slaves, from about £40 to about £10 for a female slave; for the risk of losing a slave and suffering punishment under the new laws was a factor to be reckoned with in calculating the cost and upkeep of a slave. In comparison with free labour, slave labour was becoming less attractive. Self-interest was beginning to play a part in the waning of slavery. The development of Egyptian society, increased cultural contact with Europe, the emergence of a free labour market, accelerated urbanization, and, more important, the reconquest of the Sudan, all played their part in bringing the institution of slavery in Egypt finally to an end. Lord Cromer's Report for Egypt for 1904 stated that the systematic traffic in slaves no longer existed, and that the number of Circassians brought into Egypt was decreasing. Manumissions were continuing at the rate of a hundred or so yearly.[50]

In the Sudan, following its recovery by Britain after the battle of Omdurman in September 1898, the full effect of the barbarism of Mahdist rule was evident; wars, disease and starvation had wrought their toll. The Bahr el Ghazal had been raided constantly for slaves, the region near Deim es Zubeir had been drained dry of its people, and on the White Nile it took a generation or more for the Bari people to recover from the ordeal. They were still showing the devastating effects of it in the 1920s.

The declaration issued at Cairo on 19 January 1899, signed by Lord Cromer and the Egyptian Minister for Foreign Affairs, which laid down principles for the future administration of the Sudan, contained a clause prohibiting the import and export of slaves in the Sudan, but there was no reference to domestic slavery. It was to be the policy under the Condominium that there should be a gradual reduction of slavery over a period of years. This would be attained, for example, by decreeing that persons born after the re-occupation of 1898 could not be held as slaves.

By the time the Khalifa met his death in Kordofan in November 1899, most of the Sudan had already passed into the hands of the new Sudanese government. It had the unenviable task of establishing peace and order in a vast territory where much was wrack and ruin. The eighth clause of the Memorandum instructions issued by Lord Kitchener as Governor-General, to the governors of districts in the Sudan, stated that 'Slavery is not recognized in the Sudan', but added that 'as long as service is willingly rendered by servants to masters it is unnecessary to interfere in the conditions existing between them'.[51] The Sirdar (Kitchener) did all possible to enforce regulations regarding the slave trade and slavery, but in so doing was faced with a host of problems. Nearly one-third of the petitions presented to the new government in the Sudan were requests by masters for the return of their runaway slaves. There was the question of persons bringing slaves from interior districts, so remote that they were unaware of the new slave trade regulations. In the chaos following the capture of Omdurman, liberated Egyptians sought to bring back to Egypt Sudanese women whom they had previously acquired as slaves. Children of escaping Sudanese, following the conquest of Dongola province, were easy prey to predatory slavers. And in Omdurman a considerable remnant of the old slave-trading community remained, ever on the look-out for opportunities to renew their old trade. In the few remaining months of 1898, following the capture of Omdurman, 47 persons were convicted of slave-dealing, among them a relative of the infamous Zubeir Pasha, who received a five-year sentence of imprisonment for selling a slave. In implementing anti-slave measures, the Mudir of Talodi was treacherously murdered in May 1906, along with 40 men from a Sudanese regiment.[52] Arab dissatisfaction in southern Kordofan in 1906, over the freeing and return to their homes of 120 women and children whom they had enslaved, reached the point of insurrection.[53]

Captain McMurdo, who was appointed Director of the Slave Trade Department in Egypt in 1900, extended its operations into the Sudan. Attention was first directed to the slave trade between Kassala and Suakin. The conviction and sentence to seven years' imprisonment of Sheikh Marshoud, from the notorious slave-dealing Rashaida tribe, and the apprehension of eleven minor dealers, was a salutary lesson for the Rashaida: they emigrated south to Italian territory where their slave-raiding depredations gave grave concern to the Italians. McMurdo aimed at establishing a cordon across the eastern Sudan, from the Gezireh to Suakin, and to this end, in 1901, an English slave trade inspector, based at Khartoum, was placed in charge of the Gezireh and Atbara districts, while the country between Berber, Kassala and Suakin was patrolled by camel corps, the main desert wells were guarded, and camel patrols constantly kept in touch with one another. Zeal in McMurdo's anti-slave trade policy was reflected in a ruling of 1901, whereby officers, military and civil, were empowered to arrest slave-dealers, using such force as necessary to bring them to trial.

An area of special concern to the Anti-Slave Trade Department was the frontier of Abyssinia, in the extreme south-east, where intertribal warfare was constantly throwing up large numbers of slaves. The Barun tribe, to the immediate west of the Bani Shanqul district, were the main victims of periodical raids by large parties of Abyssinians. McMurdo, in the course of a tour of the Abyssinian frontier in 1902, observed that these depredations had reduced the population in the district to the proportion of seven men to every woman. The appointment of an inspector at Roseires at the end of 1902 was a direct result of McMurdo's visit there, and the slave-raiders received a severe check when, in 1904, Colonel Gorringe, Mudir of Sennar, sentenced Ibrahim Wad Mahmoud and followers to imprisonment for slave-dealing.

The Sudan-Abyssinian Frontier Delimitation Commission of 1902/3 increased the sufferings of the Anuak tribe to the north of the Baro River, by splitting them into two sections, one in the Sudan and the other in Abyssinia. The horrors attendant on Abyssinian slave raids on the Anuak were witnessed by McMurdo during his ascent of the Sobat and Baro Rivers in June 1902. He recommended the establishment of a strong military post at Gambela, at the foot of the Abyssinian mountains, to halt raids from that direction. The delimitation of the frontier between the Sudan and Abyssinia in 1903–4 assisted in the attainment of this object.

In 1902, McMurdo turned his attention to the Kordofan Province in the west, where the Baggara and Kababash were the most tenacious of slave-dealers. The young women of their tribes taunted suitors to show their valour in slave-raiding. The price of a wife, often paid to her parents in the form of slaves, encouraged slave-raiding. In 1902, McMurdo posted an inspector and a small supporting mounted corps of local Arabs at El Obeid. The sentencing to five years' imprisonment of the slave dealer, Said Ibrahim, by Colonel Mahon, Mudir of Kordofan, in 1903 was one of the first fruits of the drive against the Kordofan slave raiders. McMurdo, following a tour of the Province, was of the opinion that little was gained in pursuing raiders on their home ground; his forces would be 'eaten up' in the fastness of the many little mountain archipelagos of Kordofan, and it was wiser to concentrate on export routes, such as that from El Obeid to the Gezireh. In 1906, the Kordofan forces were strengthened, and McMurdo, if he had sufficient resources at his command, would have extended the cordon from Roseires to El Obeid, cutting off the Jellaba slave traders from Abyssinia and the Bahr el Ghazal.

The latter region merited special attention. McMurdo, after visiting government stations on the White Nile as far as Lado in 1905, and ascertaining that the slave trade had practically ceased there, was convinced that the Bahr el Ghazal was the area to be watched. Dr Schweinfurth had for long pointed this out, maintaining that over 50,000 slaves were held there, apart from those exported.[54] The slave traffic in the northwest corner of the Bahr el Ghazal emanated from the French Congo. It was not until 1908, when posts were established on this remote frontier, that it was halted. Some pockets of slavery, however, were almost impossible to eradicate. McMurdo had no illusions as to the daunting task which faced him. It would take years to end slavery in the Sudan, for a long-standing problem remained in the east, near the Red Sea coast, from which slaves were shipped across to Yembo and Jedda for Medina and Mecca.

The Ashabab tribe, dwelling in the Atbai desert between the Nile and Red Sea, continued to pursue the slave trade until the conviction and sentence to fifteen years' imprisonment of their leader, Mohammed Nossair, in 1906. In the south, in the range of rugged mountains from Kassala to the Red Sea, the Gemelab tribe continued to enslave and pass their wares through the port of Massawa. The opening up of the district of Suakin by the Nile-Red Sea railway in 1905, with a terminus at Port Sudan, and the conviction and sentencing of fifty-eight dealers in the eighteen months January 1905 to July 1906, although a blow to the slave trade along the Red Sea coast, did not end it. The appointment of a British inspector at Suakin in 1905, and the doubling of his force of mounted men, was a recognition of the need for sustained watchfulness over the coastline from Jebel Elba to Ras Kassar.

An attempt in 1910 by French and British authorities to check the slave traffic into the Sudan from French territory by requiring passports for legitimate caravans was thwarted by a clause making it an offence for officials to intercept those not guilty of possessing slaves. Apart from this contentious issue, similar to that of the slave dhow which hoisted French colours and claimed redress for wrongful search, Kitchener was probably correct when he stated in 1912 that 'slave-trading on a large scale is clearly a thing of the past.'[55] The corresponding member of the Anti-Slavery Society at Merowe in Upper Egypt, however, estimated in 1909 that 120,000 Arabs in that Province still possessed 24,000 Sudanese slaves.

7
Northeast Africa and the Middle East

I. NORTHEAST AFRICA

The term *Habash* or *Habshi*, generally applied to the slave from Ethiopia, and possibly derived from the Arabic for 'mixed' or *Habashat*, the name of the ancient Semitic tribe from South Arabia which settled in Ethiopia,[1] denotes the heterogenous nature of the inhabitants of the Ethiopian plateaux. This region is one of the great meeting places of Africans of Bantu origin and those of Hamitic/Semitic/Cushitic stock. This amalgam produces an exotic physical type: slim, well-formed body, regular features, velvety eyes, hair long and straight, or somewhat curly, and almost blueblack or approaching to black in colour. A certain delicacy, in small hands and slender fingers, and complexions ranging from pale olive to deep brown or almost sooty black adds the final desirable touch, and explains the esteem in which the *Habash*, especially the female, slave was held in slave-owning societies in the East—

> a magnificent and sculpturesque creature, with an European profile (though some of them have slightly thick lips, and slightly prominent cheek bones). The skin is not black, but metallic and bronzed—veritable statues of Florentine bronze . . . They fetch a great price, and are much prized by the Arabs, who superstitiously believe that a Galla woman can re-animate and renew the blood of an old man: and as the Arab only lives for his wife, and would ruin himself to have one, they always find purchasers at a high price.[2]

In Turkey and Egypt they ranked first, the boys for their intelligence, and girls for their beauty. In Ethiopia itself, there were few chiefs who did not have Galla blood in their veins. The other kind of slave from Ethiopia, the *Shankalla* or *Sidi*, from the Nilotic group occupying the area between the Blue Nile and Sudan frontier, on Ethiopia's western side, was not in such great demand as the *Habash*, a term which increasingly denoted a Galla slave.

The original habitat of the Galla was probably the horn of eastern

Africa, but under Somali pressure they had been driven into the savanna country south-east of the Ethiopian plateaux, and from here had been infilitrating into Ethiopia since the sixteenth century. Their martial qualities and horsemanship gained for them an ascendancy over the more semiticised Cushites of Central Ethiopia which lasted almost three hundred years, and by the nineteenth century the Galla occupied an enormous area, from the southern tip of Tigrai to Harrar in the east, to the Tana river on the south, and to the tributaries of the Nile on the west. Although acculturated to Semitic Hamites through inter-marriage, they retained elements of their indigenous social institutions.

By the nineteenth century the Galla were no longer able to maintain their ascendancy over their Cushitic neighbours, and the tables were beginning to turn. Long centuries of Galla aggression had to be avenged. This reversal of fortunes brought for the Galla widespread enslavement, and increasingly they comprised the majority of slaves exported from the country.[3] They predominated in the great slave markets of northwestern Ethiopia, at Gondar, and at Gallabat, on the spurs of the Ethiopian massif jutting out into the Sudan, a favourite hunting-ground for Egyptian slave-hunters. Samuel Baker, journeying there in 1861-2, visited the establishments of the slave merchants at Gallabat.

> These were arranged under large tents of matting, and contained many young girls of extreme beauty, ranging from nine to seventeen years of age. These lovely captives, of a rich brown tint, with delicately formed features, and eyes like those of the gazelle, were natives of the Galla, on the borders of Abyssinia, from which country they were brought by Abyssinian traders to be sold for the Turkish harems . . . The price of one of these beauties of Gallabat was from twenty-five to forty dollars.[4]

Within Ethiopia the trade in Galla slaves in the nineteenth century was sustained by hereditary Galla chiefs, called 'kings', in the western provinces of Gojjam, Enarea and Jimma, from whence they pursued a slave trade with Muslim dealers. They raided their own and their neighbours' territory for slaves. Their brother rulers, the so-called 'Republican' Galla, in the southern and fertile highlands of Arusa, were less active slave traders, but poverty could drive them to accept the gold of the slave merchants.

When Theodore emerged as Emperor of Ethiopia in 1855, the country was in turmoil, but his campaigns of 1862 worsened the situation, and brought additional suffering and enslavement for the

Galla. A temporary resurgence of the Galla in 1865-8 was followed by renewed enslavement, and large numbers were thrown on to the slave markets. Although Theodore was acclaimed abroad as a supporter of the anti-slave trade 'cause, he was never more than its fitful votary; he was much too preoccupied in securing his own precarious position on the throne. There were also dark stories of his involvement in the slave trade, for he had pointed out to slave caravans the best and safest by-roads for their business. And Ethiopian slaves seeking refuge at the British consulate at Massawa told sorry tales of his doings, and begged that Theodore's demand for their return be not heeded.[5]

The lot of slaves in Ethiopia was much worse than under Arab masters. There was no Koranic code to ameliorate their position, nor the sense of brotherhood which always softened the relationship of master and slave under Islam. Little attention was paid to anti-slave trade legislation. When a firman of the local ruler was publicly read at Massawa, prohibiting the sale of stolen children, it was disobeyed the same day it was promulgated, and forgotten in three days' time. Slave markets throughout the country operated without hindrance from Ethiopian authorities. In 1866 thousands of Christians were sold in the slave markets at Taka and Metemma, and at the latter place 500 slaves were on sale daily, mostly young Galla destined for Jedda.[6] At Basso, in Gojjam, perhaps the largest slave market in the country, 5000 slaves were sold weekly during the high season. Ras Adal, Governor of Gojjam, regularly passed on slave children in payment of taxes to King John. And the latter in turn distributed them among his chieftains.

Galla slaves, 'Wossief', superfine goods, from the cool tablelands to the immediate north of Kaffa, were exported on a scale that caused wonderment as to their source.[7] Count Louis Penazzi, an Italian traveller, at Gedaref in 1880 reported convoys of Galla slaves, 300 at a time, travelling the road from Gallabat to Suakin, and the Governor of Gedaref received a percentage on their export.[8] The few Europeans in Ethiopia looked on with grievous concern at this spectacle of young Christian Galla slaves, in a country purportedly Christian, sold to slavers at Red Sea ports. Madam Emily Lundahl, of the Swedish Mission at Massawa, despaired over the hopeless task of retrieving them. It was with great hope that she looked forward to the day when the Italians, newly arrived in Eritrea, would take over the great work of freeing them. Commander Gissing, of HMS *Osprey*, based at Aden, reporting on the two hundred Galla slaves he had freed, noted that this was a mere fraction of the 5000 annually exported through the port of

Tajurra. Muslim slave dealers at Zeila and Tajurra supplied Galla slaves for Turkey, Arabia, and Egypt, and salved their conscience by claiming that these slaves were idolaters or Christians.[9] Ethiopian officials were bribed with ease so as allow the duty-free export of slaves from the country.

The isolated nature of Ethiopia, the precarious rule and lack of any moral sense of dereliction in the matter on the part of its leaders, made an anti-slave trade campaign exceedingly difficult. Captain Harris, at the Court of Shoa in the early 1840s, had appealed for the cessation of the slave trade there, and in 1873 the Anti-Slavery Society had made a direct appeal to King John to end the slave trade in his dominions. There was no response until 1879, when Menelik, King of Shoa, announced his willingness to abolish the slave trade in his kingdom, if the Society in turn would urge the British government to obtain from Egypt the removal of restrictions on Abysinnia's access to Red Sea ports, now held by Egypt.[10] Ensuing correspondence between the Anti-Slavery Society and the Foreign Office on the subject was unprofitable. When, on the advice of a German missionary, Johann Meyer, who acted as intermediary, a large state umbrella was made up as a present to Menelik, General Gordon warned of the umbrage its presentation would give Egypt. It was never sent.

There was also doubt as to Menelik's sincerity in ending the slave trade. He had forbidden passage to slave caravans through his country, but Galla slaves still travelled the old routes. C. W. Isenberg, in 1884, claimed that nearly 8000 slaves were annually exported from the country, and mostly from Shoa, the native province of Menelik. He received a duty of one slave for every ten exported, and was also proprietor of 2000 slaves.[11] It was apparent that there would be no quick end to the slave trade in Ethiopia.

The French at Jibuti unwittingly or wittingly abetted it, by their indiscriminate sale of firearms to slave dealers, and in lending their flag as cover for the transport of slaves across the Red Sea. Within Ethiopia traditional attitudes remained unchanged. In the late 1890s hundreds of slaves were still exacted as a form of tribute by Rases and the chieftains.[12] The announcement in December 1903 that Menelik had promulgated throughout Ethiopia a decree prohibiting the slave trade gave no great cause for jubilation at the Anti-Slavery Society.[13] Ethiopia continued to be one of the main areas giving it concern well into the twentieth century. Despite Menelik's decree, Captain R. P. Cobbold, who served in his army at the turn of the century, claimed that it was still the practice to enslave prisoners of war.

Tajurra, the Danakil capital, at the base of the great black wall of the Mabla range, with its jagged volcanic peaks and the cone of Djebbel Gudda towering over all, remained an outlet for Ethiopian slaves. Europeans hardly entered there. They were hastily brushed aside for fear they might pry to closely into the affairs of the slavers. Although slaves could not now be legally sold in Ethiopia, they might still be exchanged as gifts, and the recipient of such gifts must display good manners by reciprocating with a gift of equal value. Local chiefs continued to connive at the trade. Impoverishment of tribes through drought, disease and famine constantly threw slaves on to the market; they were often the only commodity available for sale. The vast extent of the country, great stretches of desert, the impenetrable nature of much of it, the absence of centralized authority, and the lack of enlivened public opinion, rendered the enforcement of anti-slave trade measures exceedingly difficult in Ethiopia.

A traveller at Tajurra, in 1910, noted that no stigma was attached to the slave trade, and slaves themselves willingly entered into it, for it was often held out to them as the means to a better life in rich foreign lands.[14] A slave gang on its way to the coast 'sang and laughed as they moved about . . . It required a conscious effort to pity them; nothing in their appearance or manner called for it'.[15] The worst feature of this trade was that a small proportion of slaves were young castrated boys.[16]

British contact with the Somali coast goes back to the early nineteenth century when the Indian Navy was active in establishing British influence in the Gulf of Aden, and various treaties were made with the Somali tribes for the protection of East India Company interests and 'for the harbour of their ships without any prohibition whatever'. British influence was further strengthened with the occupation of the island of Socotra (1834), Aden (1839), Perim (1857), and by treaties which Captain Robert Moresby of the Indian Navy, acting for the British government in India, made with the Sultan of Tajurra and governor of Leila. About the same time Musha Island, at the entrance to the Gulf of Tajurra, was acquired for 'ten bags of rice', and Sab Island and Aubad Island were similarly purchased by the East India Company.[17] These acquisitions, administered from Bombay, were meant to secure communications between Suez and Bombay.

It was not until October 1855 that the British concerned themselves with the slave trade in the area, and entered into an agreement with the Habr Gerhajis and Habr Toljaala tribes on the north Somali coast, whereby they solemnly proclaimed 'in the sight

NORTHEAST AFRICA AND THE MIDDLE EAST

of God and man' their intention to 'prohibit the export of slaves from Africa by every means in our power'[18] The British were to send an agent to watch over the great slave market at Berbera. No agent was however appointed, and, apart from a few visits of ships of the Indian Navy to Zeila and Tajurra in the 1850s, little attempt was made to implement the engagements of 1855. Following the reduction of the Indian Navy, and its final abolition in 1863, there was little contact with Somaliland, apart from the expedition to Harrar in 1854 of the British explorer, Burton. He saw hundreds of slaves on sale at the market at Aynterad, 40 miles north of Berbera, where 'an able-bodied male could be purchased for goods costing 15 dollars in Europe', and a woman for double that amount.[19] The slaves whom Burton saw were Galla from Ethiopia.

The Somali were comparatively free from enslavement. They were a vigorous, intelligent race, with more of the Arab than the Bantu in their make-up and appearance, a pastoral people under a patriarchal aristocracy, with a helot class at the bottom. Their reputation as fanatical Muslims, and for keeping in their country all strangers who might enter it, had left them relatively untouched by the outside world. Being Muslim, a measure of immunity from enslavement was conferred on them, but it was rather to their character and reputation for fierceness that this immunity must be ascribed.[20] And this immunity was certainly not conferred on their Galla neighbours.

Despite the barren nature of the country there was a desultory trade with the outside world in hides, beeswax, ostrich feathers, eggs, gums, camels, sheep and horses, and a bullock trade had been opened up with Mauritius by the mid-nineteenth century. The Somali were increasingly coming to Aden to work as fishermen, labourers and houseservants: they accumulated savings, and returned to their own country where they became slave-owners, and reputedly the worst of slave-masters. They had contracted new habits, were turning to agriculture, irrigating the banks of the Juba and Webi Shibeli, cultivating sugar-cane, orchella weed (used as a purple dye), and semsem (for the manufacture of a fine oil in the Marseilles market). Large numbers of slaves were required for this.

It was not generally realized by the outside world that these changes were taking place among the Somali. The contemporary view that Somaliland was a wasteland prevailed. Few travellers approaching that low-lying barren shore realized that a land so seemingly unproductive supported a large slave population.

The first intimation that this was the case came in the 1860s, when an English trader, Mr. J. Hales, at Brava, referred to the number of slaves there; many were landed from slave dhows run ashore to escape capture by British cruisers, but there was also a direct import from farther down the coast. In 1868, when Churchill in the *Star* visited the Somali coast, he noted that Somali agents were coming up from the Ozi river area where they had purchased slaves, who in turn had been brought up by the land route from Kilwa. And, in 1870, HMS *Dryad* captured a number of Arab dhows landing slaves on the Somali coast. They had avoided detection by sailing northwards from Kilwa, and to the east of Zanzibar and Pemba.[21] In 1874, Admiral Cumming put the number of slaves passing into Somaliland at 12,000 annually.[22]

When land communications were cut off by a tribal war on the Juba river in the late 1860s, there was a noticeable falling off in the number of slaves entering Somaliland, but the slave trade by sea elsewhere along the coast quickened. And when land communications were opened up with southern Somali ports in the early 1870s, the number of slaves entering there increased. Land journeys, interspersed with short sea journeys, were becoming the usual way of introducing slaves into Somaliland. In the early spring of 1871, 1900 slaves that went from Zanzibar to Lamu under the Sultan's pass were shown to have gone to Somali buyers.[23]

Somali owners of Galla slaves found it profitable to sell these valuable slaves and acquire in their stead the much less expensive Sidi slaves from farther south, who were also more docile, and less likely to run away. This Somali trade in Galla slaves joined up with the larger slave from Ethiopia which had its outlet at the Gulf of Tajurra. For it was now revealed that the old belief, current in maritime circles, and possibly fostered by the East India Company to deter competitors, that

> The wind which will carry the slave cargo rapidly up to Cape Guardafui, will take it up to the Gulf of Aden, and will be dead foul for passing up the Red Sea.

was erroneous.[24] Captain Paisley, writing from Zanzibar in August 1867, pointed out that nearly all slaves taken into the Red Sea from the East African coast were shipped during the northeast monsoon, the supposed contrary winds notwithstanding. It was a mistake to suppose that export of slaves from the East African coast was confined to the period of the southwest monsoon. If the monsoon faded out, or if slaves were surplus to requirement on the Somali coast, they were held there for a time, fattened up, and then sent north to Zeila and Tajurra, where they combined with a flow of slaves from

Ethiopian and Danakil countries. Musha Island, in the Gulf of Tajurra, was a favourite transhipping point. A network of local sultans, euphemistically termed 'Turkish authorities', were involved in the trade. The Kaimakan of Massawa and local officials, including the customs master, were notorious purchasers of Galla females. Playfair claimed that nearly all Turkish officials were culpable, and one-quarter of the proceeds of the slave trade was passed on to their overlord, the Pasha of the Yemen.

Zeila became the nodal point of this traffic. It was largely controlled by its governor, Abu Bekr, who, despite the presence of a French consul at Zeila since the 1850s, appears to have pursued a slave traffic unhindered, and to have reduced it to a systematic business. He derived a large revenue from it, and placated the Pasha of the Yemen with an annual tribute. With his family, numerous children by his many wives, Abu Bekr held sway from Obock to Berbera. His trade in slaves was his secret and lucrative monopoly. One of his sons was Governor of Tajurra, another director-in-chief of transport, and a third recruiter-general at the re-entrant of the Hawish road into Ethiopia. Abu Bekr showed much enterprise. He used the newly established telegraph communication in the Red Sea, based at Perim Island, to warn colleagues of the movements of British cruisers. M. Lucereau, a French traveller cruelly murdered in early 1881, presumably on Abu Bekr's orders, could not find words to describe the man: he was 'cunning and lying personified'. Abu Bekr collected his slaves in batches of 100 at a time, and transported them across to the Arabian side, in large undecked barges of 30 to 100 tons, at the rate of 500 to 600 per month. They were mostly young girls, and a few eunuchs (rendered as such before shipment). At the height of the season, upwards of 2000 slaves were shipped across in this fashion, and nearly all under the Turkish flag. The smoke or mast of a British steamer hailing up from Aden was the signal to run the slaves ashore; a refuge was usually assured by confederates, for the 'Mussulmans did not betray each other'. From Hodeida and Mocha slaves were shipped farther north to Jedda, and secretly smuggled into that town to avoid paying customs duty. The trade at Jedda was usually carried on during the hottest time of year when there were few British cruisers in the Red Sea.

John Kirk, at Zanzibar, drew attention to the Somali slave trade which converged at Zeila with that from Ethiopia.[25] Henceforth British officials at Aden gave closer attention to it. The appointment of a British consular agent at Berbera was urged, also the stationing of a vessel-of-war at Perim island, and protection for chiefs cooperating with the British in putting down the slave trade. These suggestions were never implemented.

An anti-slave trade campaign in the Red Sea required the collaboration of the Turkish authorities, or of their surrogates, Egyptians and Yemenese. The Egyptian government responded to British pressure and tried to check Abu Bekr's activities, but the Egyptians were in an embarrassing position. At Harrar they were blockaded by hostile tribes, and the dismissal of Abu Bekr, an Egyptian underling, would undermine Egyptian prestige. The Khedive of Egypt, Tewfik Pasha, said that Britain, with her naval base at Aden, was in a position to check the trade.

A British consul keeping watch at Hodeida and the patrol of the coast from Zeila northwards for six to eight weeks each year were quite inadequate, for the main seaports in the Red Sea were under nominal Turkish sovereignty, and at these the slave trade went on unhindered. Colonel Gordon, heartily perplexed by his own problems in dealing with the slave trade in the Sudan, recommended the deportation of Abu Bekr and his many sons; but Gordon's advice was not heeded, and he himself was soon on his way out. It was not until Abu Bekr's death in 1887 that there was any surcease from the depredations of the slavers at Zeila.

No anti-slave trade campaign in the Red Sea could fail to take account of the necessity to keep watch on Jedda, port of entry to the Hedjaz, and gateway to the holy cities of Mecca and Medina. By the 1860s dhows, flying the Turkish flag, were ferrying as many as 15,000 slaves annually across the Red Sea to Jedda during the period of the *Haj*, the pilgrimage. Slaves were sold at daily auction in Jedda and Mecca, and many changed hands privately. The valley of Naaman, near Mecca, was a favourite place for their disposal to pilgrims who came from all points of the compass. Those from Persia brought precious carpets and turquoise stones; from Damascus came those with the finest steel weapons; and from points farther East came pilgrims with rich silks and personal adornments. At Jedda articles could be exchanged for slaves who were in turn brought by pilgrims from Africa. The Anti-Slavery Society's correspondent at Alexandria estimated in 1878 that 25,000 slaves annually were thus disposed of at Mecca and Medina.[26] Mecca, a city normally of 70,000 inhabitants, doubled its population during the four months prior to the *Haj*, and took on the aspect of a great tented metropolis. Jedda, its port, literally bristled with slaves for sale.[27] Many of these slaves were taken home by returning pilgrims, but many also remained in Arabia. Taif, for example, on the plateau about 100 miles southeast of Mecca, was a luxury resort for rich Arabs from Mecca during the hottest months of the year, and they held large numbers of female slaves here. It was a pattern duplicated in many other parts of Arabia, according to Dr Schimpfer who visited there in the 1860s. He despaired of ending the slave trade in Arabia without a complete blockade of Africa.

British pressure on Turkey to end the slave trade in the Hedjaz had little success. In 1855 when the Sultan's firman was read out in Mecca and Jedda, it caused a revolution. Turkish officials, including the Kadi who read the firman, were murdered, the garrison shut, and Mecca was in a state of revolt until the Porte repealed the obnoxious order.[28] Turkish authorities in the Hedjaz were henceforth wary about taking action against the trade, and, in 1858, when the governors of Massawa and Jedda were instructed to stop the traffic there, they ignored the instructions. Captain Seymour of the *Pelorius*, at Jedda in January 1859, noted that African slaves were arriving there weekly. And when the Governor-General of the Hedjaz issued orders on 25 February 1860, forbidding the slave trade in all Turkish ports in the Red Sea, there was great excitement and fear of a recurrence of the 1855 violence. There was no Ottoman cruiser in the Red Sea capable of giving effect to this order, and Turkish officials were too frightened to enforce it.

The 1860 prohibition appears to have stimulated the slave traffic, for the trade being illegal, slave dealers were now relieved from paying the 25% duty on slave imports. Widespread smuggling and the connivance of officials kept up the normal supply of slaves for Jedda.[29] When the Sultan of Turkey's firman of August 1864, abolishing the slave trade in his dominions, was extended to the Hedjaz in March 1865, the Kaimakam was recalled for failure to implement it.[30] The Anglo-Egyptian convention of August 1877 was not binding on Turkey, but she made a show of support for it. One hundred slave-dealers were banished from Jedda, the head of the police dismissed, a number of slaves freed, and two old cruisers were stationed at Jedda. British congratulations on this apparently fine effort by the Turks proved premature. This unwonted zeal brought for the Governor-General of the Hedjaz death by poisoning in August 1878; and in May 1879, a Turkish captain who had seized four small dhows carrying 40 girls and 20 boys from the Danakil country was shortly learned to have taken four of the best slaves for himself and distributed others among his friends.[31] Feeling against Christians ran so high at the time that the British consular agent at Jedda requested stop-overs by British cruisers passing through the Red Sea, to give protection.

Nine out of every ten men at Jedda were still purchasers of slaves, and Turkish officials remained the worst offenders. It would require a herculean effort to eradicate the slave trade from the Red Sea. Rear-Admiral Corbett of the East African patrol reckoned it would take a full-scale navy.[32] Hopes were raised by the Anglo-Turkish Convention for the abolition of the African slave trade in February 1880, for it prohibited the traffic in African slaves in any part of the Ottoman empire and its dependencies, and persons concerned in acts of mutilation or dealing in children were to be prosecuted as criminals. Right of search and the detention of Ottoman vessels was granted to British cruisers. Captive ships and slaves were to be handed over to Ottoman authorities. In this last stipulation lay the great flaw in the Convention. British naval officers and the Anti-Slavery Society and its supporters had no confidence in the probity of Turkish authorities, for the latter would be lenient with slave-dealers, or exculpate them outright if bribed, and captured slave-ships would most likely end up in the hands of new slave-dealers.

To make the Convention effective it was necessary to establish Courts of Mixed Commission, as in the case of conventions with Spain and Portugal. This would ensure that there would be no one-sided dealing, or perversion of justice.[33]

Failure to insist on Courts of Mixed Commission was a grave dereliction, and there was the problem of the large number of domestic slaves accompanying pilgrims to Mecca, working as crew or passed off as the wives of crew members. The slave traffic across the Red Sea never reached the peak years of the 1860s and 1870s, but it still accounted for upwards of 3000 slaves annually entering Jedda during the Haj, when pilgrims came in tens of thousands.[34] Slaves were carried across the Red Sea in small, fast sailing dhows, *sambouks*, of two to fifty tons, lateen-rigged, and with a wild rascally crew of Zebedeeh from the Bedouin tribe, well-armed with rifles and cultasses. The crossing could be done in 10 to 18 hours, or even less in favourable conditions. The trade proved a lucrative sideline for pearl-fishing boats.[35]

Augustus Wylde, British Vice-Consul at Jedda, in August 1876 drew attention to the traffic. He had travelled widely in Ethiopia and the Sudan, and had seen slave-dealers operating at the principal markets.[36] Wylde believed that the only way to end the slave trade was to open up the African interior, and supported the proposal for a railway from Suakin to Berber, and Gordon's suggestion to establish a British trading company in the Abyssinian highlands: it would be 'the death blow of the slave trade as far as Abyssinia and Galla slaves were concerned'.[37] British officials at Aden thought the answer lay in lightly armed vessels, including a man-of-war, a few small steam launches, and two or three native dhows, operating from Aden northwards into the Red Sea. But there were many natural obstacles to such a naval patrol. It was difficult to keep watch on slavers making the short run across the Red Sea, owing to the enormous length of its shoreline, a distance of over 2000 miles. There were also extensive reefs on both the African and Arabian side, behind which native dhows could shelter, and pearl-fishing provided a good screen for their operations. There was the connivance of Turkish officials, as at Hodeida, where the Grand Shireef protected them, the Chief of Police was involved in the slave trade, and a large slave market operated openly a few miles from the town: and at Mocha lower down on the Red Sea, where 800 slaves were on sale at one time.[38]

Policing of the Red Sea was properly Turkey's concern, for she had claim to sovereignty over its shores that went back to the time of Suleiman the Magnificent. Following the evacuation of the Sudan and the rise of the Mahdi, British influence in the southern half of the Red Sea was confined to Suakin, and it was only here that she was in position to check the slave traffic on the African side of the Red Sea. The Madhist uprising in the Sudan was preceded by a rush to get slaves across to Arabia; this coincided with an unusual period of contrary winds in the Red Sea, and with British military operations at Suakin in 1883-5. The flow of slaves to the Hedjaz was thus halted, and brokers' houses at Mecca and Jedda were denuded of slaves with prices doubled.[39] The slave trade, and with it slave merchants, was diverted southwards to the Gulf of Tajurra. Mr Bergman, travelling there in 1887, reported that 2000 Galla slaves, young girls and boys (mostly eunuchs), were sold to Jedda merchants now established at the Gulf of Tajurra ports.[40] And off the coast of northern Somaliland, HMS *Bittern* dispersed numerous sambouks attempting to collect Gallą slaves; her captain however reckoned that many slaves slipped through and were taken to Jedda. Prices for female Galla slaves rose from 30 to 60 to 90 dollars apiece, such was the demand.

The Shoa Roman Catholic Mission and Her Majesty's consul at Hodeida reported in the 1880s a trade in Christian Galla children which was largely controlled by the Danakil king, Mohammed Kumfereh of Aussa; he acted as main agent for slave merchants at the coast, and sent on consignments of slaves to them. The Danakil were the most cruel of slave-dealers, rivalled only by the Baggara of Kordofan.

The ousting of Egyptian authority from the Sudan, following the rise of the Mahdi, removed what slight check had existed on the slave trade there. There was a revival of the slave trade at first, under the Mahdi, and Arab slavers returned to their former occupation. But the Khalifa, the Mahdi's successor, prohibited the export of male slaves to Arabia, fearing their lapse into religious infidelity, but permitted the export of females if wives or domestic servants.

Thus, after a brief interlude under the Mahdi, slaving recommenced. Caravans of slaves once again arrived at Suakin for shipment across to Jedda. During the period of dominance of the Mahdi and Khalifa, Suakin remained in British hands and was the headquarters of British troops in the eastern Sudan. Colonel Kitchener, commandant, 1886-8, prohibited the export of slaves, and urged that pearl-fishing, a disguise for the slave trade, be made a government monopoly. But despite Kitchener's vigilance, it was difficult to capture Suakin slave-dealers red-handed. Egyptian special anti-slave trade organization, elaborate titles, and the aid of a British man-of-war, availed little. On the Arabian side of the Red Sea, authorites in the Hedjaz, even if willing, had insufficient force to garrison its long seaboard. Two old Turkish men-of-war, stationed at Jedda, were too large and clumsy for inshore work among the creeks and numerous reefs north and south of Jedda.

As the result of a deputation from the Anti-Slavery Society to Earl Granville, Foreign Secretary, in August 1888, and a plea for the speedy appointment of British consuls at ports on the Red Sea coast and a more effective naval patrol of its waters,[41] HMS *Osprey* and *Kingfisher* were detailed to the Red Sea in early 1889. In one month the *Osprey* freed 204 slaves, and a number of slave-dealers were imprisoned.[42] British activity appears to have stirred Turkish authorities on, and they freed some hundreds of slaves held by slave-dealers at Mecca and Jedda, and on their own initiative carried out a search of slave-dealers' premises at those places.[43] The sentencing of crews of captured slave dhows to five years' imprisonment and fifty lashes each, and the conviction in 1891 of a great slave-dealer, Said Abou Sadecka of Jedda, following the conviction of his son the previous year for a similar offence, dealt a severe blow to the guild of slavers at Jedda.[44]

But the slave trade in the Red Sea portrayed the same protean character as along the East African coast: blocking its channel in one direction only served to divert it into another. Slavers divided their activities, according to the season and the whereabouts of the small British anti-slave trade patrol operating from Aden, between the northern and southern half of the Red Sea. They coasted along the shoreline between Berbera and Massawa, and on reaching the narrows of the straits of Bab el Mandeb ran their slaves across at night, to Mocha and Hodeida on the Arabian side. Shortly before the Haj there was a build-up of slaves in the markets in readiness for shipment north. A network of information existed to aid the slavers. Runners along the coast, sambuq and messenger, lookouts on the mountains, and the use of the telegraph at Perim and Obokh conveyed news of the movements of Her Majesty's ships. These clever tactics were never really countered by the naval patrol. Small, seaworthy decked steamers, with machine guns and light, long-range armament, similar to those employed by the Germans on the East African coast, would have been the answer, not the clumsy ruse of the Egyptian authorities in fitting out captured slave dhows as cruisers.

Italy's entry as a power in the Red Sea brought relief for hard-pressed British naval forces. Italy had already co-operated with Britain in 1886, when the coast near Massawa was blockaded against slavers, and the Italian corvette *Mestre*, in April 1886, had captured two dhows carrying slaves from Massawa.[45] An Italian royal decree of 3 June 1886 outlawed the slave traffic in Italy's Red Sea possessions, making enslavement a crime equal to assault with violence, and emasculation to be dealt with as a crime equal to assassination. A military tribunal at Massawa dealt with prosecutions under this royal decree.[46] Under a treaty with Britain, 14 September 1890, Italy agreed to co-operate in putting down the slave trade in the Red Sea and East African waters.[47] But her defeat at Adawa was a severe blow to the anti-slave trade campaign in the Red Sea, for it lowered European prestige, and Italy herself was now faced with renewed slave-running, especially when the Rasheida tribe transferred their activities from the British sphere and moved southwards into Italian territory.

Recognition that the Red Sea area was the last stronghold of the slave trade in East Africa was reflected in Cromer's announcement in November 1893 that the Egyptian Slave Trade Department would concentrate its efforts there. In February 1894, the British Admiralty announced a re-adjustment of the limits of the East African patrol to allow for greater attention to the Somaliland and Red Sea coast. Although effective in sealing points of departure for slaves from the African side of the Red Sea, it failed to prevent their sale at Mecca and Jedda, and twelve well-known slave merchants were still operating at Jedda in 1902. The agent of the Egyptian Slave Trade Department, at Tor, the quarantine station for travellers passing through the port of Suez, had frequently to deal with slaves accompanying pilgrims returning from Mecca and Jedda, and HMS *Scout*, during a cruise in the Red Sea in January-February 1902, captured two dhows whose fifty occupants were claimed to be pilgrims or servants of pilgrims. They were in fact slaves.[48]

Any slackening of vigilance by the naval patrol, as in 1908, when detailed for duties against the Mad Mullah at Berbera, quickly saw a recrudescence of the slave trade in the Red Sea. Throughout the early years of the twentieth century Her Majesty's ships on the East Indian Station, based at Aden, continued to make regular cruises north into the Red Sea to keep watch against slavers.

II. THE MIDDLE EAST

In Turkey, as in Egypt, the usages of society and sanctions of religion fenced round the practice of slavery so as to make it extremely difficult to obtain mitigation, let alone relinquishment of it. There was little or no out-of-door slavery in Turkey, as there was ample free labour provided by Croats, Slavs and Greeks. There was, however, a great demand for domestic slaves; personal servants, concubines, and a smaller and exclusive demand for eunuchs. Circassian and Georgian females were an established feature in most well-to-do Turkish households. In the slave markets of Turkey and Egypt, they ranked as the choicest of commodities, and commanded the highest prices.

The long-standing source of Georgian and Circassian slaves was seriously disrupted when Russia annexed the Georgian kingdom of Imeretia in 1810, and seized Circassia in 1829. By the Treaty of Adrianople, in September 1829, Russia obtained the fortresses dominating the road into Turkey from Circassia, and her occupation temporarily halted the trade from these territories into Turkey. A European traveller visiting Constantinople in 1836 noted that

> Circassians, Georgians, and Grecians were the most valued and always estimated according to their beauty. The two former being very difficult to procure, on account of the strict blockade maintained by Russia on the Circassian coast of the Black Sea, now fetch as high a price as a hundred pounds.[49]

But in the early 1840s Russia relaxed her stand against the traffic in Circassians. In four months following November 1845, a dozen Turkish vessels transported slaves from Circassia unmolested by the Russians. Russian restraint was attributed to a tacit understanding that, in return for non-interference with the slave trade, the Turks would cease their attacks on Russian forts on the eastern side of the Black Sea. The unrestricted trade in slaves caused a fall in price and a glut on the Constantinople slave market. This egregious display of slaves brought a vigorous response from the Anti-Slavery Society in Britain. A direct result of it was a firman by the Sultan of Turkey, in 1846, declaring the slave trade illegal, and promising the closing of the slave markets in Turkey. This was followed in 1847 by the prohibition of the import of African slaves through ports in the Persian Gulf.[50]

In October 1854, following unsuccessful endeavours by the Catholic Armenian Bishop to secure the liberation of Christian slaves, Lord Stratford de Redcliffe induced Sultan Abdul Majid to prohibit the open traffic in Circassian and Georgian slaves, thus striking 'a moral blow to one of the most destructive evils under which the Empire languishes'.[51] Vizirial letters sent out to governors directing them to put the firman into effect attained small result. When the co-operation of Her Majesty's navy in the Black Sea was enlisted and HMS *Tribune* patrolled the Circassian and Anatolian shores, Turkish authorities, as the *Tribune's* captain discovered, showed little enthusiasm. The Pasha of Trebizond refused to detain Circassian slaves, claiming lack of proof of enslavement.

At the time these firmans were issued the Sultan's armies were in collision with those of Russia. This had important consequences for the slave trade. The Russians, held at first by Shamyl and his Caucasian mountaineers, were finally able to take the offensive in 1854. And in the western Caucasus, and on the Araxes, General Bebutov completely defeated the Turks. In 1855, Count Muraviev, following desperate Russian losses, captured the great Turkish fortress of Kars, thus saving Georgia. The war brought Turkish armies into direct contact with the inhabitants of Circassia, and the Turkish army made the most of the opportunity. The slave traffic, previously carried on clandestinely, and in defiance of Russian prohibitions, now threw off all disguise, and was openly pursued. Circassians sold their own children, those of their relatives, and any others they could kidnap to the Turks.[52] Brigadier-General Williams claimed that:-

> If the Turks had penetrated into Georgia last campaign, very few youths of either sex would have escaped pollution. If England does not repress this trade by an effective treaty, Russia will accomplish it by force of arms, if peace leaves her in possession of Georgia.[53]

Holmes, Consul at Batoum, in 1857, reported hundreds of

Circassians imported into Turkey from the Circassian coast; Circassian females were carried on the British vessel *Kangaroo*, chartered by Ismail Pasha of Egypt. The temporary glut in Circassian and Georgian slaves thus occasioned appeared to stimulate the appetite and sharpen the demand for slaves, and soon, when these were no longer obtainable from traditional sources, there was increasing recourse to the African market. The British and Foreign Anti-Slavery Society, quick to notice the trend, complained to Palmerston in March 1856 that African slaves were included among sales of Georgian boys and girls in Turkish provinces, and black and white female slaves were sold together in the bazaars in Constantinople. The Anti-Slavery Society was agitated over the new trend, and pressed to have the subject discussed at the Peace Conference at Paris in 1856. But Palmerston was unable to bring it within the scope of the Conference.[54] But it is a strange commentary on the attitude of Circassians towards the slave trade that, even while the Conference was in progress, a deputation of Circassians in Constantinople petitioned the Porte that their country be taken under his sovereignty, and numbers of Circassians endeavoured to dispose of Circassian girls, newly arrived, in the slave markets of Turkey, in anticipation of the closure of the Caucasus by Russia. So plentiful was the supply of white slaves that black slaves were put on the market to make room for their newly-purchased competitors.

Following British pressure, a firman of December 1857 prohibited the traffic in and public sale of black slaves throughout the Sultan's dominions, with the temporary exception of the Hedjaz, exempted on the grounds of special necessity, being the seat of Mecca, where cessation would have aroused violent opposition. But the firman was habitually violated with the cognizance of the Turkish government, for it caused a rise in the price of slaves, following a decrease in their annual import from Egypt from 4000 to 2000, and from the Caucasus from 1000 to 500, and there was a keen demand to obtain them. A stout, well-formed black slave in Constantinople brought 50 to 100 dollars; and a white slave girl of beauty sold for as high as 2000 dollars.[55]

Fresh opportunity to acquire more slaves soon came the way of the Turks. The Circassians rebelled against Russian occupation, and fought a valiant but hopeless battle for independence until 1864, when their subjugation was complete. When the Black Sea ports of Poti and Batoum and part of southwest Georgia, long under Ottoman rule, were wrested from Turkey in successive wars culminating in the campaign of 1877–8, many Circassians refused to remain under Russian dominance, and nearly 500,000 emigrated to Turkey. Those who settled in Turkish territory continued to sell their daughters, ostensibly under the *nikkah*, the traditional marriage formula, prescribed by the Muslim code but really a white slave traffic in disguise. A trade in boys and girls from Circassia was carried on from territories under Russian occupation, with local chieftains the principal agents in the business. Circassian females were offered for sale on the streets of Alexandria. Turkish authorities argued that they were thus saved from prostitution, and that there was no dishonour in their being thus enslaved, for they would receive better education, and were eligible to become the wives of the greatest pasha in the land, even the Sultan himself.

Circassian females were kindly treated in harems along with negro slaves. But, being trained from childhood that she must live with man and minister to his pleasures, when emanicpated and placed in service, she usually reverted to her former habits. And since Mahommedan women, even of the lower class, were not to be exposed to the sight of any male but their husbands, female slaves (and eunuchs) were necessary attendants and servants; and it was the custom among Muslim women to bring up and educate female slaves for this purpose. Slave girls were also brought up or purchased as wives, as when a father could not afford the large expense involved in marrying his son to a free woman. A slave girl was more submissive, and there was no troublesome family in the background. Among higher class families in Turkey, three or four beautiful slaves were sometimes given as presents to sons or brothers on a birthday or other great anniversary. The slave-holding system was built into Turkish society, and the Sultan's firman of August 1864, abolishing the white slave trade, was ignored. Turkish authorities high and low continued to foster it, and gave orders to agents to procure white slaves for their harems. It was Consul Taylor's view that

> As long as the Chief of State selects his wives exclusively from Circassians or Georgians and so long as flagrant infractions of the Sultan's firmans by his own officers remain unpunished, nothing can result but a perpetuation, rather than extinction of this inhuman occupation.[56]

The trade in white slaves extended from Turkey into Egypt. The Viceroy of Egypt had an agent in Constantinople who recruited white girls for his master's harem, and those surplus to that great man's wants were given in marriage to favourites. They were brought into Egypt as wives of the importer, and disembarked at Alexandria by a gangway concealed by awnings and attended by eunuchs, who called out the potent word 'Harem' to prevent the curious from approaching. They were taken to the private houses of slave dealers and their friends, and gradually disposed of. Some were bought on commission for Egyptian residents. The *Morning Star*, of London, on 15 July 1865, reported upwards of 10,000 Circassian children, of Christian parents, exported annually from Constantinople and other Turkish ports into Egypt.

There was a reverse flow of black slaves from Africa into Turkey. There were Galla from Tajurra and Massawa, concerning the trade in which Consul Plowden, at Massawa, had appealed in 1855 to Lord Stratford de Radcliffe to prohibit their sale in the Sultan's dominions, and to confine the trade, if it must.exist, to Shankalla, that is pagan negro slaves. For, Plowden claimed 'As long as Gallas continued to be sold, Abyssinian Christian children will be mixed up with them'. The major source of black slaves for Turkey, however came by way of Egypt from the Sudan. Thousands were brought down the Nile, and many landed in view of the Viceroy's palace. Those surplus to Egyptian demands were exported to other Ottoman dominions.

In June 1867, French and British anti-slavery societies appealed to the Sultan to end the slave trade, especially that 'nameless barbarity practised upon male children'. The Paris Anti-Slavery Conference, in August 1867, re-inforced this appeal, and urged the Sultan to take action against the slave trade.[57] These appeals took on new force when, in 1869, in response to a circular sent out to consuls in the Middle East by Lord Clarendon, the Foreign Secretary, requesting information on the slave trade, a widespread trade in black and white slaves was revealed, although exact details were difficult to ascertain owing to the secrecy of the harem system, and the flat denial that a slave trade existed. A network of dealers, with branches at Constantinople, Alexandria, Cairo and Salonika, operated throughout the Middle East. People in high places, including the Persian Consul at Damascus, and certain Khans in Smyrna, were involved in the trade.[58]

The Clarendon inquiry also revealed that ships under Austrian, Egyptian, and, in a few instances, English and French ownership, were indirectly involved in the slave trade. Ships running between Smyrna and Constantinople, Jedda and Suez, brought black slaves to Egypt and Turkey; and in turn, carried white slaves back from Turkey to Egypt. The steamer *Gyptis*, owned by the Fraissinet Company of Marseilles, landed eight young black girls in almost nude state, at Salonika, and the Austrian Lloyd steamers *Aurora* and *Oreste* carried small batches of slaves from Constantinople to Alexandria. Captains of these vessels rebutted charges that they knowingly connived at the slave trade. It was, they claimed, almost impossible to check on the large suites of domestic servants and the many wives accompanying oriental gentlemen travelling on their ships. But, as so often happened, these so-called servants and many wives turned out to be slaves who were offered for sale on landing.

The Egyptian Steamship Company and the Azizieh Company, in which the Viceroy was a principal share-holder, carried black slaves to Turkey, as did many smaller vessels who ran small batches incidental to their main cargo. The Azizieh Company ran what was almost a weekly shuttle service between Alexandria and points in Turkey. Thirty to sixty Abyssinian female· slaves were carried monthly on the steamers *Schibiya*, *Tantah*, and *Mahalen*, in the period 1868–9.[59] They were landed at numerous lesser ports in Turkey, in addition to Constantinople, such as Scala Nuova, Sokia, Bainder, Tirah, Magnesia, and Cassaba. The islands of Mitylene, Cos, Laros, and Adalia were staging points where slaves were kept to improve their condition, and then taken in small numbers by boat to landing places on the Turkish coast. In the latter half of 1869 and early 1870, over 2000 black slaves were carried to Turkey from Egypt, and they shortly appeared in the slave markets of Aleppo and the fairs of Rumelia. High officials were involved in the trade, among them a judge of Scala Nuova, and the Agha of Aidan.[60] Bogus passports were issued to cover entry of black slaves and these were used a number of times over.

The import of black slaves into Turkey was increasing by the late 1860s, it being estimated that in Anatolia alone, in 1869, 3000 were imported; and Cumberbatch, Consul at Smyrna, in July 1869 noted that 'The negro importation by Egyptian steamers and by Baghdad and land is notorious'.[61] They came also with pilgrims returning from Medina and Mecca, parties of up to 100 African children accompanying less than half that number of pilgrims. African slaves seeking refuge at British consulates in Turkey had a sorry tale to tell. Slave negresses, employed by dealers, often acted as procuresses, and passed off slave children as their own to enable them to enter Turkey.

Sir H. Elliott, British Ambassador at Constantinople, reported to Clarendon in July 1869 that the Porte had been stirred into action against the slave trade. But Elliott was not optimistic. The formal promise of the Khedive of Egypt that no negro in future would be allowed to embark for Turkey unless accompanied by papers of manumission, and the announcement that public sale of slaves in Egypt was forbidden, meant only that the 'barter of human flesh took place inside a house instead of in a public market, as formerly'. In out-of-the-way streets and hidden corners of the bazaar in the Coptic quarter of Cairo, decoys inveigled manumitted slaves into their hideouts, destroyed their papers of manumission, and resold them to slave dealers.

British consular agents claimed that there was no will to end the slave trade in Cairo, despite professions of good intentions. It was impossible to change long-ingrained attitudes in Mohammedan countries, and the slave trade must be struck at its source in Africa.[62] Despite all professions of desire to end it, slavery was still a legal institution in Turkey in 1870. Letters of manumission to slaves arriving from Egypt in the Azizieh Company's steamers, and to slaves in various provinces of Turkey, giving the recipients documents of 'azad' (manumission) signed by master and countersigned by a local official and the Imam, or Mosque clerk, and with witnesses, were impressive, but had little realistic basis, as observed a Christian missionary, from Aintab in Turkey, after personally witnessing 'thirty to forty noble-looking black women' slaves on the quarter deck of a steamer bound for Constantinople.[63] Black and white slaves were sold in remote corners of Constantinople, and the Averet bazaar was a prominent slave market. Black slaves were sold as part of the estate of Fazil Mustafa, Pasha of Egypt, on his death. The Director of Customs, and Captain of the port of Rustchuk, and the Commander of the port's gunboat, possessed black and white slaves.[64] The Chamberlain of the Sultan's palace, Hamdi Pasha, was in contact by telegraph with the Imperial commissioner at Batoum, regarding the purchase for his master of a dozen girls, twelve to eighteen years of age.[65]

This was the state of affairs, which the Select Committee of 1870/71, concerned with the East African slave trade, could not ignore. The British ambassador to Turkey was instructed to make 'earnest representation to the Porte'.[66] Nothing was done, however, until a convention between Britain and the Porte was signed on 25 January 1880, to come into operation on 26 August 1881, whereby the prohibition of the slave trade in all its manifestations, throughout the Ottoman Empire, was 'absolutely' re-affirmed; the export and import of black slaves was prohibited except when domestic servants or as crew on Ottoman vessels, in which cases they must be covered by certificates duly signed by the authorities. All persons found engaged in the mutilation of children were to be severely punished as criminals.[67] British cruisers were authorized to search and detain Ottoman vessels engaged in traffic in slaves.

But as previously pointed out,[68] this convention was defective in that no provision was made for Mixed Courts to adjudicate on captured vessels, and in that penalties for wrongful seizure deterred British cruisers from making captures. A further declaration of the Porte of 3 March 1883 re-affirmed the prohibition on the import of negro slaves into Ottoman dominions. Finally, on December 30 1889, the Porte promulgated the text of a 'Law for the repression of the Negro Slave-Trade in the Ottoman Empire'. This differed very little from the Convention of 1881, apart from stating that 'In legal proceedings relating to the negro slave-trade, the public prosecutors will perform the duties attaching to their attributions, and the captain of the ship which has seized the slave-carrying vessel will appear as a party in the action'.[69]

The Anti-Slavery Society's misgivings as to this law achieving results were not belied. Few inroads were made on the slave trade in the sprawling dominions of the Sultan. Increased wealth and expensive tastes maintained the demand for slaves. Habits of thinking, the result of centuries, were not easily changed. Reader (later Sir) Bullard, arriving in Turkey in 1907 as a junior member of the Levant Service, found slavery still a recognized institution . . . 'a slave wanting his freedom could apply to the British Embassy, and, provided that he or she was black (the Circassian slave had no remedy), would be taken before a Turkish judge who was obliged to issue papers of manumission'.[70]

The oriental institution of the harem, and the tradition of placing its security in the hands of eunuchs, seems primarily to have been of eastern origin. Reference in history to white and black eunuchs at the courts of princes, pashas, and eastern panjandrums are frequent. Eunuchs were strange figures in European eyes, with their gaudy dress, pointed turbans, and flowing robes of striped silk, and their fussy charge over the seraglio, the chambers and gardens of the harem. They were 'mummified old women', a cause of wonderment and pity to western observers.

But their role as confidential secretary, and the trust and power reposed in them, enabled eunuchs to rise to high position. Many names come to mind: Narses, a famous general under Justinian, in the sixth century AD; Hermias, Governor of Atarnea in Mysia; the energetic Muhammed Kurra, who dominated his master,

Muhammed-el-Fadhl, ruler of Darfur in the early nineteenth century; and a well-known Governor of Sidam in Abyssinia in the twentieth century: all were eunuchs.

The practise of creating white eunuchs for eastern harems declined in the nineteenth century, although there is specific reference to it in Anatolia in the 1860s.[71] There is, however, continued reference throughout the nineteenth century to the trade in black eunuchs for the Middle East. The trade no doubt existed long before then, for Father Joao dos Santos, writing in the 1590s, states, as regards a tribe near Mogadishu, that 'they cut also their boys and make them Eunuchs'. The so-called *See Wee*, near Pate, on the East African coast, were reputed to mutilate their captives,[72] and Arabs in the nineteenth century still retained a wholesome fear of being shipwrecked in the vicinity of the *See Wee*. Captain Owen writing in the early nineteenth century, refers to the trade in eunuchs from the dominions of the Sultan of Muscat,

> the Red Sea and Persia and some parts of North India pay him immense sums annually for slaves to be cut for the seraglios and other faithful services for which those of the East Coast are held in the highest esteem.[73]

And Captain Harris, ambassador to the court of Shoa, recounting his journey home through Abyssinia, mentions meeting young boys who had been subjected to this savage mutilation.[74]

It is only in an understanding of the nature of the harem that the importance of the eunuch can be grasped. The Courts of the Sultan and the palaces of his pashas held large numbers of female slaves. There was scarcely a Circassian who was not expending care and money upon training a daughter, sister or niece, in the speculative expectation that at some future date he might be able to sell her for a considerable price to the Ruler of the Faithful or some 'libidinous Pasha'. The higher officials of the Ottoman Empire, the Governors of provinces, and Ministers at the Court were accustomed to show their reverence and loyalty towards their master by offering him the gift of a beautiful female slave. And that great man, the successor of the Prophet, might in turn bestow her on some Court favourite, 'an honour which is reckoned amongst the very highest of personal distinctions by the servants of the Sultan', or he might enrol her in the enormous female battalion of the Imperial household. Thus by gracious gifts and by direct imports and purchase were the harems stocked, and with it was increased demand for eunuchs to guard their inmates.[75] The institution of eunuchs was part and parcel of the harem. Most Turkish gentlemen with any claim to fashion aspired to have one or more of these capons in their establishment.[76] They were most numerous however in the imperial palaces of the Osmanli family.

The number of eunuchs in the Sultan's household had increased over the last few centuries, from 20 to 40 black eunuchs in the sixteenth century to over 200 by the early seventeenth century, and double the latter number by the nineteenth century, at which time there were 1500 women in the 'interior' and 'exterior' compartments. The Sultan's mother and his chief wife, each in turn had fifty eunuchs, and favoured concubines had their own retinue of them; in addition about 30 to 40 were used as gatekeepers.

The chief eunuch, 'master of the maidens, or, to give him his more euphonious title, 'chief of the abode of felicity', was the Sultan's most confidential adviser, and practically master of the Ottoman Empire. Life and death, revenues of State, posts of honour and influence, were more or less in the hands of this chosen bodyservant of the Sultan. The installation of a new chief eunuch was a great state ceremony, which excited the highest public interest. Great honour was accorded to eunuchs in high position.

When the chief eunuch of the household of the Khedive of Egypt came to Massawa, seeking slaves and eunuchs for royal ceremonies in Cairo, he was treated as a great personage.[77] And visitors to Turkey observed that

> When any eunuch, whether attached to the Seraglio or to a private harem, enters one of the tramcars in Stamboul, all the Turks who may happen to be in the vehicle immediately rise, salaam profoundly, and remain standing till the great man has chosen a seat for himself.[78]

Europeans might recoil in horror or cold fury at this most cruel savagery of man to man. But some Turks saw in it the translation to a higher order. Hence the honour accorded. Among eunuchs themselves, once they survived the terrible metamorphosis, there appeared to be little regret for their lot. They displayed a sagacity, cunning and conceit above the ordinary. Observing them lolling in the sun in the precincts of the palaces of the pashas, smoking cigarettes, and laughing insolently at passers-by, there was little in their mien to indicate unhappiness.

J. L. Burkhardt and R. Bowring, writing in the early nineteenth century, refer to the practice of making black eunuchs in the northern Sudan, where it was claimed nearly 300 eunuchs a year were turned out. Bowring refers to a brother of the king of Darfur, and to a Frenchman in Dongola, in the northern Sudan, who were involved in the business, and states that about 300 eunuchs per annum were sold in Cairo.[79] In North Africa, in the Atlas mountains, a certain Shereef rendered young boys into eunuchs with considerable skill, so that there were few fatal cases, and developed a lucrative trade.[80] Richard Burton dwelt on the subject in a lurid despatch to Lord Granville in December 1880, in which he described the trade in eunuchs in Kordofan, Darfur, and at Massawa.[81] Burton gave details of the gruesome operation involved in turning out eunuchs. In some cases it meant total removal. The death rate was high owing to unskilful surgery. Those surviving fetched three to five times the price of ordinary slaves. Thus, according to Wylde, every eunuch represented 'at the very least, 200 Soudanese done to death . . . say there are 500 eunuchs in Cairo today: 100,000 Soudanese had died to produce these eunuchs'.[82]

It was a hideous and revolting trade, abhorred by Europeans and Africans. The practise of making eunuchs seems to have been introduced in Africa by the Arabs. A. B. Wylde, after long years of residence in Africa, declared he had 'never seen a eunuch among the Eastern Soudan tribesmen, so they do not make the demand. If the Turkish and Egyptian Pasha did not buy the eunuch there would be no demand, consequently no supply'. In Buganda the introduction of the evil custom of castration was blamed on the Arabs. It is said that Mtesa followed their advice and castrated those of his pages who were assigned to the task of looking after his concubines.[83] Gessi, who penetrated the upper Bahr-el-Ghazal region on the fringes of the Mangbetu country in 1879, found the practice of making young male slaves into eunuchs had been introduced into that remote region by the Arabs. Yussuf Bey and his Nazir had put to death the native ruler, King Munza, and his brother. Munza's eldest son was barbarously mutilated and given as a present to Yussuf Bey's father-in-law. As soon as these loathsome deeds were done, a Mangbetuian ex-slaver employed by Yussuf Bey was proclaimed Sultan, with the special mission of producing eunuchs. So barbarously did he pursue his trade that few of his victims survived, and his master deposed him. His successors were more successful, in that a few of their poor spayed creatures survived to fetch high prices on the Egyptian market. It was Gessi's high achievement to have demolished this nest of eunuch-makers; he set to with vigour to rid the land of these vermin, and freed eleven young eunuchs held by them.[84]

British officials in the Middle East were frequently meeting cases where, among slaves imported, there were eunuchs. Captain Kemball, Resident at Bashire, in 1854 freed a small number of slaves, among them a eunuch, freshly made, still suffering, who was given medical attention. A small number of eunuchs continued to arrive at Persian Gulf ports, Boulok, Lingah, and Chahbar, well into the later nineteenth century. Among slaves seeking refuge at British consulates at Jedda, Cairo and Alexandria were usually a few eunuchs. When Cookson, consular agent at Alexandria, on instructions from the Foreign Office, approached the Khedive in the matter, the latter, while deploring the practice, claimed that to prohibit the employment of eunuchs would shock the social prejudices of the Egyptians; the number of eunuchs was diminishing anyway, they were confined to the rich, and there was now a law in effect which prohibited the making of eunuchs, and it would be rigorously enforced.

Gordon in the Sudan was the first European to take strong action against the trade in African eunuchs. He implemented the law of 1877, and inflicted the death penalty on a number of persons convicted of the crime. The Italians, with special reason to abhor the practice owing to their contact with the Danakil, noted practioners of it, declared it to be a crime equal to assassination, and as such meriting the ultimate penalty. Anti-slave trade conventions between Britain and Egypt, Turkey and Persia, in the 1870s and 1880s, decreed it a most heinous crime. And a general declaration against it by the great powers came with the Brussels General Act of 2 July 1890, which, under Article V, prohibited the mutilation of adults and male infants.

The trade in eunuchs was henceforth carried on *sub rosa* in the lands north of the equator. Hushed reference to it continued well into the twentieth century. At Tajurra, in 1910, eunuchs, young boys, were still purchased by Arab slave dealers for sale in Arabia. They were in demand not only to guard the harem, but to act as their owner's responsible servant, manager of his household and property, or as keepers of his treasury. They could be counted on never to betray their master's confidence, nor was there risk of their being tempted by a woman. Many young castrates were sent to guard the holy ground of the Khahba at Mecca, and the tomb of the Prophet at Medina; others on obtaining their freedom frequently retired to Mecca, where they were employed in keeping women out of the inner precincts of the holy places. Being 'neutrals', there was no religious stigma attached to their use for this purpose.[85] Their special position, living in a half-world of neither man nor woman, their select role as guardian of the harem, and their seclusion and narrowness imbued them with an asceticism and religious zeal of the most intense kind. With the loss of their manhood seems to have gone the warmth of humanity. They could be most steely surrogates.

The harem institution of the Sultan of Turkey with its large number of eunuchs persisted into the early twentieth century. On the eve of the overthrow of Abd ul-Hamid in 1908, his harem had 370 women and 127 eunuchs.[86] Although the fall of the Sultan at this date might be taken as the death blow to the system, one writer purports to show that the trade in eunuchs still continued in the Gulf of Tajurra, and was one of the darker chapters in the story of the slave trade there. Young boy eunuchs, between nine and fifteen years of age, were castrated 'by their parents or more exactly by the village sorcerer in anticipation of their sale.' During a heavy sleep induced by the smoke of burning leaves of a poisonous plant (*datura stramonium*) and infusions of certain other plants (possibly poppy), the genital organs were completely removed. On the wound, after a preliminary application of butter, boiling hot, the operator placed a poultice of crushed plant-leaves. The sorcerer alone knew the secret of its composition. If an infection of the bladder did not carry off the victim within six days of the operation, he was considered out of danger, and for a month was fed on raw meat and honey. At the end of the month, his recovery was pronounced complete.[87]

The rate of mortality was however high. Fully sixty per cent of those operated on died within twenty-four hours. Eunuchs thus had great scarcity value; hence their high prices in the slave markets. From eight hundred dollars to two thousand dollars apiece (from £100 to £250). In Persia where the institution had never quite attained the acceptability that it had in Turkey, they were nevertheless still much desired in upper class homes at the end of the century, as noted by J. E. Budgett Meakin, at Shiraz in 1895. While the price of slaves ranged from £16 to £18 for black females to £24 to £28 for Abyssinians, eunuchs brought as much £114 apiece.[88] By the early twentieth century, their price still stood very high. At the Gulf of Tajurra a handsome young female slave might bring £75. A eunuch would bring up to six times that amount.[89]

III. PERSIAN GULF AREA

British awareness of the slave trade in the Persian Gulf area dates from the early seventeenth century, when the East India Comany established trading interests in that area.[90] Officers of the

Company's navy, the 'Indian Navy' as it was known, until abolished in 1863, found ample evidence of an extensive slave trade in the countries of the Arabian sea and Persian Gulf. British Residents at Basra and Bushire, during the 1840s and 1850s, acquired an intimate knowledge of the slave trade in the Gulf. Basra and Baghdad were important marts for slaves who were sold in the bazaars, in hired dwellings and caravanserais, those surplus to local demand being sent inland, and up the Euphrates.

In 1842, Captain Kemball, British Resident at Bushire, estimated that 4000 to 5000 slaves were sold annually in the Persian Gulf.[91] And in 1856, the Political Agent at Muscat claimed that 13,000 slaves annually passed up the Gulf of Oman, and of these about 4000 were landed at Ras al-Hadd or Sur, and the remainder at Muscat and Persian Gulf ports.[92] An awareness of this import of slaves was reflected in the Ottoman Sultan's firman of 1846, which while closing slave markets in Turkey, was soon followed by a decree in 1847 prohibiting the import of African slaves through Persian Gulf ports into the Ottoman dominions. Ottoman vessels were ordered 'to cruise with those of Her Majesty's in order to prevent a continuance of this infamous traffic within those waters'. In 1848, to further restrict the import of black slaves into the Gulf, the Shah of Persia issued firmans to the governors of Fars and Isphahan, the two provinces adjacent to the Gulf, decreeing that 'Not a single individual will be permitted to bring negroes by sea without being subjected to severe punishment'.

By a treaty of August 1851, the Shah of Persia authorized British ships and those of the Indian Navy to search Persian merchant ships, provided a Persian officer was aboard the British cruiser instituting the search; those found guilty of slaving would be dealt with by the Persian authorities. Slaves from Persia on pilgrimage to Mecca were to carry a passport, granted by a Persian or British official. In the Persian Gulf, slaves, domestic or otherwise, could not legally be transferred by sea without passes. A scale of fines, ranging from 15 tomas per slave and 200 blows for the first offence to additional physical punishment and confiscation of the vessel for the third offence, was prescribed.[93]

To enforce the treaty an organized patrol of the Persian Gulf was instituted in 1852, and the *Tigris,* of the Indian Navy, was stationed at the entrance to the Persian Gulf. But Persian officials were not always available, nor always willing to participate in an anti-slave trade patrol; and Her Majesty's ships did not visit the Gulf during the hot time of year, April to November, when most slaves were imported into the Gulf.

Reports of 1850 indicate a pattern of widespread trade in small groups of slaves, 10 to 100 at a time, mostly from Zanzibar, being smuggled secretly into Persia. From slave entrepots at Jadder, and other small ports on the Batinah coast, they were moved up the Gulf to Bushire, and from Sharja to Bahrain. Practically all local chiefs from Bandar Abbas to Bushire had a hand in it, finding it a most lucrative sideline to fishing, pearl-diving, and gold-smuggling. To hit at the numerous speculators in the slave trade, the governor of Fars in February 1853, under pressure from Captain Kemball, imposed heavy fines on the chiefs at Lingah, Mogee and Kelat, for permitting the slave trade in their districts. Small entrepeneurs were sharing in the booty; out of 39 slaves captured from a dhow in the Gulf of Oman, 36 belonged to the crew who had obtained them by barter in Zanzibar, and planned to resell them at Lingah at a high profit; the remaining three slaves were the property of a passenger who intended that they should pay for his passage and leave him a tidy profit into the bargain. Between October and November every year, groups of slaves, mostly African females, were landed at Mukalla and Shubar on the southeast Arabian coast, and subsequently dispatched to the Yemen or Hedjaz, or shipped to Muscat and up the Persian Gulf to Lingah and Bushire.[94]

A few captures of these slavers were made. The *Tigris* and *Clive* of the Indian Navy cruised along the Batinah coast in February 1854, and a number of slaves, including Galla females, were captured.[95] In December 1856, the corvette *Falkland*, of the Indian Navy, captured a vessel under Turkish colours from Kuwait; she carried a cargo of slaves acquired at Kilwa and consigned to the Pasha of Baghdad.[96]

In May 1863, Brigadier Coghlan, Resident at Aden, obtained a treaty from the chiefs of Mukalla, Shubar, and the Jemadir of Sheher, nominally under the suzerainty of the Imam of Muscat, for the suppression of the slave traffic in their territories, and arrangements were made for an occasional visit of a British man-of-war.[97] Kemball, at Bushire, extracted a promise from the chiefs at Lingah, Mogee and Kelat that every boat touching at those places from Zanzibar would be searched. But there was widespread evasion of these restrictions which in turn were only half-heartedly imposed. Slave traders at Bushire openly connived with Persian officials by offering them slaves. When the British pressed for action against the slave trade in Persia, the British ambassador at Teheran was informed by the Persian Prime Minister that

> From Bushire to Meshed and throughout Persia, there are numbers of slaves to be found, but this is no concern of England.

The Convention has reference solely to the sea.[98]

But Persia was more efficient than either Turkey or Oman in upholding anti-slave trade treaties; the defect lay in the limitation of these treaties, and in the fact that British cruisers did not visit the Gulf regions during the hottest time of year when the slavers were running. Between 1852 and 1857, only 78 slaves were liberated by the authorities in the Gulf, and yet it was assumed that at least two thousand annually had been shipped there during that period.[99] In 1865, Lieutenant Colonel H. F. Disbrowe, the Political Agent at Muscat, and Colonel L. Pelly, Resident in the Persian Gulf, journeyed overland south of the Gulf, and observed the extensive slave trade based on small ports along the coast, from the Gulf of Oman to Ras al Kymah on the Persian Gulf. Arabs in the immediate interior, even in the Nejd, at Riyadh, were well acquainted with the latest British anti-slave trade activities, and were highly incensed by them.[100] Slave dealers from Sur, frequenting Hajee Furruj's coffee shop in Muscat, passed the time hurling abuse at Rigby, British consular agent at Zanzibar and a strong opponent of the slave trade. Bedouins, inhabiting the numerous small villages around the fortlets and date plantations near the sea shore, were involved in the slave trade. Slaves were disposed of at these places for prices ranging from 10 to 40 dollars apiece, the local chief receiving a two-dollar tax on each slave.[101]

Vessels from Matrah, to the immediate west of Muscat, went annually to Africa, taking salt fish and dates and returning with, all told, about 500 slaves. Similarly at other points, such as Al Masn'ah, 65 miles west of Muscat, about 500 were imported annually, and at Al Qashbiyah, Samh and Suhar, they were landed in small batches of 50 to 60. At Lingah, on the Persian side of the Gulf, and at small ports nearby, the total annual import would run to a few hundred.[102] Small ports might send only four or five vessels a year to East Africa. But taking in all the slaves going to these small ports, plus the 500 or so going directly to Muscat, total imports into Oman possibly reached 2000 yearly.

There was an increased import of slaves into the Persian Gulf area following the cholera epidemic which swept the western Indian Ocean and East African coast in 1869-70. It reached Bundar Abbas in 1870, and carried off so many slaves that there was an increased demand for the next few years. At Matrah, where previously small batches of slaves, totalling about 100 yearly, were imported, 300 to 400 slaves were now landed annually. Many were taken up the Gulf to Dohar on the eastern side of the Qatar peninsula, where they were purchased by the chiefs, for themselves or as presents for important personages. The purchase of these slaves might be made in exchange for wheat, at a rate working out at about 25 to 60 dollars for a slave from Kilwa or Zanzibar, and rising to about 100 dollars for an Abyssinian female. The latter in some cases might bring as much as 200 dollars.

In the face of increased slaving activity in the Persian Gulf, Britain pressed Persia and Turkey to fulfill their engagements. 'Turkey will act if we show her the particular point'.[103] By 1880, Britain had three cruisers in the Persian Gulf, but they had little freedom of action until the convention of 2 March 1882 between Britain and Persia, whereby British vessels' were permitted to detain merchant vessels under a Persian flag or belonging to Persian subjects, who if guilty were to be tried by Persian authorities. 'No person with a government passport countersigned by a British Resident or Consul who may have gone from Persia to visit places of pilgrimage, shall when returning, be interfered with, provided that they were not accompanied by more negroes, than the number mentioned in the original pass. The presence of an additional is prima facie evidence of attempted traffic in slaves'. Persia also agreed under this convention to co-operate in suppressing the slave traffic by sea.[104] This treaty was followed by another with the Sultan of Mohilla on 24 October 1882, for the suppression of the slave trade and granting Her Majesty's cruisers the right of search.

As in the convention with Turkey in the previous year, that with Persia lacked the very important executive principle which gave validity to anti-slave trade treaties with other powers, such as Spain and Portugal, namely, that all adjudications should be made by a mixed commission, or with the British consul represented ex officio at the adjudication to see that it was not one-sided. In the convention with Persia, there was also a novel but futile provision that an owner of slaves could, under the certificate of Her Majesty's Consul, take them to the great slave mart at Mecca and return with an equal number from that market, without any obligation to show that they were the original slaves taken there. Under this provision dealers were enabled to exchange aging, worn-out and less valuable slaves for the more vigorous and fresh victims of the slave hunts in Africa.

The onus of implementing these treaties fell on the inadequate British naval patrol. Her Majesty's cruisers *Osprey* and *Philomel*, in 1884 and 1885, captured three dhows in the Persian Gulf, carrying a total of 526 slaves. These captures were made at the tail end of the season;[105] many more might have been made if the patrol had been more active in the earlier monsoon period when the bulk of slaves were run north, but this being the hot season it was not the time of the year the patrol operated in Gulf waters. Other factors also explained this poor showing in the number of captures made. Slave dhows were increasingly running under the French flag which gave them immunity from seizure. And the recent anti-slave trade conventions appeared to have encouraged slave dealers to 'stock up' before more rigorous implementation took place.[106]

Slavery still remained a feature in Persia at the end of the nineteenth century. The Anti-Slavery Society in its report for January-February 1898, quoting its correspondent in Persia, stated that there were still between 25,000 and 50,000 black slaves in that country;[107] and the Reverend S. M. Zwemmer, writing in the *Missionary Review of the World* in June 1899, claimed that the Persian Gulf was still a main centre for the slave trade, despite conventions with Persia and Turkey, and the Shah's promises at the Brussels Conference, and the stationing of a Persian gunboat at Bushire. Black slaves were brought into Persia from Baghdad and landed in small numbers at ports in the Persian Gulf. News of the formation of an anti-slavery society in Teheran in 1903 gave little cause for jubilation to the Anti-Slavery Society in view of the ineffectiveness of previous Persian pronouncements in the matter.

British gunboat policy and a British naval presence in the Persian Gulf was necessary up to and past the turn of the century. HMS *Pigeon* took on board fugitive slaves at Lingah in 1899, and liberated them in accordance with Article 28 of the Brussels Conference. In September 1902 the gunboat *Lapwing*, in the Persian Gulf, after a stiff encounter with slave dhows in which a bluejacket and some Arabs were killed, freed a number of slaves.[108] And in the next two years a few dozen were landed at Qishm Island at the entrance to the Gulf and at Lingah, according to British Political Intelligence sources. How many more went up the Gulf undetected it is difficult to say. It seemed however impossible to forecast the end of the slave trade in Persian Gulf waters at the beginning of the twentieth century.[109]

Sir Edward Wakefield, who served there in the early 1940s, refers to slaves at Bahrain, privileged household servants, who, despite the fact that by merely applying to the Political Agent could obtain certificates of manumission 'whose validity was never challenged', preferred to remain in a state of slavery. But there was another form of slavery 'which was intolerably harsh'. Destitute parents in Persian coastal villages would be taken in by the plausible story of prosperity on the Arabian side of the Gulf, and send their children in charge of a dhow captain to the 'illusory land of plenty across the sea'. More frequently, children were abducted or kidnapped from their villages. Wakefield tells of a slave boy of fifteen or sixteen years of age, the son of a pearl-diver from the Makran coast, who had been abducted along with nine other children while playing along the shore, by Arabs from a dhow anchored nearby. The children were taken to Qatar, after about one month in the boat. At Dohar they were sold to an Arab at prices ranging from £22-10-0 to £75-0-0 each.

The tale of Wakefield's slave was one of infinite misery, of beatings and attempts to escape, and much longing for his home in Makran. He later died of malaria . . . 'It would take a poet, such as Simonides, to write his epitaph and convey in words the pathos of his life and death'.[110]

8
The Slave Trade in the Interior of East/Central Africa

I. THE NORTHERN INTERIOR

That slavery was indigenous to African society was the view of most European travellers to Africa in the nineteenth century. Lugard claimed that 'Slavery has been an African institution for a 1000 years,' and it was said 'you could not send three men on a mission, or two would combine to enslave the third';[1] and he questioned whether the slave suffered real anguish on the severance of family ties. Lugard's words take on an explosive character in the political climate of postured liberalism of the later twentieth century. He states that the bond between husband and wife was of a looser kind than among Europeans; a greater affection 'is said to exist between man and man then between sexes (as is often seen among the lower animals)'. African fathers and mothers

> do not feel so intense a love for their children as Europeans generally do and hence ruthless separation from relatives and family, though it may involve some grief, cannot be said to be so terrible an ordeal as we should imagine by analogy with our own feelings.[2]

Once home ties were ruptured and the slave transported miles away, he had no resource within himself, nor desire for the recovery of his freedom; thus his master's house was his sole refuge. 'His apathetic and submissive nature adapts itself to his surroundings'.[3] Captives of war not soon assimilated faced the prospect of being sold to the next passing caravan and entering into a further unknown world; thus the attainment of a master-slave relationship was a preferable and reassuring state compared to the desolation of tribelessness. Lugard himself had been embarrassed to find that a slave whom he wished to free was entirely opposed to the idea.

It was Lugard's view that slavery was

> a natural stage in the evolution from savagery to civilization . . . it prevented idleness, and enforced respect for rank, . . . which alone enables the government of a semi-savage country to be carried on.[4]

Dr Laws, of the Livingstone Mission in Nyasaland, observed that domestic slavery, as far as we knew, existed among all tribes in Africa, and varied in severity from a nominal connection to the power of life and death exercised by a master. 'Yet even where it is at the worst, there are checks of a social kind, which go a long way to modify its severity'.

Among African tribes, domestic slavery usually derived from captives of war. A district blessed, or rather cursed, by the awful and intolerable tyranny of a dominant tribe which might rise and fall only to be superseded by another, would suddenly have a supply of slaves on its hands. In Nyasaland, the Ngoni and Yao swaggered over and terrorized other tribes. In Uganda, the Baganda made life miserable for their neighbours; and the Nyoro and Hima of Ankole enslaved Toro women and children. The Tutsi dominated the Hutu in Ruanda; the Masai lorded it over the Kikuyu and Kamba, and the latter, in turn, held the Ndorobo in a kind of serfdom. The Somali enslaved the Galla, and the result was always captives of war and slaves.

Scenes of savagery wrought by one tribe over another were a frequent occurrence. In the Mbe country, in what is now Kenya, Captain Dundas RN witnessed a scene following a Masai raid:

> On our return through the Mbe country, a most harrowing sight presented itself: what only a few days before were prosperous villages, standing amid fields of grain, were now smoking ruins; bodies of old men, women and children, half-burnt lay in all directions; here and there might be seen a few solitary individuals, sitting with their head buried in their hands, hardly noticing the passing caravan, and apparently in the lowest depths of misery and despair. On questioning several of these unhappy beings, I was informed that the Masai had unexpectedly arrived one morning at dawn, spearing and burning all before them and carrying off some 250 women, and large herds of cattle. Only a few of the unfortunate people had escaped by fleeing to the mountains.[5]

Apart from captives of war and raids, there was in most tribes a floating population, made up of 'the scum of the villages, criminals and loafers', obtained by kidnapping and purchase, and fugitive slaves. There were outlaws, friendless persons, the sick left by passing caravans, ne'er-do-wells, unfaithful wives and other undesirables.

Thus, slavery was integral to African society when the Arab arrived on the scene, but he exploited the situation and gave the slave trade a new impetus by putting it on a commercial basis. His raiding for slaves, encouragement of tribal wars, and stirring up of old quarrels stimulated propensities for slaving that existed in certain African tribes such as the Yao and Manyuema, and encouraged them to become slave hunters on a large scale. When it was realized that captives of war could be exchanged for coveted trade goods, slaves took on a new value. And as the slave trade shifted north from Kilwa and the Nyasa area a vast hinterland was opened to the Arab slavers; their operations extended from the East African coast to the Congo—an area equal in size to Europe.

Kilwa retained its importance as the slave-exporting centre for the Nyasa and Zambezi area, but Bagamoyo to the north became the centre of export for slaves from the hinterland as far west as the Congo. Krapf, in the late 1860s, reported slavers moving up the coast in their search for slaves. They were stirring up tribes south of the Pangani. Only in Usambara, to the immediate west of Tanga and Pangani, were they frustrated, for Kimweri, its ruler, posed an effective barrier to their depredations. Only after his death in 1860 were they able to enter Usambara. Elsewhere, from points on the coast opposite Zanzibar, they moved into the interior as far as Unyamwezi.

The shift of the slave trade northwards from the Nyasa area was reflected in slave captures made by Her Majesty's cruisers off the East African coast in the early 1870s. Among slaves freed were Galla from Somaliland and Wajiji from the Lake Tanganyika region. Captain Prideaux reported in 1874 that nearly every caravan arriving at the coast contained a wide assortment of slaves from the interior.[6]

Slavers showed little interest in acquiring slaves from the Nyika (coastal) group—the Duruma, Digo, Giriama, and Pokomo. They were short in stature, unattractive physically, and considered by the Arabs to be dull-witted and lethargic; they were not in demand as slaves. The Wateita and Wataveta, a short distance inland between Mombasa and Kilimanjaro, on the edge of the steppe country and Wateita Hills, were careful to keep out of reach of the coast slavers, and were ready at short notice to bolt into their hilly retreats. Proximity to the Masai appears to have sharpened their wits, and this stood them in good stead in staving off enslavement.

The Masai were rarely enslaved by the Arabs, or found in a state of slavery at the coast. Pastoralists, nomadic in habit, and with an effective military organization comparable to the Zulu impis, they were formidable fighters The fear of the venom of their lash left them unmolested by slavers. In 1857, they overran the whole country to the sea, killing all in their way, forced the abandonment of the CMS mission at Rabai near Mombasa, and left a memory of their ferocity that lasted for most of the century. The reputation of the

Masai long out-lived the substance of their power, but even when they were in decline by the 1880s, it was still sufficient to deter Arab slavers from entering their country. They thus enjoyed an isolation and immunity from encroachment that was unique among East African tribes.

Following the Franco-Prussian War, when the price of ivory rose to peak heights and the search for it extended ever farther inland, Arab slavers followed in the track of the ivory hunters. Arab penetration inland was increasingly reflected in the presence of their charcoal stoves, earthenware vessels—the familiar flat-bottomed bowl with three flanges—and, occasionally, small brass cannon.[7] The latter, of more novelty value than lethal effect, were found inland as far as the eastern boundaries of the Congo.

Contrary to popular view, the ivory and slave trade had little direct connection with each other, apart from a certain sequential nature in their operation. The ivory trade, when combined with free porterage in the form of slave labour, was no doubt highly lucrative, but the phrase 'black and white ivory' is erroneous in its implication.[8] Children and women, on the whole, comprised the bulk of slaves brought to the coast in the nineteenth century, and they were not good carriers. Adult male slaves were usually in chains or slave sticks, and could not easily carry tusks of ivory. Stanley, on his way inland in 1871, meeting a slave gang on its way to the coast, noted that

> The chains were ponderous—they might have held elephants captive: but as the slaves carried nothing but themselves, their weight could not have been unsupportable.[9]

And on the Ituri River, in 1889, he met a flotilla of 57 canoes laden with 'helpless children, girls and women, and a hoard of ivory equal to about fifteen tons', but the latter was carried by professional porters. Ivory caravans in the nineteenth century consisted largely of porters hired at the coast and at depots inland.[10] At Tabora and other central points where the Arabs had settled thousands of porters were available for hire.

The way in which Arab slave traders commenced their operations in the interior developed into a familiar pattern. The Arab slave trader appeared in the guise of a friend, and with his followers settled down. His grass-roofed tembe (hut) was more elaborate than the native kind. A colourful Persian prayer rug would be spread ostentatiously and on it he made his daily obsequies to the East. His own dress—white kanzu, turban, and curved jewelled dagger at his girdle—merited deference; and his trade goods—guns, powder, merikani, silks and beads—proclaimed him a great purveyor from the outside world. The Swahili language, a lingua franca extending ever further inland, enabled some familiarity with his followers. Those chiefs in whose territory this important personage elected to make his abode were flattered by his presence, and by the hospitality and politeness with which he treated them.

At first, the newcomer's trade goods were exchanged for ivory, for the Arab was in no haste. African chiefs began to emulate his manner and dress; the white kanzu became the envied habiliment, the mark of the superior man. An Arab prefix might be added to a native name or might replace it. The real secret of the newcomer's influence, however, lay in his control of arms and powder. At first, tentative requests for these would be rejected, but generosity was soon shown by bestowing on the chief a musket in return for two females. Thus did slave trading commence. Other chiefs brought in men, women, and children in exchange for cloth, beads, and the coveted arms. A stay of a few months brought the slave trader so many slaves that he was able to send a caravan of them to the coast. At Zanzibar, the proceeds from their sale was invested in a fresh supply of arms, powder and trade goods, and a year later these were deposited at the original scene of operations. New transactions now commenced.

The Arab slave trader became a well-known figure in the area, acquainted with tribal strains, rivalries and weaknesses, which could be exploited for his own interest. Any tribe whose cause he espoused and whom he assisted with arms was assured of victory over its neighbours. In return for this help, the Arab received a share of the booty—mostly slaves. His alliance was eagerly sought; his ire must be avoided or placated at all costs. He gathered around him an armed band, swollen with new recruits, and these were directed to foray for slaves; they were as apt as their mentors:

His 'Ruga-ruga' were his dogs of war, ripe for carnage, revelling in blood, what could any individual chief or petty tribe do now?[11]

Thus did Arab slavers, in the manner described above, and affirmed by Livingstone, Stanley, Lugard and others, carry on their business. They often settled down in African districts for years. Sometimes the native ruler refused them permission to depart, as in Uganda, and often it was for the sake of gain. At their settlements were usually collected great numbers of women and children.

In Unyanyembe the Arabs had settled down as a permanent community. Stanley speaks of the dozen or more Arabs at Tabora as a fine, handsome body of men—mostly Omani Arabs, with a sprinkling of Swahili. They had set themselves up in style, supplied from the coast by their slave porters with a variety of rich food, fine clothing and amenities from the outside world. Almost every Arab of eminence displayed luxurious bedding, Persian carpets, fine copperware. The institution of the harem was well in evidence. At Unyanyembe, the Arabs were able to deploy 1,500 muskets in their slaving ventures.[12] The Wanyamwezi people were large in numbers—consisting of four great divisions, each with its own dialect, and under a warrior chief—and they were keen traders and avid travellers, readily entering into porterage for caravans, and intermarrying with coastmen. The presence of the Arabs in their midst was oppressive and tended to overshadow the great native ruler, Mirambo. The latter, to assert himself, hired Ngoni soldiers and sent small parties to Ujiji to buy slaves and ivory.[13] He opposed the organized slave trade of the Arabs, for it undermined his authority, denuded his people, and created jealousy and strife. Mirambo's death in 1884 left the field open to the Arabs.

Ujiji, lying a few miles south of present-day Kigoma, on the east side of Lake Tanganyika, and in one of the few inlets in the cliffs forming the eastern ramparts of the lake, was the great slave centre of western Tanganyika. The local tribe, the Wajiji, were inveterate slave-holders; their chiefs customarily exchanged presents with each other in the form of slaves. Arab slavers arriving at the Lake found themselves in congenial company, and soon made Ujiji their main centre after Tabora, in the interior. By the 1870s, Arabs at Ujiji possessed great numbers of domestic slaves—20 to 100 each—employing them as watercarriers, bodyguards and boatmen, and placing the females in the harem. But Ujiji was notorious for its bad climate; 'a working slave, as distinct from the female slave put in the harem, at Ujiji, did not stand the climate above a year'.[14] Thus constant replacement was needed. Slave caravans consigned to Zanzibar congregated at Ujiji, and Arab slavers met there to decide on the direction and country of their next slave hunt. Communications from Ujiji extended to Victoria Nyanza, Uganda, and to the Congo, and even little known Urundi to the north of Lake Tanganyika was tapped for slaves; in 1881, Said bin Habib brought down many boatloads of slaves from there to Ujiji.

> The Arab system extended to great distances, and octopus-like, grasped every small unprotected village community, making the whole country a vast battlefield wherein no one was safe outside the stockades.[15]

The Arabs turned the whole of Ulungu into a wilderness. The

Wafipa, from the east side of Lake Tanganyika, soon caught on to the basics of the slave trade. They brought over grain to the west side to purchase slaves from the Arabs there—one 60-pound load of grain for a boy, and one 120-pound load for a girl; old men and women, however, were unmarketable, for they could not stand the long march to the coast.

Père Guilleme, writing from Lake Tanganyika in 1888, described the great slave market at Ujiji. The large square, surrounded by grass-roofed mud huts, was crowded with slaves. They were fastened in long lines—men, women and children—in frightful disorder, some tied with cords, others with chains. A few from Manyuema had their ears pierced and a slender cord passed through so as to keep them together. In the streets were living skeletons at every step.[16] Scars of ill-treatment were well in evidence. Slaves were cheap at Ujiji, especially those worn out from the long journey, and too weak to run away. Near the slave market lay an uncultivated piece of ground, the cemetery, where not only the dead, but the dying, too, were cast. Hyenas, very numerous, gorged on human flesh, and were so sated that bodies were left half-devoured.

Père Guilleme came to Ujiji to ransom captives, but he was too poor to ransom the scores that awakened his compassion. 'Here at present, it is almost entirely women and children that are sold: the men are killed'. Lovat Cameron, who visited Ujiji, told a similar tale. Cameron was disappointed that the Germans 'newly arrived on the scene in Africa' had not done more to put down slave trading, and the devastation it caused in their territory. But he was expecting too much; the Germans were still busy at the coast. By the time they penetrated as far as Ujiji, the worst excesses associated with the slave trade there had ended.

The Arabs pressing inland had reached the plateau region between the basins of the Congo and Zambezi, occupied parts of Katanga, and as they advanced set up petty sultanates which were little more than pockets of brigandage under their direction. They introduced their religion, dress and manners wherever they penetrated. Their richest field of operations lay in the Manyuema country to the west and north of Lake Tanganyika, an area some 400,000 square miles in extent. Nyangwe, its principal town, on the right bank of the Lualaba River, was the centre of an Arab settlement by 1870. Although tribes between the coast and Lake Tanganyika began to acquire arms and were less fearful of the Arabs by the 1870s, and Kimweri, ruler of Usambara, and Mtesa of Uganda stood up to them, and Mirambo had harried them out of

Unyanyembe, the Manyuema were as yet strangers to these new weapons of the outside world. And when the Arabs appeared among them they were viewed as superior beings and their muskets struck terror in their hearts. 'They believe that the Arabs have stolen the lightning, and that against such people the bow and arrow can have little effect'.[17]

The Manyuema were deferential, shy and eager for trade. They were an attractive people, with physical characteristics akin to the finest Habash slaves of Abyssinia. Female slaves from Manyuema commanded high prices. Their very light colour, fine noses, well-cut and not over-full lips, and absence of prognathous jaw, made them eagerly sought after as wives by the half-castes of the East African coast. Even the pure Omani Arabs did not disdain to take them in marriage. In addition to these exotic physical attractions, the Manyuema were an industrious and artistic people. They cultivated the Mwili palm, and from its fibre manufactured the finest cloth, superior even to that of the famed barkcloth of the Baganda. They had mastered the art of dyeing. Their homes satisfied more than mere functional use, and their habiliments were elegantly fashioned.

But this superior tribe offered a potential vineyard of slaves, which was not left long untilled by the Arabs. And it was in their midst that there took place the massacre described by Livingstone, when, in July 1871, a half-caste Arab, Tagamoyo, aided by a notorious slave, Manilla, launched an attack on the market place at Nyangwe. In an attempt to escape by canoe, hundreds lost their lives. Livingstone had arrived in Manyuemaland when the slave trade there was just gathering impetus, and the ivory trade was still at its peak. But when Cameron arrived at Nyangwe in 1874, the ivory trade was giving way to the slave trade. In 1878, Abd bin Salim despatched a large caravan of Manyuema slaves and 350 tusks of ivory to the coast. In 1883, when H. M. Stanley arrived at Stanley Falls, he witnessed the widespread desolation wrought by slavers:

> Every three or four miles we came in view of the black traces of the destroyers. The scarred stakes, poles of once populous settlements, scorched banana groves, and prostrate palms, all betokened ruthless ruin ... The bodies of two women bound together with a cord were pulled out of the river.[18]

Arab and Swahili slavers, who throughout the previous year had been raiding between the Congo and Lubirianzi, had now turned their attention to the region between the Aruiwimi and the Congo, and ensconced themselves at strong palisaded points whence they sent out parties of trained Manyuema slave hunters. The fruits of these forays were gathered at these central points and then shipped to the coast by way of the great trade route from Nyangwe to Zanzibar which crossed Lake Tanganyika at Mtowa, and thence ran from Ujiji by way of Tabora to the coast.

The Manyuema outdid their mentors. The result of their depredations in the region to the immediate west of the Semliki River was observed by Stuhlmann and Lugard in 1891. The Manyuema slavers had demoralized surrounding tribes, destroying crops, and famine reigned everywhere, so much so that Stuhlmann gave up his attempt to reach the savannah country to the north-east, 'our porters being on the point of dying of hunger'. But Lugard saw much in the Manyuema slave hunter to admire; they were 'civil and respectful', they treated him 'most hospitably', and they repudiated their custom of cannibalism when they took service with Europeans. They were brave, generally trustworthy, and loyal, and along with the Wanyamwezi were possibly the best porters in Africa. It was their superiority in many ways which made them successful tools in the hands of the Arabs. 'One could only regret that they had not been taught in a better school than that of the Arab slave raiders'.[19] The Manyuema set a wide area of country in turmoil. They seized ivory, levied blackmail, playing off one tribe against another, or, espousing a quarrel between tribes, fell on the unoffending tribe and carried off captives as slaves. As a result of their few years' contact with the Arabs the Manyuema could put 2000 guns into the field, largely breech-loaders. They became so addicted to slavery that Sir Harry Johnston swore they had Arab blood in their veins. Their village, Lupanzula, in the Mbuta country in the eastern Congo, was astonishingly Arab in character—'The whole place might have been a village on the island of Zanzibar'. But accompanying these signs of Arab civilization were the worst ravages and cruelties. Natives had been horribly mutilated, hands and feet lopped off, and women's breasts cut away, the work of the Manyuema slave trader 'done sometimes out of wanton cruelty, sometime as a punishment for thieving or absconding'.

The avidity of the Manyuema for slave raiding encouraged the view that slaves became more numerous the farther inland the Arabs penetrated. But the halcyon period was soon over. Arab expansion was checked by the emergence of the Congo Free State. By the early 1890s, European rule and administration had severely curtailed the activities of the slave raiders in the Congo.

The acknowledged leader of the Arab slavers up to 1876 was Tippu Tip. Originally a poor coast slaver, he had become a wealthy and powerful figure in the trading and commercial world of East Africa. By storming and capturing the stronghold of the Tabwa chief, Nsama, midway between Lake Mweru and Lake Tanganyika, in May 1867, Tippu Tip acquired a fortune in ivory and slaves which he sent back to Unyanyembe with his brother, while he continued on to Nyangwe with 500 guns, ravaging the countryside on the way. Approaching the district known as Mtotila, according to Stanley's account, Tippu learned that its King had disappeared mysteriously many years before, and he artfully conceived the plan of palming himself off as the long-lost ruler. By the time Tippu arrived at Mtotila he had so steeped himself in the details of the King's ancestry, names of living relatives, and general circumstances of the kingdom, that he was greeted by the elders as the missing ruler. He was showered with abundant presents of ivory and invited to reclaim his inheritance. This re-invested ruler, however, soon displayed an unaccountable appetite for ivory and slaves and his henchmen scoured the surrounding countryside, seeking these commodities by any means.[20]

Within the next few years Tippu Tip acquired another fortune from the ivory and slaves of Manyuemaland. He was firmly established in the country by 1880. Basing his headquarters on a large island in the river near Stanley Falls, in conjunction with his nephew, Rashid, he farmed the area for slaves. Von Wissmann, on his second journey from the Congo to the Zambezi, 1886-7, ran into the 'rapacious' expeditions of Tippu Tip's slave hunters;[21] and in 1882, A. J. Swann, missionary, writing from Mpwapwa on his way to Lake Tanganyika, saw the fruits of their forays in Tippu Tip's annual caravan headed coastwards. There were long files of slaves, chained by the neck, some were in forks about six feet long, and many women were carrying babies on their backs.

> They looked at us with suspicion and fear having been told, as we subsequently ascertained, that white men always desired to release slaves in order to eat their flesh like the Upper Congo cannibals.[22]

The slaves were in a filthy state and many were scarred by cuts of the 'Chikote' hide whip. They had already travelled 1000 miles from the Upper Congo, and were faced with another march of 250 miles to the coast. Von Wissmann, meeting the caravans heading coastwards, noted the hundreds of slaves fastened together with long chains and neck-yokes, in sets of ten to twenty. The weaker women and children, who were not expected to escape, were only tied with ropes or left unfettered, for they seldom went astray, but those who had to be especially watched were walking by twos in the 'mukongua,' the slave-fork in which the neck was fastened. They were in a miserable and lamentable condition.

> Their arms and legs almost fleshless, their bodies shrivelled up, their looks heavy and their heads bent, while they were marching along eastward into an unknown future, farther and farther away from their homes, separated from wife and child. The slaves were mostly bound together according to their powers of marching, without the least regard to sex.[23]

Mr Walter Hutley, of the London Missionary Society, who had resided at various points on the main slave route to the coast during the years 1878-81, was well placed to speak of the nature of the slave trade.[24] The greatest problem was that of feeding the thousands of slaves marched coastwards. It was the custom to ration out to them every five days an allowance of five cowrie shells (a form of native currency) per head. One cowrie shell was equivalent in value to a potato or a maize cob, and a slave was expected to subsist for a march of ten to fifteen miles a day for a period of five days on this very inadequate sustenance. This inevitably wrought a heavy toll among the slaves. There was outright starvation, or death caused by eating poisonous fungi to supplement the meagre diet. And in their weakened state, disease was rampant among the slaves. Hutley referred to a caravan of 1000 persons which was decimated by smallpox.

Although caravans such as those of Tippu Tip might raid along the route of march, and clear away the villages and crops of those natives who protested, they tended to leave in their wake many dead slaves. Even before they set out on the long trek from Ujiji to the coast, they were seriously depleted in number. In crossing Lake Tanganyika, slaves were made to sit doubled up in the bottom of the canoes, so closely packed that by the time Ujiji was reached a quarter had succumbed, although the distance across the lake, depot to depot, was scarcely 200 miles. Of the 300 slaves brought from Manyuema by Said bin Habib, only 50 reached Unyanyembe alive.

The pattern of the slave trade along the route of march was not a straightforward transit of slaves from the interior to the coast. Tippu Tip, Juma Merikani and Arabs from Nyangwe shipped their slaves as far south as the upper Zambezi, where they were sold to the Portuguese. They also often sold their slaves in ones and twos along the way, or traded them for oxen, the value of a male adult slave being equivalent to that of an ox. And there was a type of slaver who lay in wait on the road, seizing straggling slaves, and who, offering provisions for sale in the slavers' camps, would induce other slaves to run away so that they might take them in hand themselves and later sell them at Ujiji or Unyanyembe.[25] Large caravans leaving Manyuema were often accompanied by numbers of free natives with one or two slaves of their own for sale, or to be hired out as porters to carry ivory for the Arabs.

At Unyanyembe, in Unyamwezi, there were unaccountable aspects of the slave trade—at least in the eyes of humanitarians in England. For the Wanyamwezi had entered into the business of slaving with gusto, and were either slavers on their own, or acted as agents for the Arabs. They captured slaves in tribal wars and obtained them by purchase. The price of a green or raw slave was that of a good Tower musket, a great article of barter among the Wanyamwezi, who had imbibed a passion for firearms and obtained these from the Arabs in return for slaves. Caravans arriving at Unyanyembe from Ujiji made up their losses by obtaining fresh supplies of slaves from Unyanyembe. By 1881, despite the excessive mortality, about 4000 slaves reached Unyanyembe annually, and since Manyuema slaves were in great demand among the Wanyamwezi, many were disposed of there, and fresh supplies replaced them. At this date, at least a quarter of the population of Unyamwezi was estimated to be slaves.[26] The Wanyamwezi were cruel masters compared to the Arabs, and treated their slaves as if they were on the level of animals. The slaves, however, did not seem to mind this much and, although apparently feeling keenly the separation from friends, rarely attempted to run away. And slaves emulated their masters in the matter of slave-holding, and themselves possessed slaves. A slave might own a slave in the person of a small boy or girl, who would wait on him as a personal servant, bringing him drinking water and preparing his food. The slave system spread throughout Unyamwezi almost as by a process of osmosis, so thoroughly had it become ingrained in the social life of the Wanyamwezi.

In far-away Uganda, cut off from communications with the coast, and with apparently no outlet for slaves, it came as a dolorous surprise to the first Christian missionaries there that slavery was a long-standing institution in that advanced kingdom of Bantu agriculturalists. They commented on the large number of slaves at the King's court, and the cheapness with which life was held. Speke, who visited Mtesa's court in 1862, described the cruelty that lay beneath the polished surface. Every day, two or three slaves from

Mtesa's harems were dragged away to death for some minor transgression. The Reverend Father Levesque personally witnessed the death by mutilation of a female slave on Mtesa's orders. Protestant and Catholic missionaries inveighed against the slave trade in Buganda and endeavoured to dissuade the Kabaka and chiefs from slave trading. Mackay, of the CMS, recounts that when some Arab traders arrived in Buganda to purchase slaves, offering cloth in exchange, he opposed them vigorously. He lectured Mtesa on physiology and asked, 'Why should such an organism as a human body, which no man could make, be sold for a rag of cloth which any man could make in a day?' According to Mackay, the result of this discussion was not only the refusal of the Arabs' immediate demand but the King issued a decree forbidding any person in Buganda to sell a slave on pain of death. This caused bitter enmity on the part of the Arabs against the mission.[27] Slaves were one of the main articles Buganda could offer the Muslim traders, both for domestic use and for sale at the coast. Kagwa writes that in Buganda many women slaves were captured in war, and before the Arabs arrived these were usually distributed among the chiefs. One chief, Mende, possessed 700 female slaves. Following the wars of King Suna, there were so many women captives that Suna presented 2000 to his mother, 80 to Sebowa, the Katabalwa, and the remainder were taken to the Court and distributed among his wives who ruled over them as they pleased. But with the coming of the Arabs, an alternative market was opened, and the Buganda now found they could use women captives as an article of exchange:[28]

In Buganda society there was a lower stratum of slaves. The Mukopi, of the same race as the Baganda, but a form of retainer in that he accompanied his master to war, was comparable to the churl or serf of feudal society in Medieval Europe, an *adscriptus glebae*. This serf-like class in Buganda was fairly well treated, enjoyed a certain civil status, and the Mukopi with his wife and family lived on his master's estate. He grew his own food and, in return for protection, tendered produce at stated intervals to his master. In Buganda society there was also the real slave, the Baddu (Muddu) captured in war or acquired by purchase, who was the chattel of his owner, and subject to hard usage, and whose women were degraded to the level of mere playthings. The Baddu class of slaves was continually augmented by fresh captures in war.

The wars between Buganda and Bunyoro constantly brought in slaves, for the history of these two kingdoms was one of intermittent strife and mutual enslavement throughout most of the nineteenth century. The arrival of Europeans in Uganda coincided with the decline of Bunyoro, when hundreds of slaves from there were paraded at Mtesa's court. Busoga, east of Buganda, supplied it with slaves as a form of tribute; they were a form of currency, used to palliate and strike *bon accord*. Emin Pasha, while in Buganda, saw hundreds of women brought in from Busoga. Buddu, a district of Buganda, was long recognized as a slave-producing area; the term Muddu, which gained wider currency as designating a slave, originally denoted an inhabitant of Buddu.

Slaves from Uganda appear to have reached the coast at about the mid-nineteenth century, or shortly after. The explorer, Grant, arriving at Unyanyembe in 1861, noted that among the diversity of slaves gathered there awaiting the long trek to the coast were Hima female slaves from Karagwe in Uganda. They were highly desired for their beauty and intelligence, and ranked well above the ordinary run of slaves in the estimation of the Arabs. When the first Arabs reached Buganda and Bunyoro in the second half of the century, slaves were abundant, owing to the recent raids and counter-raids of Mtesa and Kabarega. Pretty Hima female slaves were also in evidence in Buganda and were much sought after there as concubines and wives. Nyoro girls, whose lower incisors had been extracted, were less valued, and so also were Ganda females, owing to a deformity, possibly a small pelvis, which made childbirth difficult. Peters, Schweinfurth and Emin Pasha all commented on the attractive Hima women with their 'pretty orthogonous' faces. An ordinary slave in Uganda would fetch as much as 10,000 cowrie shells, but a beautiful Hima woman would bring twice that amount. The diminishing fertility of Ganda women resulted in the increasing import of women from adjoining tribes.[29]

Arab slavers came to Mwanga's court with their arms and powder for the purpose of purchasing these slaves. Mackay estimated that 2000 slaves were exported annually from Uganda, and a similar number from Bunyoro. Slaves acquired in Uganda were taken by the Arabs southwards by land across the Kagera River or by way of Lake Victoria, and thence to Unyanyembe and the coast. Mr Wilson, of the CMS, saw something of this brisk trade in slaves going down Lake Victoria in canoes furnished by Mtesa, as many as 200 slaves at a time. At least 1000 slaves a year were exported from Uganda by this route.[30] That slave raiding was widespread in Uganda was personally confirmed by Bishop Tucker after observing a fifteen-mile-wide stretch of country in Kavirondo devastated by Swahili slavers from the coast. They had co-opted local chiefs into the business by bribing them with trade goods.[31]

The first attempt to check the slave trade in Uganda was that made by General Gordon when, in 1875, he sent the Frenchman, Ernest Linant de Bellefonds, to Uganda to obtain Mtesa's promise to forbid the buying and selling of slaves. The latter, alarmed at Egyptian intervention, gave his consent. There is little indication, however, that he intended to keep his promise. In a satirical gesture, he sent slaves to accompany Felkin and Wilson back to Europe, under the pretext that they were taking back chiefs. Treaties between Britain, Buganda, Bunyoro and Ankole, following the establishment of a British protectorate in the 1890s, contained clauses providing for the extinction of the slave trade and slavery. In the treaty with Mwanga of 30 March 1892, Lugard obtained from the latter a declaration that 'Slave-trading or slave raiding, or exportation or importation of people for sale or exchange as slaves is prohibited'.[32]

Lugard refused to acknowledge the long-standing practice in Uganda that captives of war were reduced to the status of slaves, and following the submission of the Mohammedans and their leader, Mbogo, he freed their prisoners. In full baraza (council) in 1892, he enacted a law whereby captured prisoners of war held in Buganda were freed from any status of slavedom. They were manumitted without ransom money being paid for them and given papers of freedom and protection.[33] Before Lugard departed from Uganda in 1892, he had personally freed 50 slaves under this order, and a number of them accompanied him to the coast.

During his stay in Uganda, Lugard was much absorbed in thought over the problem of the disposal of freed slaves. He proposed establishing villages for them, much along the lines of what he had done on the Sabaki River. These freed slave villages would be in the vicinity of mission stations, with a resident missionary and a headman in charge. But he differed in opinion from the Protestant missions who would have in turn handed over these freed slaves to individual well-known and trusted Protestants, 'who adopted them into their households with good results', for this smacked too much of 'compulsory religion' for Lugard. He reluctantly acceded to this plan only on the stipulation that all such slaves handed over to the Missions should be listed, and that the Missions should account for their whereabouts when requested by the administrative authorities.

Lugard's work on the redemption of slaves was continued by Major Macdonald. During the year following Lugard's departure, he liberated over 2000 slaves.³⁴ Sir Gerald Portal, who arrived in Uganda in April 1893, attempted to carry out Lugard's scheme of the rehabilitation of freed slaves, but with the assumption of a British protectorate in 1894, the status of slavery was abolished completely and the absorption of freed slaves into the general population was quietly and smoothly effected in Buganda. Outside that kingdom, however, the slave trade lingered on for some years. Missionary extension outside Buganda, in some cases, was specifically undertaken as a positive effort to end this state of affairs. The White Fathers moved into the districts of Koki and Ankole, on the border of German East Africa, so as to acquire 'moral ascendancy' over the natives and 'to put a stop to the Slave Trade, which still continues to this day to carry off many victims among our Christians'.³⁵

Bunyoro, the kingdom to the immediate northwest of Buganda, continued to be the focus of an extensive slave trade for a number of years after it ended in Uganda. Kabarega, King of Bunyoro, carried on an extensive trade with the Arabs, obtaining from them arms and ammunition in exchange for slaves. Colonel Colvile's attack on Kabarega's capital in 1894 was intended as a blow against 'the only remaining great slave trade centre of this part of Africa'. At the end of this campaign, when Kabarega and his forces were on the run, many slaves were abandoned (including Baganda women of such 'mountainous proportions' that they moved about with great difficulty), and they became a glut in the market.³⁶ The price of an adult female slave in Bunyoro fell from one load of beads or two guns, to 'three goats with an extra goat thrown in for her child'.

Kabarega's capitulation did not end the slave trade in Bunyoro. At Kitangole, one day's march south of the Kagera River, a settlement of 800 Arabs and Swahili traders continued to trade with Bunyoro for slaves. At the end of the nineteenth century a regular traffic in captured Buddu women continued into German East Africa, and the British administration in Uganda was somewhat mortified to find that a Sudanese company which they had stationed at Mbarara, in southwestern Uganda, was deeply involved in this slave trade and had to receive due punishment.

The extent of slave-raiding inland as far as the fringes of the Kenya highlands was substantial in the early 1890s. When the Imperial British East Africa Company set up a post at Machakos under its agent, John Ainsworth, in the early 1890s, he discovered it to be the centre of a substantial and long-standing slave trade.³⁷ And following the occupation of Ulu by the Company, Kitui became the principal rendezvous of slave traders in that part of the country. In the mid-1890s similar slave depots were revealed at Quambola, Mola and Nzawi, in what is now Kenya. Ainsworth blamed much of the slave raiding on the young bloods 'who look on this raiding as a very simple means of obtaining wives and shamba workers on the cheap'.[38] The ramifications of this slave trade were widespread. It extended from the Samburi in the north, and linked up with a slave route to the north of Mount Elgon and the trade in slave concubines originating in the district east of Kitui, and then ran down to the Sabaka River to Takaungu at the coast, and thence south to Pangani in German East Africa. Ukambani, north of Kitui, was an important centre of Wakamba slave traders, particularly during the great famine of the 1890s when hundreds of Masai women were sold to the Kikuyu. On the other hand, the Kikuyu would not risk bringing them into Kitui, and so the Swahili were the middlemen. Their caravans made regular journeys into the interior to purchase slaves from the Kikuyu. Swahili slavers would then sell these slaves at Kitui for cattle, and would take these to Mumoni and sell them for ivory. Masai women also trekked to the coast for the purpose of selling themselves and their children in order to survive. During this period the price of a good-looking girl was three goats. The Uganda Railway Survey, 1891-2, revealed the extent of this slavery.[39] In Sotik, runaway slaves from Swahili caravans joined the railway survey party, and reported they had been enticed to sell food to these caravans and had then been seized. People from half-starved villages were encouraged to attach themselves to caravans, being assured of plenty of food a few miles ahead. The promised land never arrived, and they ended up in slavery. In time of famine, it was not uncommon for parents to sell their children in exchange for food to passing caravans.[40]

The more remote areas of what is now Kenya were not penetrated by Arab slave traders from the coast until these regions were opened up by European explorers, such as Count Teleki, in the Rudolf area. Arab and Swahili slavers were quick to transfer their activities to these new routes. Chanler, who entered the region of northern Kenya in the mid-1890s, describes their methods. Slaving parties from the coast, headed by Arabs or Swahili, and consisting very often of slave porters, spent a year inland on their trading expeditions. Several Arabs would enter into a loose partnership, each furnishing a number of slave porters to make up a party. They would then give promissory notes to an Indian merchant for trading goods, generally at an interest of 12 per cent or more per annum. Each caravan had its

Mchawi, a wizard-cum-guide, with knowledge of the black arts and able to tell future events and ward off evil. At the head of the expedition was carried a white flag, the *kome*, covered with curiously wrought figures, triangles and circles, and many phrases from the Koran. This flag supposedly possessed occult power. The makers of these *kome* were great medicine-men who had made long journeys into the interior during their youth, and were well steeped in the lore of the safari. In their old age, highly respected and held in considerable awe, they derived a large income from the manufacture of these totem flags.[41]

At the end of the trading journey the profits were shared out. Each partner received payment according to the number of porters he had contributed to the enterprise. These porters were given a round sum for the journey, one-third in advance, and the remainder on the completion of the journey. During the safari they were furnished with trade goods on account for their own trading, and this opportunity for private gain was one of the most attractive features of the enterprise for them. It was all a respectable and matter-of-fact business, from their viewpoint. Count Teleki blamed the Africans more than the Arab slavers for the slave trade in the interior. They were constantly at war and enslaving each other and would sell their captives to the Arab and Somali traders. Slaves, in turn, regarded such sales as a blessing, saving them from cruel native masters, and they went willingly and gladly to the coast. The declaration of the British East Africa Protectorate in 1895, and the establishment of outlying posts, checked much of this slave trade.[42]

The Uganda Railway, European settlement, and the establishment of effective administration, all played their part in bringing slavery and the slave trade to an end. But in northeastern Kenya, in Tanaland Province, a trade in slaves continued into Italian Somaliland well into the twentieth century. The defeat of the Italians at Adowa, in 1896, lowered European prestige in the Horn of Africa and, followed shortly after by the rise of the Mad Mullah, gave an impetus to the slave trade in this region. Little check on the slave trade in these remoter areas could be effected by European administrations.

The Abyssinians were the last practioners of the slave trade in the early part of the twentieth century. They raided south, as far down as Lake Rudolf, and attacked Turkana tribes in the Turquel River area. A raiding party of 400 Abyssinian soldiers and followers, in 1904, captured 20,000 head of stock and over 100 Turkana women and children in one foray. Abyssinian soldiers received no pay on these raiding excursions, but were permitted to take as many slaves as they pleased, provided that every soldier presented the Ras with one slave. Commissioner Sadler of the British East Africa Protectorate, in 1904, was so incensed over Abyssinian slave raids in this area that he proposed occupation of the Lake Rudolf region to end the slave trade there, but Lansdowne was 'entirely opposed to occupation of more advanced posts'. Stable and contracted frontiers were more important than pursuing moral causes.[43]

The Germans, on taking over the coastal strip from the Sultan of Zanzibar in 1888, found domestic slavery firmly established and legally recognized under Islam, and they did not interfere with it. Domestic slavery meant stability, good order, and an available labour supply. The Sultan's decree of August 1890 received no parallel pronouncement in German territory; German officials expressed sympathy with its principles but stated they were not as yet in a sufficiently strong position to enforce a similar decree.[44]

The Germans were, in fact, less restrictive in their attitude towards domestic slavery than the Sultan of Zanzibar, who was forced by British pressure into making concessions to the anti-slavery cause. The Germans, for example, permitted slaves to be inherited not only by the children of the owner, but by lawful heirs. Sale of domestic slaves, provided these slaves were not exported abroad, was not inquired into too closely.[45] Most German officers would probably have agreed with the Governor, Baron von Schele, who remarked in 1894

> It is another matter to root abruptly domestic usages which are interwoven with the whole life of the natives and not necessarily inhuman. Born slaves do not feel their condition any hardship. After all we had serfdom, which is much the same thing as this mitigated slavery, in civilized Europe not 100 years ago.[46]

In German territory, if a slave was subjected to cruelty, he could complain to the German authorities, and they, if his case justified it, would manumit him. The Liwali (Arab magistrate appointed by the Germans) could also free any slave who had just cause for complaint. The Germans allowed every slave the unfettered power of purchasing his freedom, a facility not available to domestic slaves in the Sultan's domains. Slaves were not restive under their purported bondage, and it was the Governor's opinion that they 'preferred Arabian bondage to European freedom'. German leniency in regard to domestic slavery did not extend to slave raiding. The 'raw' slave trade meant disruption of law and order, and must be suppressed at all costs. The Germans almost invariably inflicted the punishment of death for this offence. It was their ruthless action in this respect that was one of the main causes which led the Arab, Bushiri, to revolt against German rule in 1889. The Germans would not permit caravans to leave the coast for the interior without being searched for gunpowder and arms. Slave traders were tried under summary justice and hanged on conviction.[47] The hanging by the Germans of a number of Arab slavers in the Taveta region in 1890, followed by the hanging of another batch at Lindi in 1891, gravely shocked British sensibilities at Zanzibar. Sir Arthur Hardinge commented that he would have been satisfied with life imprisonment for the culprits.[48]

A German Society for the Abolition of Slavery had been formed in 1848, and it was active in opposing the slave trade in German colonies in Africa in the mid-1880s. It was largely as a result of the Society's efforts that the Reichstag, in January 1889, voted 2,000,000 marks for the suppression of the slave trade.[49] The Society introduced the novel feature of lotteries to raise funds for its work. In 1892, it sent out representatives to the colonies to work for the suppression of the slave trade and to care for freed slaves. Its endeavours in this respect in German East Africa were largely ineffectual, owing mainly to an unfortunate choice of representatives. Oscar Baumann, who journeyed from Pangani through Masailand to Ruanda and Urundi, left a reputation for cruelty akin to that of Karl Peters in the Kilimanjaro region.

It was the Committee's intention to construct stations at strategic centres to intercept slave caravans, and to supervise patrols of the Central Lakes. But the French traveller, Lionel Dècle, who visited the Committee's post on Ukerewe Island in Lake Victoria, noted that the fine station had been constructed by forced labour, and that the Committee's African subordinates were guilty of extortion and depredation. The failure of the Committee to fulfil expectations was reflected in the withdrawal of its agents within a year of their arrival in East Africa, and the handing over of their stations and equipment to the government and to the White Fathers' Mission. Christian Missions henceforth took on the responsibility for the disposal of freed slaves. In May 1892, a number of freed slave girls were handed over to the Protestant and Catholic Missions at Dar es Salaam and Bagamoyo. The Missions of the White Fathers on Lake Victoria and Lake Tanganyika also took on the task of looking after freed slaves. The Government supported this work by contributing £1.5.0 for each freed slave taken into their care.

Major Herman von Wissmann, in charge of German military

forces in German East Africa, 1889-90, and later Governor, 1894-6, was active in his efforts to suppress the slave trade. He had crossed Africa from west to east in 1886-7, and had accompanied one of Tippu Tip's large slave caravans from the interior; thus he was no stranger to the devastation caused by the slave trade in Africa. Von Wissmann was largely responsible for placing steamers on Lake Nyasa and Lake Tanganyika on behalf of the German Catholic African Society, in an attempt to check the slave trade, and he also founded the station of Langenburg, at a strategic point at the north end of Lake Nyasa. Military action against slavers was taken by von Wissmann and Baron von Eltz, his second-in-command, in the region between Lakes Nyasa and Tanganyika in 1892, and they gave most valuable assitance with forces and steamers to Harry Johnston in the suppression of Arab slavers in the Lake Nyasa region. Similarly, Captain Langheld, in charge of the German station at Bukoba, on the western shore of Lake Victoria, was assiduous in suppressing the slave trade in that area. His enthusiasm for the anti-slave trade cause led him into breaching the boundaries of the British sphere and advancing northwest as far as Lake Albert Edward in 1894.

Anti-slave trade legislation in German East Africa, as in British East Africa, was a piecemeal process. A Bill submitted to the Reichstag in 1891 to end the institution of slavery and to deal with slavers was dropped when the committee to whom it was referred hesitated to recommend immediate action. Colonial authorities were then asked to provide more information on the subject, and, in the meantime, to step up the campaign against the slave trade.[50] These were delaying tactics, and at the end of 1894 instructions circulated by von Wissmann authorized station and district officers to examine all caravans travelling to the coast, to check whether so-called porters were actually slaves and, if they were found to be so, to take them into custody. Caravan leaders were also ordered to obtain permits from superintendents of stations in the interior before leaving for the coast.[51] So effective were these measures that in April 1895, the British Admiralty noted that

> The vigilance of the German authorities and severity with which they punish slave dealers has seriously checked the traffic in the territory under their jurisdiction.[52]

The Germans also took limited action against the slave trade at sea and, in May 1895, the German cruisers *Seeadler* and *Condor* patrolled the German East African coast. Naval regulations for the 'suppression of the Slave Trade at Sea' were laid down. Slave dhows captured at sea were taken to Dar es Salaam and handed over to the Imperial authorities.

There were certain areas in the German sphere which were a cause of special concern to German authorities because of the active slave trading centred there. The northern portion of the coast near Tanga was the locale of numerous slave traders who kidnapped or stole slaves from villages and then smuggled them across in canoes to Pemba at night. The region adjacent to the Uganda border was also the centre of traffic in slaves, especially female slaves from Uganda, who were exchanged for power and arms. This latter trade caused embarrassment to both German and British administrations. The German advance into the interior along the Bagamoyo, Tabora and Ujiji line of march appears to have diverted the slave trade southeastwards into the populous districts of Kilwa and Lindi on the coast south of Dar es Salaam where, as the result of the shallowness of its waters, it was infrequently visited by men-of-war. The harbours along this coast were quite inadequate for naval vessels, and they had to lie well off shore, but slave dhows could hug the inner shore to evade detection. The long-standing slave routes terminating at Kilwa and Lindi merged into the plantations behind these towns, and from these slaves were smuggled at night by canoe through numerous creeks leading to the sea and thence loaded on to slave vessels. Local officials connived at this trade; the Liwali at Lindi was himself a large slave-owner, having 70 to 80 slaves in his possession, and augmented his miserable administrative salary with proceeds from slaving. Similarly, the Liwali of Kilwa was in league with a notorious slaver, Hasan bin Omar.

In 1894, the Germans attempted the eradication of the slavers in the Lindi/Kilwa region, and sent two companies of soldiers there to disperse them. But they were soon diverted from this task by the Wahehe uprising, and it was not until November 1895 that they were able to launch an offensive against the slave trader, Hasan. His capture, following a raid on his headquarters, struck a severe blow at the slave trade in the Kilwa region. But the port of Kilwa still continued to be the outlet for the export of slaves captured by Arab slavers, who now concentrated their efforts at the northern points on Lake Nyasa. During the famine conditions of 1898-9, there was also a recrudescence of inter-tribal slavery, resulting in the sale of women and children to stave off starvation. Although this state of affairs was largely confined to the eastern and central districts which were easily accessible to the coast, there is no evidence that it developed into an external slave trade.[53] Sporadic incidents of the kidnapping of children from the German coastline for sale in Pemba and Zanzibar continued into the first years of the twentieth century. But by 1900 it might be said that regularized and traditional export of slaves from the German coastline had ceased.

But this could not be said of the institution of domestic slavery. Although pressure from humanitarians at home was insistent on its termination, officials in German East Africa were disinclined to tamper with the institution. A bill to end domestic slavery was brought before the Reichstag in January 1895. But Dr Kayser, head of the Colonial Department in the Foreign Office, had no intention of listening to 'philanthropic old women'. The abolition of domestic slavery would bring economic ruin to colonies just emerging from a primitive past,

> Things must go on as they are for at least ten years to come. It would be time enough then to see what could be done towards modifying a system which is indigenous to the country, and without which all agricultural labour would come to an absolute standstill.[54]

With a revolt on their hands, the German administration had more important matters to think about than doing away with the institution of domestic slavery. And, as elsewhere in East Africa, it had a tenacious life. Although a Bill passed in the Reichstag in July 1895 reaffirmed the death penalty for 'raw' slave trading, it legally recognized the status of household slavery.[55] There appeared to be a growing reluctance to tamper with the institution. This arose from the realization of the expense involved in compensating slave owners if their slaves were freed, and also the failure to recruit coolies from Singapore to German East Africa in 1896. There was increasing need to rely on domestic slavery for the coconut plantations in the Mafia Island group, and for the newly established sugar plantations along the Pangani River. Increasingly, domestic slaves were hired out to Indian sugar planters, and after a period of three years they were eligible to purchase their freedom. This was a policy encouraged by the German administration, both to provide adequate labour for sugar cultivation and as a gradual form of amelioration of the lot of domestic slaves. In the period July 1898 to June 1899, 845 letters of emancipation were granted to freed slaves under this arrangement, without affecting a stable labour supply in the territory.

The subterfuge resorted to in February 1898, whereby the title of 'slavery' was done away with and the term 'serfdom' substituted for it (harking back to the institution which existed in Prussia before the reforms of Stein and Hardenburg in the early nineteenth century), was meant to disarm hostile criticism on the part of persons ignorant of African affairs and necessities at home, rather than to produce any real change in the status of the slaves, who would remain in their present condition under the new and less objectionable designation of serfs'.[56]

Hence, after 1899, slaves were to be referred to as 'retainers', and owners as 'masters'. Hostile criticism at home was not so easily taken in by this ruse, however, and following continued pressure for the abolition of domestic slavery, an imperial decree of November 29 1901 set out detailed conditions for its amelioration. No one should be placed in a condition of slavery, and every domestic slave was to be allowed to work on his own account for two days of the week, and was empowered to terminate his slavery by purchase, the amount of the purchase price being fixed by the official authority. The owner of a domestic slave must support him in old age, and could forfeit his ownership by lack of duty towards his slave. No slave was to be sold without his or her consent and the sale of married couples and children under 12 years of age was forbidden. Limited rights of inheritance of domestic slaves, the right of freedom by ransom, manumission, the official grant of letters of freedom in case of ill-treatment, automatic freedom if five years had elapsed without working as a slave, and on the death of an owner without heirs, all were detailed in the decree of 1901. A female slave was freed if she married a freeman, or if a bride price was paid to her owner, or if an owner acknowledged a child by her as his offspring. Infraction of these regulations was punishable by a fine and imprisonment.[57] This decree of November 1901 began the erosion of the system of domestic slavery in German East Africa.

In 1904, another decree of the Imperial Chancellor declared all slaves born after 31 December 1905, of slave parents, to be *ipso facto* free; slaves born prior to that date could purchase their freedom at prices determined by courts of law.[58] This decree furthered the process towards gradual extinction, but even at this date it was estimated that this would not be reached before 1930, or even 1940, for it was not desired to make an abrupt break with the existing institution, as this might cause grave embarrassment to the local administration.

The number of domestic slaves in German East Africa at the turn of the century is difficult to assess accurately. But in the Ujiji district, in 1913, the Germans estimated the number of slaves there at 20,000; and in the Songea and Iringa districts, a total of 15,000 slaves was recorded in 1913. It is more difficult to arrive at a number for the coastal strip, for slavery there was of such a fluid nature under a mild Swahili master that it is not easy to distinguish the free from the unfree, but the number of domestic slaves probably reached nearly 20,000. Thus a total of some 50,000 slaves in German East Africa on the eve of World War I would probably not be far off the mark. During World War I, many deaths, the opportunity to sever connection with unpopular masters, and the recruitment for the services of the military, so reduced the overall number of slaves that in the districts mentioned above they were practically non-existent at the end of the war, when the British took over the administration. Domestic servitude, however, was still prevalent in the coastal belt at the end of World War I. Long association with Zanzibar, Arab influence and the strength of Islamic tradition all tended to support its continuance there.

The terms of the mandate under which Britain administered the ex-German colony following World War I provided for 'the eventual emancipation of all slaves and for as speedy an elimination of domestic and other slavery as social conditions will allow'; and all forms of the slave trade were to be suppressed. In pursuance of this, legislation enacted in 1922 under Sir Claude Hollis, acting Governor, brought in an Involuntary (Abolition) Servitude Ordinance to end the status of domestic slavery. It provided that no rights arising out of such relationship should be enforced by any civil or criminal court or by any other authority within the Territory. This effectively ruled out any question of compensation to owners for loss of slaves freed under the Ordinance. The Ordinance further enacted that no person who had acquired property by his own industry or by inheritance should be dispossessed of it on the grounds that he was a slave. There were penalties under the Ordinance for the detention of any person as a slave against his will. In certain parts of the Territory 'voluntary servitude' continued to exist, based on the earlier form of household slavery. In the Mafia Island group, however, a form of 'involuntary servitude' lingered on almost up to World War II.[59]

The generations of slavery which formed part of the social history of East Africa seem to have left little bitterness or recrimination among its native peoples. There is no inferiority complex in regard to their former status as slaves, nor does there appear to have been any attempt to exploit or create such a feeling for political reasons, except possibly in Zanzibar during the events leading up to the January 1964 revolution, when the Arab élite was ousted. It is doubtful whether memories of slavery in East Africa are sufficiently strong to foster a feeling against the Arabs comparable to that directed against descendants of other slave-holders in other parts of the world.

II. THE SOUTHERN INTERIOR

When that remarkable man, Livingstone, seeking to establish a mission station, penetrated north into the territory of the Makololo chief, Sebebwane, in 1852, he found that Portuguese slavers from the west coast had already arrived there. They had introduced the Makololo into the business of slaving, having recently purchased from them 200 boys captured in raids. According to Livingstone, the Makololo declared that they had never heard of people being bought or sold till then. But their avidity for trade goods had led them into it.[60] During his journey to Luanda, on the west coast, in the period November 1853-June 1854, Livingstone continued to meet evidence of Portuguese slaving. They were driving gangs of slaves to the west coast, and their demoralizing influence was seen in that 'wherever slave-traders have been, the natives are more difficult to deal with, and more exorbitant in their demands. There is a universal curse in slavery'.

On his return journey from Luanda, retracing the course of the Zambezi river eastwards, Livingstone witnessed the activity of Portuguese slavers from the east coast of Africa. A slave trader with whom he had perforce to travel, had two chain gangs of slaves 'full of women going to be sold for ivory'. For the vigilance of British cruisers off the east African coast was forcing the Portuguese into taking their slaves in a southeasterly direction, selling them for ivory, and the ultimate purchasers would be Transvaal Boers. The Portuguese governors at Tete and Quelimane were involved in the slave trade. And this was quite inexplicable, for Major Sicard, Governor of Tete, was a 'good man', and the Portuguese 'do not seem at all bigoted in their attachment to slavery, nor in their attitude towards colour'. But they did not regard the slave trade as immoral, and seemed to ignore 'the dreadful amount of misery and woe to which it gives rise'. According to Livingstone 'The Portuguese home government has not generally received the credit for sincerity in suppressing the slave-trade which I conceive to be its due',[61] but it was frustrated by men on the spot, especially that worst product of all, the Portuguese half-caste, to whom Livingstone so frequently and so contemptuously refers in his later travels.

He arrived back in England in December 1856 to receive a joyous welcome, for he was already being accepted as Africa's great saviour, the medical missionary-explorer unparalleled. In March 1858, he returned to Africa accompanied by his wife. The years 1858 to 1862 were devoted to various journeys on the Zambezi and the discovery of Lakes Nyasa and Shirwa. After much trouble with the little river steamer, *Ma-Robert*, it was abandoned, and replaced by a larger vessel, the *Pioneer*, and he was able to proceed with his explorations. But the slave trade dominated all other considerations, for Livingstone now witnessed the way in which, like a cancerous growth, it had spread out from stockades at the mouth of the river Shire. Half-caste Portuguese, heading gangs of black slave hunters, had forayed up the farthest reaches of the river. They were a law unto themselves, raiding at will. One of them, Mariano, previously imprisoned for slaughtering Portuguese troops, had used his considerable wealth to such good effect as to secure his freedom. And now, by the time Livingstone entered the country in 1858, he was heading a band of armed slave raiders, and ravaging the country south and east of the Shire cataracts. Fugitives were crowded along the Shire river, and famine followed in their wake; dead bodies floated downstream, and slave dealers from Tete bought up the living.

Entering the country of the Manganja tribe in July 1861, Livingstone found a regular system of slave hunting set up by the Portuguese, some of whom were acting as agents of the governor and commandant at Tete. They had armed the Yao who then attacked the Manganja, enslaving their women and children and selling them to the Portuguese. Buyers also came from the Makololo country farther west, to purchase female slaves from the Yao at the rate of one 60 lb. tusk of ivory per slave.

Proceeding up the Shire river, Livingstone left the *Pioneer*, and passing the Murchison Cataracts sailed into the hitherto undiscovered Lake Nyasa. Marching along its western shore, while his boat sailed up its west side, he noted that

> The population on the shores of the lake exceeds all I have seen in Africa for numbers. Numerous bays of the lake make an extended coastline affording access to a very large tract of slave-producing territory.[62]

Arab slavers were active on the lake. Livingstone espied an Arab dhow full of slaves heading across the lake to the eastern side, and the booming of the small brass cannon which Arabs used, more for their alarmist than their deterrent effect, could be heard along the southeastern shore. Taking stock of the overwhelming extent of the slave trade in the Nyasa area, Livingstone estimated that 20,000 slaves annually were taken from there, and 'There has never been such an export of slaves from the Zambezi since we entered it as now'.[63]

Livingstone returned from this journey up the Lake resolved to do his utmost to stir up the civilized world against the slave trade. The Portuguese were the chief culprits behind the traffic. Although they never used the lower Zambezi nor entered the Shire river, they kept close watch against the entry of other nations. They had set up what was almost a private slave preserve, between Cape Delgado and Delagoa Bay, 'some nine hundred miles where Britain had not one free avenue'.

> This conduct on the part of the Portuguese has a more depressing effect on the mind than scorching suns, long marches, hunger or thirst, or even the fever itself . . . I see more plainly than ever that, without an alternation in the exclusive system of the Portuguese, the beneficial effects of HM's cruisers can never be realized here, as they have been on the West Coast. The question assumes the greatest importance to me, inasmuch as if they are to follow us into the Lake region, our labours will be in vain. The idea takes the pith out of one's heart; but we shall go on with our road-making.[64]

The Portuguese government had assured Lord Clarendon of all possible support for Livingstone, and would allow him 'to carry all his goods up to Tete without paying any import duties and thence freely into the interior.' But the Portuguese were naturally disquieted at the irruption of a wandering British missionary into their sphere, especially one who was sending out reports to his government which were derogatory to Portuguese rule. They tried to prevent Livingstone from ascending the Ruvuma river in the *Pioneer* in early 1861, and no doubt it was Portuguese pressure which influenced the Foreign Office into recalling Livingstone's expedition, before he had carried out his plan to place a steamer on Lake Nyasa.

Despite the death of his wife, Mary, from fever at Sharpanga, at the mouth of the Zambezi, in April 1862,[65] Livingstone was soon busy again with his accounts of the terrible desolation caused by Portuguese slave agents on the Zambezi, and with his own plans for further exploration. He took his small steamer, the *Lady Nyasa*, to Bombay, where, after a journey of 45 days, most tempestuous and adventurous, she was sold—a mere footnote to the larger enterprise on which he was soon to embark. Back in England, in 1864, he was persuaded by Sir Roderick Murchison, President of the Royal Geographical Society, to return to Africa to report more extensively on the slave trade, and to carry out further exploration, this time as regards the sources of the Nile.

To this end, after revictualling at Zanzibar, he landed at the mouth of the Ruvuma river, from where he penetrated the interior, on what was to be his last great journey in Africa. Working his way up the Ruvuma, and mentally plagued by the many signs of the slave trade, dead slaves, abandoned sick slaves, and slave sticks strewn along his path, he reached the district of Mataka, an influential chief on the watershed between the coast and Lake Nyasa. Here, *mirabile dictu*, the natives had turned on Arab slavers, forcing them to seek shelter across the Lake. Would that this sort of thing happened more often in Africa! But momentary rejoicing over this turning of the tables on the Arabs was soon superseded by the sight of the ravages of the Mazitu (or *Mavitu* and *Maviti*, as variously termed). A country 100 miles broad had been depopulated by them, and a 'woeful system flourished three hundred miles of the coast'.[66]

Rounding the southern end of Lake Nyasa, Livingstone headed northwestwards, to the southern end of Lake Tanganyika. On the shores of Lake Nyasa, coast Arabs had set up depots of ammunition and calico to trade for slaves. Marauding parties of Yao under native or Arab leaders attacked Wyanyassa' villages, and enslaved their inhabitants. Those who escaped these raids usually died of starvation. It was a story similar to that in the Shire valley. Concerned lest he be thought to exaggerate, Livingstone reminded Lord Clarendon, 'I beg your Lordship to remember, wherever my statements have been tested on the spot, they have been found within not beyond the truth. Even the grand Victoria Falls were put down at less than half their size.'[67]

During this expedition Livingstone found himself in the anomalous position, owing to his bad health and dire need for food, of being succoured by those whose trade he loathed. The Arabs treated him kindly, with courtesy and dignified beneficence. As for the African chiefs, when Livingstone expostulated with them for selling their own people, there were 'uneasy excuses' . . .

> If so and so gives up selling, so will we. He is the greatest offender in the country . . . It is the fault of the Arabs who tempt us with fine cloths, powder, and guns . . . I would like to keep all my people to cultivate but my next neighbour allows his people to kidnap mine . . . I must have ammunition to defend them.[68]

In December 1866, Livingstone again crossed the path of the Mazitu.[69] Their 'customary marauding propensities' were again revealed, in that the country had been swept clean of provisions and cattle, and its people had emigrated 'beyond the bounds of those ferocious plunderers'. Moving northwards, Livingstone, by the time he reached Ujiji on the east side of Lake Tanganyika, was wearied in body, 'a ruckle of bones'; foot-slogging was a chore, and he was depressed in mind. Although he had left behind him the Nyasa area and the appalling scenes of slavery witnessed there, he was still to witness, in July 1871, 'the most terrible scene I ever saw', the onslaught of the Arab slavers on the market place at Nyangwe, to the west of Lake Tanganyika.

Few observers were to succeed Livingstone in the Nyasa area, and none quite so able to describe the horrors of the slave trade as he, despite his brief and roving consulship there. British official contact with the area was practically non-existent. Lyons McLeod, appointed British consul in 1857, to reside at Mozambique, who was to enlist Portuguese assistance in suppressing the slave trade, was a tactless man. The Portuguese were opposed to his presence, and he 'struck his flag' after little more than a year there.[70] Following his departure, Britain had no official contact with the territory for fifteen years. A motion carried in the House of Lords in 1866, to appoint a consul for Mozambique and Madagascar, was never acted on. But the recommendations of the Select Committee on the East African Slave Trade, 1870/71, supported by the Political Agent and Vice-Consul at Zanzibar, resulted in the latter himself, Captain Elton, being appointed British official representative on the Portuguese East African coast.

Elton was an able, lively man, tactful and on good terms with the Governor-General of Mozambique. He was also familiar with the slave traffic on the northern section of the east African coast from his experience at Zanzibar. He now became 'a zealous collector of information on that trade on the Portuguese East African coast. Evidence of the traffic was everywhere; in the stockaded forts, *Aringas*, of slavers such as Morães and Bongo, on the Zambezi, from which rapacious bands of armed slavers sallied out to obtain their catch of slaves; women and children, in gangs of 100 at a time, were brought down the Shire, and then to Quelimane; a slave trade was carried on with Madagascar; and there was a movement of slaves along the coast. Large launches, manned by Portuguese officers, kept up communication between Inhambane, Bazaruto, Sofala, Angoche and Mozambique, and there was a constant, secret conniving at the slave trade.

All this Elton reported, and, as a result of his urging, British cruisers were directed to the Mozambique Channel. During Elton's consulship there was something like real activity on the part of the Portuguese. Their gun boats patrolled the coast; Arab dhows were burnt in the Umfussi and Kirolane delta; Africans, inspired by this unwonted demonstration on the part of the Portuguese, took their cue from them, and destroyed an Arab slave dhow, and became so aggressive that Arab slavers were unwilling to face this unexpected display of resistance.

But this short-lived demonstration of fervour for the anti-slave trade cause relaxed after Elton's death while on a journey to the northern end of Lake Nyasa, in 1877. His journals, published posthumously, provide much information on the slave trade in Portuguese East Africa. There were good and bad Portuguese officials, much mismanagement on the part of the government in Lisbon, pretence at full control, and a refusal to admit the existence of a slave trade in their East African colony. It was difficult to whip up enthusiasm for an anti-slave trade crusade among the Portuguese. There were no influential, well-connected humanitarians, no enlightened anti-slave trade societies to spur on Portuguese officials. Elton, after much pondering, was of the view that only a concerted British attack on the slave trade at its source could end it. But as to how this attack should be implemented, he had little to offer apart from the suggestion that a British commissioner should be appointed to the Nyasa area to work against Arab slave trade influence there, and to attach native chiefs to a policy of legitimate trade and progress. This suggestion was also supported by Elton's successor, Lieutenant H. O. O'Neil.[71]

O'Neil had a less successful rapport with the Portuguese than Elton, but he was assiduous in collecting information on the slave trade. He visited the coast between the town of Mozambique and Cape Delgado, and discovered the hideouts of slave dealers and native chiefs who connived with them. And at points on the Angoche river and Bay of Tungi, Indians, British subjects from Zanzibar, were financing the trade. O'Neil also learned that the inhabitants in many places along this coast had never seen a Portuguese official. He noted that along the coastal strip between Cape Delgado and the Lurio river there was increasing plantation cultivation for the development of oil seed; small estates, 50 to 100 acres, were being turned to this use, and large numbers of slaves were required. The lot of these slaves was not a hard one; they had their own plots to cultivate, and they were under easy surveillance. So much so that there was a constant drift away from these plantations; in the eighteen months prior to July 1880, over 500 had escaped from the Kissanja area. Constant replenishment was thus necessary.

O'Neil's reports on the slave trade were coming in at an auspicious time. The abolition decree of 1878 had just come into effect, and along with the recent Hova Emancipation Edict in Madagascar, it brought about a noticeable falling off in exports of slaves across the

Mozambique Channel. The Portuguese king had recently expressed perturbation over reported atrocities by slave dealers in Portuguese East Africa, and when Lord Salisbury, British Foreign Secretary, made a plea in March and July 1879 for Anglo-Portuguese cooperation against the slave trade,[72] the Portuguese responded favourably. They were now freed from a recent Zulu war, and the need to keep watch in Delagoa Bay. The Governor-General and the Portuguese officials (despite their pay being nine months in arrears) were surprisingly enthusiastic in the anti-slave trade cause.[73] At long last they appeared to be alive to the scandal of an export of thousands of slaves annually from the territory they were administering.[74] Portuguese gunboats were now directed to search out hitherto undisclosed barracoons, and during July 1880 they launched an attack against the slave dealers in the Umfussi-Kivolani district.

Despite these fine augurs of a new approach by the Portuguese towards the slave trade along the coast of their territory, inland a different state of affairs prevailed, for the densely populated Nyasa area, including both sides of the Lake, the Shire and Mlanje country, had become a great catchment basin from which slaves could be tapped at will. Tribal movements earlier in the century and far to the south in the African continent had contributed to this state of affairs. The violent energies and superior military tactics developed by the great Zulu king, Shaka, in the 1820s, had set in motion a northward migration of the Nguni peoples. One group crossed the Zambezi river in 1835, made its way up the western side of Lake Nyasa, and pushed through the gateway between Lakes Nyasa and Tanganyika, almost as far as Lake Victoria, until its thrust was blunted by the powerful Unyamwezi ruler, Mirambo. Another offshoot, the Matabele, under Mzilikazi settled in what is now Rhodesia. To the east, wedged in between the Matabele and the Sabi river, and also affected by these powerful reverberations, were the Mashona.

In the 1850s and 1860s, the Yao, from the Ruvuma river area, settled along the northern and eastern side of the Lake, and in the highlands of the upper Shire, and added a new dimension to the turbulence. The Yao were slavers of old; their own social system was riddled with domestic slavery. From previous contact with the Arabs on the Ruvuma river, they closely emulated the latter 'in all things innocent and evil', wore Arab clothes, lived in Arab-type habitations, and set themselves up almost as partners with the Arabs in the business of slaving. They attained a dominance over surrounding tribes, meted out brutal punishment to all who opposed them, and exploited the displacement of the peoples in the Nyasa basin. The latter, defenceless in the face of the warlike tactics and superior weapons of the Yao, their villages and food supplies destroyed, and cut off from escape, were enslaved wholesale. The name 'Yao' recurs all too frequently at the coast and in Zanzibar, when slaves were interrogated as to the circumstances of their original enslavement.[75]

Similarly the Bemba, originally from the Congo area, and occupying the great plateau of what is now north-eastern Zambia, raided the Mwamba and Senga to the east and north of Lake Nyasa, and played a part in this general displacement of peoples, forcing them to crowd down into the Nyasa basin. And when to the movements of Yao, Bemba, and Nguni, in exerting a containing pressure on the lake people, with Chewa and Tongo on the west, and Nyanja (or Manganja) in the south, there was added the ravages of the Arab slavers, the victims were caught in an intolerable dilemma. They suffered grievously.

It has been asserted that the Arabs followed Livingstone in his journeyings, and traded on his good name, but Livingstone found Arab slavers already in residence on Lake Nyasa when he arrived there. They had pushed up from the Ruvuma river to Lake Nyasa by the mid-century.[76] After enslaving the peoples on the east side of the lake, they crossed over to its western shore and established themselves under a coast Arab, Jumbe, who was nominally the representative of the Sultan of Zanzibar, but who refused in any way to be controlled by him. Captain R. R. Patterson of the 1st Royal Lanark Militia, on special mission to the Matabele country in the early 1880s, noted extensive slave raiding on the upper Zambezi. Bands of slaves were driven coastwards in chains, and attempts to escape were punished by cutting off the ears and depriving the men of their manhood. And all done under the flag of a European nation! In the Shire country where the Portuguese sold guns and powder, Patterson observed those rapacious 'dogs of war', and their mentors, the Arabs, who were capturing young girls near Blantyre. From their bases on the lake shore the Arabs directed their slave forays, stirred up native wars, distributed firearms, and corrupted native chiefs with presents of cheap calico and trade goods, receiving slaves in return. Looting, kidnapping and famine were consequent on these depredations.

During the 1880s, the Arabs, led by half-castes Mlozi, Kopa kopa and Msalema, practically controlled the west side of the Lake, and operated from there what was practically a shuttle service across it. They had at least twelve slave dhows on the northern half of the Lake, and at its southern end, a Baluchi, Kabunda, a notorious slaver, had five dhows and 500 armed men engaged in sweeping the shores in search of slaves. From their stockaded villages, extending from Kota Kota up to the Lakes Company trading station at Karonga, with slave routes extending along the lake shore and into the interior, a veritable spider's web had been laid to entrap their victims.

Livingstone and Rigby anticipated that the entry of missionaries, the beginning of steam navigation on Lake Nyasa and the resulting commerce would bring the slave trade to an end there. They were over-optimistic. It was some years before the Free Church Mission, at Bandawe on the western shore of Lake Nyasa, had a moderating effect on Ngoni slavers; and officials of the African lakes Company at Karonga, in 1884, were beleaguered by slavers, and forced to take refuge at the north of the Lake. The British received small support from the Portuguese in checking the slave trade in the interior. The presence of the British Christian missions and the African Lakes Company in Nyasaland was seen by the Portuguese as an attempt to usurp the 'hinterland'. And when Captain C. E. Foot, RN, was appointed in 1883 as British consul for 'the territories of the African Kings and Chiefs in the districts adjacent to Lake Nyasa', they were confirmed in their suspicions.

Foot died within a year of taking up his post. His successor, A. G. S. Hawes, who arrived in 1885, sent an armed force against Yao slavers in the Shire highlands, but soon realized that the challenge he faced required far more military strength than he possessed. What were needed were armed steamers on the Lake, and a planned strategy on a grand scale to oust the Arabs. For throughout East/Central Africa the years 1887-90 were witnessing a period of Arab resurgence, encouraged by large imports of arms and powder, in a last bid to withstand European encroachment. Possibly stirred up by the harshness of German rule, an attempt was being made to repel Europeans once and for all from the domain long considered to be an Arab preserve. Hawes' brief three years of consulship were depressing. The home government did not appear to take his reports seriously, nor even to care about the extent of Arab slaving in the Nyasa area. It was difficult to convince the outside world that Lake Nyasa was a miniature of the Indian Ocean world as far as slave trading was concerned.

John Buchanan, who succeeded Hawes, was thrown into the

maelstrom unprepared. He was surprised to find that 'caravan after caravan of slaves passed down from Nyasaland by the Mlanje and Matapwiri route',[77] and that slaves were ferried in unceasing procession across to Chitesis, on the eastern side of the Lake, and taken along the slave routes from Kota-Kota and Mpenda's to the southern end of the Lake, whence they passed to the coast. Buchanan observed that Zanzibar slavers who had come inland by way of Kilwa were no longer returning that way; German vigilance was forcing them to return to exit ports on the northern stretch of the Portuguese coast. Buchanan, throughout his short career, appears to have been nonplussed at the extent of the slave trade in the Nyasa area and to have made no contribution towards ending it. The first concerted effort to crush the slavers was made by Captain F. D. Lugard, who took over the forces of the African Lakes Company in May 1888.

Lugard had seen much evidence of the slave trade. On the Kakwa river he met a large barge of slaves, he had witnessed the devastation around Lake Shirwa where the few remaining inhabitants had crowded on to a small island, and there were well-beaten paths with 'semaphore like signs' of the progress of the slave trade. Lugard was not given to wholesale condemnation of the Portuguese as was Professor Drummond, who, writing about the same time, had stated that 'They had done nothing for the people since the day they set foot in Africa', but he had few illusions as to their probity in the matter of the slave trade. Portuguese authorities at the coast had attempted to prevent ammunition reaching him at Karonga and he had constantly run into that 'worst of European productions: the Portuguese half-caste'.

The worst devastation was witnessed at the northwest corner of Lake Nyasa. The Nkonde, a prosperous people inhabiting a beautiful and fertile country, and with a high degree of art and craft work, (their finely wrought and many-patterned spear heads were famous), had recently been the victims of the Ngoni. The Nkonde valley, a stretch of country 24 miles long, and previously a garden of fertility and flourishing villages, was now a 'Jungle of dense grass and blackened ruins'. The Ngoni were

> The terror and curse of all this country. Swooping down by night in their fantastic garb of war, with unearthly yells, grunts and groans with which they accompanied their attack, they fell upon villages and looted everything. When the dread cry was raised that the Angoni were coming, a blind panic seized the helpless villagers; each thought only of flight and concealment unless, as more often

happened, the surprise was complete by night, and there was no time for escape.[78]

And now, when Lugard entered the scene, the Arabs had joined in the pillage of the Nkonde. Mlozi and his followers had destroyed what remained of their villages, and the inhabitants had been driven into hiding in caves in the more inaccessible parts of the mountains; they were too frightened to return to their cultivation. The woes of the Nkonde were not complete, for they were soon to suffer grievous losses from cattle plague in the 1890s. And to mark their demise, as it were, Mlozi arrogantly proclaimed himself 'Sultan' of Nkonde, and demanded tribute from the African Lakes Company of Karonga. And its officials, in the face of Arab attack, were forced to withdraw to the north end of the Lake. The Arabs held the field, and this was the position when Lugard arrived.

Lugard's first task, however, to which he set himself in May 1888, was to lay seige to the immensely strong fortress of the Arab chief, Kopa Kopa, near Karongo, which commanded the road to Tanganyika. The first attempt to dislodge the slavers from their formidable stockade, with its towering walls and protecting embankments, was unsuccessful, and in the attack Lugard was seriously wounded. During the long delay while he was convalescing and waiting for the arrival of a seige cannon from South Africa, Lugard made an unsuccessful attempt to drive the Arab slavers off the Lake. The failure of an envoy from the Sultan of Zanzibar to wean the Arabs from their pursuits (they claimed the so-called envoy was a 'mere Swahili' of inferior standing), and the failure of the cannon when it finally arrived in January 1889 to breach the stockade resulted in Lugard leaving for England to seek additional support in ousting the Arabs. With his departure, they were left apparently as strongly entrenched as ever.

It was left to Harry Johnston, who suceeded O'Neil as consul at Mozambique in the autumn of 1889, to see out the last phase in the assault against the Arab slavers in the Nyasa area.[79] Although caught up in Cecil Rhodes' grand plan of an all-British Cape-to-Cairo strip, and in frustrating Portuguese extension into the Nyasa and Shire country, he was inevitably drawn into the campaign against the slavers. Following the signing of an Anglo-Portuguese convention in August 1890 and June 1891, and the Anglo-German Agreement of July 1890, the demarcation of the British sphere of influence in the Nyasa area left Britain's role in carrying out an anti-slave trade campaign there clearly defined. Johnston was soon aware that a treaty of peace which he had concluded with Mlozi in the

THE SLAVE TRADE IN THE INTERIOR

autumn of 1889 meant little to the latter. And when, in February 1891, Johnston was appointed 'Her Majesty's Commissioner and Consul General to the Territories under British influence to the north of the Zambezi', he was directed, as his first task, 'to suppress the Slave Trade by every legitimate means' in his power.

Johnston was faced with a resurgence of the slave trade because the gradual extension of German rule into the interior of their sphere of influence and the stern treatment they meted out to slavers were driving the latter south into the Nyasa area. Johnston, however, could not move against the Arabs at the north of the Lake until he had cleaned up the slavers' nests to the immediate south of the Lake. Yao slavers raided along the east bank of the Shire, and prowled 'round the very precincts' of the British Residency at Zomba. The great mountain massif of Mlanje, east of the Shire, was the site of an active slave trade carried on by a chief, Chikumbu. Captive slaves from the Mlanje area were driven through a deep gap between the hill Mwananyani and the detached cone of 'Machesa, and thence to Quelimane at the coast. In late 1891, Johnston and Captain Cecil Macguire, with a small force of Sikhs and native recruits, moved against the slave dealers on the Shire and at southern points on the Lake.

Stockades were destroyed, slave sticks burnt, and the numerous victims freed. Macguire, in order to 'lesson' the slavers, placed on their own necks the slave sticks taken from their victims, but he soon relented, for he could not bear the sight of their fetterment, and out of sympathy he removed the slave sticks. The slavers immediately escaped. Macguire's death in December 1891 marked the loss of a redoubtable, if too chivalrous, opponent of the slave trade.[80] In the same year, Johnston planned his move against Kota Kota, where Jumbe, despite a treaty with Johnston and an annual subsidy of £300, still connived at the slave trade. He had around him turbulent underlings, Arabs and Yaos, committed to slaving. It was not until 1895 that all Arab stockades on both sides of the southern portion of Lake Nyasa were destroyed. But already Johnston had moved to clear the northern portion of the Lake of the Arab slavers, who were making a last bid to preserve it as the scene of their slave trading interests. In the early 1890s they were farming it intensely for slaves. Dr Cross, of the Free Church Mission, had reported in late 1892, 'Slave-dealing Arabs are predominant all over the country . . . there never was a time in the history of the lake, when so many guns and so much powder were in circulation'.[81]

Cargoes of guns and powder were run across the Lake to Deep

Bay, and from here a steady stream of slaves left the Nyasa region, and caravans headed for the coast. The Ngoni kept the country to the northwest of the Lake in a state of upheaval, and added the finishing touch to the horrors of slaving perpetrated by the Arabs. An account of an Ngoni raid is given by a member of a garrison of the African Lakes Company stationed at Karonga in November 1892.

> Last Friday night, 18th November, the Angoni came down to the Lake in great numbers, and attacked the village of Kayuni. They entered the village silently, and each warrior took up his position at the door of a hut, and ordered the inmates to come forth. Every man and boy was speared as he emerged and every woman captured. News of this disaster soon reached the three white men stationed at Karonga's in the employ of the Lakes Company. One of their number set out immediately with fifty guns to recapture the women, who, to the number of 200 or 300 were being carried off. In the afternoon they met the Angoni and opened fire. Taken by surprise, the raiders made off, but, not being able to carry both the booty and the women, they began immediately to spear the latter. A horrible scene then ensued. In half an hour they were beaten off and the women rescued. I was at the scene of the disaster three days after, and counted forty-seven wounded. The others had either died or been carried off by friends. One man had fifteen spear-wounds; a child of two years had seven. What impressed me most was the number of young girls and children (even on the breast) who were speared. The poor creatures were afraid to go to their village, and were living in the reeds lining the lake shore. As far as can be ascertained, the following is the list of dead: Men 29; women about 100; girls 32; boys 16; Angoni about 30.[82]

In view of the temporary rebuff of the Ngoni by the African Lakes Company, Johnson now moved against the northern Arabs. In this he was assisted by the Germans. A German expedition under Major von Wissmann, on behalf of the German Anti-Slavery Society, had launched a steamer, the *Wissmann*, on Lake Nyasa in 1892; this was now placed at Johnson's disposal and in addition to this he had an armed steamer of his own by June 1893. Captain Prager of the German Anti-Slavery expedition sent into the Nyasa area, supported by a small Sudanese detachment and a Hotchkiss gun, rallied to Johnston's support. This united front, German and British, was most salutary in its effect on the minds of Arab slavers and Africans alike.

Johnston's last efforts were directed against Mlozi, at Karonga. Mlozi openly defied the British, and his cohorts raided the Nkonde, while the Bemba were armed by the Arabs and encouraged to extend their slaving operations to the northwest of the Lake, and pass on the fruits of these raids to the Arabs. The end came quickly, when on 3 December 1895 Johnston stormed Mlozi's stronghold. It was successfully scaled and captured and Mlozi was taken prisoner. On 4 December 1895, amid Nkonde chiefs and nearly 600 slaves freed from his stockade, this archetype of slavers, Mlozi the Arab half-breed, was hanged. And on 24 January 1896, Johnston informed Lord Salisbury that, as far as he was aware, 'there does not exist a single avowedly slave-trading chief within the British Central Africa Protectorate, nor any one who is known to be inimical to British rule'.[83]

Despite Johnston's complacent statement, there was much mopping up of slavers still to be undertaken. It took the combined efforts of British and German forces to check the Bemba, prime collaborators with the Arabs, in their attempts to enslave the Sengo. And Arab stockades in the north Nyasa district had still to be destroyed, expeditions carried out against slave dealers in the Mzimba country to the immediate west of Kota Kota, and Yao robber chiefs driven out of central Ngoniland district. In 1896 and 1897, punitive expeditions were carried out against the Ngoni in the southwest of the protectorate, and Fort Manning erected to guard these approaches. A strong fort, constructed in 1895 on the site of the town of the former slave dealer, Zarafi, on Mangoche mountain, guarded the eastern approaches.

Constant slave raiding in the Nyasa area had left the territory depopulated by the end of the nineteenth century. The encouragement of native settlements, the issue of certificates of claims to land and approved freehold titles, and later large scale immigration from Portuguese East Africa tended to make good the earlier loss of population. Yao slave raiding chiefs, who had fought against the government in the early days, lived on into the twentieth century. Two of them, Nyasera and Namwanda, died only a short time before 1908, Matipwiri and Chikumbo still lived in the Tuchila valley in 1908, but now loyally assisted the district government and appeared to have quite forgotten their earlier slave raiding proclivities, while Tambala, the tough old Yao slave raider of Central Ngoniland, who finally surrendered in 1908, was pardoned and re-instated in an honourable position by the British.[84]

9
The Last Phase of the Anti-Slave Trade Campaign

I. AT INTERNATIONAL LEVEL

It was well into the late nineteenth century before the problems of the East African slave trade were grappled with at an international level. Attempts by the Anti-Slavery Society to raise the question at the Conference in Constantinople in 1876-7, and to bring a motion before the House of Commons in 1878, seeking a declaration from the Berlin Conference of that year to outlaw any nation condoning slavery within its boundaries (a direct reference to Turkey), were set aside as extraneous to the business of these Conferences.

More successful were the Society's efforts to bring the matter before the West African (Berlin) Conference, 1884-5. A memorial to Prince Bismarck who hosted the Conference, and pressure on Lord Granville by the Society, resulted in a declaration from the Conference which, in Article 9 of its General Act, adjured powers exercising sovereign rights in the Congo basin to prohibit the slave trade in the territories under their control, and employ 'all means' to bring it to an end. Although weakened by the exemption of the Sultan of Zanzibar's dominions from the meaning of the Declaration—for he had specifically exempted them fearing that free trade in the Congo basin, as decreed by the Conference, would adversely affect his revenue—nevertheless, the Declaration was an important gain for the abolitionists.

And it was timely. Africa was now opening up under European influence and administration. A rash of reports from officials, travellers and missionaries was at hand, and there was dire news of the barbarism in the Sudan, under the rule of the Mahdi and his successor. There was sharpened need for action against the slave trade. The vigilance of British cruisers, and the occasional presence of ships-of-war of other nations, availed little against the increasing resort to the French flag as cover for running slaves. Penalties for slavers when caught were derisive, and far too mild. The culprits suffered more in pocket than in person. A captured slave dhow might be confiscated and her slaves freed. But her captain and crew were usually landed at the nearest point on the coast, or set aboard a passing dhow, and left free to recommence their nefarious work. There was also a new problem facing the abolitionists in the great demand for porters for large caravans going into the interior. About 20,000 porters monthly were estimated to leave the coast for the interior in the late 1880s and early 1890s. Slave owners found it a profitable business to hire out their slaves as porters to these caravans. A slave himself might take the initiative, often without indicating his slave status to his new employer, the caravan leader. During the slave's absence in the interior, often a year or more, his wife, children and plot of ground were looked after by his master. The slave received a quarter of his earnings, the master the remainder. A half of the master's share was paid at the time the bargain was struck, and the remainder on the return of the slave from the interior. This arrangement might be made with the master directly, or through an agent. With the money thus received, the master purchased fresh slaves, and hired these out in turn. It was a profitable and easy business, appealing to the languid Arab slave owner. Willoughby, at Zanzibar in the late 1880s, witnessed this hiring out.

> Many of these big fellows were led up by tiny Arab boys, who claimed them as slaves, and who promptly annexed half their wages as soon as they were paid.[1]

Often unwittingly, European explorers and inland Missions were employers of slave labour. Three-quarters of Stanley's 680 porters on his 1888-9 expedition were slaves, the Uganda Railway survey party consisted largely of slave porters, Sir Gerald Portal's mission to Uganda in 1893 employed slaves as porters, and Horace Waller remarked that if one wished to see well-beaten slave routes one had only to look at the British East Africa Company's caravan routes—the Company had over 1300 Zanzibar porters (mostly slaves) in its employ. Vessels on the anti-slave trade patrol were coaled at Zanzibar by slave labour, and a German steamer, transporting so-called labourers to the Congo in 1892, and stopped outside Zanzibar harbour by a British cruiser, was found to be carrying slaves.

This hiring out of slaves as porters brought for them a new experience, far beyond what their meagre earnings would indicate. European caravan leaders often made no distinction, or were aware of none, between free and slave labour, treating both as of equal status. A slave porter might be raised to the position of head porter, and given responsible duties entailing extra trust and dignity. European attitudes towards the slave trade and slavery had a salutary effect on slave porters. Hitherto dominated by the idea that slavery was his natural state, an attitude instilled into him by his Arab master, the slave porter under a European caravan leader, after participating in or witnessing the freeing of slaves from a slave caravan, would never again see slavery in quite the same light.

The Sultan's proclamation of 9 December 1888, forbidding the practice of hiring out of slaves (it was made on the advice of the British consul, and was meant to halt the drain of labour from Zanzibar), had little effect until registration and control over porterage was affected by government regulations in the later 1890s. Caravans now going inland were increasingly under the auspices of European firms, such as Boustead, Ridley and Company, and Smith, Mackenzie and Company, who contracted to supply stores for the new government administration. Regulations for the Treatment of Porters, 1895 and 1899, and the appointment of an Inspector of Caravans[2] made the lot of the porters easier, and prevented what had long been known, that raw slaves were often included among the so-called porters returning with caravans from the interior.

In this last phase of the campaign against the slave trade in East Africa, the abolitionists found their standard-bearer in Cardinal Lavigérie, the great French ecclesiastic and ardent anti-slave trade spokesman. He played a part similar to that of Livingstone in the 1860s. Lavigérie's humanity and range of conception cut across narrow sectarian views, despite a bitter feud at the time between Catholics and Protestants in Uganda.[3]

Stirred by letters from Catholic missionaries at Ujiji and Karema on the east side of Lake Tanganyika, describing the atrocities of the slave traders at those places, and the flood-like proportions of the slave trade in the interior, Cardinal Lavigérie undertook a campaign in Europe to awaken public feeling against the slave trade in East Africa. Between 1888 and 1890 he toured a number of European cities, including London, making stirring addresses on behalf of anti-slave trade societies. His talk of ringing the Sahara with 'Armed Brethern', 're-incarnating the spirit of Old Testament Judaism', who would divide their life between prayer, work, and bearing arms, and would only 'pull the trigger or draw a sabre' to repulse attack, his launching of anti-slavery societies in France, and the generous gift of a large sum of money to the Anti-Slavery Society in Britain, made the hearts of the abolitionists vibrate. To Lavigérie largely goes the credit for the convening of the Anti-Slavery Conference at Brussels in 1890.

At a meeting in London on 31 July 1888, held under the auspices of the Anti-Slavery Society, presided over by Lord Granville, and attended by important figures, including Cardinal Manning, Lavigérie directed attention to East/Central Africa, 'the high plateaux of the interior—invaded by slavers from Egypt and Zanzibar'. Quoting letters from missionaries in the Lake Tanganyika region, he dwelt on the horrors of the slave trade, and made an inspiring appeal for a crusade against it. On a motion from Cardinal Manning, the meeting passed a resolution that a conference of the Powers should be convened to seek measures to secure 'the abolition of the fearful slave trade.' The Marquess of Salisbury, to whom the resolution was forwarded, lost no time in contacting Lord Vivian, British Ambassador at Brussels, to see if Léopold, King of the Belgians, would convene an Anti-Slavery Conference in his capital.

His Majesty was willing to do so, and the necessary invitations were sent out. Meanwhile Mr Sidney Buxton had brought the Resolution before the House of Commons. An important debate followed, occupying the whole evening sitting of 26 March 1889, the like of which had not been heard in the House since 30 June 1871, when Mr Charles Gilpin, on behalf of the Anti-Slavery Society, obtained from the Government the appointment of the Select Committee which had resulted in Sir Bartle Frere's Mission to East Africa. The ensuing Resolution of the House on 26 March 1889 supported the motion for a Conference of the Powers for the purpose of devising measures for the suppression of the slave trade.

In the summer of 1889, serious discussion also took place between the India Office and the Foreign Office on an all-out campaign against the slave trade in Persian Gulf waters. But it was soon realized that little could be done to prevent slavers leaving Oman for Zanzibar, for there was no way of identifying them as such; their fittings gave no clue to their business. The problem must be tackled at the African end.

Thus the problem of suppressing the slave trade shifted to East Africa. The Germans in their territory, by their tactlessness, had shaken the Sultan's authority, and it was to this that Kirk attributed native unrest and the increase in enslavement of the late 1880s and '90s. When General Mathews, in the Sultan's employ, attempted to intercept the coastwise slave trade, the Germans misrepresented this as a political move to contest German claims to the interior. The Germans were soon faced with armed revolt in their territory. A joint Anglo-German blockade of the coast instituted in November 1888, ostensibly against the slave trade, had as its main object the halting of the flow of arms to the rebels challenging German rule.[4] But the blockade imposed a serious strain on German resources, and so seriously affected the health of German sailors not inured to the tropics that within a year the German sought to end it. But German prestige must not suffer in the process.

A way out was soon found. In August 1889, during the Kaiser's visit to England, an understanding was arrived at whereby Germany promised to lift the blockade, so injurious to the Sultan of Zanzibar's commerce, if he in turn would take steps to halt the slave traffic in his dominions. The time was auspicious for such a move. The Sultan had recently prohibited the sale of slaves related by family ties,[5] and agreed, 'in secret engagements' with the British consul at Zanzibar, to the right of search over the vessels of his subjects, in his territorial waters; Kirk, the Germanophobe, was no longer at Zanzibar, and Sir Gerald Portal, acting-Consul, favoured a 'striking measure' to soothe German feelings irritated over the 'Lamu Award'. Thus a magnanimous German gesture would be passed on to the Sultan through a friendly British intermediary.

The blockade was ended on 1 October 1889, and Sultan Khalifa concluded an agreement with the British whereby all slaves brought into his dominions after 1 November 1889, and all children born in his dominions after 1 January 1890, would be freed. Although the Sultan's proclamation embodying these provisons was largely ignored by his subjects, it was a timely achievement in view of what was at hand.

The Conference which assembled at Brussels on 18 November 1889, in response to Léopold of the Belgians' invitation, was to concert measures for

> the gradual suppression of the slave trade on the continent of Africa, and the immediate closing of all the external markets which it still supplied.

The Anti-Slavery Society sent a deputation to it, and provided a large map of Africa, on which were shown slave routes, together with a large slave yoke from Central Africa, which was forwarded to the President of the Conference, Baron Lambermont. Its exhibition occasioned much surprise; many delegates were unaware of the use of these instruments of torture. On 2 July 1890, a general act was signed by delegates to the Conference, subject to the ratification of the various governments represented, and, in the case of France, with certain reservations.

While the Berlin Act of 1885 dealt with the coastlands under the suzerainty of European powers, and laid down rules for the effective occupation of the interior, the Brussels Act of 1890 dealt with the obligations incurred by the Powers who had acquired possessions in the interior between 1885 and 1890. Seventeen Powers, including the USA, took part in the Conference's deliberations. The Conference struck a high moral note, and enjoined signatories to safeguard the welfare of the peoples of Africa by putting an end to the crimes and devastations of the slave traffic, thus ensuring for that vast continent the benefits of peace and civilization.

The Powers signatory to the Act undertook to carry out its provisions; they might delegate these engagements to chartered companies, but they remained nevertheless responsible. They bound themselves to establish strongly occupied stations in the interior, to check slave hunting and to construct roads, and particularly railways, to permit easy access to the interior. The General Act established a zone across Africa between the 20th parallel of north latitude and the 22nd parallel of south latitude, within which the importation of firearms and ammunition was forbidden, apart from those for administrative needs and the import of flint-locks with unrifled barrels. It also prohibited the importation and manufacture of spirituous liquors. (This latter provision pertained more to the west coast, for traffic in liquor was never a serious problem on the east coast, where Muslim influence precluded the use of alcohol).

The Act provided for systematic measures to prevent the transit of slaves by sea. There was to be a mutual right of visit and search within a limited zone off the coast of Africa, except for vessels flying the French flag, and a slave seeking refuge on a man-of-war of the signatory powers was automatically freed.[6] There should be homes for freed slaves. An international slavery bureau was to be established at Brussels, with a branch at Zanzibar.[7] The Act was not effectively ratified and in force until April 1892. Along with the Berlin Act of February 1885, it was abrogated (with the exception of Article I) by the Convention of St Germain in September 1919.

The Brussels General Act was most timely in coming shortly after the Anglo-German agreement of July 1890, which had placed the Sultan of Zanzibar in a defenceless position. So long as Zanzibar was an independent Mahommedan state, and slavery was recognized as a legal institution under Mahommedan law, Britain could only check it by exerting pressure on the Sultan, a difficult and slow process. But the assumption of a British protectorate over Zanzibar, which followed the Anglo-German agreement of 1890, forced the Sultan to face up to the abolition of the slave traffic. On 1 August 1890, Ali bin Said signed an Anti-Slavery decree prohibiting the exchange, sale or purchase of slaves, and limiting the rights of inheritance and ownership.

The decree took his subjects entirely by surprise. Despite the angry response of the Arabs, who claimed they would rather die than submit to the enactment, and their threat to abandon Zanzibar, the decree was received without major incident. The decree did not touch the institution of slavery itself. This would gradually disappear, it was hoped, since natural increase would be insufficient to maintain the slave numbers, and many clauses of the decree, ameliorating the harsher aspects of slavery, were designed to bring about its gradual end. The decree declared the immediate closing of houses of slave brokers. Slaves were to be inherited at the death of their owner only by the lawful children of the deceased. If there were no heirs, the slaves became *ipso facto* free. Owners habitually ill-treating slaves were to be punished, and in flagrant cases of cruelty slaves would be forfeited. Slaves were given the right to bring complaints before the Qadi. There was a clause prohibiting British Indians from keeping slaves in the names of their Arab or Swahili wives, a practice which had been increasing since the 1873 decree. Every slave was entitled to purchase his freedom at a just and reasonable tariff, to be fixed by the Sultan's authorities.

The Anti-Slavery edict of 1 August 1890, if fully implemented, would have effected a substantial and immediate improvement in the position of slaves, and in course of time would have brought about the disappearance of domestic slavery without prejudice to the vested rights of owners. But a proclamation by the Sultan on 20 August 1890 annulled some of its most important clauses.

> If any slave runs away from his master, or does anything wrong, punish him as before. If any slave does great wrong, kills anyone, or steals, send him to the Liwali who will punish him. You will see it and be pleased. If any slave brings money to the Qadi to purchase his freedom, his master shall not be forced to take the money.

Henceforth no court could compel a master to manumit his slave unless it was shown that the slave was ill-treated. The Sultan's proclamation of 20 August 1890 removed the possibility of self-redemption or otherwise for all slaves in his dominions. This supplementary proclamation of 20 August 1890 received very little publicity, although the leading Arabs in Zanzibar seemed to have been well aware of it. Two years later, the administrator of the British East Africa Company stated that he was never officially informed of it. And when Lugard, on his return from the interior in 1892, endeavoured to use the wages earned by his porters (hired slaves) to purchase their freedom, he found, to his surprise, that this supplementary decree made his gesture fruitless. It was argued that feeling in Zanzibar ran so high over the 1 August decree that the

Sultan's supplementary concession was necessary to prevent an uprising. Lugard, however, believed that if promulgation of the 1 August decree had been backed by the presence of a man-of-war there would never have been a supplementary decree of 20 August.

Unlike the edict of 1873, the enforcement of which lay with the British naval anti-slave trade patrol, the enforcement of the edict of 1890 lay with the Sultan and thus it remained largely a dead letter. A commentary on its effectiveness is that a few months later his steamer, the *Kilwa* was employed in the slave traffic.

The 1 August decree, once it had been grievously weakened by the Sultan's supplementary proclamation of 20 August, was received with great relief by the Arabs, for general emancipation had been staved off.

Turning to the implementation of the Brussels Act, which applied to the territories outside the Sultan's dominions, this required an entirely new approach to an anti-slave trade campaign. Lugard, fighting Mlozi and the Arab slavers in the Lake Nyasa area in 1888-9, had turned his mind to the problem. He was critical of the establishment of a British consulate in Nyasaland, for the consul was accredited to no local authority, had no legal standing nor jurisdiction, and small influence at home. He was backed by no force, and, as in the case of Consul Hawes, could suffer personal humiliation at the hands of the slavers. As for the anti-slave trade patrol, it had been operating for years, but results were meagre. Supervision of the coast was expensive and fruitless. The evil must be attacked at its source. Lugard realized this, and had joined the expedition on the Nyasa because

> I felt myself to be on the path which should lead me to verify by fuller experience the theories I have already formed.

Lugard's grand scheme for the suppression of the slave trade in the interior called for a coercive force, a body of soldiers with headquarters on the plateau between the southern end of Lake Tanganyika and the northern tip of Lake Nyasa. There would be armed steamers, about 65 feet long and 30 tons in weight, of light draught, one on Lake Tanganyika, and one on Lake Nyasa, as transport and trading steamers. There would be small subsidiary garrisons at strategic points on the lakes. Communication would be maintained with headquarters by means of heliographs, the hills along the lake shores offering excellent facilities for this.[8] There would be a system of spies furnishing information on the movement of slave caravans, headquarters would direct the armed steamers to the nearest point to the spot indicated, and a well-directed attack by disciplined and armed troops by land, supported by steamers on the lake, would turn the tables.

> Any village caught *in flagrante delicto* would have its stockade levelled, and prohibited to reconstruct them, while all dhows and sea-faring canoes would be destroyed.[9]

The steamers when not engaged in transporting troops could ply a peaceful and remunerative trade. The land garrison would continue to be on the lookout for caravans marching directly by land to the coast.

Lugard would thus establish an 'impassable barrier' along the length of Lake Tanganyika, across the intervening plateau to Lake Nyasa, along that lake and down the Shire to Murchison Rapids, a total distance of over 1100 miles. With additional boats and steamers patrolling the lower Shire and the Zambezi, the cordon could be drawn practically to the sea. The naval patrol at sea would be maintained, for it tended to keep alive national enthusiasm for a noble and disinterested cause.

Lugard was so fired with this problem of suppressing slavery and the slave trade that he had

> a strong desire to throw into the fire, the mere tale of my personal travels—to abandon my intention of writing on the commercial profits of East Africa to 'slide' the story of 'adventure' and of sport, and to limit myself to this engrossing subject of the slave trade.[10]

There was little sentimentality in his approach to the abolition of the slave trade.

> So much nonsense and 'bunkum' is talked. Vivid appeals are made to imagination and to mere sentiment and horror-mongery, as though, forsooth, we must have our palates tickled by a few blood-curdling atrocities (though of these, as I and others have shown, there are plenty) and our pharisaical philanthropy quickened by pictures of agonized slaves in impossible fetters (which would anchor a man-of-war) pleading with clasped hands, before we can put our hands in our pockets and produce the coin which stamps our sympathy as sincere, or give our efforts to the advocacy of a cause, which without these embellishments of blood and thunder and clanking of chains, should appeal to mere humanity, simply because it is the cause of those who have no champion—nay, who do not even know the depths of their own degradation, because they have never experienced its contrast.[11]

How far British government policy saw the issue of slavery as part of its imperial mission is difficult to judge. There were humanitarians in the Foreign Office and in the overseas administration who were supremely well connected, and versed in the art of exercising influence, in an active and open manner, or as an unseen hand quietly determining the lines of policy and deftly adjusting the balance in favour of their own views. Their intervention and pressure on the government largely explains the attitude towards slavery and the slave trade which characterized Britain as distinct from other powers. Humanitarians were prepared to take a much stronger line than was the government against the Sultan of Zanzibar. In 1873 they would have blockaded Zanzibar, even though it would have meant an act of war. And now in 1890, Britain should take

> a strong stand worthy of a Great Power whose men-of-war were capable of sinking the whole island in an hour.

Not a few abolitionists admired the strong measures of the Germans, who hung on the spot Arabs caught red-handed in slave dealing. In the British sphere they got off lightly, with their threatened attacks on fugitive slave settlements and mission stations, their open mutiny and street riots in Mombasa. In contrast to German severity, Britain replied to these overt acts of hostility by negotiation and the ransoming of slaves.

The Imperial British East Africa Company complained that it had never been consulted in the matter of enforcing anti-slave trade decrees in the territory leased from the Sultan, and this was an eventuality it had never anticipated. Experience of the African Lakes Company and the South African Company, saddled with similar responsibilities and expense in implementing anti-slave trade laws, was fresh in their minds, and Sir Francis de Winton, Adminstrator General for the Company, protested earnestly against being forced to apply these measures. The Company did not have the means to implement them. Anti-slave trade decrees had caused a wave of hostility towards Europeans along the coast, and the Company would have to fight the Arabs at Takaungu, Gazi, Lamu and Malindi, if they endeavoured to enforce them. So little was known in Takaungu about the provisions of the decrees—so the company claimed—that, on the death of the ruling sheikh there, his successor presented his cousin with his father's fighting slaves, and this cousin, last of the fighting Mazrui, maintained a hideout in the nearby Shiba hills from which he regularly sold slaves to Pemba.

There was also difficulty for the Company in determining whether the ten-mile wide coastal strip leased by it was to be calculated from the head of creeks or estuaries, or as against the general headland. It was impossible to guard an unmarked inland frontier against incursion of slaves, and the Company could not attempt to do so. Its request for subsidies from the British government to enforce the decrees was refused.

Defects in the decrees continued to be revealed. The clause freeing all slaves on the death of their owner, except those inherited by direct lawful heirs, weighed heavily on indirect heirs, and upon old and broken-down slaves, especially women, who, when their master died without children, were thrown out penniless.[12] Their numbers sensibly increased, both at Zanzibar and along the coast. The decrees in fact did them a great disservice, for Islam looked upon the care of slaves as a responsibility continuing into their old age; it might be disregarded, but the Qadi could always invoke punishment for its violation.

The decrees were expected to end the sea traffic, but the smuggling of slaves continued, usually in small batches of twos and threes. A renewed blockade of Pemba was ineffectual, for the same reasons as had made previous blockades ineffectual. The two steam pinnaces were far too slow, with their speed of a couple of knots per hour, and an inadequate supply of fresh water for their boilers—salt water quickly clogged them. It was not until 1892 when the cruiser *Blanche* was added to the patrol, and look-outs were posted on shore, that the blockade became anything more than a paper one. But the mainland could not be watched effectively. Africans were abducted quite brazenly from points along the coast.[13]

The 1890 decree, and the edict of the Sultan of 11 September 1891, prohibiting the enlistment of slaves as soldiers, porters or coolies outside the Sultan's dominions, and the November 1893 requirement to register dhows, if fully implemented, should have effectively ended the slave trade. But the number of slaves on the clove estates increased. For many years following the great hurricane of 1872 clove production had greatly diminished; in consequence, the renewed planting of clove trees had taken place during the ten years up to 1896, and had literally converted Zanzibar and Pemba into a clove forest. Demand for labour during the clove-ripening season raised the price of a slave to 240 dollars, an all-time high, which encouraged the smuggling of slaves to Zanzibar and Pemba from the mainland.

The northern slave trade also remained vigorous. In April 1893, it was revealed that children were kidnapped in Zanzibar town. At smaller coastal villages, and in hideouts along the numerous creeks and bays of Pemba and Zanzibar, slaves were kept in hiding awaiting the arrival of a slave dhow, and then shipped north.[14] This was a smaller, diversified slave trade, but most difficult to check, and the removal of traditional bonuses for slaves captured at sea and the substitution of a special allowance for officers and men on detached boat service was heartily disliked. It reduced the ardour of the chase.

The abolitionists who looked forward to the declaration of a British protectorate over Zanzibar in 1890 as

> a step of the highest importance in obtaining the suppression of the maritime slave traffic and the extirpation of slavery itself

were disappointed that it had not accelerated the pace towards complete emancipation. A vigorous campaign in press and parliament, and country-wide protest meetings were instituted to achieve this end. In an address by the Anti-Slavery Society in August 1892 to the Foreign Secretary, Lord Rosebery, it was pointed out that wherever Britain had assumed protectorates, one of her first actions had been to abolish the legal status of slavery. This should now be done in Zanzibar.

Throughout the summer of 1893, the Anti-Slavery Society kept up its pressure.[15] Sir Rennell Rodd, acting Consul-General in Zanzibar, sympathetic to their demand for total emancipation, saw many obstacles in the way of it. Did not the Anti-Slavery Society realize that many slaves preferred to remain with their masters, and that there was a lack of administrative officials to enforce emancipation decrees? Any sudden measure for complete emancipation would be calamitous for Zanzibar's economy. Freed slaves were notoriously lazy, and were the worst characters in Zanzibar.[16] Industrial Missions, Boustead, Ridley and Company, and General Mathews could adduce much evidence in support of this. Violence would follow general emancipation, there would be increased expense from an enlarged police force to cope with it, a mass exodus from the clove estates would force Arab owners into bankruptcy, and Arabs would go over to German East Africa where slavery was still permitted and where there was no sentimental nonsense in regard to it, as now existed in the British sphere. Hardinge, who took up the post of Consul-General at Zanzibar in May 1894, not only sustained Rodd's views but gave them a strenuous boost, and added suggestions of his own.

II. THE FRENCH FLAG AND RIGHT OF SEARCH

The use or, more correctly, misuse of the French flag posed perhaps the most contentious and persistent obstacle faced by the British naval patrol in suppressing the slave trade on the East African coast in the nineteenth century. It arose from the French claim to immunity from search and capture for ships flying the French flag. France had fallen in line with most of the great powers in the general policy of prohibiting the slave trade and slavery, but would never concede the right of search, which was basic to an effective anti-slave trade patrol at sea. Her refusal was upheld in 1817 by the British jurist, Sir William Scott (later Lord Stowell), in the famous case of the French slaver *Le Louis,* when he reversed a previous judgement on the grounds that France had not entered into any convention for right of search over her vessels.

> No authority can be found, which gives any right of visitation or interruption over the vessels and navigation of other states, on the high seas, except what the right of war gives to belligerents against neutrals . . . No government could force the way to the liberation of Africa by trampling on the independence of other states in Europe . . . If this right be imported into a state of peace, it must be done by convention.

A similar decision was given by the US Supreme Court in the case of the *Antelope.*[17]

For the remainder of the nineteenth century Britain had to wrestle with this problem of the French flag. Commodore Nourse in 1824 proposed to the French authorities at Bourbon a scheme for 'reciprocal searches and detentions', but the British Admiralty did not take the suggestion seriously. The French would never 'under any circumstances' accept such an arrangement. The matter was touched on in 1826, at the time of the Commission of Enquiry into the State of the Mauritius slave trade, but it was not pressed.[18]

Conventions with France, in 1831 and 1833, conceded to Britain a limited right of search. But conditions for exercising it were so restricted, intricate and delicate that supreme restraint was necessary to avoid an international incident. The joint treaty of 1841 between the major powers of Europe, for mutual right of search, was signed by the French plenipotentiary but never ratified, owing to the Eastern Crisis and Palmerston's ill-timed criticism of the French treatment of the native population of Algeria. A deputy from Nantes, a maritime centre with an interest in the slave trade, led the opposition to the treaty in the French Chamber. The limited right of search under the 1831 and 1833 conventions was sustained by the ten-year convention of May 1845; Britain and France engaging to prohibit 'for ever' slave trading in their colonies and France agreeing to the right of visit to verify her flag.

It was evident from the latter convention that French reluctance to grant a full right of search arose from the question of prestige. French public opinion would never countenance the right of search by Britain, her traditional rival on the seas, and there was also French suspicion that British naval power was expanding behind the humanitarian guise of an anti-slave trade patrol.

French claim to immunity from search for her vessels took on special significance on the East African coast following a French treaty with Muscat, 17 November 1844, whereby France was granted extraterritorial jurisdiction and immunity from entry or visit for French domiciles in the Omani Sultanate. The French government contended that this immunity extended to all vessels flying the French flag in the territorial waters of the Sultanate, even against the authority of the Sultan himself. When in 1850 the Sultan granted to Her Majesty's vessels of war the right of seizure of vessels engaged in the slave trade in his territorial waters, France fell back on her immunity under the 1844 treaty. The Omani Arabs were quick to exploit this new situation. And by the mid-nineteenth century, the British naval patrol was faced with a new and most exasperating problem, and, in meeting it, went beyond the bounds allowed by treaty, in a manner highly prejudicial to Anglo-French relations.[19]

Following an approach to France, it was agreed in March 1859 that, although the 1845 Convention had lapsed, verification of the French flag might be carried out if there was doubt as to the true nationality of a vessel.[20] But British Admiralty instructions in 1859 urged extreme caution.

> To inquire into the nature of the cargo, or the commercial operations of the vessel, or any other fact, in short, than that of nationality of the vessel, is prohibited; every other search and inspection whatever is absolutely forbidden.[21]

This was most galling. British parties, boarding intercepted vessels, verified the flag midst the noise of Arabs endeavouring to drown the clamour of slaves below, but no right of search was admissible. The Arabs were

> well aware that under it the right of search is denied to us, and it has now become the great object of their desire to obtain a French register.[22]

And in September 1861 Rear-Admiral Walker reported

> A brisk and increasing Slave Trade with all its attendant horrors, has been for some time past carried on under the protection of the French Imperial Flag.[23]

Captain Gardner, in July 1862, ingenuously remarked that when British cruisers hoisted the French flag to see if they could get close to suspected vessels, it 'always worked'.[24] Both Livingstone and Horace Waller personally witnessed the way the French flag was used as cover by Arab slavers in the Mozambique Channel; the Arabs sneeringly challenged the British to do something about it.

The granting by the United States of the right of search to Great Britain, on 7 April 1862, gave Earl Russell the opportunity to belatedly point out to the French that

> slave-traders, driven out of the shelter they have hitherto obtained under the protection of the flag of the USA may have recourse to the French flag as a cover.[25]

In response to Russell's overtures, the French government, in 1863, instructed her consuls to keep stricter watch on the use of the French flag, and French certificates of registry were no longer to be available merely on paying a fee. French papers in future were to be granted only to Arab vessels whose proprietors were domiciled in a French colony, and who gave proper guarantees as to the legal nature of their trade. Her Majesty's Government expressed satisfaction with this step, not realizing that it left the door open to widespread abuse.

As a result of the French ruling, Arab dhow owners now fulfilled domicile requirements by acquiring small patches of land in Madagascar, Réunion, the Comoro Islands and, later, in French Somaliland, and were then granted papers to fly the French flag.[26] Playfair bitterly complained of the ease with which the French flag could be obtained. An Indian, a British subject, flew the French flag over his vessel because his wife came from the French island of Nossi Bé, and in 1864 a subject of the Sultan of Zanzibar, to escape his authority, flew the French flag to show, according to his own admission, his defiance. Numerous remonstrances from the British government in the 1860s and 1870s always drew the French reply that they were doing their best to uphold their treaty engagements in the matter of suppressing the slave trade, and that their consuls exercised exquisite discretion in granting the use of the French flag.[27] They also pointed out with relish that Mr Sunley, British Consul at Johanna in the Comoros, employed large numbers of slaves on his sugar estates. It was a telling charge not easily countered by the British reply that these slaves were hired out to Mr Sunley by Arab slave owners.

French touchiness on the subject of use of their flag brought from the British Admiralty further instructions to officers on the naval anti-slave trade patrol. They were reminded that

> There is no Treaty in force between Great Britain and France for the suppression of the Slave Trade. None of the general instructions therefore are applicable to French vessels. Your conduct therefore towards vessels hoisting French colours shall be regulated exclusively by the confidential instructions with which you have been furnished by the Admiralty.[28]

The Clarendon inquiry into the slave trade in 1869 revealed that the use of the French flag by slavers was spreading. There was a feeling on the part of the British that the French were using the loan of their flag and a differential duty of 10%, in favour of goods carried under the French flag, to expand their trade, prestige and influence in the Indian Ocean. Evidence before the Select Committee of 1870/71, showed that Arabs would no longer risk placing a dhow under the Arab flag, if the French flag were obtainable. On the high seas a dhow flying the Arab red flag was immediately suspect, and might be exposed to search half a dozen times in succession while passing up the coast from Zanzibar, and compelled to lower sails, perhaps at a critical spot between dangerous reefs. Thus even the honest Arab dhow master found it beneficial to fly under the tricolour, for it exempted him from annoyance and interference.

Captain Tucker, of HMS *Columbine,* reported that slave dhows under the Arab flag sailed in concert with those flying the French flag, and, if overhauled, would transfer their slaves to the latter. The Sultan referred to this preference for the French flag on the part of his subjects in 1870,

> most of them have taken French protection, and are now quiet and we also shall be spared their complaints of the oppression of the British government towards them.[29]

Sir Bartle Frere visiting Zanzibar in February 1873 observed that at that port, where there was scarcely any French trade, the French flag was flying over a large proportion of Zanzibar shipping, simply because under it vessels were free from search and could carry slaves unchallenged.

But from the French viewpoint one sees the question in an altogether different light. It was discussed in the French National Assembly in December 1872. France was doing her utmost to guard the use of her flag: Arabs who abused it, many of them, were subjects of the Sultan of Zanzibar. Why then did Britain not put pressure on the Sultan with whom she had a special relationship? It was astounding, in French eyes, that Britain, a country which produced a Clarkson, a Wilberforce, a Buxton, and others who brought glory upon Britain through their efforts to abolish the slave trade, should have concluded treaties with the Sultan of Zanzibar who tolerated the slave trade and slavery. This was all very much tongue in cheek! The French Minister of Marine, speaking in the Assembly, said that dhows were apprehended and handed over to the French authorities if there was a suspicion of misuse of the French flag. Nevertheless he had issued new and precise instructions for scrupulous care in the matter of use of the French flag.[30] It was, he said, all a question of from what side, French or English, one viewed the subject.

A British request to France in 1872 for periodical communication of lists of all dhows furnished with French registry was never acted upon. It would have availed little anyway in view of the ease with which papers of registration were bandied about among Arab dhow owners. Despite French claims that they exercised great care in granting their flag, once an Arab dhow was in possession of that flag they had little or no control over it. An instance of this was the capture in August 1880 of a dhow in Zanzibar harbour with 99 slaves on board; they had been embarked an hour or two after the French consul had signed papers granting the French flag. The captured vessel was duly handed over to the French consul; it was burned on the spot, and the accused were sent for trial to Réunion, but the consul then upbraided the Sultan for acting contrary to the 1844 treaty.[31] When the incident was reported to the French government, deep regret was expressed for the affair.

> The Slave Trade was utterly repugnant to the feelings of the French Government and the French nation and that it concerned the honour of France to repress vigorously such an abuse of the French flag as appeared to have occurred.[32]

But the abuse continued. Rear-Admiral Jones of the East Indies Squadron claimed that but for the French the slave trade would have ceased long before.[33] British feeling in the matter was brought to a high pitch by the savage and cowardly murder of Captain I. C. Brownrigg and four seamen from HMS *London* in December 1881, in a fight with the crew of an Arab dhow flying French colours, and boarded off Pemba for the purpose of checking her papers. A report in August 1888 from the German officer in charge of the Lindi district that principal Arabs at that place sailed their dhows under the French flag, which they received from the French consul in

Madagascar, in having their ships registered there, and information gained by British cruisers visiting the western ports of Madagascar in 1888 to check on the slave trade there, confirmed the British view that the French exercised very little or no restraint in issuing their flag, 'even the Portuguese were more co-operative'. Cynicism and exasperation in the matter was expressed by Euan-Smith, British Consul at Zanzibar, in 1889. The presence of a French man-of-war on the East Coast, he claimed, was a rare occurrence; he knew of no instance of the capture of a slave dhow by a French warship. The service was wholly distasteful to the officers of the French navy; the French man-of-war *Bouvet*, sent out at the beginning of 1889 for the avowed purpose of suppressing the Slave Trade, had remained at anchor in Zanzibar harbour for six months 'doing abolutely nothing'. The French rarely admitted the truth of any charge against a French dhow; it would be tantamount to admitting the flaws in their own administrative machinery. They always demanded 'impossible proof'. They would not take the mere statements of officers and men; they challenged and questioned these endlessly. In the majority of cases the English officer concerned was inclined to throw up the case in disgust.

> Long before the preliminary inquiry is finished the dhow will have finished her voyage and landed her cargo of slaves; and their owners and crew knowing they have been reported will disappear till the case blows over. By the time that a decree of condemnation and punishment would have been issued by the responsible French official there would neither be slave to liberate, dhow to condemn, nor crew, captain, or owner to punish. They will all have disappeared, and once again the Arabs will in their own minds, conclude that the French officials are virtually on their side . . . Unless a dhow is searched from stem to stern, it is impossible to ascertain whether or not she has slaves on board. Such a search can never be made by British cruisers, not one dhow in a thousand is so searched by French men-of-war.[34]

At the Brussels Conference, 1890, France maintained her attitude in the matter of the right of search, but promised not to grant her flag to vessels fitted out and owned by persons other than her subjects and protégés. Even Cardinal Lavigérie, with his great influence, was unable to effect a change in the attitude of the French government towards the right of search, and the use of her flag. The Congress of Anti-Slavery Societies which he convened at Paris in September 1890 glossed over the question. In debates in the French Chamber in June 1891 French sensitivity in the matter was clearly revealed. France had already conceded much in permitting the verification of papers.

She had given Great Britain everything she had asked in the partition of Africa, in the conversion of the Egyptian debt, and in the matter of a British protectorate over Zanzibar. True, Britain had officially recognized a French protectorate over Madagascar, but she had hedged this, and surrounded it with a network of difficulties and restrictions. That she should persist in requesting so fundamental a concession as the right of search was more than France could brook.

Anti-slave trade legislation and the Sultan of Zanzibar's important decree of August 1890 greatly enhanced the value of the French flag. Sir Rennell Rodd, British Consul-General at Zanzibar, estimated that at least one-third of the dhows carrying slaves ran under the French flag, despite a warning from the Sultan of Zanzibar to his subjects against their use of it. The widespread kidnapping and smuggling of slaves from Zanzibar was carried on by Suri Arabs who, sailing under the French flag, came down on the northeast monsoon, lodged in the Malindi quarter of Zanzibar town for a few months, and from there carried on their activities. Rodd was stirred into exclaiming in April 1893,

> I do not wish to be understood to imply that the French flag is issued without any apparent reason, simply on payment of fees, but the Arabs seem thoroughly to understand that it is easy to procure it if they are willing to face an expense which the lucrative business of slave-running with impunity well repays. There are various ways in which the French flag can be secured, but the simplest and surest is the purchase of a hut or a few square metres of land in Nossi Bé or some other French island. It is thus not too much to state that French protection can actually be purchased for a few rupees, and it would be strange if the slave traders and all whose hands are against the Local Governments did not avail themselves of this resource, as we find to our cost that they do . . . It is by such means as these, if not on even less warrantable grounds, that scoundrels from the Persian Gulf and the Gulf of Oman, from regions which have as little connection with France as the planet Jupiter, are enabled to carry havoc into this Protectorate and to foster a trade which all the rest of civilization is loyally co-operating to suppress.[35]

For France it was a simple matter. She acknowledged the civil status of natives of Madagascar and the Comoro Islands, and accorded them the rights of French subjects. Madagascar-domiciled slave dealers could thus claim French protection as French subjects. For Britain it was a delicate question; and she was averse to pressing it too far. The British themselves enjoyed extraterritorial rights in Turkey and Egypt which they jealously guarded. A pronouncement by the Lord Chancellor, in October 1893, leaves an impression that the law officers of the Crown considered the whole question best left alone.

> It appears to me to involve the maintenance on our part of propositions in relation to Treaties and usage and the bearing one upon the other of a very perilous character, when our Capitulations with Turkey and other Powers are borne in mind.[36]

And had not Britain, after the declaration of a British protectorate over Zanzibar in July 1890, agreed that it would not affect 'any rights or immunities enjoyed by French citizens' in Zanzibar?

Thus the vexatious question continued. The Commander of a British cruiser would inform the French consul that there were grounds for search of a suspected vessel under the French flag, and would place before him any evidence gained to support this deduction, but beyond this he could do nothing. These proceedings were well illustrated in the case of the capture of an Arab dhow under French colours in Zanzibar harbour by HMS *Philomel* in April 1893. It turned out that she had 67 slaves on board, mostly children, but owing to the refusal of the French consul to admit the right of search, she was handed over to him, and he sent the vessel to Réunion where she was acquitted by the French authorities. This acquittal in which a number of prominent Arabs were involved produced a profound impression at Zanzibar in view of the encouragement it would give Arab slavers to obtain the French flag. In another case, in November 1896, Commander Baker reported,

> All the time the officers were on board the Arabs continued to make as much noise as possible by shouting and stamping their feet, but notwithstanding this the presence of living creatures could be distinctly heard from below the hatches; that, combined with the stench, convinced me that she was also full of slaves. Nevertheless under the circumstances and the very delicate nature of the instructions I reluctantly allowed her to proceed.[37]

Immunity from search and increased profits from the sale of slaves encouraged the extension of the use of the French flag. A slave purchased for 15 dollars on the East African coast, and transported at a cost of about 15 dollars to Sur, could be sold there for from 70 to 100 dollars. By 1896 it was estimated that 100 Suri dhows were sailing under the French flag; all were presumed to be slavers.[38]

The Sultan's further decree of April 1897 abolishing slavery in his dominions was soon bypassed. When the French delegate to the International Maritime Bureau at Zanzibar (set up under the Brussels Conference of 1890),[39] announced that only natives with consular authority or under French protection were to embark Africans on board dhows under French colours, Suri Arabs hired impersonators who, declaring they were voluntarily proceeding to Arabia, received a consular pass. On the day of sailing, the real slaves were taken on board, and since they were found to correspond with the passenger list no further questions were asked. The French consul, in 1897, attempted to defeat this device by having fastened round the wrist of every African passenger a cord, on the knot of which the wax seal of the French consulate was stamped,[40] but this practice was unfortunately dropped by his successors.

The British anti-slave trade patrol was plagued by the obstacle of 'the French flag' right up to the turn of the century, apart from a temporary respite in 1898 when a smallpox epidemic deterred Arab dhows from landing at Pemba, Zanzibar, and mainland points. Sir Arthur Hardinge, Consul-General at Zanzibar, perturbed that the practice of using foreign flags might spread to the use of the German flag—there were already reports to this effect—imposed a strict watch on Zanzibar and Pemba, and dhows, once having cleared Zanzibar harbour, were forbidden to stop at Pemba, or any other point on Zanzibar. But the French immediately claimed this to be an infringement of the rights of French subjects under their 1844 treaty with Muscat.[41]

The whole question began to shift to Muscat, where the French had recently obtained from its ruler a naval base at Bandar Jessa, a few miles southeast of Muscat. This, Britain claimed, violated the 1862 declaration guaranteeing Muscat's independence, to which Britain and France were party, and the 1891 treaty between Britain and Muscat to the same end. Faced with a British ultimatum and appearance of a British naval force in his harbour, the Sultan in May 1898 withdrew the concession made to the French.[42] The French were left smarting, and when, in June 1900, the Sultan supported by the British political agent attempted to dissuade his subjects from using the French flag, there was swift action from the French consul, who lectured the Sultan in person, and reassured Arab dhow-owners that they might unfurl their French flags.[43] And in the Spring of 1902, when several dhows under the French flag flouted the Sultan's authority in territorial waters, the French flagship *Inferne* was sent to enforce their claim to French protection. The Sultan then appealed to the British government. The matter quickly escalated into a bitter crisis when, in the summer of 1903, a native sailing vessel under the French flag was forcibly detained by the Sultan's officer at the port of Sur. The French claimed indemnity for this 'illegal' detention, and asserted protective rights over members of the crew. There were all the makings of a *crise de nerfs*. But a report and recommendations from Lord Curzon, who was visiting the Persian Gulf at the time, helped to allay tension, and both governments agreed to refer the dispute to the Court of Arbitration at the Hague. Lively interest in the matter, in the House of Commons and at the Anti-Slavery Society, showed the importance of the issue at stake.[44]

The 'Muscat Dhows' arbitration award, of 8 August 1905, favoured the British case. Its substance was that, while recognizing French rights under the 1844 treaty with Muscat and her claim to inviolability from search for her flag, these rights had been altered by France herself, in her ratification of the Brussels Act on 2 January 1892. Under Article 32 of that Act, 'the facility of the Signatory Powers to grant their flag to native vessels was limited for the purpose of suppressing slave trading and in the general interests of humanity'. And, in addition, the term 'protégé' had been restricted in its application by France herself, in a convention with Turkey and Morocco in 1863. 'This pretended right', according to the Award, must now be abandoned 'in relation to other Oriental States by analogy'. Only subjects of the Sultan of Muscat, deemed to be under special French protection as of 1863, could fly the French flag, and this right was not transferable to other persons or vessels.[45] This ruling undercut the claims of practically all dhow owners to be French protégés. France henceforth had to exercise close supervision over the granting of her flag to the subjects of other powers. The Hague Tribunal decision of 1905 is a landmark in the long catena of events culminating in the suppression of the East African Slave Trade at sea.

10
Sir Arthur Hardinge and the Abolition of Slavery

The goal of complete abolition of the slave trade at sea, anticipated in the Sultan's decree of 1 August 1890, might have been reached much sooner but for the slave trade carried on under the French flag. Similarly, the abolition of the institution of slavery in Zanzibar might have been more quickly attained but for the appointment of Arthur (later Sir Arthur) Hardinge as British consul in Zanzibar. Hardinge's opposition to the sudden abolition of slavery explains the continued existence of this institution in the Sultan's dominions for nearly a decade after the 1890 decree.

Sir Arthur Hardinge was one of a remarkable group of pre-World War I diplomatists, which included such men as Sir Francis Younghusband, and, later in time, Sir Ronald Storrs. Hardinge, like Sir Lloyd Mathews, was half-oriental in his mode of thought. Few British officials could have been less English in their approach to the question of slavery. A scholar, a Fellow of All Souls College, Oxford, an intellectual, he had held consular posts in Constantinople, Bucharest and Cairo, and had travelled widely in Asia and Turkestan, and his heart, so he claimed, was in the 'Mohammedan East'.[1]

During his career in Zanzibar, 1894–1900, he managed to hold off the Foreign Office in its endeavours to end slavery. On taking up his appointment as Consul-General, in May 1894, Hardinge was instructed to recommend measures for facilitating total abolition, provided that slave owners were not treated unjustly. In November 1894 he was requested to examine whether the India Act of 1843, abolishing the legal status of slavery, could be applied to Zanzibar. But Hardinge soon made it clear that he was in no hurry to end the institution of slavery. His instructions to Dr O'Sullivan, Vice-Consul at Pemba, in December 1894, warned the latter against a hasty or ostentatious crusade against it. And in a continuous stream of brilliant memoranda, Hardinge regaled the Foreign Office with the virtues of Islamic slavery: there seemed almost a note of wistful regret that non-Muslims were debarred from the delights of this institution which tolerated concubinage and exalted the role of the male. Hardinge was skilful and imaginative, a writer of most persuasive prose, and abolitionists and aggressive missionaries, such as Bishop Tucker, more than met their match in this eccentric personality.²

Domestic slavery, according to Hardinge, was a fundamental principle of the social system of Islam, with a close resemblance to that established by the Levitical Law, and for a person who regarded that law as of divine authority, slavery, as sanctioned by the Bible and the Koran, was lawful. 'Arabs had not been touched by Christianity and western civilization, their political institutions and family life were still that of the Books of Judges and Kings, and the patriarchical system of slavery was as natural to them 'as it was to their ancestor Abraham'. The state of Islamic slavery was similar in all respects to that depicted in the Old Testament. Thus any interference with a master's rights over his slave was, in Islamic eyes, contrary to the law of God.³

Hardinge maintained that the Arabs, on the whole, were not cruel to their slaves. The lot of slaves in East Africa was not so harsh as the public in England imagined. Missionaries in East Africa, men who had spent a decade or more in the field, were usually more tolerant towards slavery than those in England who had never been to Africa, and were constantly prating about the 'moral continuity' of British policy. And critics at home if they wished to understand Mahommedan domestic slavery and family life must banish from their minds all the associations of 'Uncle Tom's Cabin' and similar works, and transport themselves in imagination to the familiar scenes of the Bible. Had not Captain Colomb admitted that before he came to East Africa he had sentimental notions about slavery?

> a mental picture of a very black negro, with a peculiarly gentle upturned face, standing hoe in hand in a grove of sugar canes, and humbly receiving vigorous castigation at the hands of his driver.⁴

This view, according to Hardinge, was nonsense. That conditions for the slave were not over-strenuous was evident in that his working life was as long as that of the free man; Hardinge had seen 'many grey-haired old men and women among them, over 60 years or more, who may well have been imported over 30 or 40 years ago'.

The work on clove estates was less severe than agricultural work in England. All the slave had to do was weed the ground round the clove trees, and when the crop was ripe, during two or three months in the year, he sat on a branch or on the bars of a ladder, in a wood protected from the sun by the clove trees, and picked the fruit which he threw into a basket. Tales of his working under the lash were ridiculous; the master 'in order to wield his instrument of torture with effect would have to be constantly climbing with monkey-like agility from tree to tree'. In Zanzibar, according to Hardinge, slavery was an easy thraldom. The slave preferred to hand over half his pay to his master rather than purchase his freedom with it. In ill-health his master looked after him, and in a row with other persons a master took his part. The slave was so imbued with his master's rights over himself that he considered it wrong to run away.

The lot of an African slave under an Arab master was much kinder than under tribal slavery in the interior, where slaves were treated with harshness and cruelty. Hardinge's views were supported by Sir Lloyd Mathews, who had resided for many years in Zanzibar, and claimed that

> Mohammedans were not the monsters of cruelty they were painted by those who aimed at publicity 'by preaching a "jehad" against the Arabs from their comfortable arm-chairs in England.' There were, of course, exceptions; but even the worst Arab masters treated their slaves 'far better than many householders at home treat their so-called "slaveys", or husbands their wives in the East End of London'.[5]

Hardinge detailed all the benefits accruing to a slave. With his master's consent he could own property. In practice, out of clove time, he was allowed two days a week (Thursday and Friday) on his own plot—usually rented to him by his master. Here he grew maize, sweet potatoes, and coconuts, which provided 'God's Drink'. The slave woman, when not engaged in work for her master, might weave mats used for drying cloves, and these could be sold for a few pice each. Every six months the slave was entitled from his master to one shirt. And when, as was the case with the Zanzibaris almost without exception, he wished to satisfy 'his extraordinary craving for travel, which possesses these people almost like a mania,' he could leave his wife and child in his master's safe-keeping during his absence. And Hardinge instanced that strange phenomenon, so incomprehensible to those unfamiliar with slavery in the East, whereby slaves owned slaves, and freed slaves were especially ambitious to acquire them.

> A curious instance came before me recently, as showing how completely the system of slavery has permeated the whole life of this people. A slave who had slaves of his own, complained to me that his master wished to take them away from him because he had given him enough labour and I found on further inquiry that the master in question was himself a slave of the well-known Tanganyika Arab—Mahomed-bin Khalifan, or Rumaliza.[6]

Miss Balfour noted, regarding Zanzibar, that 'The curious thing about Slavery here is that Slave-owners are frequently Slaves themselves, and their Slaves may also own other Slaves.'[7] A visitor to an hotel in Zanzibar in 1891 cited the case of a 12-year-old servant who was the slave of another 16-year-old servant, who took all his earnings, leaving him only what he felt necessary for his minimum wants.[8]

Apologists for slavery under Islam argued that Islam had found slavery an established human institution, but had ameliorated its harsher aspects, making it more beneficent as a result of the strong religious sanctions which could be applied against a cruel master. The Qadi could compel him to forfeit his slaves if he ill-treated them, or the Sultan might intervene. The Mohammedan Law encouraged manumissions as a laudable act, but required, with very few exceptions, that it should be the master's own free and spontaneous act. A person committing certain specified sins, however, such as breaking the Ramadhan fast, might be ordered by the Qadi to manumit a slave in atonement.

In Zanzibar there was the practice known as 'Tadbir', whereby the master promised that on his death his slave should go free, and likewise all the slave's children born subsequent to the promise. A master at the point of death might manumit his slaves as a last means of seeking divine favour. A slave thus manumitted possessed a deed of freedom, written by the Qadi, which he wore in a silver case hung around his neck. Devout Muslims claimed that they purchased slaves with the specific object of emanicpation, for did not the Prophet say

> Whosoever shall free a Moslem slave, God will free every member of his body, limb by limb, from the fire of Hell.

Hardinge maintained that emancipation by a foreigner of slaves purchased with this religious intention was strongly resented, as depriving the owners of the merit of their contemplated act, defrauding them, so to speak, of an investment in the world to come. Hardinge's arguments are not too convincing, but there were instances to which he could point to uphold them. The new Sultan, in 1893, granted their freedom to 300 slaves whom he inherited, and in 1896 O'Sullivan, Vice-Consul at Pemba, referred to slaves who owed their freedom to the observance of the Koran's teachings, in this respect, by their former Arab masters.[9]

In addition to Arab wives, many of the richer Arabs kept concubines (suria) chosen from their female slaves. This practice was recognized by the sharia, the religious and secular law of Islam. When a concubine bore her master a child, the concubine achieved near-equality with his Arab wives, and was entitled to her liberty on her master's death. While the Bible made the children of the concubine the legal inferiors of those of the wife, 'Islam, as becomes the creed of the children of Hagar, puts the offspring of the concubine on the same level as the offspring of the wife, and treats Ismael as equal to Isaac'. The children born of concubines were regarded as legitimate, and no distinction was made between them and the children born of the Arab wives. Seyyid Barghash, Khalifa, and Ali, sons of Seyyid Said, who succeeded him as Sultans of Zanzibar, were born to concubines.

Abolitionists in England demanded that concubinage be made illegal. Mathews and Hardinge argued that to abolish it would upset Muslim family life and their social organization, and stir up intense feeling against Britain. Soon after his accession to the Sultanate, Seyyid Hamoud begged Mathews to save his people from a fate to which 'death would almost be preferable',[10] namely, the surrender of their concubines. Hardinge pointed out that the attachment of Arab and Swahili towards their concubines was generally far stronger than towards their wives. For the concubine was selected by her master or lover for her personal attractions, while the wife he had never spoken to, 'he has not indeed even seen her face, until after the marriage ceremony is complete, he enters the recesses of the harem, and for the first time himself removes her veil.'

> concubines are in all Muslim communities in which slavery is widespread more prolific as a general rule than wives.[11]

Harding and Mathews argued that the Muslim system of slavery, which secluded large numbers of girls in harems, afforded a guarantee against their becoming public harlots; Mohammedan concubinage could not be compared with the sights seen in the thoroughfares of some European cities. In Zanzibar a slave woman could not be made a concubine against her will, and the practice of keeping concubines was not so widespread as imagined, chiefly owing to the expense of maintaining more than one wife.

Finally Hardinge, ending on an idyllic note, portrayed a picture of the slave treated as a member of the Arab family, eating and living with them on terms of considerable intimacy. There was a closeness of ties which could never exist between a slave and an infidel.

> To a man who is well off and given to Eastern hospitality the supplying of the simple wants of native Africans is not a very serious expense, two or three pairs of small black hands more or less in the rice dish will not ruin him.[12]

But Hardinge, in portraying the attractive side of domestic slavery, ignored the depressing features. The concubine, on the death of her master, lost her immunity if she had not borne him a child, and she might be inherited by children born of legal wives of her late master. Subject to the jealous vengeance of the other wives, she could be turned out on the death of her master, to lead a life of prostitution as her only means of livelihood. As for the life of the ordinary slave on clove plantations in Pemba and Zanzibar, it might not be too onerous so long as the slave was able-bodied, but at the end of his productive career he was often discarded. There were many starved miserable derelicts throughout the islands and on the coast, left to scavenge as best they could, or dependent on alms, and finally left to die of starvation or disease. Friday was recognized as an official begging day in the island of Pemba and Zanzibar. On the coast, instances were known where old slaves were picked up trying to struggle back into the interior. Finally Hardinge ignored the fact that over half the slaves in Zanzibar and Pemba were owned by non-Arabs, who were certainly not imbued with the patriarchal tendencies ascribed to the Arabs.

Abstract questions of freedom and legal rights, the Englishman's championship of 'liberty and independence,' meant little to Hardinge, or for that matter to many British administrators and missionaries on the spot. Lugard, in his early years at least, was perhaps an exception, but even he was remarkably candid and lacking in sentimental approach to the question of slavery. He certainly did not support its continuance but was against any sudden emancipation that would cause social chaos or generate ill will. For the slave master was

> wholly dependent on slaves to cultivate his estates, and for household service, for there is little free labour available, and ruin and starvation would result from their loss.

Lugard favoured a period of adjustment to make provision for freed labour, as in the Portuguese colonies, where it was decreed in 1858 that the abolition of slavery would have twenty years to work itself out.

Hardinge and Lugard would prevent slave raiding by the enforcement of existing decrees. This would bring an end to slavery by freeing an increasing number of slaves each year, over a period of time, until all were emancipated. This would require a system of registration of slaves. Hardinge would divide Zanzibar into four coastguard districts, and Pemba into three, each under an 'English retired warrant or petty officer', with 50 askaris to assist in patrolling the coast. He did not agree with the hard line of the Germans who hanged those guilty of 'raw slave-trading', but he would imprison for life.[13] He envisaged the end of the status of slavery in possibly ten to fifteen years' time, but as for concubinage, 'so long as we permit polygamy and the harem system,' it would continue.

To end the institution of domestic slavery by gradual stages, so as not to upset the social system of Islam, Hardinge also favoured a system of self-redemption for slaves. This would avoid paying out substantial compensation, as would be the result if slavery were abolished suddenly, for it was only fair that owners should be recompensed for the loss of their property, as in the case of the West Indies planters. The cost of such compensation, the expense of slave courts, and additional police to enforce the abolition decree would place a great burden on the Sultanate, already saddled with paying down £200,000 for the re-possession of the Imperial British East Africa Company's lease of the coastline. The declaring of Zanzibar a free port in 1892 had already seriously affected its revenue. Hardinge argued that compensation money would not go to the planters but, as in the West Indies, into the hands of money-lenders, in this case Indians who held mortgages on the clove estates. The dire result of all this would be a great population of unemployed freed slaves, and a crowd of indigent Arab ex-slave owners.[14] Thus the longer abolition was delayed, the fewer slaves there would be and the less compensation would be payable. It is significant that Hardinge's estimate of the number of slaves for whom compensation would be payable, if there were immediate abolition, was much higher than that of his critics.[15]

As for the argument that free labour would be attracted from the mainland, Hardinge asserted that this was unlikely. The Nyika, the narrow belt a few miles inland from the coast, although thought to be an arid and sparsely inhabited stretch, was in Hardinge's view actually fine country, and in some parts highly populated and fertile. Its people were passionately attached to its 'waving fields of Indian corn studded here and there with pineapples and mango trees, and the dome-shaped cottages nestling in the thick bush or behind their bomas, of thorn and cactus', and in order to earn wages in Zanzibar they would have to cross the sea, 'which they regard with superstitious horror'. The few who had been persuaded by railway contractors to work on the Uganda railway had usually run away the very moment they received their first instalment or advance of pay.

When Hardinge's 'fine old crusted-long-in-bottle arguments' failed to disarm his opponents, he stated there was a need for a Royal Commission to inquire into the whole question of slavery in East Africa. He was certain it would vindicate his views on the

HARDINGE AND THE ABOLITION OF SLAVERY   249

subject. It would find that slavery did not weigh heavily on the African, and there was no alternative to slave labour.

But the Foreign Office was not interested in the appointment of a Royal Commission. It was perturbed that the 1890 decree had had little effect in the Zanzibar dominions, and that the institution of slavery still flourished there with vigour. In Pemba, only one-quarter of the island's 2000 Arabs had responded to the decree. The remaining 1500 retained their slaves, on an average 30 slaves each, though in some cases possessing up to three and four hundred. On the mainland, as the time drew near for the withdrawal of the Imperial British East Africa Company, the question would have to be faced whether slavery could be permitted to continue there; it might possibly revive, unrestrained, under Islamic rule. The administration of the hinterland of the British sphere was currently under discussion. Any proposal for placing it under the Sultan's authority would certainly be vetoed, on the grounds that this would extend and legalize Islamic slavery in a wide area of East Africa. It would become an open hunting ground for slavers. Much of this argument was picked up by the Foreign Office from the British and Foreign Anti-Slavery Society, which was relentless in its pressure to end slavery in the Sultan's dominions.

It produced figures, much exaggerated, to show that 40,000 to 50,000 slaves left the East Africa mainland yearly, and that Admiralty figures indicated only 5% to 6% of this number were captured by the anti-slave trade patrol.[16] The British government must take action, not only against the Arabs, but also against the rich 'Hindis' of Zanzibar,

> Who advance thousands to the Arabs to carry on their work—and here, you would perhaps strike a more vital part of this horrid system than you imagine, and bring to account subjects of our Queen who disgrace our name.[17]

The Anti-Slavery Society, increasingly exasperated by Hardinge's and Mathews' delaying tactics, requested Donald (later Sir Donald) Mackenzie, who was visiting East Africa on behalf of the Liverpool Chamber of Commerce to report on the commercial prospects, to combine this with an on the spot investigation of slavery there. Mackenzie was an ardent supporter of the Society, and a founder of the freed slave settlement at Cape July on the west coast of Africa.

Mackenzie arrived in Zanzibar on 2 March 1895, and spent scarcely a month in Zanzibar and Pemba, apart from a few days' visit to German East Africa. He was very active in this brief tour, storing impressions, and garnering statistics and telling facts for later use. He visited plantations in Pemba, and met large slave-owners, the Wali (Governor), and a sheikh who possessed 2000 slaves in Pemba, in addition to holding 800 in Zanzibar. There were conversations with the Sultan, Hardinge, and hard-liners such as Mathews and Pigott, the latter, an ex-IBEAC officer, pouring into his ears on several occasions the tale that slaves were only fit for bondage. Other officials, and some missionaries too, Mackenzie admitted, were of the same view. It was all a complicated question!

Mackenzie ascertained that there was 30% mortality among slave porters, that few children were born to slaves, that imports of slaves into Zanzibar and Pemba from the mainland still ran at 6000 annually, and that Indian merchants still had a hand in underwriting slave trade transactions.[18] This was all ammunition for the Anti-Slavery Cause. It was what he had come out to get. In his report to the Anti-Slavery Society, Mackenzie maintained that there were many vocal vested interests in slave labour who feared that abolition would interfere with their profits. He pointed out that, owing to the scarcity of free labour in Zanzibar and Pemba, Europeans and Indians were hiring slaves from their owners, to work as domestic servants and labourers. They were paid wages, but half their earnings were handed over to the masters from whom they were hired. Mackenzie accused Hardinge of having allowed the arguments of those interested in maintaining slavery to affect his judgement. Immediate emancipation would not disturb the prosperity of the country, freed slaves would still have to work for their living, and, if paid adequate wages, would be more industrious.

Meanwhile the abolitionists at home, impatient with the procrastination of the Foreign Office, organized meetings up and down the country, and resolutions were passed expressing indignation at the existence of slavery under the British Crown. As Lugard pointed out, so long as Zanzibar was under an independent Sultan, there was no invective sufficiently strong to condemn slavery, but now that Zanzibar was a British protectorate, and the yield of cloves determined financial prosperity for the government, it was a different tune; there was almost a half-hearted apology for the necessity of retaining slavery.

Mackenzie's enthusiastic reception on his return home and his rousing speeches on the need to abolish slavery in Zanzibar were marred by the interjections of an 'unknown' correspondent from East Africa, who, in three articles in the *Pall Mall Gazette* in the autumn of 1895, attacked the unctuous zeal of the Anti-Slavery

Society, and defended domestic slavery as practised by the the Mohammedans in East Africa. Who was this mysterious African correspondent, Pigott, Mackenzie, or Hardinge? No one knew. It was all wishful spite, for nothing now could halt the movement towards abolition.

On 8 March 1895, when the House of Commons was in Committee of Supply, an animated debate developed over a supplementary vote of £500, for expenses incurred in the suppression of the slave trade. Mr J. A. Pease, a prominent Quaker and influential member of the Anti-Slavery Society, moved a reduction of this vote, on the grounds that it was meaningless, for the slave trade still flourished in East Africa, and slavery was still permitted in the Zanzibar protectorate. In the debate which followed strong views were expressed on both sides of the House in favour of immediate abolition, even if this necessitated an Imperial grant to make good the deficit that might result in Zanzibar revenues.[19] Lord Kimberley, forced by the demonstration of feeling in Parliament, immediately wired Hardinge to expedite his recommendations for dealing with the institution of slavery in Zanzibar.[20]

In June 1895, Lord Salisbury formed his third Ministry, following the resignation of Lord Rosebery. It was not long before the new Government was questioned as to its proposals for dealing with slavery in Zanzibar. On 21 August, Mr G. N. (later Lord) Curzon, Under-Secretary of State for Foreign Affairs, assured the House that the Government was 'in communication' with Hardinge on the subject.[21] Hardinge, however, was still playing for time, and advising caution; he asked that a final decision be deferred until he expressed his own views in person at the Foreign Office.[22] Before he left for England on leave in late June 1896, Hardinge, in a long despatch to Salisbury, controverted recent remarks of Lugard on his (Hardinge's) failure to criticize more severely the evil effects of Islamic slavery, for example, the fact that many slave girls supported their owners by the wages of prostitution. But, claimed Hardinge, very few Zanzibar negro slave girls earned money this way from the Arabs or other fairly well-to-do Moslems. Such earnings as they made by immorality were derived mainly from Europeans, many of whom in Zanzibar and along the coast kept black mistresses, and in many cases purchased their freedom for them.

While Hardinge was absent in England, there took place the succession dispute in which Sayyid Khalid made a bid for the throne. His predecessor, Sayyid Hamid, had been increasingly restive under British control. The payment of £200,000 in June 1895 out of Zanzibar funds, in compensation to the IBEAC on its withdrawal from the mainland, was sharp practice at the Sultan's expense, and it cast doubt in his mind on the probity of British intentions. Sayyid Hamid had used the opportunity when the British were absorbed in suppressing the Mazrui rebellion on the mainland to build up a palace force of over 1000 men. The reduction of this bodyguard at the rate of 25 each month to what Hardinge considered was an adequate force, and closer surveillance over his household finance, had irked the Sultan exceedingly. And when in August 1896, following Hamid's death, a rival claimant, Sayyid Khalid, noted for his animus towards the British, made a bid for the throne and seized the palace, a British naval force bombarded the palace and inflicted severe losses on its defenders: Khalid fled to the German consulate. Following the bombardment the British placed their own nominee, Sayyid Hamud, on the throne. They were now in firm control. The first and major result of this assertion of authority was the immediate step taken towards abolishing the legal status of slavery. Mr (later Sir Basil) Cave, acting-Consul while Hardinge was on leave, reported to Salisbury, following the bombardment, that the Arabs had 'received a lesson which they will not forget for many years', and it might prove of great value in bringing about the abolition of slavery.[23] The British were now arbiters of the Sultanate. Slavery could be promptly disposed of.

Hardinge, at home on leave, in deep conversation with the Foreign Office, in the autumn of 1896 argued strenuously for a phased-out emancipation to give slave-owners time to adjust to the new state of affairs. Outright abolitionists, so Hardinge claimed, were alarmists of the worst sort, and very gullible in believing atrocity stories; it was up to him to set the record straight, and to plead the cause of the Arabs. He must obtain justice for them. Hardinge fought to the last against outright abolition. He referred to the defeat of the Italians at Adowa, the unsettled state of affairs in East Africa and the Horn: there was the threat of the Khalifa in the Sudan, and the recent rise of the Mad Mullah in Somaliland. Abolition of slavery, a direct challenge to the Islamic world, would cause all these dangers to coalesce and converge on the British. And, finally, there would be left in the Arab mind a strong sense of injustice if, in British territory, Arab slave-owners were penalized, while in neighbouring German East Africa the institution of slavery was permitted to continue. The Germans would not be slow to exploit this situation and win over Arab sympathy. Thus did Hardinge with persistent advocacy retail his case against any sudden abolition of slavery in the Zanzibar dominions.

But his eloquent and unceasing advocacy was beginning to pall; it was too much even for the colossal patience of Lord Salisbury. Hardinge was finally forced to yield to overwhelming opposition, though he never changed his views.

But he won his case in two respects. He convinced Lord Salisbury, in the face of Anti-Slavery Society opposition, that slave-owners should receive compensation for loss of their slaves: 'the English nation and Parliament should be ready to share with the subject race, on whom they are forcing it some portion of the inconvenience which it entails'.[24] Hardinge also won his case in that slave-owners were allowed to retain their concubines. At a meeting at the Foreign Office with Mr (later Lord) Curzon and Clement Hill, head of the African Department, a plan was worked out for the abolition of slavery and compensation to slave-owners. There was difficulty in arriving at a number of slaves for whom compensation was payable. Figures varied, from those of Hardinge at 70,000 slaves, to those of acting-Consul Smith at 4500 to 7000 slaves. At four dollars per head, this meant anything from 28,000 dollars (£5,600) to 280,000 dollars (£56,000) total compensation.

Before Hardinge returned to Zanzibar, the decision on abolition was hastily wired out to acting-Consul Smith, almost it seems through fear that Hardinge might frustrate the decision at the last moment. The acting-Consul was informed that after Ramadhan (the long Muslim fast) he was to invite His Highness the Sultan of Zanzibar to issue a Decree by which the legal status of slavery in Zanzibar and Pemba would be abolished, and compensation paid to owners proving legal tenure for their slaves as at August 1890. No interference was contemplated with Arab family rights.[25] The decree would be promulgated after Ramadhan, presumably because Arabs would then be in better humour to accept this trenchant blow.

The decree abolishing the legal status of slavery was signed by the Sultan on 5 April 1897, and the chief Arabs from Pemba and Zanzibar were summoned the following day to hear the pronouncement. The substance of the decree was as follows. In the future, local courts would decline to enforce 'any alleged rights over the body, service, or property' of any persons on the ground that such a person was a slave. Compensation would be paid to owners who could prove legal tenure in slaves as at August 1890, and whose services were thus lost to them; compensation money would be unseizable for past debt. The status of concubines as 'inmates of the Harem in the same sense as wives' was not affected by the decree.

They could only claim their freedom on grounds of cruelty or, if they had borne no children, with the sanction of the court. The administration of the decree would be carried out by District Courts presided over by Arab Walis. A vagrancy clause bound freed slaves, on pain of being declared vagrants, to show they possessed a regular domicile and means of subsistence. The practical effect of the decree was to throw the onus of obtaining freedom on the slave himself. A slave, other than a concubine, who wished to acquire freedom had to apply to the District Court, and would be issued with freedom papers.[26]

News of the abolition decree appears to have leaked out beforehand. A number of Arabs endeavoured to ship their slaves off to Arabia and the Persian Gulf shortly before the announcement was made and, in the month following the decree, there was a considerable exodus from Zanzibar and Pemba of Arabs with their slaves, for whom freedom papers had been obtained. It was discovered that these freedom papers were used a number of times over, to cover various batches of slaves shipped north to Arabia. It was very difficult to prevent erstwhile slaves, once formally freed, from accompanying their employers,[27] so habituated had they become to the master-slave relationship. But, on the whole, the news of the decree was taken calmly in Zanzibar, almost with a sense of resignation. Hardinge was prepared for trouble, but apart from a brief panic among Indian traders in Zanzibar the whole thing passed off quietly. A number of slave girls left their mistresses, declaring they were now free, and would do no more work, 'but not getting their usual supper they reconsidered their position and returned this morning to their ordinary avocations'.[28]

As for the Arabs they had long enjoyed a moratorium, and now apparently realized that the forces working against them could no longer be held back. The lesson of the bombardment also had its effect in dispelling 'all ideas of any forcible resistance to the will of the Protecting Power'.[29] The Sultan demonstrated his sincere intentions, and set a good example, in ordering that his own plantation slaves who declined to apply for their freedom papers would, in future, work for him three days a week, as rent for their holdings, and on the remaining days could either work for themselves or receive wages if they worked for him. As a reward for acquiescence to British wishes in issuing the decree, the Sultan was appointed honorary Knight Grand Cross of the Star of India.

To effect the administration of the decree, A Wali was appointed to each of the five districts into which Zanzibar and Pemba were divided, three in Zanzibar and two in Pemba. Two European Slavery Commissioners, Mr J. T. Last and Mr J. P. Farler, were to oversee the work of emancipation in Zanzibar and Pemba respectively. The decree was published in each district, and messengers were sent into the countryside to spread the news of it, notices were placed in public places, and the European commissioners made tours of inspection. Slaves and Arabs in Zanzibar and Pemba were slow to realize the import of the decree.

There was no great rush for freedom. During 1898, 2735 slaves claimed their freedom; in 1899 the figure was 3659; it dropped to 1720 in 1900, to 844 in 1901, and continued to decline until, in 1907, only 85 sought their freedom. By this final date, compensation paid out for freed slaves stood at 487,530 rupees (£8125).[30] Relevant statistics showing a reduction in the slave population during the period 1897-1901 are as follows:

Freed.............. 12-13,000
Died—ordinary deaths ... 10,000
Died—small pox   20,000
Disappeared...........5,000 (kidnapped, or to German territory and mainland as porters.)

47,000

Thus, out of a total slave population in Zanzibar and Pemba of 100,000 in 1897, there were still 53,000 remaining in slavery at the end of 1901; about 12% had been emancipated under the 1897 decree, an average of 3000 to 3500 per annum. Of the total number of about 55,000 slaves still remaining in 1901, the Arabs possessed no more than 15 to 16 thousand; the original inhabitants of Zanzibar—the Hadimu in the eastern part of the island, Pemba and Tumbatu, scarcely distinguishable from the slave population—possessed some 20,000 slaves; and 15,000 to 18,000 slaves were held in small batches by natives from the Comoros, and other persons.[31] There were many instances where slaves themselves held slaves. In Zanzibar and Pemba, ex-slaves and their descendants, who regarded themselves as 'Shirazi', and were mostly Muslim, easily merged into the rest of the population on attaining their freedom.

The prophecies of Hardinge and some missionaries as to the adverse results which would follow abolition were partially fulfilled.

There was 'wholesale immorality' following the decree; 'nearly every freed female slave became a prostitute'. Farler, Commissioner for Pemba, and with years of experience as missionary with the Universities Mission to Central Africa, stated,

> Since the restraints imposed by their Arab masters have been removed, Pemba has become one huge brothel, the women being worse than the men. They seem to have but half-human souls, and with the subtlety of savages, the passions and physical strength of adults, they have only the intelligence of the child to restrain them.[32]

In Zanzibar numerous brothels were set up, the occupants of which were mostly freed female slaves. When British administrators insisted that young girls and unmarried women must have proper homes to go to before being freed, they came under criticism, notably from the Friends' Mission in Pemba and a zealous young Quaker, Mr Theodore Burtt. The Society of Friends and the Anti-Slavery Society claimed that British officials were frustrating the abolition decree, and the Walis were not honestly implementing it. An investigation by Hardinge showed that although some Walis were sluggish in seeing that the decree was observed, Burtt's charges on the whole were groundless. When freed slaves, intoxicated with their new-found freedom, roamed over the island of Pemba, drunk and irresponsible, indulging in terrorism and petty thieving, a special police force was formed to check the menace; but when Article IV of the decree, which made the right to freedom dependent on 'a regular domicile and means of subsistence,' was invoked, the Friends' Mission and the Anti-Slavery Society appealed to the Foreign Office, and this ruling was dropped. There followed an increase in vagrancy, and Hardinge's and Farler's prognostications were more than fulfilled.[33] It was the persistent criticism from the Quakers which elicited from Hardinge the remark that he could well now understand why apparently otherwise humane Roman Emperors 'so cruelly persecuted the early Christians'.[34]

Predictions by the anti-Abolitionists as to the adverse effects which would result from the decree continued to be fulfilled. Freed slaves refused to work; in some cases they preferred to starve. Clove plantations were derelict, and, since compensation money was not seizable for debt, Indian moneylenders foreclosed mortgages on the estates, but were unable to obtain labour to work them. The excellent clove harvest of 1900 was thus lost. Indian owners did not help matters when they informed erstwhile slaves that, since they were now free and not compelled to give a portion of their pay to their masters as formerly, their wages would now be reduced.

New habits of energy and self-help were discernible on the part of some Arabs, and in a few instances they used the compensation money to repurchase estates at fair prices. But for a large section of the Arab commercial and planter community in Pemba and Zanzibar the decree meant financial collapse. Those Arabs who foolishly incurred new loans at very high interest, on the expectation of their compensation money, were soon helpless in the hands of Indian moneylenders, paying them from 75 to 150 per cent compound interest on these loans.

The decree came under criticism from abolitionists in England, as being a too 'cumbersome procedure', and Hardinge was blamed for the meagre results accruing from it, for had he not stated that slavery was the 'best form of social organization for the blacks'? Immediate and complete abolition was urged.[35] This is what the Anti-Slavery Society had urged, but it overlooked the fact that only legal slavery had been abolished under the decree, and that a slave was not freed until he applied for and received freedom papers, terminating his legal status as a slave. Curzon, still Under-Secretary of State for Foreign Affairs, explained that no slave was held against his wishes, but he must take a positive approach and *claim* his freedom. The fact that many slaves had not come forth to claim their freedom must be interpreted as indicating they were satisfied with their lot.

Justification for Hardinge's policy of gradualism was expressed in Salisbury's dispatch of June 1898, published as a White Paper in the same year.[34] It refuted any suggestion of withholding freedom from slaves, or of dishonesty on the part of the walis in implementing the recent decree. Emancipation was taking place as anticipated, and without undue shock to the social economy of the islands. It rebutted charges by those, like Mr Burtt, who in misguided enthusiasm hampered the work of emancipation.

The pace of emancipation slowed up markedly after the first flush of exhilaration of new-found freedom. Slaves, aware that freedom was theirs by merely applying for it, were in no hurry to claim it. Their lot was an easy one. They were careful not to be overworked, and could invoke the threat of applying for their freedom to extract better terms from their masters. There were a few instances of freed slaves requesting a return to slavery, and being disappointed to find that this was impossible. Many freed slaves were re-employed by their former masters. Those who crossed to the mainland to work on the Uganda Railway or with the Uganda Transport department found their lot as porters, toiling along the Uganda road, with a 60 lb load on their heads, up over the cold Masai steppes, under the strict discipline of a European caravan leader who was impatient of malingering or idleness, more onerous and hard than life under an indolent Arab master, midst the coconut and spice trees of Zanzibar. The establishment of a labour bureau in Zanzibar and Pemba in 1901 placed labour recruitment on a more firm and orderly basis, but a chronic shortage continued for the next few years, only partially relieved by immigration from the mainland.

The freeing of slaves, fluctuating with dry or rainy seasons, good or bad harvests, harsh or mild masters, worked itself out slowly, much too slowly for the British and Foreign Anti-slavery Society. It pressed for a speeding up of emancipation. It also pointed out that the legal status of slavery was still recognized in the Sultan's mainland coastal strip, now leased to and under British administration. Sir Charles Eliot, Hardinge's successor as Commissioner for the East Africa Protectorate, was averse to extending the provisions of the emancipation decree with its implications of compensation to the mainland strip. There was no adequate administration there as yet to enforce these provisions. Britain was also involved in a long-drawn-out campaign against the Mad Mullah in Somaliland, and could not afford to face more antagonism in East Africa. Eliot, also using Hardinge's argument, opposed immediate abolition on the grounds that it would provoke more ills than it would solve, and the longer it could be staved off, the less compensation would be payable to ex-slave-owners.

Turning to the campaign against the slave trade at sea, the Admiralty continued its watch along the East African coast. Occasional cases of slave-running continued to be reported up to and after the turn of the century. On 29 April 1899, an Arab slave dhow carrying 60 slaves was captured off Wasin Island, some 60 miles south of Mombasa. She was heading for Muscat. An Arab Qadi in Pemba was implicated in the affair, and fled to Sur to avoid apprehension. On 4 May 1899, another Arab dhow, flying the French flag, was captured in Zanzibar harbour, with 20 slaves on board; fourteen of these had been kidnapped in Zanzibar. Numerous instances of slave ships sailing north in 1901 were reported, and HMS *Red Breast*, in the spring of 1901, after landing Sir Charles Eliot at Aden, re-coaled there before proceeding to intercept Arab dhows known to be operating off the coast.[37]

As long as a dhow trade existed with East Africa, attempts would be made to carry slaves northwards. The slave trade continued to be recognized as a shady, but secondary branch of the dhow-master's main trade. Disreputable characters from Muscat and the

Hadhramaut did not scruple to steal legal slaves from brother Muslims in East Africa, and petty slavers prowled the beaches of Zanzibar and Pemba, hoping to snatch a few children and smuggle them into canoes standing close by the shore. They were then transferred to dhows lying in wait, and when wind and darkness were favourable they slipped away to the north. Africans, slaves and free, were picked up from fishing boats, and the Wali of Lamu lost a number of his slaves in this fashion. Other slaves were ensnared by numerous stratagems, taken secretly by canoe into the open sea, and thence transferred to dhows which took them north. Watchfulness against the smuggling of slaves north continued well into the second half of the twentieth century. In the 1960s, East African port regulations, aimed originally at curbing impressment and slavery, still limited crew numbers to those considered reasonable for the working of a ship: eight to ten for small dhows, fourteen to twenty for medium-sized dhows, and twenty-one to thirty for larger dhows. The largest dhow crew recorded in 1961 was fifty-three in number.[38]

It had been argued that abolishing slavery in Zanzibar and Pemba, while allowing it to exist in the Sultan's coastal strip on the mainland, would encourage a slave traffic from there to the islands. This had not taken place, apart from a few slaves smuggled across from the mainland in canoes. There were only a few cases of illegal imports in Zanzibar and Pemba from the mainland. In the mainland coastal strip, slavery was a declining institution; the census of slave population for the two mainland provinces, Seyyidieh and Tanaland, in February 1902 revealed a total of 15,039 slaves (8160 in Seyyidieh, and 6879 in Tanaland). The legal status of slavery on the mainland was not terminated until 1907. And various aspects of the slavery question were still being tidied up in June 1909, when a decree provided that compensation would not be paid after 31 December 1911. Concubines were allowed to claim their freedom but forfeited their rights over their children. Compensation courts were set up in Mombasa, Lamu and other coastal towns in 1910.[39]

In retrospect, Hardinge was sensible in supporting gradual emancipation as a period of adjustment for both slaves and masters, so as to avert excesses known to have taken place in other slave-owning societies as a result of outright abolition. Hardinge's successors were the first to recognize the wisdom of his views.[40]

Recount and Summary

It is a formidable task to establish an overall figure for slave exports from Eastern Africa during the nineteenth century, much more arduous than a similar undertaking for the West African slave trade. The new world markets of the latter are well known and well documented; those for the Eastern Africa slave trade are obscured in a haze of mystery, and singularly lacking in written sources. To arrive at even a rough approximation of the number of slaves going to them is an exercise in hazarding, much extrapolation, and the weighing of disjointed evidence.

At the beginning of the nineteenth century, the number of slaves exported from the East African coast north of the Ruvuma river was about 4000 annually,[1] and this had risen to between 10,000 and 17,000 by the 1820s. There was also an annual export of 10,000 to 15,000 slaves from the Portuguese East African coast during the same period. Thus the total annual export of slaves from the East African coast during the 1820s probably ran at between 20,000 and 30,000.

Following the transfer of Sultan Said's court to Zanzibar in 1833, and the institution of custom house returns for slave imports and exports, the number of slaves 'legally' shipped north can be calculated on more reliable data, and would appear to be about 20,000 annually. This was Captain Cogan's and Colonel Hamerton's estimate in the late 1830s and early 1840s, and also that of Rigby at the mid-century. But they also averred that another 10,000 slaves were shipped north 'illegally', without duty being paid on them, and '3000 to 4000' were brought into Zanzibar by the Sultan and his family, on which no duty was paid.[2]

Thus, allowing for the substantial decline of the slave trade on the Portuguese East African coast at this date, the total annual export of slaves from the East African coast at the mid-century was probably running around the 30,000 mark, and this was sustained into the 1870s.

RECOUNT AND SUMMARY

After 1873, when the slave traffic at sea had been curtailed, slavers were resorting to the land route, and custom records are no longer available, it is more difficult to compute the number of slaves going northwards. Kirk and Vice-Admiral Macdonald put it at about 12,000 annually.[3] But many slaves taken north by the land route were absorbed in the plantation cultivation that was developing along the East African coast, and in Somaliland. Naval officers and British officials claimed that up to 10,000 passed into the latter territory each year.[4] Meanwhile the demand for slaves in the Middle East did not abate. Import there continued to run at between 6000 and 8000 annually,[5] mostly under cover of the French flag, until its use was curtailed at the turn of the century. The total export of slaves from the East African coast, south of the Horn, was thus probably running at about 20,000 annually well into the 1870s.

But to these figures must be added those for the rest of Eastern Africa. In Egypt, where the annual caravan from the Sudan brought in 5000 to 6000 slaves during the early nineteenth century, import had risen to between 20,000 and 30,000 by the second half of the century,[6] a figure which was sustained into the 1870s. About one-third of these were shipped to Turkey, but this was offset by an import into Egypt of slaves from Turkey.[7] There was also an import of 15,000 to 20,000 slaves annually into Mecca and Medina from the African side of the Red Sea, sustained well into the later nineteenth century, until it dropped to about 1500 annually during the last decade.[8] Thus, for the period from the 1820s to the 1870s, overall export from Eastern Africa was running at about 40,000 slaves per annum.[9]

In the 1880s, annual export from the East African coast, as recorded by missionaries at Unyanyembe and Mwapwa, stations admirably placed for assessing the volume of slaves proceeding coastwise, and at Kilwa, Lindi, Bagamoyo and Pangani, was between 4000 and 5000 annually.[10] In addition, another 2000 were shipped northwards by the land route. Thus total export of slaves from the East African coast in the 1880s was running at between 4000 and 7000 annually.

Thus, averaging out figures for the export of slaves from Eastern Africa for the nineteenth century as a whole: for the fifty years of the middle portion of the century (1820s to 1870s), export from the coast south of the Horn was about 20,000 annually; and from the northern half of Eastern Africa during the last 25 years of the same period (1850s to 1870s), about 30,000 to 40,000, say 35,000 annually. Adding to these totals those for Eastern Africa as a whole, for the first years of the century when figures were rising and at the end when they were tailing off, and taking these at 5000 a year for 50 years, we get an overall calculation:-

$(50 \times 20{,}000) + (25 \times 35{,}000) + (50 \times 5000) = 2{,}125{,}000$

And the above does not take into account the 'fringe numbers'—those slaves going in driblets of a few hundred a year to Madagascar well into the later part of the century, into South Arabia from across the Gulf of Tajurra, and the continuing trade in slaves from Ethiopia up to the turn of the century. Even allowing for an overestimate in the calculation of the above figures, it would seem fair to say that the export of slaves from Eastern Africa during the nineteenth century reached at least the two million mark.

NOTES

S.P. = Sessional Papers
F.O.C.P. = Foreign Office Confidential Print
F.O. = Foreign Office

CHAPTER 1

1. Wheeler, Sir Mortimer, *Rome Beyond Imperial Frontiers*, London 1953, p. 128.
2. Hourani, G. F., *Arab Seafaring in the Indian Ocean in Ancient and Early Medieval Times*, Princeton, 1951, pp. 1-24. Villiers, A., 'Dhow Builders of Kuwait', *Geographical Magazine*, p. xx, 1948.
3. Thompson, L. A., and Ferguson, J., *Africa in Classical Antiquity*, Ibadan, 1969, p. 26.
4. Cary, M., and Warmington, E. H., *The Ancient Explorers*, London, 1963, p. 101, pp. 123-4.
5. Jones, H. L., *The Geography of Strabo*, Harvard, 1959. Vol. VII. p. 341, Vol. XVI, p. 48. Cary and Warmington, p. 94.
6. C. Plinius Secundus, (transl. Holland, P.) *The Natural History*, Bk VI, London 1962, p. 65.
7. Breasted, J. H., *Ancient Records of Egypt*, Vol. II, New York, 1962, p. 486.
8. Fraser, P. M., *Ptolemaic Alexandria*, Vol. I, London, 1972, p. 74.
9. Seneca, *Letters*, LXXXVII, p. 9.
10. Roman Law, Digest of, (rescript concerning eastern trade) XXXIX, p. 5, XV, p. 7.
11. Strabo, *Geography*, IV, p. 16. V, p. 2.
12. Hj. Frisk, *Le Périple de la mer Erythrée*, Göteberg, 1927.
13. Various sites mentioned in the *Periplus* have been tentatively identified with points along the East African coast. The Cape of Spices is probably Cape Guardafui; Raphta is somewhere between Pangani and Kilwa Kisiwani; and Menouthias is possibly Zanzibar, Pemba or Mafia; Nikon is likely to be Port Durnford (Mathew, G., *History of East Africa*, Vol. I, London, 1963, p. 95.)
14. Freeman-Grenville, G. S. P., *The Medieval History of the Coast of Tanganyika*, Chapter I, 'The Times of Ignorance', London, 1962, pp. 28-9.
15. *The Christian Topography of Cosmas Indicopleustes*, edited by

Winsted, E. O., London, 1909: Mathew, G., *History of East Africa*, p. 98.
16. There is no evidence that Chinese traders personally visited East Africa; although they were capable of doing so in their large ocean-going vessels, and in that they were using the mariner's compass by 1000 A.D. (Needham, *Science and Civilization in China*, Vol. III, Cambridge 1959, p. 552, pp. 559-60: Lane, F. C., 'The Economic Meaning of the Invention of the Compass', *The American Historical Review*, LXVIII, 1963, pp. 605-17: Kirkman, J. 'China and Africa in the Middle Ages', *The Journal of African History*, Vol. IV, 1963, p. 297: Tibbetts, G. R., *Arab Navigation in the Indian Ocean Before the Coming of the Portuguese*, London, 1971, pp. 290-1).
17. Duyvendak, J. J. L., *China's Discovery of Africa*, London, 1949, pp. 13-14, pp. 23-4. Mathew, *History of East Africa*, pp. 107-8.
Huzayyin, S. A., *Arabia and the Far East*, Cairo, 1942, p. 213.
18. Duyvendak, p. 29.
19. Duyvendak, ibid. During the fifth voyage of Cheng Ho, 1417-19, envoys from Malindi were returned to East Africa after chaperoning two giraffes sent to China. The Chinese associated the giraffe with the fabulous unicorn, and composed a flowery hymn of praise in its honour (Duyvendak, p. 34; Hirth, F., 'Early Chinese Notices of East African Territories', *Journal of the American Oriental Society*, XXX, 1909, pp. 47-8: Filesi, T., *China and Africa in the Middle Ages*, London, 1972, pp. 21-2).
20. Hitti, P. K., *History of the Arabs*, London, 1971, pp. 467-8. The Muslim empire was flooded with slaves as a result of this upheaval. 'Even a pirate in the Syrian army at the battle of Siffin had from one to ten servants waiting on him' (Hitti p. 235).
21. Ibid.
22. Wilson, A. T., *The Persian Gulf*, London, 1928, p. 88.
23. Smith, V. A. *The Oxford History of India*, London, 1958, p. 272.
24. Barros J. de, *Decadas da Asia*, ed. A. Baiao, Coimbra, 1930, quoted in Kirkman, J. S., 'History of the Coast of East Africa to 1700', paper presented at Makerere, 1963. See also the same author's *Men and Monuments on the East African Coast*, London, 1964, wherein the history and atmosphere of the coast are woven into a rich tapestry.
25. According to oral tradition, orthodox Sunnis, from the Persian Gulf, fleeing from persecution by the Caliph of Bagdhad, founded Mogadishu and Barawa. Other arrivals referred to are the Dabuli, possibly from the ancient port of Dhabol on what is now the coast of Pakistan; Shirazis from Persia supposedly intermarrying with the local Bantu (Kashur) are connected with the legendary Kingdom of Shungwaya in southern Somaliland.
Claims to Persian descent, a form of self-flattery not uncommon on the Swahili coast, has some support in traditional history, and in blue-glazed pottery of post-Sassanian type found at various places in East Africa, and dating from the ninth century.
26. Chittick, N., 'Archaeological Research by the British Institute of Eastern Africa'. A Paper submitted to the International Congress of Africanists, 3rd Session, December 9-19, 1973, Addis Ababa, Ethiopia.

27. *Zanj*, the term given to the East African coast by medieval Arab writers, from the Persian *Zang* for Ethiopia; hence *Zanjibar* or *Zanzibar* (Hitti, p. 467).
28. Freeman-Grenville, G. S. P., *The East African Coast: Select Documents*, London, 1962, p. 10. Van der Lith, P. A., *Kitab al-Ajaib al-Hind* Leiden, 1883-6, p. 22.
29. Jaubert, P. A., *Géographie d'Edrisi* Paris, 1836-40, Vol. I, pp. 58-9.
30. Freeman-Grenville, *Select Documents*, p. 32.
31. *The Book of Duarte Barbosa*, Hakluyt Society, 1918-21, Vol. I, pp. 19-21.
32. Freeman-Grenville, *Select Documents*, p. 106.
33. Ibid, p. 109.
34. Ibid, p. 125.
35. Axelson, E. V., *Portuguese in South-East Africa 1600-1700*, Johannesburg, 1960, p. 55.
36. Livingstone, D., *Missionary Travels and Researches in South Africa. Including a Sketch of Sixteen Years Residence in the Interior of Africa*, London, 1857, p. 540.
37. Linschoten's Voyage, Hakluyt Society i 1885 pp. 24-33.
38. The appearance of Dutch and English slavers in East African waters in the seventeenth and eighteenth centuries were rare occurrences. An English pinnace in 1629, which captured 126 slaves from a Portuguese vessel in the Mozambique Channel; the *London*, carrying slaves from Madagascar to Barbados, wrecked on the Mozambique bar in 1682; the *Good Hope*, which sailed to East Africa in 1686 for slaves; the *Mercury* which carried slaves from Natal to Virginia in 1719; and a Dutch ship, the *Jagstrust*, which, in 1779, spent two months in Zanzibar collecting slaves; these about exhaust the list.
39. Boxer, C. R., *Fort Jesus and the Portuguese in Mombasa*, London, 1960, p. 84.
40. Ibid, p. 62.

CHAPTER 2

1. Duffy, J. *Portuguese Africa*, London, 1961, p. 146.
2. Hutchinson, E., *The Slave Trade of East Africa*, London, 1874, p. 18.
3. It was not yet overshadowed by nearby Chinde, which, after it was discovered in 1899 to be on the banks of a river navigable from the ocean, became the great port for the area.
4. Barnard, Lieutenant (RN) *A Three Year Cruise in the Mozambique Channel for the suppression of the Slave Trade*, London, 1848, p. 18.
5. Owen, W. F., *Narrative of Voyages to Explore the Shores of Africa, Arabia and Madagascar*, London 1833, Vol. I, p. 296.
6. Prior, J. *Voyage of the frigate Nisus*, London, 1819, p. 29.
7. Tete, 300 miles up the Zambezi, founded in 1531, and with a cathedral dating from 1563, was the only place of consequence in the interior; Zumbo, a mere outpost, marked the limits of Portuguese occupation in the interior. Nearby Borama, centre of early Jesuit activity, was an abandoned ruin.
8. Prior, pp. 25-45, noted that recent British conquest of the Mascarenes and vigilance of naval patrols had reduced the annual

output to about 3000; 'quite enough to shock any mind but that of a slave-trader. I am afraid we are not in great favour here ... A British man-of-war seldom is ... an Englishman's mind is supposed to be filled with designs against their commerce'.

9. Newitt, M. D. D. *Portuguese Settlement on the Zambezi*, London, 1973, p. 221.
10. Buxton, T. F. *The African Slave Trade*, London, 1839, pp. 28-9.
11. Owen, Vol. I, pp. 292-3.
12. For a study of the prazeros see Newitt, M. D. D. *Portuguese Settlement on the Zambezi*, London, 1973; and Isaacman, A., *Mozambique, the Africanization of a European Institution, the Zambezi Prazos 1750-1902*, London, 1972.
13. S.P. XXXIX 1852/53, Select Committee Report, Q. 1624.
14. Coupland, Sir R., *East Africa and its Invaders* Oxford, 1938, p. 172.
15. Barnard, p. 13.
16. S.P. IX 1850, p. 113.
17. S.P. XXXIX 1852/53, Select Committee, Q. 1627.
18. S.P. LXI 1862, No. 102, Rigby to Russell, 5 Oct. 1861.
19. S.P. XXXIX 1852/53, Select Committee Q. 1627.
20. Treaties of alliance in 1809 and 1810 between Portugal and Britain affirmed their intention of working towards abolition of the slave trade. At the Congress of Vienna, 1815, Portugal was a signatory with Britain to a convention forbidding her subjects to carry on the slave trade north of the Equator; and by a convention of 1817, with Britain, she prohibited the use of the Portuguese flag as cover for the slave trade outside Portuguese possessions; mixed Commissions were set up at Rio de Janeiro and Sierre Leone to adjudicate on captured slave vessels, and limited right of search was conceded to Britain. The latter right however availed little, for a vessel could not be condemned unless slaves were on board, or there was 'clear and undeniable proof that slaves had been on board for the purpose of illegal traffic'. Usual evidence of slaving, extra decks, slave-chains, etc., was not admissible. The slave trade was made unlawful for Portuguese vessels after January 1823 (later extended to 1830, when the traffic was declared piracy) with severe punishment and confiscation of their ships decreed for slave traders. The most substantial gain was that of December 1836, which forbade export of slaves from Portuguese possessions.
21. Livingstone, D. *Missionary Travels*, p. 342.
22. Buxton T. F. *The African Slave Trade*, London, 1839, p. 15.
23. Ibid. p. 29.
24. Bennett N. R. and Brooks G.E. *New England Merchants in Africa*, Boston, 1965, p. 192.
25. Quoted in Mathieson, W. L. *Great Britain and the Slave Trade*, London, 1929, pp. 20-1.
26. Under the treaty Courts of Mixed Commission were set up at Loanda and Mauritius.
27. *Anti-Slavery Reporter*, Vol. 5, New Series, 1850.
28. Bennett and Brooks, p. 258.
29. Hill, P. G. *Fifty Days on Board a Slave Vessel in the Mozambique Channel*, London. 1844, p. 54.

30. In 1819 the Seychelles and Mauritius were transferred from the naval control of the 'Indian Station' to that of the 'Cape Station'; and in 1820, one ship was specifically directed to be stationed at Mauritius for the purpose of assisting its governor in suppressing the slave trade at that island (S.P. VIII, 1820, 911, C. 191).
31. Devereux, W. C. *A Cruise in the Gorgon,* London, 1869, p. 57, p. 61.
32. Report of Commissioners at the Cape, 1848.
33. His most notable seizure was the *Progresso,* a well-known slaver, captured near Quelimane after a seven-hour chase, which only hove to when musketry reached her sails. The slaves on the *Progresso,* following its capture, broke loose from their confinement, opened casks of *aqua ardiente,* and gorged themselves on salt food to the extent that fifty died the first night. It took fifty days to get the *Progresso* to the Cape; during the passage more than half the original number of slaves died (S.P. LVI 1851, Part I. See also Barnard, p. 40.)
34. Sulivan, G. L. *Dhow Chasing in Zanzibar Waters,* London, 1873, p. 21.
35. Burton, R. F. *Zanzibar,* London 1872, Vol I, p. 476.
36. S.P. LVI 1854/55, No. 123, Commodore Talbot to Secretary to Admiralty, 31 Jan. 1854.
37. S.P. LVI 1854/55. Correspondence between the Commissioners, Cape of Good Hope, the British Admiralty Courts and British Naval Officers respecting the slave trade; April 1854 to March 1855 (H.M.'s Commrs to Clarendon, 27 Mar. 1854).
38. Bethel, L., *The Abolition of the Brazilian Slave Trade,* London, 1973, p. 334, (Appendix) gives an import of 'well over one million slaves' during the first half of the nineteenth century; but does not indicate what proportion of this came from East Africa.
39. Colomb, P. *Slave Catching in the Indian Ocean,* London, 1873, p. 447.
40. S.P. LXII 1870, p. 801. Colomb, p. 447.
41. Coupland, Sir Reginald, *The British Anti-Slavery Movement,* London, 1933, p. 164.
42. The American Ambassador at Paris, General Cass, author of *An Examination of the Right of Search,* probably influenced the French government in its stand against ratifying the Quintuple Treaty which conceded full right of search.
43. S.P. LXIV 1867/68 No 80, 8 Apr. 1867. The loss sustained by its owners when the Spanish barque, *Duke of Tetuan,* ran ashore in 1864 set them back a year.
44. In 1856 Commodore Trotter, rejoicing over the decline of the emigré slave trade and that fewer slaves were now carried round the Cape, was unaware that seven large clippers, including the notorious *Minnetonka,* were on their way to Mozambique (S.P. LXIV, 1857/58, No 60, 6 June 1857: ibid, No 70, 15 Jan. 1858: S.P. LXIV 1861, Commander Oldfield's report, 30 June 1860).
45. S.P. LXI 1862, No 98, Commander Oldfield to Secretary to Admiralty, 31 Dec. 1860.
46. S.P. LXI 1862, No 99 Commander Buckley to Keppel, 31 Dec. 1860.

S.P. LXI 1862, No 97, 14 May 1861: ibid, No 98, 12 July 1861.
47. Malloy, W. M., 'Treaties and Conventions', U.S. Documents, No 5646, I, pp. 674–87.
48. S.P. LXXI 1863, No 192, Earl Russell to Mr Herries (Ambassador at Lisbon) 28 July 1862.
49. In April 1875, Portugal ordered the abolition of the servile condition of the *Libertos*, one year from that date; and in 1878 the Lisbon government decreed abolition of slavery throughout Portuguese possessions.
50. S.P. LXVI, 1864, No 84, Playfair to Bombay Government, 16 Nov. 1863.
51. S.P. LXI 1862, No 105, Sir A. Magenis to Russell, 16 Feb. 1861. Ibid, No 106, 16 Apr. 1861.
52. Ibid, No 97, 8 Aug. 1863.
53. S.P. LXI 1873, No 31, Frere's Report, 27 Feb. 1873.
54. Bissell, *A Voyage from England to the Red Sea 1789-9* London, 1806, pp. 38–41; Bennett and Brooks, p. 520.
55. Nicholls, op. cit. p. 96.
56. Freeman-Grenville, *Select Documents*, p. 191.
57. Ibid. pp. 195–6.
58. Freeman-Grenville, G. S. P., *The French at Kilwa Island*, London, 1965, p. 216.
59. Gray, Sir John Milner, *History of Zanzibar from the Middle Ages to 1856*, London, 1962, pp. 99–101.
60. Freeman-Grenville, *Select Documents*, p. 206.
61. Prior, pp. 80–1.
62. S.P. LXXV 1829, Report of Commissioners of Inquiry upon the Slave Trade at Mauritius.
63. Confiscation of the ship concerned, and suspension of officers from service for ten years, as compared with the severe penalties under the British act of 1811. Under the Abolition Act of 1807 slave ships captured by the British anti-slave trade patrol were forfeited to the Crown; a penalty of £100 imposed for every slave captured; and generous bounties awarded to officers and men concerned in the capture of the slave vessel. The Penal Act of 1811 declared slave-trading a felony punishable by transportation for fourteen years. A Consolidating Act of 1824 (Geo IV, c 113), declared slave-trading to be piracy and punishable by 'death without benefit of clergy': this was repealed in 1837 in favour of transportation for life. An Act of 1843 extended these penalties to wherever British subjects were domiciled.
64. S.P. VIII 1820/21, pp. 259–387.
65. Graham, G. S. *Great Britain in the Indian Ocean*, London, 1967, pp. 54–5.
66. '400 soldiers' caps, shoes, and clothing, 100 barrels of gunpowder, 100 English muskets, and 10,000 flints'.
67. S.P. VIII 1820/21, p. 331, pp. 353–4.
68. S.P. XXIII, 1821, pp. 5–6.
69. S.P. XXXIX, 1852/53, No 7. Report of Select Committee on the Slave Trade.

70. It was not ineffective, as witness the case quoted in the *Observer* of 22 Feb. 1969, a reprint from the *Observer* of 22 Feb. 1819: 'Philip Caday alias Phillibert, Amand Clarensac, and Joseph Ann Tregrosse, were arraigned at the Old Bailey on Saturday to take trial for having feloniously taken a number of Negroes from the Mozambique Islands, on the coast of Africa, and carried them to the Isle de France, in the Mauritius, for the purpose of being dealt with as slaves, contrary to the statute etc. the *Magicienne* frigate was stationed off the Isle de France to suppress the traffic in slaves. The captain saw a schooner, of which the prisoners were part of the crew, in the harbour, and suspected it was in the slave trade. He sent some of his men in pursuit and it was discovered that 92 human beings had been landed for the purpose of sale. The prisoners were afterwards apprehended. They were found guilty and sentenced to three years' confinement in the House of Correction, and to hard labour.'
71. Hansard, 1826, XV, p. 1031.
72. S.P. XXXV, 1829, Report of Commissioners of Inquiry.
73. S.P. XXXVII 1849, Report on Mauritius.
74. S.P. LXI 1857/58 No 186, Captain Lyster to Rear-Admiral Sir F. Grey, 24 Nov. 1857.
75. S.P. LXI 1857/58, Commodore Trotter to Admiralty, 10 Dec. 1856.
76. Guillain, M. *Documents: l'Afrique Orientale,* ii, Paris, 1856 pp. 52-3 p. 124.
77. Scott, R. *Limuria, The Lesser Dependencies of Mauritius,* London, 1961, p. 126.
78. Zanzibar Archives: Hamerton to Bombay Government, 13 Aug. 1841.
79. *Anti-Slavery Reporter,* Vol. 2, Dec. 1840.
80. Zanzibar Archives: Willoughby J., Chief Secretary, Bombay Government, to Hamerton 30 Nov. 1841. An attempt by Mauritian planters in November 1844 to offer premiums for recruitment of labourers from East Africa was quickly disallowed by the British government.
81. In all the literature on the subject, there is little evidence of the return of these engagés to Africa on the expiry of their term of contract.
82. Zanzibar Archives: Hamerton to Bombay Government, 12 Nov. 1851.
83. S.P. XIV 1857, No 130, 30 Nov. 1856.
84. S.P. LXI 1857/58, Commodore Trotter to Admiralty, 10 Dec. 1856.
85. S.P. XXXIV 1859, Consul Sunley to Grey, 3 Oct. 1858.
86. Ibid.
87. Russell, C. E. B. *General Rigby, Zanzibar and the Slave Trade,* London, 1935, pp. 145, 186.
88. It was supposedly his revulsion at the suffering on the field of battle at Solferino which led to the founding of the Red Cross.
89. S.P. LXXI 1863, No 126, Incl. Commander Stirling to Rear-Admiral Sir B. Walker, 30 June 1861.
90. S.P. LXI 1862, No 102, Rigby to Russell, 5 Oct. 1861.
91. S.P. LXVI 1864, Incl. Playfair to Bombay Government, 16 Nov. 1863.

92. S.P. LIV 1868/69 No 37, Consul Pakenham to Lord Stanley, Tamatave, 16 June 1868.
93. S.P. LXXV 1866 No 108, Incl. Consul de Castro to Mr Lytton, 11 Sept. 1865.
94. S.P. LXXV 1866, No 35, Wm. Sunley's report, 5 Jan. 1865.

CHAPTER 3

1. An excellent account of the coast for this period is that by Nicholls, C. S., *The Swahili Coast, Politics, Diplomacy and Trade on the East African Littoral 1798–1856*, London, 1971.
2. These letters are referred to in a Paper, 'The External Relations of the East African coast: before 1800', presented by Freeman-Grenville, G. S. P., at the Colston Symposium, University of Bristol, April 1973.
3. *Voyages of Sir James Lancaster to the East Indies*, Hakluyt Society, London, 1877, pp. 6–8. p. 26.
4. The *Union* and *Ascension* in 1609-1610; an English pinnace which took off slaves from a Portuguese slaver in the Mozambique Channel in 1629; the frigate *Good Hope* in 1686; the *London* wrecked on the Mozambique bar in 1682; the *Mercury* carrying slaves from Natal to Virginia in 1719; these about complete the list.
5. *A New Account of the East Indies* Edinburgh 1727, by Alexander Hamilton, who had not visited there, also refers to East Africa. Nicholls, op.cit. p. 94.
6. Bissell, A., pp. 31-7. See also Coupland, *East Africa and Its Invaders*, pp. 162-70; Gray, *Zanzibar*, p. 98; *Africa Pilot*, Part III, South and East Coast of Africa, London, 1929.
7. Freeman-Grenville: *Select Documents*, pp. 198–200.
8. India Office Library: Maritime Records: Misc. 586 (Smee's account of Zanzibar). See also his *Voyage to the Eastern Shores of Africa, 1811*, Transactions of Bombay Geographical Society, Vol. VI, 1844.
9. Aitchison, C. U., *A Collection of Treaties, Engagements and Sanads Relating to India and Neighbouring Countries*, Vol. X, Delhi, 1933, p. 128.
10. Gray, *Zanzibar:* p. 232.
11. Jones, M. K., 'The Slave Trade at Mauritius 1810-1829' B. Litt. Thesis, University of Oxford, 1938, p. 194: Ad 1/69 Captain Moresby to Rear-Admiral Lambert, 30 Sept. 1821.
12. Edwardes, S. M. *Rise of Bombay*, London, 1902, p. 163.
13. Banaji, D. R. *Slavery in British India*, Bombay, 1933, pp. 73-5.
14. Especially to Charles Grant, a leading member of the Clapham sect, who served 17 years in Bengal.
15. In 1805 the Bombay Government issued a regulation declaring that 'the importation and exportation of slaves for the purposes of traffic at the port of Bombay and at other ports subject to the immediate authority of this Presidency stand prohibited' (Bombay regulation, May 14, 1805); in 1807 it was legislated that masters or owners of all ships except the Company's must make declaration that they were not carrying or intending to carry slaves, subject to imposition of a

fine of 500 rupees for infringement of the prohibition. (Bombay regulation, 22 Sept. 1807). In 1811 a similar measure enacted in Bengal 'for preventing the importation of slaves from foreign countries and the sale of such slaves in the territories immediately dependent on the Presidency of Fort William' provided that importation should be punished by imprisonment for six months and a fine not exceeding 200 rupees or another six months' imprisonment, and required that 'captains and supercargoes of vessels, with the exception of the Honourable Company's ships, importing at Calcutta shall, previously to being permitted to land any part of their cargo or goods, execute a bond, rendering themselves liable to the payment of a penalty of rupees five thousand in the event of their disposing of any persons as slaves' (Bengal Regulation X, 6 Aug. 1811). In 1813 this regulation was adopted also in Bombay. (Bombay Regulation of 5 May 1813.)

16. St. Helena was under East India Company control until 1834 when it was placed under Crown Colony government.
17. F.O.C.P. 6805/211, Memorandum on Slavery in India, Kirk, J. 13 Dec. 1895. All questions of emancipation and compensation were avoided by refusing to recognize that slavery had any legal status in India. About 200,000 slaves were affected by this legislation; the number of these who were African slaves is not indicated.
18. The French had a factory at Basra by the beginning of the eighteenth century, a Residency at Basra in 1755, and had carried out a survey of the Persian Gulf in 1785.
19. This occupation did not take place until the threat of the Napoleonic advance on India in 1808.
20. Wilson, A. T., *The Persian Gulf,* Oxford, 1928, pp. 189-91.
21. India Office Records: Bombay Political and Secret Consultations, Vol. 32, 1812, pp. 388-90: Secretary to Bombay Government to Said, 4 Mar. 1812.
22. Miles, S. B., *The Countries and Tribes of the Persian Gulf,* London, 1919, p. 276, pp. 312-26.
23. India Office, Bombay Political and Secret Consultations, 1815; 3685, Nepean to Said, 26 July 1815.
24. Aitchison, Vol. X. p. 128.
25. C.O. 167/58, Farquhar to Bathurst, 14 Apr. 1821, Moresby to Farquhar, 4 Apr. 1821, Farquhar to Moresby, 5 Apr. 1821.
26. C.O. 167/58, Farquhar to Hastings, 28 Sept. 1821.
27. C.O. 167/58, Hastings to Farquhar, 4 Dec. 1821.
28. India Office: Bombay Political and Secret Consultations, Government of Bombay to Said, 7 Aug. 1821. C.O. 167/58 Farquhar to Said, 11 May, 1821, enclosure in Farquhar to Bathurst, 4 Dec. 1821.
29. C.O. 167/62, Farquhar to Bathurst, 29 Feb. 1822.
30. C.O. 167/62, Said to Governor of Bombay, 13 Dec. 1821; Governor of Bombay to Said, 22 Jan. 1822; Farquhar to Said, 15 Mar. 1822; Farquhar to Bathurst, 29 Feb. (sic) 1822.
31. C.O. 167/62, Bruce to Governor of Bombay, 20 Feb. 1822.
32. Admiralty Records (Public Records Office) i, 2188: Farquhar to Moresby, 3 June 1822, Ibid., Farquhar to Moresby. 10 June 1822,

C.O. 167/63, Farquhar to Said, 10 July 1822.
33. Admiralty, i, 2188, Farquhar to Moresby, 10 June 1822.
34. Letters from Wilberforce to Moresby, 28 May 1822; quoted in letter to *The Times* of 1 Aug. 1933, from Admiral Sir Fairfax Moresby. Coupland *East Africa and its Invaders*, p. 214.
35. Admiralty, i, 2188, Moresby to Admiralty, 9 June 1822.
36. ... you may seize every (Arab) vessel you may fall in with beyond Madagascar, and in the sea of Mauritius, after four months from the date of the permission ... and you may carry in to me for my disposal any ship you may meet even on this side (the Isle de France), provided she have not the written statement required from the governor of the port whence she sailed' (Answers under His Highness the Imaum of Muskat's Hand and Seal, to the Requisitions made by Captain Moresby, of His Majesty's ship *Menai*, Commissioner etc. 7 Sept. 1822, Bombay Records, pp. 655-6: Graham, p. 200).

There was no competent interpreter present when Said signed the 'requisition and answers' version in Arabic of the proposals presented to him to limit the slave trade; this Arab version, later translated into English at Bombay, revealed significant differences from the original proposals in English. The version in Arabic to which Said assented was listed as official by Aitchison, at the end of the nineteenth century (Aitchison, Vol. XI, p. 289: B.P.C. 385/26 Proc. 18 Sept. 1822, Moresby to Farquhar, 11 Sept. 1822: B.P.C. 385/26 Proc. 25 Sept. 1822. See also Selections from Bombay Records, XXXIV, pp. 654-7, 1856.) In Moresby's version culprits were to be sent to Said for punishment, but in the Arabic version officers involved in the capture were to inflict this punishment themselves, and vessels east of the stated line were to be treated 'in the same manner as if they were under the English flag' (Nicholls, pp. 223-4).
37. Zanzibar Archives: Hamerton to Bombay Government, 1 Feb. 1843. (Crowns here mean Maria Theresa thalers).
38. P.P. XVIII Nourse to Admiralty, 5 Jan. 1823.
39. Owen, W. F., *Narrative* Vol. i, p. 366. When Owen decided to publish his account of the expedition, Boteler allowed him to use the journal he had kept on the voyage. Boteler's journal and notes, largely ascribed to Owen, were published in 1833. Boteler's narrative was published in its own right in 1835 as *Narrative of Discovery to Africa and Arabia*, 2 Vols., London, 1835.
40. Gray, *Zanzibar*, p. 117.
41. Owen's Report to Admiralty, i, iii 24 (Adm i 2269).
42. In 1814 they sent him a derisory gift instead of the munificent offering usually accorded him.
43. Encouraged by the visit of Captain Vidal with HMS *Barracouta* and *Albatross* in 1823, (they were also part of Owen's expedition). Vidal was hailed as a deliverer, and pending arrival of Owen, he sailed in the *Barracouta* to Pemba. (Boteler, T. *Narrative of a Voyage of Discovery to Africa and Arabia* London, 1835 Vol. ii, pp. 1-12. For an account of the affair see also Gray, Sir John M., *The British in Mombasa, 1824-1826*, London, 1958.)
44. Owen, *Narrative*, Vol. i, p. 368.
45. Owen left East Africa in February 1825; the remainder of his career

was spent in climes far removed from East African waters, in survey work on the great lakes of Canada.

46. Although offset to some extent by the acquisition of Socotra (1834) and Aden (1839), regret for the missed opportunity was expressed in 1842 by the Political Agent in the Persian Gulf. 'The shortest and simplest check we shall ever be able to impose is to obtain possession of the seaports or line of coast of Africa whence the slaves are imported and to prevent the arrival there of slaves from the interior or the sale of them' (Zanzibar Archives: Hamerton to Bombay Government, 6 July 1843). A similar view was expressed to the Select Committee on the Slave Trade in 1871. In 1883, faced by a German irruption in East Africa, Sir John Kirk ruefully remarked 'It is a pity we hauled down the British flag at Mombasa when we held it under cession in 1823. Had we kept Mombasa and the whole coast then ceded to us, the slave question would have been settled and by this time we should have had dominion over tropical Africa' (Coupland, *The Exploitation of East Africa* London, 1939, p. 387).

47. Horace P. Putnam who visited Zanzibar in July 1847 described his approach to the island by sea—
'I never beheld a more beautiful sight than this island presented to the eye. As we sailed along the shores for miles we beheld nought but was the most grand to gaze upon; fruits of the most delicious kinds we saw in abundance. The cocoa nut and the orange tree were laden with their rich treasure, and almost sunk beneath their burden. The air was fresh and cool; which being scented with the rich perfumes of the shore or land breezes made it truly an acceptable treat to the mariner who had not seen the least particle of vegetable life for 70 days'.
A closer view was less attractive—
'The appearance of the city is anything but inviting. The houses are mostly low thatched hovels built of clay mud and timber, with a few rocks to keep together the structure. The buildings in which the nobility and the foreigners residence are more respectable in their appearance. The streets (if they deserve the name of such) are mear paths of some six or ten feet in width, dirty and filled with rubbish ... it is the most despicable looking place I have yet seen. Herds of Slaves were continually going about the streets with their drivers following in their rear urging them to the market where they were to be sold like cattle. The whole island is covered with slaves. They are brought from the African coast where they are obtained in large numbers and at small cost'. (Bennett and Brooks, *New England Merchants in Africa* p. 400. See also Isaacs, Nathaniel, *Travels and Adventures in Eastern Africa*, 2 vols., London, 1836; Roberts, Edmund, *Embassy to the Eastern Courts of Cochin China, Siam and Muscat, 1832-4*, New York, 1837; Ruschenberger, S. W., *Voyage round the World*, 2 Vols. Philadelphia, 1838.)

48. S.P. XXVII, 1838/39, p. 886 (Cogan's memorandum, 5 Dec. 1839).

49. Zanzibar Archives: Hamerton to Bombay Government, 13 July 1841. Ibid. 5 Sept. 1844. Burckhardt, J. L., *Travels in Nubia*, London, 1819, p. 314, puts the annual export of slaves from the 'eastern side of Africa to Egypt and Arabia' at 15,000 to 20,000.

50. For an estimate of number of slaves imported into the Persian Gulf area see Kelly, J. B., *Britain and the Persian Gulf, 1795-1880,* Oxford, 1968, pp. 414-7. These average out Hamerton's and Bruck's figures:

Exports north from Zanzibar	10,000 to 15,000
To Muscat and Sur	8,000 to 10,000
To Hadhramaut and Red Sea	2,000 to 5,000

Perhaps 5000 to 8000 were absorbed in Oman, Piratical Sheikhdoms, and the interior of Arabia. About 3000 to 5000 to the upper Gulf (including those brought by pilgrims); and another 1500 to 2000 going to Sind, Kutch and Kathiawar.

51. Dr T. Mackenzie, Acting Resident in the Persian Gulf in 1840, stated that 4000 slaves were annually shipped up the Gulf from Muscat and Sur, and that 100 vessels were involved in the slave trade at Muscat. (F.O. 84/387 Mackenzie to Sec. Bombay Government, 16 Oct. 1840). Commodore G. B. Brucks, of the Gulf Squadron of the Indian Navy, in October 1842, placed the number of slaves exported from Said's dominions to Red Sea ports, Jeddah and Muscat, and ports in southern Arabia, at between 10,000 and 15,000; of this number, 4000 to 5000 went to Muscat; with probably another 500 going to southern Arabian ports between Aden and Mukalla. The number of vessels involved in the trade being about 100 (F.O. 84/501 Brucks to Aberdeen, 5 Oct. 1842).

52. Captain Haines of the Indian Navy, in 1838, had seen exposed for sale at Mokhara, in one lot, 799 Nubian girls at £7 to £25 apiece (Haines, S. B. 'Memoir to Accompany a Chart of the South Coast of Arabia'. *Journal of the Royal Geographical Society*, Vol. 9, 1839, p. 150. See also Wellsted, J. R. *Travels in Arabia,* London, 1838, Vol. i, p. 388.

53. Colomb. J. R. p. 125 'the most unhappy looking coast we had visited', Owen *Narratives* Vol. i, p. 346.

54. Owen *Narratives,* Vol. i, p. 339.

55. *The Times,* 14 Feb. 1839.

56. Badger, G. P. *History of the Imams and Seyyids of Oman by Salil ibn Razik* Hakluyt Society. 1871, p. 93.

57. Miles, S. B. *The Countries and Tribes of the Persian Gulf,* London, 1919, p. 265.

58. Maurizi, V. *History of Seyyid Said*, London, 1819. p. 29.

59. Selections from the Records of the Bombay Government, 633, No XXIV, New Series, Bombay, 1856. The effect of this East African infusion of blood is seen today in the 'polyglot Salala suq where the numbers of black people attest Oman's centuries of contact with East Africa' *National Geographic,* Vol. 143, Feb. 1973. In some areas the population ranges from the almost pure negro type to the Arab with woolly hair and thick lips.

60. Bennett and Brooks, p. 435.

61. Owen, *Narratives* Vol. 1, p. 336.

62. Sheikh Mansur, *History of Seyd Said,* London, 1819, p. 131.

63. Keppell, G. (Major) *A Journey from India to England,* Vol. 1, London, 1834, pp. 21-2.

NOTES

64. Wellsted, J. R., *Travels to the City of the Caliphs,* Vol. 1, London, 1848, p. 58.
65. Hughes, W. *The Country of Baluchistan,* Bombay, 1877, p. 45.
66. Indian Office Pamphlet, P.W./4046.
67. Carroll, M., *From a Persian Tea House,* London, 1960, p. 158.
68. Lugard, F. D., *Rise of Our East African Empire*, Vol. I, London, 1893, p. 183.
69. This did not prevent the transport of Somali female slaves to the Persian Gulf in 1841. Their release was effected by the Resident in the Gulf, and they were returned to Berbera in the same year. F.O. 84/444 Hennell to Willoughby, 16 Oct. 1841.
70. Zanzibar Archives, Hamerton to Bombay Government, 13 July 1841. Hamerton had been directed by the Bombay Government, in December 1840, to proceed to Zanzibar 'with as little delay as possible for the purpose of ascertaining all the particulars of the aggressions attributed to the French'.
71. F.O. 84/342, Memo by Palmerston, 12 Dec. 1840: and see Harris, W. C. *The Highlands of Ethiopia,* London, 1844, Vol. I, pp. 227-9. Vol. II, pp. 208-9.
72. F.O. 84/387 Leveson to Cabell, 8 June 1841.
73. F.O. 84/444 Said to the Queen, 11 Feb. 1842. F.O. 84/425 Aberdeen to Ali ibn Nasir, 9 Nov. 1842. Zanzibar Archives: Hamerton to Bombay Government, 28 Dec. 1842.
74. Zanzibar Archives: Hamerton to Foreign Office, 2 Aug. 1842.
75. Zanzibar Archives: Hamerton to Foreign Office, 28 Sept. 1846.
76. Zanzibar Archives: Hamerton to Foreign Office, 28 Sept. 1846.
77. Aitchison, *Treaties,* Vol. xi, pp. 68-70. F.O. 84/647, Hamerton to Aberdeen, 28 Sept. 1846.
78. Aitchison, Vol. X, pp. 133-4.
79. Zanzibar Archives: Hamerton to Foreign Office, 4 Oct. 1845.
80. F.O. 84/647, Palmerston to Hamerton, 6 Dec. 1846.
81. Zanzibar Archives: Hamerton to Bombay Government, 5 Sept. 1846. (The Sultan's fleet consisted of one 74-gun ship, one 50-gun ship, one 26-gun frigate, two corvettes of 14 and 10 guns, and one 'schooner yacht': all were destroyed in the great hurricane of 1872.)
82. Zanzibar Archives: Hamerton to Foreign Office, 27 Mar. 1849.
83. Zanzibar Archives: Hamerton to Bombay Government, 23 Jan. 1847.
84. Zanzibar Archives: Captain Parker to Foreign Office, 18 Feb. 1848.
85. Zanzibar Archives: Hamerton to Palmerston, 21 Aug. 1850.
86. Aitchison, *Treaties,* Vol. X, Appendix 46, Vol. XI, Appendix 4.
87. F.O. 84/737 Hamerton to Palmerston, 13 Nov. 1848.
88. Zanzibar Archives: Hamerton to Bombay Government, 27 June 1850.
89. Krapf, J. L. *Travels, Researches, and Missionary Labours in Eastern Africa,* London, 1860, pp. 112, 411, 423-4.
90. Said was succeeded at Zanzibar by his second surviving son, Majid, and in Oman by his eldest surviving son, Thwain; but when the latter claimed the East African dominions of his father, and threatened to send an expedition against Majid in 1861, Lord Canning, Governor-General of India, intervened, and by the 'Canning Award' of the same year, confirmed Majid as Sultan of Zanzibar, and Thwain as ruler of Oman: but the Sultan of Zanzibar was to pay Muscat 40,000

dollars (£8500) annually as compensating for loss of Zanzibar. The Anglo-French Declaration of March 1862 confirmed this arrangement.
91. Bennett and Brooks, p. 415.
92. Russell, *General Rigby,* Appendix II.
93. S.P. LXXI 1863, No. 126, Incl. Report by Captain Oldfield, 20 Nov. 1861.
94. *Anti-Slavery Reporter,* Vol. 9, No. 1, 1861. The Sultan, on 6 July 1850, had issued an edict forbidding Indians from buying or selling slaves in his African dominions; but this remained a dead letter. Report of Charles Ward, Bennett and Brooks p. 462.
95. When Rigby left Zanzibar the French representative reported that the Indian residents, because of the British official's harsh regulations rejoiced as if it were 'the termination of a great catastrophe'. Jablonski to Thuvenel, 7 Sept. 1861, Bennett and Brooks, p. 518.
96. Zanzibar Archives: Rigby to Chief Sec., Bombay Government, 14 May 1861.
97. S.P. LXI, No. 102, Rigby to Russell, 5 Oct. 1861.
98. S.P. LXIV 1867/68, Hillyar to Sec. to Admiralty, 8 Apr. 1867.
99. S.P. LXXV 1866, No. 75. Playfair to Russell, 30 May 1865.
100. Zanzibar Archives: Playfair to Chief Sec. Bombay Government, 23 May 1863.
101. Zanzibar Archives: Playfair to Chief Sec. Bombay Government, 1 Jan. 1864.
102. S.P. LXXIII 1867, No. 91, Incl. 2, Captain Bedenfield to Commodore Hillyar, 12 May 1866.
103. A dhow captured by the *Lyra* and condemned at Cape Town in January 1868, carried bogus passes and papers from both the Sultan of Muscat and Sultan of Zanzibar. S.P. LVI 1868/69, No. 18, H.M. Commrs to Stanley, 1 Feb. 1868.
104. S.P. LXXIII 1867, No 79, Commander Latham to Sec. Admiralty, 19 Jan. 1866.
105. S.P. LXXXV 1866, No 75, Playfair to Russell, 30 May 1865.
106. Zanzibar Archives: Churchill to Chief Secretary, Bombay Government, 22 Dec. 1867.
107. See Ruete, Emily (Salma binti Said), *Memoirs of an Arabian Princess,* Berlin 1886.
108. *Anti-Slavery Reporter,* Vol. 16, No 10, 1 July 1869.
109. S.P. LVI 1868/69, No 93, Churchill to Stanley, 21 Aug. 1868.
110. Bennett and Brooks, p. 535. At the same time as the duty on slaves was raised, the Sultan abolished the tax of two pice annually on every fruit-bearing cocoanut tree. The tax on slaves was much easier to collect.
111. Bennett and Brooks, p. 261.
112. Ibid.
113. Playfair, R. L. 'Report on the various Countries around Zanzibar' *Transactions of the Bombay Geographical Society,* Vol. XVIII, 1865, p. 263, describes the slaves of Zanzibar as 'the gayest and happiest class of the community'.
114. Bennett and Brooks, p. 427. Ruschenberger, *A Voyage round the*

World, Vol. 1. p. 34, states that in the public square at Zanzibar, slaves were sold from a wooden cage every day at sunset to the highest bidder. 'The cage is twenty feet square and at one time during our short visit there were no less than one hundred and fifty slaves, men, women and children locked up in it'. I have found no other reference to this 'wooden cage'.

115. S.P. 1868/69 No. 17, Livingstone to Clarendon, 11 June 1866
116. Colomb, pp. 392-3.
117. Ibid.
118. S.P. LXI 1873, No 56, 29 May 1873. Sir Bartle Frere's Report on his visit to East Africa. Elton who visited the Zanzibar slave market in 1873, placed the price of slaves at 11-14 dollars for a shamba (garden worker) slave; 30-45 dollars for Surias (concubine slaves) sold for misconduct; and 24-25 dollars for domestic slaves and girls. These high prices were likely consequent on the recent cholera epidemic which had created a great scarcity of slaves.
119. Ibid.
120. A slave rising did take place in Zanzibar in the summer of 1840. It appears to have been confined to members of the Zigua tribe, originally from the African mainland, a few miles inland from the coast opposite Zanzibar. A number of these slaves seized Arab dhows at Zanzibar and escaped to the mainland; others held out in Zanzibar for some months until the arrival of mercenary troops from the Hadhramaut suppressed the uprising. (Gray, Sir John Milner *History of Zanzibar,* pp. 141-2.) The whole affair occasioned little concern in Zanzibar. Hamerton, arriving as British Consul the next year, makes scarcely passing reference to it. There was nothing in East Africa comparable to the great slave rising that took place in the Euphrates Valley in the ninth century.
121. Bennett and Brooks p. 427.
122. Prior, pp. 75-7.
123. S.P. LXI 1870, Report of Clarendon Committee, 1869/70.

CHAPTER 4

1. 'dhow'—from 'dau', the small sailing craft native to Zanzibar waters—but more widely applied to all lateen rigged vessels plying the Arabian Sea and Indian Ocean: see Steere, E., *Handbook of the Swahili Language as Spoken at Zanzibar,* London, 1870.
2. But see the experience of an American, Ephraim A. Emmerton, who journeyed on an Arab dhow in the Mozambique Channel in June 1849: 'This is the greatest specimen of navigation that I have ever yet seen. They have a compass but no charts, quadrants nor anything that are of use to the navigator. They know the course from one place to another, and steer for it, but if the wind be not fair, or the current strong, they then are lost to their own reckoning and know not where they be. How they ever find their port of destination is more than I can tell'. Bennett and Brooks, p. 426.
3. Colomb, p. 35.
4. The larger dhows—buggalows—might carry a second mast, a copy of the first and placed near the stern.

5. S.P. LXXIII, No. 84, Captain Purvis to Admiralty: 19 May 1866.
6. Villiers, 'Dhow Builders of Kuwait'
7. See Naval Intelligence Division Handbook: Geographical series: Iraq and the Persian Gulf: Oxford 1944, plates 65 and 66 showing shipbuilding at Kuwait; and the decorated poop and stern of an ocean-going dhow from the Persian Gulf.
8. Dhow construction was carried on to a small extent on the East African coast at Msimbati Island—near Kilwa, Rufiji, Tukuni, and near Pate. Coastal dhows, known as *sambuqs,* were little more than small boats of 30 to 50 tons with very little superstructure. A few had long projecting sterns and graceful prows. They carried square-rigged sails of coarse matting but in shoal water generally pulled with sixteen oars or paddles, or were propelled by means of long slender poles (the dhows referred to by Owen, Vol. i, p. 384, were probably from Muscat.)
9. MacMaster, D. N., 'The Ocean-Going Dhow trade to East Africa' *The East African Geographical Review:* No. 4, April 1966, pp. 13-24.
10. *Anti-Slavery Reporter,* Vol. 16, No. 10, 1 July 1869, Commander Dowell to the Secretary to the Admiralty, 4 July 1868.
11. Graham, *Great Britain in the Indian Ocean,* Appendix: Changing Boundaries of the Cape and East Indies Stations, 1810-1850, p. 455.
12. India Office, Vol. 90, No. 412, Hennell to Malet, 23 Sept. 1847.
13. S.P. LVI 1865, No. 152, Rear-Admiral Walker to Secretary to the Admiralty, 17 Nov. 1863.
14. S.P. LXIII 1867, No. 216, Acting Consul Seward to Secretary to Bombay Government, 19 Sept. 1866. S.P. LXIV 1867/68, No. 81, Memo by Commodore Hillyar, 8 Apr. 1867.
15. Kelly, *Britain and the Persian Gulf,* p. 610.
16. Colomb, p. 194.
17. Ibid., p. 185.
18. S.P. LXXI 1863, No. 15, H.M. Commrs to Russell, Cape Town, 8 Nov. 1862.
19. S.P. LXXIII 1867, No. 92, Incl. 2, Bedenfield to Hillyar: 25 June 1866.
20. S.P. LVI 1865, No. 152, Rear-Admiral B. Walker to Secretary to Admiralty, 17 Nov. 1863.
21. S.P. LVI 1865, No. 5, Report of Commissioners, Cape of Good Hope, 4 Feb. 1864. Two other cases reported by Lt. Commander H. R. Purvis in May 1866 concerned a dhow which was run ashore and most of her slaves drowned; in the other case a dhow was beached and 162 slaves were run ashore and taken into the interior. The fierceness of the Somalis was borne witness to when one of the *Gorgon's* boats was wrecked on the Somali coast; two of its crew—West Africans—were captured and sold into slavery for three bullocks apiece, but they were later ransomed and returned to the *Gorgon.* The *Lyra* in 1865 pursued a dhow near Port Tola and she was run ashore, and all but 40 slaves were drowned, the surviving slaves being run ashore and later shipped in another slave dhow to Brava. (S.P. LXI 1873, No. 26, Sir B. Frere to Granville, 13 Feb. 1873; S.P. LXXV 1866, No. 98, Commander Parr to Admiralty, Port Tola, 23 June 1865: Colomb, p. 190).

NOTES

22. Kelly, p. 621.
23. S.P. LXVI 1864, No. 82, Playfair to Earl Russell: 20 Sept. 1863.
24. The Sultan's clearance certificate translated from the Arabic read:—
    'From (the Sultan of Zanzibar).
    'Know by these presents all our benevolent and most respectable friends who are resident on men-of-war, and travelling from east to west and from west to east continually, (may God give a helping hand to you!) that this is the vessel—belonging to—coming from—going to—. Beside the captain and owner, there are on board—seamen and—passengers.
    'Do not throw any obstacle in their way, but fulfil all the obligations of friendship, and all the respects of familiarity.
    'Dated
    (Colomb, p. 217)
25. S.P. LXXIII 1867, No. 92, Incl. See Lt. Garforth's Report: 30 June 1866.
26. Colomb, p. 70.
27. Ibid., p. 197.
28. S.P. V. 1873, No. 167, Slave Trade Consolidation Act 1873, Seizure of Slave Ships.
    Prima Facie evidence as set out here was:—
    Hatches with open gratings instead of usual closed hatches.
    More than usual division of bulkheads etc.
    Spare planks for second or slave decks.
    Shackles, bolts or handcuffs.
    Larger quantity of water than usual.
    Mess tins.
    Extraordinary quantity of rice, etc.
    Mats or matting.
29. Colomb, p. 229.
30. *Anti-Slavery Reporter,* Vol. 16, No. 10, 1 July 1869, Consul Churchill to Lord Stanley, Zanzibar, 21 August 1868.
31. Bounties were apportioned as follows: to the agent for the prosecution a commission of $2\frac{1}{2}\%$, to the naval prize balance account 5%, and to Greenwich Hospital 5%. One-third of the remainder went to the commander-in-chief of the station, one-tenth to the captain of the capturing ship, the remainder was divided into shares—a boy receiving one, a servant two, subordinate and petty officers seven to twelve, and commissioned officers twenty to forty-five shares. A very active ship in one year might claim from the Treasury £2000—giving the Admiral £60, the Captain £170, the remainder being divided among the officers and men.
32. *Anti-Slavery Reporter,* Vol. 16, No. 10, 1 July 1869, Consul Churchill to Lord Stanley, Zanzibar, 21 August 1868.
33. S.P. LXXI 1875, No. 66, Captain Prideaux's Memo. 28 July 1874. Colomb, pp. 262-3.
34. Zanzibar Archives: quoted in Hamerton to Secretary, Bombay Government, 8 Aug. 1844.
35. *Anti-Slavery Reporter,* Vol. 3, Fourth Series, Sept. 1883.
36. S.P. LXXV 1866, No. 97, Captain Bowden to Commodore Montresor, *Wasp,* 30 June 1865.

37. Colomb, pp. 267, 274.
38. Devereux. *The Cruise of the Gorgon.* p. 71.
39. *Anti-Slavery Reporter* Vol. 11, 22 Sept. 1841. Harris, J. E., *The African Presence in Asia,* Evanston, 1971, pp. 67-79.
40. Sulivan, *Dhow Chasing,* p. 196. S.P. LXXV 1866, No. 97, Captain Bowden's report, 30 June 1965. Colomb, pp. 262-3.
41. *The Times,* 18 Apr. 1962, quotes this letter.
42. *Anti-Slavery Reporter,* Vol. 1. 4 Nov. 1840.
43. Ibid., Vol. 15, No. 9. 16 Sept. 1867.
44. Ibid., Vol. 14 Third Series. 1866.
45. Ibid. Vol. 18, No. 5, 1 Apr. 1873.
46. S.P. LXI 1873, No. 40, Captain Elton's report.
47. F.O.C.P. 5770/600. Memo on freed slaves, 20 Nov. 1888.
48. Lugard, F. D. Vol. 1, p. 198.
49. Hardinge, Sir A., *A Diplomatist in the East,* London 1928, p. 141.
50. Lugard, Vol. I, p. 224. The number of runaway slaves in these independent colonies, Fulladoya, Pentagoa, and Makongeni, increased after 1880, when Kirk rebuked the Missions for harbouring runaway slaves. See Temu, A.J. *British Protestant Missions,* London, 1972, p. 21.
51. Lugard, Vol. I, p. 222.
52. Temu, p. 29.
53. Lugard, Vol. II, pp. 55-8. See also Ashe, R. P. *Two Kings of Uganda,* London, 1889, p. 98.

CHAPTER 5

1. Anti-Slavery Conference, Paris, 1967. Proceedings, p. 134.
2. S.P. LXI 1868/69, No. 17., Dr Livingstone to Earl of Clarendon: 11 June 1866.
3. Special report on the Anti-Slavery Conference held in Paris. 26-27 August 1867. *Anti-Slavery Reporter,* Vol. 15, No. 9. 16 Sept. 1867.
4. Parl Papers 1870, LXI, pp. 899-907 (C. 209). Report of Committee on the East African Slave Trade addressed to the Earl of Clarendon. The Committee included Henry A. Churchill (Pol. Agent Zanzibar), Henry Fairfax, J. Wm. Kaye (Pol. Sec. F.O.), Wm. Robinson, H. C. Rothery, W. W. Wyle, and C. Vivian (Head of Slave Trade Department F.O.)
5. Most of the 196 slave ships captured between January 1864 and December 1869 were taken off Port Durnfurd or Cape Guardafui; they were all described as 'name unknown', and condemned at the Cape of Good Hope. The Spanish ship, *The America,* captured on 5 April 1864 off the east coast of Africa, was taken to the British and Spanish Mixed Commission Court, Sierra Leone, where she was condemned on 25 August 1864.
6. British Sessional Papers, House of Commons, 1871, Vol. XII (I) Report from the Select Committee on the Slave Trade (East Coast of Africa), together with the Proceedings, Minutes of Evidence, Appendix and Index, ordered to be printed by House of Commons, 4 Aug. 1871 (No. 420).

7. Majid had refused to pay the subsidy after Thwaini, ruler of Muscat, was murdered by his son, Salim, in 1866. Salim's overthrow two years later, by another branch of the family, the Azzan ibn Qais, strengthened Majid in his refusal, and in 1868 he sent a mission to England to seek formal release from the payment. Lord Clarendon was not unsympathetic, for he felt that the ursupation of power by the Azzan ibn Qais had released Majid from the obligation. This was also the opinion of a section at the India Council, and it was largely owing to the intercession of Sir Bartle Frere that India and Britain took over payment of the subsidy. (R. J. Garvin, 'The Bartle Frere Mission to Zanzibar,' *The Historical Journal,* Vol. V (1962). India Office: Home Correspondence [Sec] Vol. 62, Minute by Frere, 15 July 1868, and Vol. 63, R. Olway to Merivale, 29 May 1869, and C. Spring Rice to Merivale, 1869.)
8. The Select Committee included: Viscount Enfield, Mr Percy Wyndham, Mr Kennaway, Mr Kinnaird, Mr Robert Fowler, Sir John Hay, Sir Robert Anstruther, Sir Frederick Williams, Mr Crum-Ewing, Lord F. Cavendish, Mr Shaw Lefevre, Mr John Talbot, Mr Gilipin, Mr O'Connor. Witnesses included the Hon. Crespigny Vivian of the Foreign Office, Sir William Kaye, Henry Adrian Churchill, Sir Bartle Frere, Major-General C. P. Rigby, Sir Leopold Heath, Mr H. C. Rothery, Sir William Coghlan, Rev Horace Waller, Rev Edward Steere, Rear-Admiral Chas. F. Hillyar, Captain Philip Colomb, Mr Charles Allington, Mr Edward Hutchinson.
9. HMS *Daphne,* in April 1868, overhauled 50 to 60 dhows; all carried 'domestic' slaves. (Sulivan, p. 201).
10. The cost of the upkeep of the squadron over twenty years prior to 1890 was estimated at four millions sterling. This did not take into account the large amount of work imposed on consular and judicial staff at Zanzibar in adjudication and dealing with reports, etc.
11. In 1872, the British Steam Navigation Company established a monthly mail service between Aden and Zanzibar, and a telegraph cable was laid down from Aden to Zanzibar in 1879.
12. Sessional Papers; House of Commons, 1871, Vol. XII (II), Report from the Select Committee on the Slave Trade (East Coast of Africa) together with the Proceedings and Minutes of Evidence, Appendix and Index. Ordered to be printed by the House of Commons, 4 April 1871 No. 420.
13. *Anti-Slavery Reporter.* Vol. 17, No. 1, 31 Mar. 1870.
14. S.P. LIV 1872, No. 24, Kirk to Granville, 22 Feb. 1871.
15. E. F. Berlioux, *The Slave Trade in Africa,* prefaced by J. Cooper London, 1872.
16. Hansard: House of Lords, 23 July 1872.
17. Garvin, 'The Bartle Frere Mission to Zanzibar', pp. 122-48.
18. India Office, Home Correspondence (Sec) Vol. 71. Memo by Kaye. 5 Oct. 1872. Kelly pp. 631-2.
19. 'Frere is a strong and able, and a plausible man. It is true that his strength is akin to obstinacy and self-will, that he is rather too plausible, and that he will gain his ends by crooked paths when he has tried the straight in vain. He is a dangerous agent, but I should think a useful adviser'. *Letters of Lord Acton to Mary Gladstone,*

London, 1904, p. 17.
20. The Mission included; Reverend G. P. Badger, Secretary and Confidential Adviser; Major C. B. Euan-Smith, Military Attaché; Captain Fairfax, RN Naval Attaché; Mr C. Hill, Secretary; Mr Gray, Attaché.
21. S.P. LXI 1873, No. 20, Frere to Granville, 18 Jan. 1873.
22. F.O.C.P. 7077/49, 3 Jan. 1899.
23. S.P. LXI 1873, No. 26, 13 Feb. 1873.
24. Martineau, J. *Life of Sir B. Frere,* 2 vols. 1895, Vol. II, pp. 82ff.
25. S.P. LXI 1873, No. 46, Earl Granville to Dr Kirk, 15 May 1873.
26. F.O.C.P. 7077/49, 3 Jan. 1898.
27. Lyne, R. N. *Zanzibar in Contemporary Times,* London, 1905, pp. 82-3.
28. *Anti-Slavery Reporter,* Vol. 19, No. 2, 1 Apr. 1874.
29. Martineau, *Life of Sir B. Frere,* p. 113.
30. Ibid.
31. S.P. LXXI 1875, No. 91, Major Miles to Earl of Derby: Muscat, 2 Oct. 1874.
32. 2,000 slaves held by Indians were freed and issued with freedom papers.
33. S.P. LXII 1874, No. 2, Elton to Captain Prideaux, 26 Dec. 1873.
34. S.P. LXII, No. 3, Report by Elton, 7 Jan. 1874.
35. S.P. LXXI 1875, No. 114, Rear Admiral Cumming to Admiralty, quoting from the Catholic Mission at Bagamoyo, 4 May 1874.
36. *Anti-Slavery Reporter,* Vol. 21, No. 2, May 1878.
37. S.P. LXX 1876, No. 33, Report on Zanzibar, 1874/75.
38. F.O. 84/1547, No. 69, 1 May 1879. S.P. LXIX 1880, No. 300, Lt. O'Neil's report on the Slave Trade in the Dar-es-Salaam district, Jan. 1879.
39. *Anti-Slavery Reporter,* Vol. 19, No. 3, 1 July 1874.
40. *Anti-Slavery Reporter,* Vol. 19, No. 8, 1 Sept. 1875.
41. F.O.C.P. 5977/66 Euan-Smith, 19 July 1889.
42. F.O. 84/1574, No. 20, Kirk to Salisbury, 23 Feb. 1880.
43. S.P. LXXI 1875, No. 105, Rear-Admiral Cumming, Commander in Chief of the East Indies Squadron, Report for 1873.
44. She was a wooden ninety-gun two-decker, of 2598 tons—3580 tons displacement—with a complement when fully manned of 850 officers and men, and cost £90,000. She gained renown at the bombardment of Sebastopol in October 1854, in the Crimean War, Captain Charles Eden being then in command of her. Mathews Biography, p. 35.

CHAPTER 6

1. Budge, Sir Ernest A. Wallis *A History of Ethiopia, Abyssinia, and Nubia,* London, 1928, p. 8.
2. F.O. 78/381, Report on Egypt, Dr Bowring, 1838.
3. Kinglake, A. W., *Eothen,* London, 1845, p. 65.
4. S.P. LVI 1854/55, No. 592, Consul-General Bruce to Earl of Clarendon, 1 Jan. 1855.
5. It was from Darfur that Napoleon, in 1798, replying to the

congratulations of its ruler, Abd-er-Raham, on the defeat of the Mamelukes, requested that ruler to send to him by the next caravan 2000 black slaves 'upwards of sixteen years old, strong and vigorous'.
6. F.O. 78/381, March 1839, Dr Bowring's Report, 1838.
7. F.O. 78/381, The Mss. draft of a report on Egypt by Dr John Bowring, March, 1839.
8. The Nilotes include the Dinka, Nuer and Luo, east of the Upper Nile, with branches of the Luo extending down the eastern shore of Lake Victoria. To the south-east of the Dinka and Nuer, along the east bank of the Bahr el Jebel, are the Bari, and on its west bank are the Nilo-Hamitic speaking Kuku, Kakwa, Pajulu and Nyangbara, a mixture of Bari stock and other Sudanic elements.
9. S.P. LXXV 1866, No. 216, 12 Jan. 1865.
10. Shaikh Ahmad al-Aqqad had bought out his competitors, and sheltering under a Khedival decree which permitted official personnel to bring their concubines and children to Khartoum, and using this as a pretext, shipped thousands of slaves northwards down the Nile.
11. S.P. LXX 1863, No. 324, 31 Oct. 1867.
12. Schweinfurth, G. *The Heart of Africa: Three Years' Travels and Adventuring in the Unexplored Regions of Central Africa, 1868-1871,* Vol. II, London, pp. 365-6.
13. S.P. LXX 1863, No. 324, 31 Oct. 1862.
14. S.P. LXXIII 1867, No. 68, 31 Jan. 1866.
15. Also, *The Nile Tributaries of Abyssinia,* 1867.
16. S.P. LXIV 1867/68, No. 45, Lord Stanley to Reade, 31 Aug. 1867.
17. S.P. LXIV 1867/68, No. 50, Incl. 2, 6 Nov. 1867.
18. S.P. LXIV 1867/68, No. 50, Incl. 4, 5 Nov. 1867.
19. Tugay, Emine F. *Three Centuries: Family Chronicles of Turkey and Egypt* London 1963, p. 179, p. 191.
20. F.O. 84/1472, Vivian to Derby, Cairo, 14 Apr. 1877. W. D. Mackenzie, *Egypt and the Egyptian Question,* London, 1883, pp. 269ff.
21. S.P. LXI 1873/74, No. 56, Sir Bartle Frere's Memorandum, 29 May 1873.
22. Although the attempt to establish a foothold at the mouth of the Juba failed, the city of Harrar was captured by an Egyptian force under Raouf Pasha, and remained in the possession of Egypt until 1885, when its garrison was withdrawn to face the Mahdi revolt in the Sudan. Ismail revived Said's project of a railway linking the Sudan with Massawa on the Red Sea. Little came of these plans; by 1877, only 50 miles of rails were laid, at a cost of £450,000. Ismail, in a sense, anticipated the 'scramble', but it brought him no more than a steady wastage of Egyptian resources, and little in the way of territorial gains apart from the southern Sudan. His war with Abyssinia merely served to aggravate the slave trade on Egypt's south-eastern frontier.
23. F.O. 84/1389 Frere to Granville, 1 Jan. 1873.
24. S.P. LXI, 1870, No. 34, 24 Nov. 1869.
25. F.O. 141/63, Reade to Stanley, 9 Aug. 1867.
26. F.O. 84/1389 Frere to Granville, 1 Jan. 1873.

27. Zubeir, a Jalli Arab, educated at Khartoum, established himself in the Bahr el Ghazal in 1856. He married the daughter of a powerful Azande Chief, Tikimia, and enslaved the members of his wife's tribe. He built Deim Zubeir, a zeriba, strategically placed to tap the slave trade. In 1866, by an alliance with the Rizeiquat Arabs, a cattle-owning tribe inhabiting the area north of Bahr el Arab, he secured the Kordofan route for his slave caravans. Zubeir could throw a thousand armed men into the field.
28. Gordon, on taking up his administration in 1872, had declared all the ivory in the region under his sway to be a monopoly of the government.
29. Gessi, R. *Seven Years in the Soudan,* London, 1892, states that in the space of fourteen years more than 400,000 slaves were taken from their native country and sold in Egypt and Turkey, and that thousands more were massacred. See also *Anti-Slavery Reporter,* Fourth Series, Vol. 12, Jan.-Feb. 1892.
30. Hill, G. B., *Colonel Gordon in Central Africa, 1874-9,* London, 1881, pp. 348-9.
31. F.O.C.P., 7402/15, Lt. Col. Martyr's report on the Nile District, 15 Apr. 1899.
32. F.O. 84/1370, Elliott to Granville, 8 July 1873.
33. F.O. 78/3188, Minute by Tenterden, 22 Dec. 1875. F.O. 84/1450, Tenterden to Rourke, 3 Feb. 1875.
34. S.P. LXII 1886, Nos. 18 and 28, Oct. 1885.
35. *Anti-Slavery Reporter,* Vol. 21, No. 1, 14 Feb. 1878.
36. F.O. 141/140, della Sala to Riaz Pasha, Cairo, 12 Sept. 1880.
37. S.P. LXXXV No. 64, Malet to Granville, 16 June 1880.
38. S.P. LXXVIII 1889, No. 57, 2 Apr. 1889.
39. S.P. LXV 1882, No. 35, 21 May 1881.
40. S.P. LXV 1882, No. 19, Incl. 3, Schweinfurth's letter, 11 Oct. 1880.
41. *Anti-Slavery Reporter,* Fourth Series, Vol. 7, Nov.-Dec. 1887.
42. *Anti-Slavery Reporter,* Fourth Series, Vol. 13, No. 1, Mar.-Apr., 1893.
43. Wingate, Major F. R., *Mahdism and the Egyptian Sudan,* London, 1891. p. 478.
44. Wingate, Major F. R. *Ten Years Captivity in the Mahdi's Camp, 1882-1892* (from original manuscripts of Father Joseph Ohrwalder, late priest of the Austrian Mission at Delen in Kordofan) London, 1892, p. 22, pp. 382-6.
45. Wingate, *Mahdism and the Egyptian Sudan* p. 286.
46. *Anti-Slavery Reporter,* Fourth Series, Vol. 14, No. 5, Sept.-Oct., 1894.
47. Ibid., Fourth Series, Vol. 20, No. 4, Aug.-Oct. 1894.
48. S.P. XCVII 1896, Treaty Series, No. 16.
49. See account of Wilfred Jennings-Bramly in *Geographical Journal* Dec. 1897.
50. Parl. Papers, Egypt, No. 1, 1895.
51. *Anti-Slavery Reporter,* Fourth Series, Vol. 20, No. 2, Mar.-May 1900.
52. Memorandum as to position of Slavery Department in the Sudan, Intelligence Report II, 43/365, pp. 5-6, 1925.

53. *Anti-Slavery Reporter,* Fourth Series, Vol. 23, No. 1, Mar.-May, 1907.
54. *Anti-Slavery Reporter,* Vol. 19, No. 5, 1 Jan. 1875.
55. Holt, P.M. *A Modern History of the Sudan,* London, 1961, p. 121.

CHAPTER 7

1. Budge, Sir E. A. Wallis, *A History of Ethiopia,* pp. 120-1.
2. *Anti-Slavery Reporter,* Vol. I, 1 May 1881, Letter from M. Lucereau, 6 July 1880.
3. According to Shack, W. A. *The Gurage,* London, 1966, p. 137, the majority of slaves in pre-Menelik times were captured in war or purchased, the chief source being the negro tribes from the west Nile region, and Sidama and Galla tribes.
4. Baker, S. W., *The Nile Tributaries of Abyssinia,* London, 1867, pp. 349-50.
5. S.P. LXXI 1863, No. 305, 8 Oct. 1861.
6. *Anti-Slavery Reporter,* Vol. 19, No. 1, June 1874.
7. Ibid.
8. S.P. LXXXV 1881, No. 79, Malet to Salisbury, 15 Nov. 1880.
9. S.P. LXI 1873, No. 17, 10 Jan. 1873, S.P. LXXII 1889, No. 25, 13 Feb. 1889.
10. *Anti-Slavery Reporter,* Vol. 21, No. 9, Aug. 1879.
11. Ibid, Vol. 5, Feb. 1884.
12. Ibid, Vol. 22, Fourth series, Aug. 1902.
13. Ibid, Vol. 23, No. 5 Dec. 1903.
14. Montfried, Henri de, *Pearls, Arms and Hashish,* New York, 1936, pp. 106-15.
15. Ibid.
16. Ibid.
17. Aitchison, *Treaties,* VII, pp. 178-81.
18. Ibid, XI, Third Edition.
19. Burton, R. F. *First Footsteps in Africa,* Vol. 1, London, 1894, p. 90.
20. According to the Koran, a Mussulman cannot be made a slave, if he is able to say 'There is no God, but God, and Mohamet is the Prophet of God': slavery can only be inflicted on unbelievers. The treaty with the maritime chiefs of the Persian Gulf in July 1839 stated: 'As the selling of males and females, whether grown up or young, who are 'hoor', or free, is contrary to the Mahomedan religion, and whereas the Soomali tribe is included in the 'ahtar' or free, I do hereby agree that the sale of males and females, whether young or old, of the Soomali tribe, shall be considered as piracy, and that after four months from this date all those of my people convicted of being concerned in such an act, shall be punished the same as pirates' (Low, C. R. *History of the Indian Navy, 1613-1863,* London, 1877, Vol. II, p. 323) The Wadigo, south of Mombasa, reputedly embraced Islam to avoid slavery. Muslims might evade the Koranic injunction by enslaving purportedly fellow-Muslims on the ground that they were heretics, as in the case of Sunni taking as slaves Shias, a heretical sect.

21. S.P. LXXI 1875, Correspondence on the Slave Trade, p. 159.
22. S.P. LXXI 1875, No. 120, July 1874.
23. S.P. LIV 1872, No. 49, Kirk's report, 2 June 1871. F.O.C.P. 5370/65 Incl. Report from Mr R. M. Lloyd, Lindi, 20 Sept. 1886.
24. And so also the long-accepted view that it was impossible to cross the Arabian Sea during the southwest monsoon. Captain Brucks, of the Indian Navy, 'a hardy seaman of the old school, in whose vocabulary "impossible" was an unknown term', in 1838 miscalculated the power of the engines of his ship to force her through the mountainous sea and high wind that prevails between the months of June and September. Having patched up the boilers of the *Semiramis,* he quitted Bombay with the mails for Suez on 15 July, and for eight days strove his utmost to fulfil his pledge to take his ship to the Red Sea. But all was in vain, and after splitting his fore and aft sails and shipping 'blue sails', which threatened to put out the fires, or swamp the ship, he felt himself reluctantly compelled to adopt the advice of his officers, and bore up to Bombay. (Low, Vol. II, p. 53.)
25. F.O. 84/1547 No. 46, Kirk's report, 1 Apr. 1879.
26. *Anti-Slavery Reporter,* Vol. 21, No 2, 14 May 1878.
27. Ibid, Vol. 19, No 4, 1 Oct. 1874 (from correspondent at Jedda).
28. S.P. LIV 1857, Vice-Consul Page to Secretary, Bombay Government, 2 July 1856.
29. F.O. 84/1144 Consul Stanley to Russell, 17 Apr. 1861.
30. S.P. LXXV 1866, No 224, Sir H. Bulwer to Earl Russell, 9 Apr. 1865.
31. S.P. LXXII 1884/85, No 63, Commander Domville to Sec. Admiralty, 24 Sept. 1884.
32. S.P. LXIX 1880, No 408, Rear-Admiral Corbett to Sec. Admiralty, 8 Aug. 1879.
33. *Anti-Slavery Reporter,* Vol. 22, No 1, 1 Mar. 1880.
34. S.P. LXXXV 1881, No. 218, 23 Aug. 1880. Ibid, No 221, 25 Sept. 1880.
35. S.P. LXV 1882, No 48, 4 Mar. 1881.
36. A. B. Wylde, Vice-Consul at Jedda, December 1875 to January 1878, and with long and varied experience in the Red Sea, Sudan and Abyssinia (author of *'83 to '87 in the Soudan,* London 1888) was the son of W. H. Wylde, highly respected head of the Slave Trade Department at the Foreign Office. Father and son were active members of the Anti-Slavery Society.
37. F.O. 84/1450, 25 Nov. 1876: F.O. 141/117, 23 Jan. 1878 (Reports by Wylde).
38. S.P. LXV 1882. No 123, 28 Feb. 1881.
39. S.P. LXXII 1884/85 No 56, Consul Jago to Granville, 12 May 1885.
40. *Anti-Slavery Reporter,* Vol. 3, Fourth Series, 17 Apr. 1886.
41. *Anti-Slavery Reporter,* Vol. 1, No 9, 15 Sept. 1888.
42. In October 1885 two dhows carrying Zanzibar slaves were captured in Suakin harbour (S.P. LXII 1886, No 85, 11 Nov. 1885). In November 1886, British cruisers captured two dhows in the Red Sea (S.P. LXXVIII 1887, No 49, 12 Nov. 1886). Captain Gissing of the *Osprey* captured three dhows, and landed 204 slaves at Aden (S.P. LXXII 1889, No 25, 13 Feb. 1889).
43. S.P. LXXII No 89. 12 Mar. 1889.

44. *Anti-Slavery Reporter,* Vol. 12, Fourth Series, Jan-Feb. 1892.
45. Ibid, Vol. 6, Fourth Series, June 1886.
46. *Anti-Slavery Reporter,* Vol. 7, Fourth Series, Sept-Oct. 1887.
47. S.P. LXII 1890/91, No 19, Incl. Commander Gardiner to Vice-Admiral Fremantle, 9 Feb. 1891.
48. Parl. Paper, Report on Egypt, No 3, 1899. *Morning Post,* 29 Nov. 1902.
49. Spencer, Edmund, *Travels in Circassia,* London, 1839, p. 157
50. Zanzibar Archives: Foreign Office to Colonel Sheil, Inward letters 1847-52.
51. S.P. LVI 1854/55, No 570, Lord Stratford de Redcliffe to Clarendon, 9 Oct. 1854.
52. S.P. LVI 1854/55, No 594, Consul Brant to Stratford, Erzeroom, 19 Nov. 1854.
53. S.P. LVI 1854/55, No 596, Brigadier-General Williams to Clarendon, 6 Feb. 1855.
54. *Anti-Slavery Reporter,* Vol. 4, Third Series, Apr. 1856.
55. Marie Theresa dollars.
56. S.P. LXI 1870, No 94, Consul Taylor to Clarendon, 20 Sept. 1869.
57. *Anti-Slavery Reporter,* Vol. 15, Third Series, Aug. 1867.
58. S.P. LXI 1870, No 89, Consul Wilkinson to Clarendon, Salonika, 11 Oct. 1869. Ibid Nos 88 and 95, Vice-Consul Reade to Clarendon, 12 Oct. 1869.
59. S.P. LXI 1870, No 1030, 5 Aug. 1869. *Anti-Slavery Reporter,* Vol. 17, No 3, 30 Sept. 1870.
60. S.P. LXI, 1870, No 106, 29 July 1869, Ibid, No 17, 25 June 1869.
61. S.P. LXI 1870, No 88, Consul Cumberbatch to Clarendon, 12 Oct. 1869. Ibid No 112, 28 Aug. 1869.
62. S.P. LXI 1870, No 58, Elliott to Clarendon, 13 July 1869, Ibid. No 92, 21 Nov. 1869.
63. *Anti-Slavery Reporter,* Vol. 21, No 3, 28 Aug. 1878.
64. S.P. LXII 1871, No 114, British Consul at Rustchuk, 21 Mar. 1871.
65. Anti-Slavery Reporter, Vol. 21, No 4, Oct. 1878.
66. F.O. 84/1341 Granville to Elliott, 10 Aug. 1871.
67. S.P. LXVI 1883, No 110, 30 May 1882, See also Aitchison, *Treaties,* Vol. X, Convention between Britain and the Porte, 25 Jan. 1880.
68. See Page 158.
69. *Anti-Slavery Reporter,* Vol. 9, Fourth Series, Nov-Dec. 1889.
70. Bullard, Sir Reader, *The Camels Must Go,* London, 1961, p. 53.
71. S.P. LXI 1870, No 106, 29 July 1869.
72. See page 78.
73. Owen, *Narrative* Vol. 1, p. 342.
74. *Anti-Slavery Reporter,* Vol. 4, Third Series, 1843.
75. For an account of the Harem, see Penzer, N.M., *The Harem,* London, 1967.
76. And so also the Sultan of Zanzibar: The American, Horace B. Putnam, visiting there in 1847, noted that the Sultan's harem of 40 concubines was guarded by two eunuchs (Bennett and Brooks, p. 402).
77. *Anti-Slavery Reporter,* Vol. 1, No 2, May 1887.

78. Ibid. Vol. 20, No 9, Mar. 1881.
79. Burkhardt, J. L. *Travels in Nubia,* pp. 329-30. F. O. 78/381, Report on Egypt by Dr John Bowring, Mar. 1839. See also Lane, E. W., *The Manners and Customs of the Modern Egyptians,* London 1836, p. 137.
80. S.P. LXVI 1882, No 110, 30 May 1881.
81. S.P. LXVI 1882, No 32, Lister to Malet, 10 May 1881. Ibid. No 41, Cookson to Granville, 8 July 1881.
82. Wylde, A. B. *'83 to '87 in the Soudan,* Vol. 2. p. 257.
83. Oded, A. 'The Muslim Factor in Buganda (c. 1850-1884)' Ph.D. thesis, Tel Aviv University, 1972, p. 80.
84. S.P. LXXV 1882, No 83, Incl. Gessi Pasha to Gordon Pasha, 21 Jan. 1880.
85. S.P. LXV 1882, No 95, Consul Zohrab to Mr Goschin, 22 Dec. 1880.
86. Penzer, p. 20. See also McCullagh, F. *The Fall of Abd ul-Hamid,* London, 1910 pp. 276-8.
87. Monfried, Henri de, p. 115.
88. *Anti-Slavery Reporter*, Fourth Series, Vol. 16, No 2, Mar-Apr. 1896.
89. Monfried, Henri de, pp. 115-16.
90. The East India Company established a factory at Bandar Abbas in 1616, acquired the island of Ormuz in 1622, in 1640 established a factory at Basra, and in 1763 at Bushire (headquarters of the British Political Resident in the Gulf after 1778). A Resident was stationed at Baghdad in 1798, and at Muscat in 1808.
91. Bombay Records: Inward Letters; from Resident in Persian Gulf, 9 July 1842. Special Report of the Anti-Slavery Conference, Paris, Aug. 1849, p. 149.
92. Bombay Records, XXIV, 1856. Extracts from Records of Bushire Residency.
93. The Convention was renewed in 1862, but superseded by the Convention of 2 Mar. 1882.
94. S.P. LXXIII 1854, Correspondence respecting the Slave Trade, No 277, Captain Kemball to Lieutenant Colonel Justin Sheil (British ambassador at Teheran) 1 Feb. 1853.
95. S.P. LXXIII 1854, Correspondence respecting the Slave Trade, No 279, Report by Commodore Robinson, Feb. 1854.
96. S.P. XLIV 1857, No 614, Incl. Lord Stratford's despatch, 1 Jan. 1857.
97. S.P. LXVI 1864, No 83, Brigadier Coghlan, 18 May 1863.
98. S.P. LVI 1854, No 280, 25 May 1854.
99. Select Committee on the East African Slave Trade, 1870/71.
100. Report of Colonel Lewis Pelly, Bombay Records, 1866.
101. S.P. LXIV, 1867/68, No 124, Incl. Disbrowe to Sec. Bombay Government, 13 Sept. 1866.
102. Parliament Papers, 1867, Class B. p. 123.
103. S.P. LXXXV 1881, No 349, Rear Admiral Jones to Admiralty, 24 Sept. 1880.
104. S.P. LXV 1882, No 2, 2 Mar. 1882.
105. *Anti-Slavery Reporter,* Vol. 4, Fourth Series, Dec. 1885.
106. S.P. LVII 1890/91, No 1, Report for 1890, Vice-Admiral Fremantle.

Ibid, Incl. 9, Commander Gardiner to Vice-Admiral Fremantle, 9 Feb. 1891.
107. *Anti-Slavery Reporter,* Vol. 18, Fourth Series, No 1, 1898.
108. Ibid Vol. 22, No 4, Aug.-Oct. 1902.
109. Sykes, Ella C., *Persia and its People,* New York, 1910, p. 69, speaks of negresses being expensive slaves in Persia, 'though many are still being introduced by pilgrims from Mecca'.
110. Wakefield, Sir Edward, *Past Imperative: My Life in India: 1927-1947,* London, 1966. pp. 189-91.

CHAPTER 8

1. Lugard, Vol. I, p. 181; *The Dual Mandate in British Tropical Africa*, London, 1922, p. 366.
2. Lugard, Vol. I, p. 191. It is not easy to see how Lugard could know the feelings of Africans in these matters.
3. Ibid.
4. Ibid p. 171.
5. Dundas R. N. *Scottish Geographical Magazine* Mar. 1893.
6. S.P. LXXI 1875, No. 74, Captain Prideaux to Derby, 19 Sept. 1874.
7. As used on Arab dhows and introduced from South Arabia to the East African coast by the fifteenth century.
8. Livingstone may be partially responsible for the popular view that 'Black ivory carried white ivory'. But Livingstone states 'those Arabs who despair of white ivory invest their remaining beads and cloth in slaves'. *Last Journals,* Vol. I, London, 1867, p. 232: Cameron stated that Tippu Tip preferred porters to slaves for transport of goods. F.O.C.P. 6039/86, Inc. 1, p. 93: 'slaves are acquired for their own value, and any conveyance of ivory by them is a mere accidental advantage.'
9. Stanley, H. M., *How I found Livingstone,* London, 1890, p. 92.
10. Porters carried staggering weights on their heads—from 50 to 80 pounds. Livingstone speaks of a porter carrying 200 pounds of ivory from Tabora to the Indian Ocean.
11. Lugard, Vol. I, pp. 90-2.
12. S.P. LXXI 1875, No. 74, Captain Prideaux to Derby, 19 Sept. 1874.
13. S.P. LXIX 1880, No. 369, Kirk to Salisbury, 7 Jan. 1879.
14. Von Wissman, Hermann *My Second Journey Through Equatorial Africa from the Congo to the Zambezi in the Years 1886 to 1887* London, 1891, p. 246.
15. Swann, A. J., *Fighting the Slave Hunters in Central Africa*, London, 1910, p. 62.
16. Cardinal Lavigerie, *Slavery in Africa* Boston, 1888.
17. Stanley, *How I found Livingstone* p. 381.
18. Stanley, H. M. 'Slavery and the Slave Trade', *Harpers New Monthly Magazine* March, 1893, p. 622.
19. Lugard, *Rise of Our East African Empire,* Vol. II, pp. 412-14.
20. Stanley 'Slavery and the Slave Trade' p. 29.
21. Von Wissmann, *My Second Journey,* p. 162.
22. Swann, A. J. *Fighting the Slave Hunters* p. 48.
23. Von Wissmann, *My Second Journey,* pp. 245-6.

24. *Anti-Slavery Reporter,* Vol. 2, Fourth Series, June 1882.
25. Von Wissmann, *My Second Journey,* pp. 244-5.
26. *Anti-Slavery Reporter,* Vol. 2, Fourth Series, June 1882.
27. *Church Missionary Intelligencer,* 568, Sept. 1879. O'Flaherty to Hutchinson, 12 July 1881. C.M.S. Archives, O'Flaherty to Wigram, 9 Aug. 1882.
28. Kagwa, A. *Ekitabo Kya Basekabaka Be Buganda* (London, 1927 [first edition 1901]), p. 102. (Abbreviated as above *Basekabaka.*)
29. The accumulation of female slaves to increase the population in a matrilineal society, where the existence of the tribe depended on the productive capacity of the female, encouraged enslavement of women from other tribes. See Alpers, E. A. 'The Yao in the 19th Century,' *Journal of African History,* Vol. X, 1969 p. 3.
30. *Anti-Slavery Reporter,* Vol. 2, Fourth Series, No. 5, pp. 279-80.
31. *Church Missionary Intelligencer,* Apr. 1893.
32. C-7708 Africa No. 7 (1895) Papers relating to Uganda, No. 38, Incl. 2, Mgr. Hirth to Colonel Colvile, Rubaga, 27 Apr. 1894 (Transl.): 'I saw by experience how easily the Protestants sold so many Catholic prisoners during the first three months of 1892. Four of our Missions, stationed from the Kagera up to Tabora, are still occupied in the work of redemption.'
33. A large number of Mohammedan slaves were brought down by Lugard from Lake Albert in 1891, with Sudanese and followers based at Kavalli's. Nearly 9000 persons were led back from Kavalli's by Lugard. Many deserted on the march, and these were left with the garrisons at Fort Wavertree and Fort George. The remainder, half the original caravan, stretched over seven miles in length when on the march.
34. *Zanzibar Gazette,* 13 June 1894.
35. C-7708 Africa No. 7 (1895) Papers relating to Uganda No. 38, Incl. 2. Mgr. Hirth to Colonel Colvile, Rubaga, 27 Apr. 1894. (Transl.).
36. A product of these raids and counter-raids between Buganda and Bunyoro in the 1890s was Erastus Karamii, a prince of Bunyoro, captured during a slave raid, and still living in the 1900s at Bunyoro High School. See Erastus Karamii, *Slave Prince, A True Story of Uganda,* Hattersley, C.M.S., 1910.
37. *Anti-Slavery Reporter,* Vol. 14, Fourth Series, No. 2, Apr. 1894 Letter from John Ainsworth, Machakos Station, 1 Jan. 1894.
38. F.O. 2/97, No. 49, 4 May 1895. Report from Superintendent, Machakos and Kikuyu.
39. S.P. LXII, 1893-94, *Uganda Railway Survey Report,* Chap. III, 'The Slave Trade in Connection with the Projected Railway.'
40. Pledging children, especially girls, in return for food, in time of famine, was a custom which continued into the nineteenth century. They might be redeemed at a later date on repayment of the original price. This practice was fairly common among the Masai and the Turu of central Tanzania, and it might develop into slavery during famine conditions when parents were forced to sell their children for food. In the famine of 1961, a clerk in Singida, in central Tanzania, was offered a twelve-year-old girl by her mother in exchange for a sack of millet.

NOTES

41. Chanler, W. A. *Through Jungle and Desert,* London, 1896, p. 214.
42. F.O. 2/97, No. 49, 1 May 1895. Minutes by Kimberley, 'When we take over the territory we must consider what can be done to put a stop to the slave-raiding'.
43. Entebbe Archives, A-24, Item 4, Abyssinian Raids, 1904-5, 19 Feb. 1904, 2 Mar. 1904.
44. *Anti-Slavery Reporter,* Vol. 10, Fourth Series, Mar. 1890. F.O.C.P. 6261/133 Euan-Smith to Salisbury, 5 Aug. 1891.
45. F.O.C.P. 6717/186, Hardinge to Kimberley, 27 Apr. 1895.
46. F.O.C.P. 6617/380 Hardinge to Kimberley, 23 Aug. 1894.
47. In respect to the German attitude towards slave raiding and slavery in East Africa, the British Embassy in Berlin reported in 1894 that 'It would appear that the German administration in East Africa has not interfered, to any great extent, with the prevailing customs in regard to domestic slavery, which is generally speaking of a mild form, and against which there is no movement amongst the slaves themselves. Domestic slaves are passed on from father to son, or to any lawful heir of the origianl owner. On the other hand, very stringent measures are taken to suppress slave raiding and dealing. Any Arabs or natives caught *flagrante delicto* are condemned to death'. Foreign Office Report on German Colonies for 1894, No. 346 [C7582-7], pp. 34-44.
48. F.O.C.P. 6693/284, Hardinge to Kimberley, 26 Feb. 1895.
49. F.O.C.P. 5770/163, Memorandum on Slave Trade in German Colonies, 29 Jan. 1889.
50. F.O.C.P. 6717/97, Memorandum on Slavery in German Colonies, Apr. 1895.
51. *Kolonialblatt,* 15 Jan. 1895.
52. F.O.C.P. 6693/37, Admiralty to Foreign Office, 8 Apr. 1895.
53. F.O.C.P. 7690/50, Report on German East Africa, Jan. 1901.
54. F.O.C.P. 6717/97, Memorandum on Slavery in German Colonies, Apr. 1895.
55. F.O.C.P. 6761/148, Sir E. Malet to Salisbury, 9 Aug. 1895.
56. F.O.C.P. 7159/83, Hardinge to Salisbury, 27 Feb. 1898.
57. *Reichsanzeiger,* 6 Dec. 1901.
58. Foreign Office Report on German Colonies for 1903-4, No. 3519 (C7582-7): 'The Institututon of slavery is, however, clearly dying out in German East Africa, and will disappear when the country is provided with better means of communication'.
59. According to the Mafia *District Book* formal slavery was not abolished there until 1923. This information has kindly been provided by Dr G. S. P. Freeman-Grenville.
60. Livingstone, D. *Missionary Travels* p. 79. On the other hand, Livingstone states that among the Chiboque tribe slave-trading was an honoured institution; and the Mambari were outright kidnappers of children (pp. 258, 297).
61. Ibid. p. 342. Portuguese Companies were putting abolition of the slave trade prominently in the terms of their prospectuses. (p. 564.)
62. Report of the Anti-Slavery Conference, Paris, 1867, p. 70.
63. S.P. LXXI 1863, Nos. 198 and 214, Livingstone to Lord Russell, 10 Nov. 1861.

64. Ibid.
65. The calmness of manner with which Livingstone took the death of his wife, and leaving her buried under a baobab tree, immediately proceeded with his own plans, might seem to indicate a certain insensitivity, a self-seekingness: but the inner grief was real, despite his dour expression of it.
66. S.P. LVI 1868/69, No. 17, Livingstone to Clarendon. 18 Aug. 1866.
67. S.P. LVI 1868/69, No. 19, Livingstone to Clarendon, 20 Aug. 1866.
68. Ibid.
69. The Mazitu, a branch of the Nguni, driven north in the great migration of the early nineteenth century, were entrenched in the region between the mountain range overhanging the northeastern side of Lake Nyasa, and the Ruvuma river. They ranged far afield. They stormed Kilwa in 1868, causing its local Indian population to flee for its life; and routed a party of Arabs and Africans who endeavoured to repulse them. Their presence in the vicinity of Kilwa in the late 1860s temporarily disrupted the business of slave traders there.
70. McLeod, L. *Travels in Eastern Africa; with the Narratives of a Residency in Mozambique,* (2 vols.), London, 1860.
    S.P. XXXIV, 1859, No. 169, 2 July 1858.
71. Rhodes House Library; G. 21, Consul O'Neil to Foreign Secretary, 3 Feb. 1878.
72. S.P. LXIX 1880, No. 84, Salisbury to Morier, 13 Mar. 1879. Ibid, 18 July 1879.
72. S.P. LXIX 1880, No. 84, Salisbury to Morier, 13 Mar. 1879. Ibid, 18 July 1879
73. S.P. LXXXV 1881, No. 145, Incl. 2, 9 Mar. 1880, quoting *O'Africano,* 1 Feb. 1880.
74. S.P. LXXII 1884/85, Correspondence respecting Portugal, 7 Feb. 1884.
75. See the story of the Nyasa boy, Richard Kanyema, taken in slavery by the Maviti, sold to the Yao, passed on by them to the Arabs, and thence to Kilwa. The slave dhow taking him to Muscat was captured by a British cruiser and the young lad could scarcely believe, when he was safe in British hands, that he would not be eaten. The Arabs had convinced him that the British were cannibals. (Madden, A. C. *Kiungani,* 1887, quoted in Lyne, R. N., *Apostle of Empire,* London 1936, pp. 25-33.) Although seldom enslaved themselves, the Yao did receive a taste of their own medicine, when, in 1884, the Angoni invaded the Shire highlands, and returned home from the foray with 800 Yao captives. (Stigand, C. H., *The Land of Zinj,* London 1913, p. 118.)
76. In their advance on the interior, the Arabs penetrated almost to the west coast. About 1870 two Arabs from Kilwa appeared in Angola, having crossed the continent. See precis on *The Slave Trade in the Gulf of Oman and Persian Gulf, 1873-1905:* India Office Library, vol. 27, C246.
77. S.P. LXXII 1889, No. 4, Acting-Consul Buchanan to Salisbury, 29 Jan. 1889.
78. Lugard, Vol. I, p. 86.

79. Oliver, R., *Sir Harry Johnston and the Scramble for Africa*, London, 1957, pp. 205-68.
80. S.P. LXXXV 1893/94, Papers re Suppression of the Slave Trade in British Central Africa: No. 2, Incl. Johnston to Rosebery, 19 Oct. 1892. S.P. LXXXIV 1892, No. 5, Papers relative to Suppression of Slave Trading: Johnston to Salisbury, 21 Nov. 1891, 20 Feb. 1892.
81. *Free Church Monthly*. Nov. 1892.
82. *Glasgow Herald*, 21 Dec. 1892.
83. S.P. LVIII 1896, No. 3, Johnston to Salisbury, 24 Jan. 1896.
84. In 1919, the Mambari, apparently quite unaware that they were living in the twentieth century, and in a different climate of opinion as regards the slave trade, sent slaves to the Lunda country in Barotseland, for sale to the Portuguese, and were nonplussed to find that they no longer held the same currency value nor were acceptable in trade transactions. Hardinge, C., *In Remotest Barotseland*, London, 1924, p. 33.

CHAPTER 9

1. Willoughby, Sir J., *Sport in East Africa*, London, 1890, p. 224.
2. F.O. 107/19 Cracknall to Rosebery, 16 Mar. 1894: Incl. 1, Mathew's memorandum on Treatment of Porters. F.O.C.P. 7402/38 Ternan to Salisbury, 1 June 1899.
3. In a letter to an English correspondent shortly before his death in November 1902, Cardinal Lavigérie blamed himself as being the cause of the troubles in Uganda, 'since I first sent them [the Catholic Missionaries]'. *Anti-Slavery Reporter*, Vol. 12, Fourth Series, Nov.-Dec. 1892.
4. F.O.C.P. LXXIV 1888, No. 1, Memorandum by Count Leyden, 8 Oct. 1888.
5. F.O.C.P. XCIII 1888, No. 30, Foreign Office to Holmwood, 21 Jan. 1887.
6. Admiralty Instructions of 10 August 1876 had already stated that any fugitive slave taken on a British ship, or seeking protection there, was not to be surrendered.
7. The Office of the International Anti-Slavery Bureau at Zanzibar was to register dhows transferred to a foreign flag; to inflict penalties for offences against the Brussels Act; to exchange information relating to slavery, such as the number of slaves who had been freed during a given period in each European dependency. Throughout the period of its existence 1890-1914, the President of the Bureau was one or other of the Foreign consuls at Zanzibar; however, Sir Arthur Hardinge, the British Consul-General at Zanzibar, 1894-1900, stated that during the entire period of his stay there neither he nor any other Englishman was asked to act. This probably sprang from the idea that the Protecting Power was already too strong, and that continental countries should combine to restrict British authority 'in order to prevent perfidious Albion from being mistress of the Bureau as well as of the sea'. Hardinge, Sir A., *A Diplomatist in the East*, pp. 107-8.

From its foundings in 1890 till it ended in 1914, the Bureau received little publicity: the contentious issue of the use of the French flag no doubt hampered its effective working. It was formally abolished in 1920 but its history still remains to be written.

8. Lugard, Vol. I, pp. 63-4, pp. 210-11.
9. Ibid. p. 205.
10. Ibid. p. 210-11.
11. Ibid., p. 211.
12. F.O.C.P. 6761/172 Hardinge to Salisbury: 12 June 1895.
13. India Office: Political and Secret Department: 1 May 1892.
14. F.O. 107/3 No. 122, Rodd to Lord Salisbury, 14 Apr. 1893. F.O. 107/4 No. 133, Rodd to Lord Salisbury, 2 May 1893.
15. Correspondence Respecting Slavery in Zanzibar (C-7707), Africa No. 6, 1893.
16. F.O.C.P. 6497/217 Rodd to Rosebery: 31 Dec. 1892.
17. Colombos, C. J. *International Law of the Sea,* New York, 1962, pp. 415-16.
18. See page 30.
19. S.P. XXXIV 1859, No. 122, Grey to Admiralty, 16 Oct. 1858. Ibid. No. 174, 19 Oct. 1858.
20. S.P. LXVI 1864, No. 82, Playfair to Russell, 20 Sept. 1863.
21. Hertslet, vii, pp. 345-6.
22. S.P. LXVI 1864, No. 82, Lt. Col. Playfair to Russell, 20 Sept. 1863.
23. S.P. LXI 1862, Rear-Admiral Sir B. Walker to Sec of Admiralty, 19 Sept. 1861.
24. S.P. 4. LXXXI 1863, Captain Gardner to Rear-Admiral Walker, 3 July 1862.
25. S.P. LXXI 1863, No. 132, Earl Russell to Earl Cowley, 24 May 1862 LVI 1865, No. 61, Earl Russell to Earl Cowley, 9 Feb. 1864.
26. S.P. LXVI 1864, Incl. 8 No. 82, M. Jablonski to Lt. Col. Playfair: 15 Sept. 1863, gives an extract of 'Acte de Francisation' granted to Seleman bin Djouma, domiciled at Ambanourow.

'In the name of the Emperor of the French, the Commandant of Nossi-Bé declares that Sieur Selemani bin Djouma "Français domicilié" at Ambanourow is entitled to be the proprietor of the boat "Ambanourow" below described, which has been registered at the port of Hellville (Nossi-Bé)' *Seen* the Acts establishing the measurement of the boat, the said boat is French property, and that the oath has been received. *Seen* also the recognisance and the security bond deposited in the Post Office, Nossi Bé, on the 27 Nov., relating to the registry of 'Francisation', exceptionally granted in the colony. The present Act is given by us in order to confer the privilege of navigating under the French flag.

In consequence we pray and require all Sovereigns etc.

27. S.P. LVI 1865, No. 61, Earl Russell to Earl Cowley, 9 Feb. 1864. S.P. LIV 1872, No. 1, Lord Lyons to Earl Granville, 11 Jan. 1872, No. 4, 21 May 1871.
28. F.O.C.P. 5867/280, 11 Feb. 1869: Handbook for the East African Slave Trade: *Instructions for the Suppression of the Slave Trade.*
29. S.P. LXII 1870, No. 2, Barghash to Churchill, 6 Nov. 1870.

NOTES 295

30. *Anti-Slavery Reporter,* Vol. 18, No. 4, Jan. 1873.
31. S.P. LXXXV 1881, No. 90, Lord Lyons to Earl Granville 14 Oct. 1880.
32. Ibid.
33. S.P. LXV 1881, No. 295, Miscellaneous: Lord Lyons to Granville, 9 Dec. 1880.
34. F.O.C.P. 5977, No. 113, Euan-Smith to Salisbury, 19 July 1889.
35. F.O.C.P. 6454/180, Rodd to Rosebery, 14 Apr. 1893.
36. F.O.C.P. 6497/17, Memorandum of Lord Chancellor on Right of Search of French vessels in Zanzibar waters, 9 Oct. 1893.
37. F.O.C.P. 6913/140, Admiralty to Foreign Office, 17 Nov. 1896.
38. F.O.C.P. 6913/164, Admiralty to Foreign Office, 24 Nov. 1896.
39. See page 225.
40. F.O.C.P. 7024/124, Memorandum by Sir John Kirk, 9 Mar. 1898.
41. India Office, Pamphlets PW/4, Muscat Precis, 1892-1905.
42. F.O.C.P. 7077/81, Salisbury to Sir E. Monson, 13 May 1898.
43. Whigham H. J. *The Persian Problem,* London, 1903, p. 20.
44. *Anti-Slavery Reporter,* Vol. 25, No. 4, Aug.-Dec. 1905. Parl. Paper, *Muscat* No. 1, 1905.
45. Award of the Arbitration Tribunal appointed to decide in the grant of the French Flag to Muscat dhows, The Hague, 8 August 1905. Herstlet *Commercial Treaties,* Vol. XIX, p. 289. 'Some principal Aspects of the British efforts to crush the African Slave Trade 1807-1929, Wilson, H.H. *American Journal of International Law* 1950.

CHAPTER 10

1. Hardinge, Sir A., *A Diplomatist in the East,* p. 350.
2. Sir George Rendel, who served under Hardinge when the latter was Ambassador to Spain, states 'he was, I suppose, one of the vaguest and most impractical men ever to enter the service of the Crown.' Rendel, Sir George, *The Sword and the Olive (Recollections of Diplomacy and the Foreign Service),* London, 1957, pp. 42-3.
3. 'To the Arab the holding of slaves is legal, sanctioned by his religion and the custom of his forefathers for ages. The Koran, while recognizing the domestic institution of slavery—as also does St. Paul—and the right to enslave infidel captives of war, does not support the raiding of slaves *per se*. On the contrary, it condemns it specifically. The Arab's social standing is estimated by his number of slaves. He received them as actual property from his father, representing a certain market value. His inalienable right to them is implanted in his mind, and has grown up with him from childhood, just as in your opinion, the property left you in his will by your father is yours fairly and legally, and arbitrary deprivation would be regarded by you as manifest despoliation.'
F.O. 107/43 Hardinge to Kimberley, 28 Mar. 1895.
4. Colomb, p. 465.
5. F.O.C.P. 7401/41, Sir L. Mathew to Hardinge, 17 Mar. 1899.
6. F.O.C.P. 6717/184, Hardinge's Report. 27 Apr. 1895.

7. Balfour, A. B., *Twelve Hundred Miles in a Waggon*, London, 1895.
8. Sienkiewicz, H. *Letters from Africa*, 1891, translation by Bojarski, E. A., p. 101.
9. F.O.C.P. 6717/186, Hardinge to Kimberley, 27 Apr. 1895. F.O.C.P. 6861/37, O'Sullivan to Hardinge, 30 May 1896.
10. Correspondence respecting the Abolition of the Legal Status of Slavery in Zanzibar and Pemba (C-8858) Africa No. 6, 1898, pp. 76-7. F.O. 107/57 Mathews to Hardinge, 14 Nov. 1896.
11. F.O.C.P. 7077/103, Hardinge to Salisbury, 3 Apr. 1898.
12. F.O.C.P. 7090/22, Hardinge to Salisbury, 13 June 1898.
13. In an amusing colloquy with the Sultan in April 1895, Hardinge argued that since the whole mainland of Africa was held by European governments who were at amity with Islam it had become a 'Dar-al-Aman', a land at peace with the Muslims, and therefore its inhabitants could not legally be enslaved. The Sultan replied that they were already enslaved by their fellow idolaters; and in a state of bondage when sold to Arabs; and also the condemnation of the sons of Ham to slavery was a tradition among Muslims. F.O.C.P. 6717/184, Hardinge to Kimberley, 17 Apr. 1895.
14. F.O. 107/35, No. 50, Hardinge to Kimberley, 13 Mar. 1895. F.O.C.P. 6849/192, Hardinge to Salisbury, 4 May 1896.
15. F.O.C.P. 6538/8, Memo by Consul C. S. Smith, 4 Jan. 1894. In February 1895, the total population of Zanzibar and Pemba was estimated at 208,000, of which 140,000 were slaves; according to Hardinge, 60,000 were legally held, but his critics claimed that only those acquired prior to 1873 and 1876 were legally held, and their number was only 9000.
16. F.O.C.P. 6490/27, Admiralty to Foreign Office, 5 Mar. 1893.
17. F.O.C.P. 6339/94, British and Foreign Anti-Slavery Society to Salisbury, 16 Feb. 1892. The view that the Indians were behind the slave trade died hard: Euan-Smith stated in 1890: 'Among the whole body of Arabs there will probably be found none more anxious for a return of the whole system of trade in its former channels—with the concomitant horrors of slavery and the slave trade, the ivory trade, and all that it involved, than the British Indian merchants enjoying the protection of Her Majesty's Government.' F.O.C.P. 6093/310, Euan-Smith to Salisbury, 24 Feb. 1890.
18. F.O. 107/35, No. 57, Hardinge to Lord Kimberly, 26 Mar. 1895. *Anti-Slavery Reporter,* Vol. 15, Fourth Series, No. 2, June-Aug. 1895.
19. Hansard Vol. XXXVI, 1895, pp. 664-7.
20. F.O. 107/40, Telegram 17, Lord Kimberley to Hardinge, 9 Mar. 1895.
21. Hansard Vol. XXXVI, 1895, p. 503.
22. Correspondence respecting the Slavery in Zanzibar Dominions, C-8275 Africa No. 7, 1896, p. 31.
23. F.O. 107/54, No. 244, Cave to Lord Salisbury, 29 Aug. 1896.
24. F.O.C.P. 6861/115, Memo by Hardinge, 10 Aug. 1896. F.O.C.P. 6861/154, British and Foreign Anti-Slavery Society, 19 Aug. 1896.
25. F.O.C.P. 6951/25, Salisbury to Mr Cornish, 18 Jan. 1897.

NOTES

26. C-8433, Africa No. 2 (1897) Abolition of the Legal Status of Slavery in Zanzibar and Pemba, Incl. 3 in No. 1.
27. F.O.C.P. 6964/115, Hardinge to Salisbury, 18 May 1897.
28. C-8433, Africa, No. 2, 1897, No. 1 Hardinge to Salisbury, Zanzibar, 9 Apr. 1897.
29. F.O. 107/77, No. 78, Hardinge to Salisbury, 9 Apr. 1897.
30. Despatch from HM Agent and Consul-General at Zanzibar transmitting a New Slavery Decree Cd. 4732 (1909) PP LIX, 577.
31. F.O.C.P. 7946/158, Mr Cave to F.O., 21 Jan. 1902. It was extremely difficult to get accurate numbers of slaves in the islands or on the mainland. One method was to count the number of houses and multiply this by the average number of inmates. But it was not easy to distinguish between slave and freeman. Native huts were scattered promiscuously over the shambas, and there was constant migration from district to district.
32. F.O.C.P. 7823/47, 19 Apr. 1901.
33. F.O. 2/194, Telegram 71, Salisbury to Cave, 10 Nov. 1899. F.O. 286/110, Incl. 2, Hardinge to Salisbury, 9 Apr. 1900.
34. F.O. 107/90, Hardinge to Salisbury, 29 Jan. 1898.
35. Hansard, Vol. LIII 1898, pp. 293-8.
36. Correspondence respecting the Abolition of the Legal Status of Slavery in Zanzibar and Pemba. C-8858 Africa No. 6, 1898.
37. F.O.C.P. 7823/147; Admiralty to F.O., 4 June 1901.
38. MacMaster, D. N., 'The Ocean-Going Dhow Trade to East Africa,' *East African Geographical Review*, No. 4, April 1966, pp. 13-24.
39. Cd-4732, Africa No. 3 (1909); Cd-4816, Africa No. 4 (1909); Hollingsworth, L. W., *Zanzibar under the Foreign Office 1890-1913*, London, 1953, p. 158.
40. Despatch from HM Agent and Consul General at Zanzibar (Cd-4816), Africa No. 4, 1909.

RECOUNT AND SUMMARY

1. See pages 13, 17-18, 24-6, 38
2. See pages 44, 48, 55, 96-8, 104
3. See pages 115-17, 154
4. See page 154
5. See pages 58-60, 78, 175-7
6. See pages 123, 132, 135, 164-7
7. See pages 155-9
8. See pages 150-9
9. See pages 119, 122-3, 127-9, 132, 135, 151
10. This was also the estimate of von Wissman, and the Anti-Slavery Society: see pages 117, 119, 154-5, 191-4

Bibliography

PRIMARY SOURCES

Foreign Office: F.O. 84 (Slave Trade) These volumes contain correspondence relating to East Africa up to 1892.
Foreign Office General Correspondence: F.O. 107/18 to 107/105 (Matters concerning Zanzibar and the East African Protectorate).
Foreign Office Confidential Prints: These contain the majority of despatches relating to East Africa, but not usually the minutes thereon.
British Sessional Papers, House of Commons: Correspondence relating to the Slave Trade on the East African coast.
Selections from the Records of the Bombay Government in the nineteenth century.
Anti-Slavery Reporter.
Court Minutes of the East Indian Company.
Zanzibar Archives: Letter books in the Zanzibar Secretariat.

OTHER PRINTED SOURCES

Admiralty: Handbook for the East African Slave Trade: *Instructions for the Suppression of the Slave Trade,* 1869.
Hertslet, E. *The Map of Africa by Treaty*, London, 1909, Vols I and II.
Lorimer, J. G. *Gazeteer of the Persian Gulf, Oman and Central Arabia*, Calcutta, 1908.
Naval Intelligence Division: Handbook, *Iraq and the Persian Gulf,* Geographical Series, Oxford, 1944.

JOURNALS & NEWSPAPERS

Das Deutsche Kolonialblatt, Berlin, 1890-1914.
Die Deutsche Kolonialzeitung, Berlin, 1884-1920.
Free Church Monthly.
Glasgow Herald.
Morning Post.
O'Africano.
Reichsanzeiger,
Tanganyika Notes & Records, Dar es Salaam, 1936–

The Times.
Uganda Journal.
Zanzibar Gazette.

PARLIAMENTARY PAPERS

Papers relating to the Mombasa Railway Survey and Uganda, C.6555 (1892).
Correspondence respecting Slavery in Zanzibar, C.7707 (1895).
Correspondence respecting Slavery in the Zanzibar Dominions, C.8275 (1896).
Instructions to Mr Hardinge respecting the Abolition of the Legal Status of Slavery in Zanzibar and Pemba, C. 8858 (1898).
Correspondence respecting the Status of Slavery in East Africa and the Islands of Zanzibar and Pemba, C. 9502 (1899).
Correspondence respecting Slavery and the Slave Trade in East Africa and the Islands of Zanzibar and Pemba, Cd.-96 (1900): Ditto Cd.593 (1901): Ditto Cd.1389 (1902).

ARTICLES

Alpers, E. A., *The Yao in the 19th Century,* Journal of African History, X, 3, 1969.
Dundas, R. N., *Slavery in East Africa*, Scottish Geographical Magazine, March 1893.
Freeman-Grenville, G. S. P., *The External Relations of the East African Coast: before 1800*, Colston Papers, No. 25; Foreign Relations of African States, London, 1974.
Garvin, R. J., *The Bartle Frere Mission to Zanzibar,* The Historical Journal, V, 1962.
Haines, S. B., *Memoir to Accompany a Chart of the South Coast of Arabia*, Journal of the Royal Geographical Society, vol. 9, 1839.
Hattersley, S., *Erastus Karamii, Slave Prince, A True Story of Uganda,* London, 1910.
Hirth, F., *Early Chinese Notices of East African Territories,* Journal of the American Oriental Society, XXX, 1909.
Jennings-Bramly, W., *A Journey to Siwa,* Geographical Journal, December, 1897.
Kirkman, J., *China and Africa in the Middle Ages*, The Journal of African History, IV, 1963.
Lane, F. C., *The Economic Meaning of the Invention of the Compass,* The American Historical Review, LXVIII, 1963.
McMaster, D. N., *The Ocean-Going Dhow Trade to East Africa*, The East African Geographical Review, No. 4, April 1966.
Pankhurst, R., *Ethiopia's Economic and Cultural Ties with the Sudan from the Middle Ages to the Mid-Nineteenth Century* A Paper submitted to the International Congress of Africanists, 3rd Session, Addis Ababa, 1973.

Playfair, R. L., *Report on the various Countries around Zanzibar,* Transactions of the Bombay Geographical Society, XVIII, 1865.
Tibbetts, G. R., *Arab navigation in the Red Sea,* Geographical Journal, cxx vii, London 1961.
Villiers, A., *Dhow Builders of Kuwait,* Geographical Magazine, xx, 1948.
Wilson, H. H., *Some Principal Aspects of the British efforts to crush the African Slave Trade 1807-1929,* American Journal of International Law, 1950.

BOOKS

Abbas, I. M. A., *The British, the Slave Trade and Slavery in the Sudan 1820-1881,* Khartoum, 1972.
Aitchison, C. U., *A Collection of Treaties, Engagements and Sanads Relating to India and Neighbouring Countries,* Delhi, 1933.
Ashe, R. P., *Two Kings of Uganda,* London, 1899.
Axelson, E. V., *Portuguese in South-East Africa 1600-1700,* Johannesburg, 1960.
Badger, G. P., *History of the Imams and Seyyids of Oman by Salil ibn Razik,* Hakluyt Society, 1871.
Baker, S. W., *The Albert Nyanza: Great Basin of the Nile, and Exploration of the Nile Sources,* London, 1866.
—*The Nile Tributaries of Abyssinia,* London, 1867.
—*Ismailia: a narrative of the expedition to Central Africa for suppression of the slave trade,* 2 vols., London, 1874.
Balfour, A. B., *Twelve Hundred Miles in a Waggon,* London, 1895.
Banaji, D. R., *Slavery in British India,* Bombay, 1933.
Barnard, (Lieutenant RN), *A Three year Cruise in the Mozambique Channel for the Suppression of the Slave Trade,* London, 1848.
Barros, J. de, *Decados da Asia* (ed. Baiao, A.,) Coimbra, 1930.
Barrow, R. H., *Slavery in the Roman Empire,* London, 1969.
Baumann, H. and Westermann, D., *Les Peuples et les Civilisations de l'Afrique* (traduction française par L. Homburger), Paris, 1948.
Bennet, N. R. & Brooks, G. E., *New England Merchants in Africa —A History Through Documents, 1820 to 1865,* Boston, 1965.
Berlioux, E. F., *The Slave Trade in Africa,* London, 1872.
Bethel, L., *The Abolition of the Brazilian Slave Trade,* London, 1973.
Bissell, A., *A Voyage from England to the Red Sea, 1798-99,* London, 1806.
Breasted, J. H., *Ancient Records of Egypt,* New York, 1962.
Brode, H., *Tippu Tip,* Berlin, 1905.
Boteler, T. (Lieutenant), *Narrative of a Voyage of Discovery to*

Africa and Arabia, London, 1835.
Boxer, R. F., *Fort Jesus and the Portuguese in Mombasa,* London, 1960.
Budge, Sir Ernest A. Wallis, *A History of Ethiopia, Abyssinia, and Nubia*, London, 1928.
Bullard, Sir Reader, *The Camels Must Go,* London, 1961
Burckhardt, J. L., *Travels in Nubia*, London, 1819.
Burton, R. F., *The Lake Regions of Central Africa*, 2 vols., London, 1860.
—*Zanzibar, City, Island and Coast,* London, 1872.
—*First Footsteps in Africa*, London, 1894.
Buxton, T. F., *The African Slave Trade*, London, 1839.
Cameron, V. L., *Across Africa*, 2 vols., London, 1877.
Carroll, M., *From a Persian Tea House*, London, 1960.
Cary, M., & Warmington, E. H., *The Ancient Explorers*, London, 1963.
Casati, G., *Ten Years in Equatoria, and the Return with Emin Pasha* (transl. Clay, J. R., and Landor, I. W. S.) 2 vols. London, 1891.
Chaille-Long, C., *Central Africa: naked truths of naked people,* London, 1876.
Chanler, W. A., *Through Jungle and Desert*, London, 1896.
Christie, J., *Cholera Epidemics in East Africa*, London, 1876.
Colombos, C. J., *International Law of the Sea*, New York, 1962.
Colomb, P., *Slave Catching in the Indian Ocean,* London, 1873.
Coupland, Sir Reginald, *The British Anti-Slavery Movement*, London, 1933.
—*East Africa and Its Invaders,* Oxford, 1938.
—*The Exploitation of East Africa*, London, 1939.
De Cosson, A. E., *Cradle of the Blue Nile,* London, 1877.
Devereaux, W. C., *A Cruise in the Gorgon*, London, 1869.
Douin, G., *Histoire du règne du Khedive Ismail,* Tome III, *(L'Empire africain),* Cairo, 1941.
Duarte Barbosa, *The book of Duarte Barbosa* (ed. M. L. Dames), Hakluyt Society, London, 1918
Duffy, J., *Portuguese Africa*, London, 1961.
Duyvendak, J. J. L., *China's Discovery of Africa*, London, 1949.
Edwardes, S. M., *Rise of Bombay*, London, 1902.
Eliot, C., *The East Africa Protectorate*, London, 1905.
Elton, J. F., *Travels and Researches among the Lakes and Mountains of Eastern and Central Africa,* London, 1879.
Ferrard, G., *Relations de voyages et textes géographiques*, Paris, 1913.
Filesi, T., *China and Africa in the Middle Ages*, London, 1972.
Fitzgerald, W. W. A., *Travels in the Coastlands of British East Africa and the Islands of Zanzibar and Pemba*, London, 1898.

Fraser, P. M., *Ptolemaic Alexandria*, London, 1972.
Freeman-Grenville, G. S. P., *The Medieval History of the Coast of Tanganyika*, London, 1962.
—*East African Coast: Select Documents*, London, 1962.
—*The French at Kilwa Island*, London, 1965.
Frisk, H. (ed.), *The Periplus of the Erythraean Sea*, Göteberg, 1927.
Galbraith, J. S., *Mackinnon and East Africa 1878-1895*, London, 1972.
Gessi, R., *Seven Years in the Soudan*, London, 1892.
Giraud, V., *Les Lacs de l'Afrique Equatoriale; voyage d'exploration exécuté de 1883 à 1885*, Paris, 1890.
Graham, G. S., *Great Britain in the Indian Ocean*, London, 1967.
Grant, J. A., *A Walk across Africa*, London, 1864.
Gray, J. M., *The British in Mombasa*, London, 1957.
—*History of Zanzibar from the Middle Ages to 1856*, London, 1962.
Gray, J. R., *A History of the Southern Sudan, 1838-1889*, London, 1961.
Gregory, R. G., *India and East Africa*, London, 1971.
Guillain, M., *Documents sur l'histoire la géographie et le commerce de l'Afrique Orientale*, Paris, 1856.
Hamilton, A., *A New Account of the East Indies*, 2 vols., London, 1727.
Hardinge, Sir A., *A Diplomatist in the East*, London, 1928.
Hardinge, C., *In Remotest Barotseland*, London, 1924.
Harris, J. E., *The African Presence in Asia*, Evanston, 1971.
Harris, W. C. (Major), *The Highlands of Ethiopia*, London, 1844.
Hill, G. B., *Colonel Gordon in Central Africa, 1874-1879*, London, 1881.
Hill, P. G., *Fifty Days on Board a Slave Vessel in the Mozambique Channel*, London, 1844.
Hinde, S. L., *The Fall of the Congo Arabs*, London, 1897.
History of East Africa; vol. I ed. Oliver, R. & Mathew, G., London, 1963.
—Vol. II ed. Harlow, V., Chilver, E. M., & Smith, A., London, 1965.
Hitti, P. K., *History of the Arabs*, London, 1971.
Hogg, P. C., *The African Slave Trade and its Suppression. A Classified and Annotated Bibliography of Books, Pamphlets and Periodical Articles*, London, 1973.
Hohnel, L. von, *The Discovery of Lakes Rudolph and Stephanie*, (transl. N. Bell) 2 vols. London, 1894.
Hollingsworth, L. W., *Zanzibar under the Foreign Office, 1890-1913*, London, 1953.
Holt, P. M., *A Modern History of the Sudan*, London, 1961.
Hore, E. C., *Tanganyika, Eleven Years in Central Africa*, London,

1892.
Hoskins, G. A., *Travels in Ethiopia*, London, 1835.
Hourani, G. F., *Arab Seafaring in the Indian Ocean in Ancient and Early Medieval Times*, Princeton, 1951.
Hughes, W., *The Country of Baluchistan*, Bombay, 1877.
Hutchinson, E., *The Slave Trade of East Africa*, London, 1874.
Huzayyin, S. A., *Arabia and the Far East*, Cairo, 1942.
Ingham, K., *History of East Africa*, London, 1962.
Isaacman, A., *Mozambique, the Africanization of a European Institution, the Zambezi Prazos 1750-1902*, London, 1972.
Isaacs, N., *Travels and Adventures in Eastern Africa*, London, 1836.
Johnston, H. H., *The Uganda Protectorate*, London, 1902.
Jones, H. L., *The Geography of Strabo*, Harvard, 1959.
Jones, M. K., *The Slave Trade at Mauritius 1810-1829* B. Litt. thesis, Oxford, 1938.
Junker, W., *Travels in Africa, 1875-1886* (transl. Keene, A. H.) 3 vols. London, 1890-1892.
Kagwa, A., *Ekitabo Kya Basekabaka Be Buganda*, 4th edn. London, 1953.
Kelly, J. B., *Britain and the Persian Gulf, 1795-1880*, London, 1968.
Keppell, G. (Major), *A Journey from India to England*, London, 1834.
Kersten, O., *von der Deckens Reisen in Ost-Afrika*, Leipzig, 1869.
Kirkman, J. S., *Men and Monuments on the East African Coast*, London, 1964.
Kinglake, A. W., *Eothen*, London, 1845.
Krapf, J. L., *Travels, Researches and Missionary Labours during an Eighteen Years' Residence in Eastern Africa*, London, 1860.
Lancaster, J., *The Voyage of Sir James Lancaster, Ktd., to the East Indies*, (ed. C. R. Markham) Hakluyt Society, London, 1877.
Langheld, W., *Zwanzig Jahre in deutschen Kolonien*, Teil 1, *Deutsch-Ostafrika 1889-1900*, Berlin, 1909.
Lane, E. W., *The Manners and Customs of the Modern Egyptians*, London, 1836.
Lavigérie, Cardinal, *Slavery in Africa*, Boston, 1888.
Linschoten, J. H. van, *Linschoten's Voyage*, Hakluyt Society, 1885.
Livingstone, D., *Last Journals*, London, 1867.
—*Missionary Travels and Researches in South Africa, Including a Sketch of Sixteen years Residence in the Interior of Africa*, London, 1857.
Lloyd, C., *The Navy and the Slave Trade*, London, 1949.
Low, C. R., *History of the Indian Navy, 1613-1863*, London, 1877.
Lugard, F. D., *The Rise of Our East African Empire*, London, 1893.

Lyne, R. N., *Zanzibar in Contemporary Times*, London, 1905.
—*Apostle of Empire*, London, 1936.
Macdonald, J. R. L., *Soldiering and Surveying in British East Africa, 1891-1894*, London, 1897.
Mackenzie, W. D., *Egypt and the Egyptian Question*, London, 1883.
Madden, A. C., *Kiungani*, London, 1887.
Malloy, W. M., *Treaties and Conventions*, US Documents, New York, 1962.
Mangat, J. S., *A History of the Asians in East Africa*, London, 1969.
Martineau, J., *Life of Sir B. Frere*, London, 1895.
Mathieson, W. L., *Great Britain and the Slave Trade*, London, 1929.
Maurizi, V., *History of Seyyid Said*, London, 1819.
McLeod, L., *Travels in Eastern Africa: with the Narratives of a Residency in Mozambique*, London, 1860.
McCullagh, F., *The Fall of Abd-ul-Hamid*, London, 1910.
Miles, S. B., *The Countries and Tribes of the Persian Gulf*, London, 1919.
Montfried, Henri de, *Pearls, Arms and Hashish*, New York, 1936.
Muller, F. F., *Deutschland-Zanzibar-Ostafrika: Geschichte einer deutscher Kolonial-oberung, 1884-1890*, Berlin, 1959.
Mungeam, G. H., *British Rule in Kenya, 1895-1912*, London, 1966.
New, C., *Life, Wanderings and Labours in Eastern Africa*, London, 1873.
Newitt, M. D. D., *Portuguese Settlement on the Zambezi*, London, 1973.
Newman, H. S., *Banani, The Transition from Slavery to Freedom in Zanzibar*, London, 1898.
Nicholls, C. S., *The Swahili Coast, Politics, Diplomacy and Trade on the East African Littoral 1798-1856*, London, 1971.
Oded, A., *Islam in Uganda*, Tel Aviv, 1974.
Oliver, R., *The Missionary Factor in East Africa*, London, 1952.
—*Sir Harry Johnston and the Scramble for Africa*, London, 1957.
Owen, W. F., *Narrative of Voyages to Explore the Shores of Africa, Arabia and Madagascar*, London, 1833.
Pearce, F. B., *Zanzibar, the Island Metropolis of East Africa*, London. 1920.
Penser, N. M., *The Harem*, London, 1967.
Perham, M. F., *Lugard: The Years of Adventure, 1858-1898*, London, 1956.
Peters, K., *New Light on Dark Africa*, London, 1891.
—*Die Grundung von Deutsch Ostafrika*, Berlin, 1906.
Petherick, J., *Egypt, the Soudan and Central Africa*, Edinburgh, 1861.
Plowden, W. C., *Travels in Abyssinia and the Galla Country with an*

Account of a Mission to Ras Ali in 1848, London, 1868.
Portal, G. H., *The British Mission to Uganda in 1893* (ed. Rennell Rodd), London, 1894.
Prins, A. H. J., *The Swahili-speaking Peoples of Zanzibar and the East African Coast, Arabs, Shirazi and Swahili: Ethnographic Survey of Africa*, London, 1961.
Prior, J., *Voyage of the Frigate Nisus*, London, 1819.
Pruen, S. T., *The Arab and African*, London, 1891.
Rendel, Sir G., *The Sword and the Olive (Recollections of Diplomacy and the Foreign Service)*, London, 1957.
Roberts, E., *Embassy to the Eastern Courts of Cochin China, Siam and Muscat, 1832-34*, New York, 1837.
Robinson, R. E. & Gallagher, J., with Alice Denny, *Africa and the Victorians*, London, 1961.
Rodd, R. J. Rennell, *Social and Diplomatic Memories, 1884-1893*, London, 1922.
Roscoe, J., *The Baganda*, London, 1911.
Ruschenberger, S. W., *Voyage round the World*, Philadelphia, 1838.
Russell, C. E. B., *General Rigby, Zanzibar and the Slave Trade*, London, 1935.
Ruete, Emily (Salma binti Said), *Memoirs of an Arabian Princess*, London, 1907.
Schmidt, R., *Geschichte des Araberaufstandes in Ostafrika*, Frankfurt, 1892.
Schramm, P. E., *Deutschland und Ubersee*, Berlin, 1950.
Schweinfurth, G., *Emin Pasha in Central Africa*, London, 1888.
—*The Heart of Africa: Three Years' Travel and Adventuring in the Unexplored Regions of Central Africa, 1868-1871*, London, 1873.
Scott, R., *Limuria, The Lesser Dependencies of Mauritius*, London, 1961.
Schack, W. A., *The Gurage*, London, 1966.
Sienkiewicz, H., *Letters from Africa*, 1891 (transl. by Bojarski, EA).
Smee, T. (Capt.), *Voyage to the Eastern Shores of Africa*, London, 1811.
Smith, I. R., *The Emin Pasha Relief Expedition, 1886-1890*, London, 1972.
Smith, Mackenzie & Co Ltd, *History of Smith, Mackenzie and Company Ltd*, London, 1938.
Speke, J. H., *Journal of the Discovery of the Source of the Nile*, London, 1863.
Spencer, E., *Travels in Circassia*, London, 1839.
Stanley, H. M., *In Darkest Africa*, London, 1890.
—*How I Found Livingstone*, London, 1872.
—*Through the Dark Continent*, London, 1878.
Steere, E., *Handbook of the Swahili Language as Spoken at*

Zanzibar, London, 1870.
Stevenson, J. S., *The Arabs in Central Africa and at Lake Nyassa*, Glasgow, 1889.
Stigand, C. H., *The Land of Zinj*, London, 1913.
Strandes, J., *Die Portugiesenzeit von Deutsch- und Englisch-Ostafrika*, Berlin, 1899.
Stuhlmann, F., *Mit Emin Pasha ins Herz von Afrika*, Berlin, 1894.
—*Die Tagebucher von Dr. Emin Pasha*, Hamburg, 1919-27.
Sulivan, G. L., *Dhow Chasing in Zanzibar Waters*, London, 1873.
Swann, A. J., *Fighting the Slave Hunters in Central Africa*, London, 1910.
Sykes, E. C., *Persia and its Peoples*, New York, 1910.
Temu, A. J., *British Protestant Missions*, London, 1972.
Theal, G. M. (ed.), *Records of South-Eastern Africa*, 9 vols. London, 1898-1903.
Tibbetts, G. R., *Arab Navigation in the Indian Ocean Before the Coming of the Portuguese*, London, 1971.
Thomson, J., *Through Masailand*, London, 1885.
Tippu Tip, *Maisha ya Hamed bin Muhammed el Murjebi yaani Tippu Tip* (transl. W. H. Whiteley) East African Swahili Committee Journals, 28, ii, 1958 and 29, i, 1959.
Tucker, A. R., *Eighteen Years in Uganda*, London, 1908.
Tugay, E. F., *Three Centuries: Family Chronicles of Turkey and Egypt*, London, 1963.
Valentia, G., *Voyages and Travels to India, Ceylon, the Red Sea, Abyssinia and Egypt*, London, 1811.
Vandeleur, S., *Campaigning on the Upper Nile and Niger*, London, 1898.
Villiers, A., *Monsoon Seas*, London, 1952.
Wallon, H. A., *Histoire de l'esclavage dans l'antiquité*, Paris, 1879.
Wellsted, J. R., *Travels in Arabia*, London, 1838.
—*Travels to the City of the Caliphs*, London, 1848.
Wheeler, Sir Mortimer, *Rome Beyond Imperial Frontiers*, London, 1953.
Willoughby, Sir J., *Sport in East Africa*, London, 1890.
Whigham, H.J., *The Persian Problem*, London, 1903.
Wilson, A. T., *The Persian Gulf*, London, 1928.
Wilson, C. T. & Felkin, R. W., *Uganda and the Egyptian Soudan*, London, 1882.
Wingate, F. R. (Major), *Mahdism and the Egyptian Sudan*, London, 1891.
—*Ten Years Captivity in the Mahdi's Camp, 1882-1892*, London, 1892.
Winsted, E. O. (ed.), *The Christian Topography of Cosmos Indicopleustes*, Cambridge, 1909.
Wissmann, H. von, *My Second Journey Through Equatorial Africa*

from the Congo to the Zambezi in the Years 1886 to 1887, London, 1891.
Wylde, A. B., *'83 to '87 in the Soudan*, London, 1888.

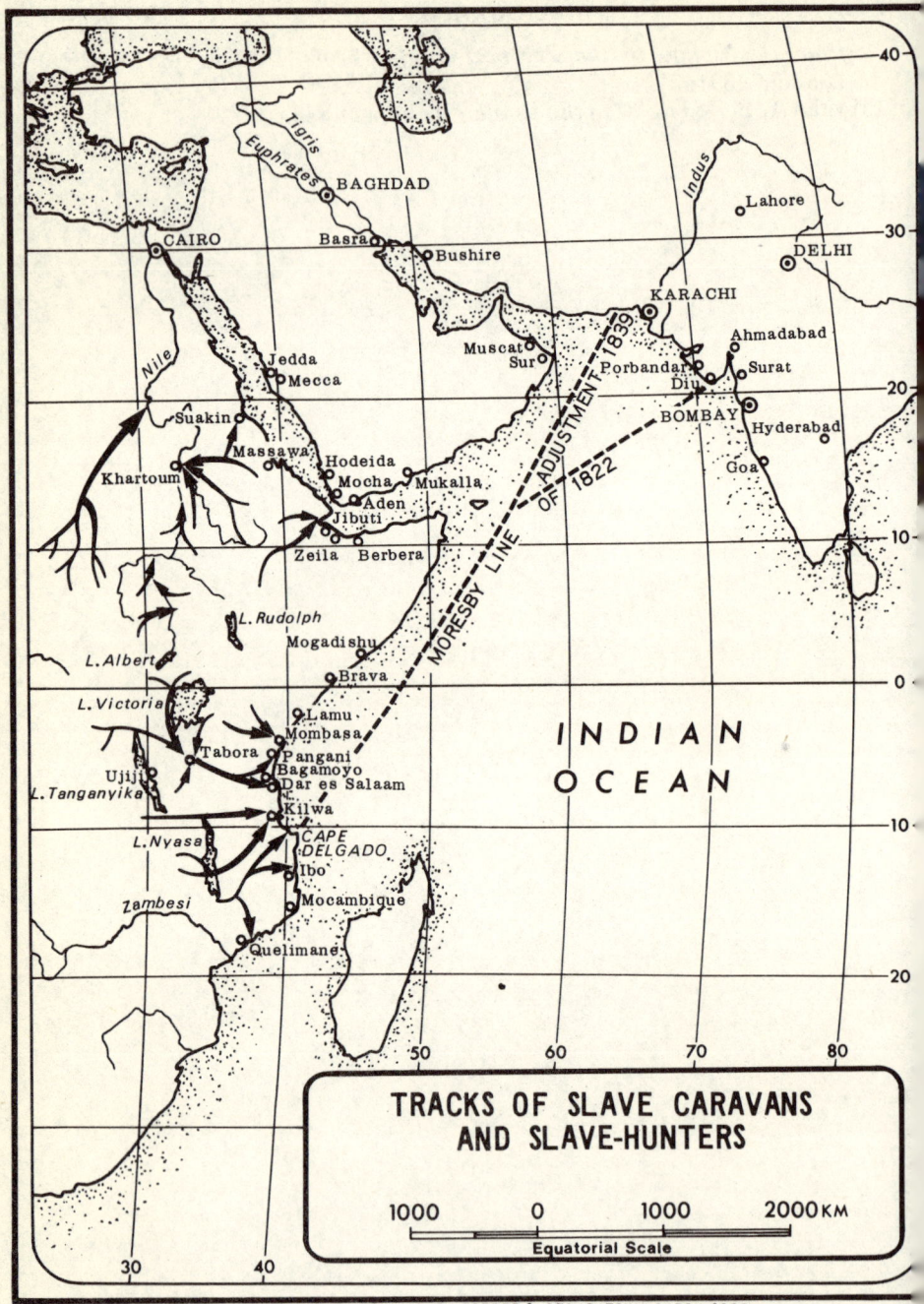

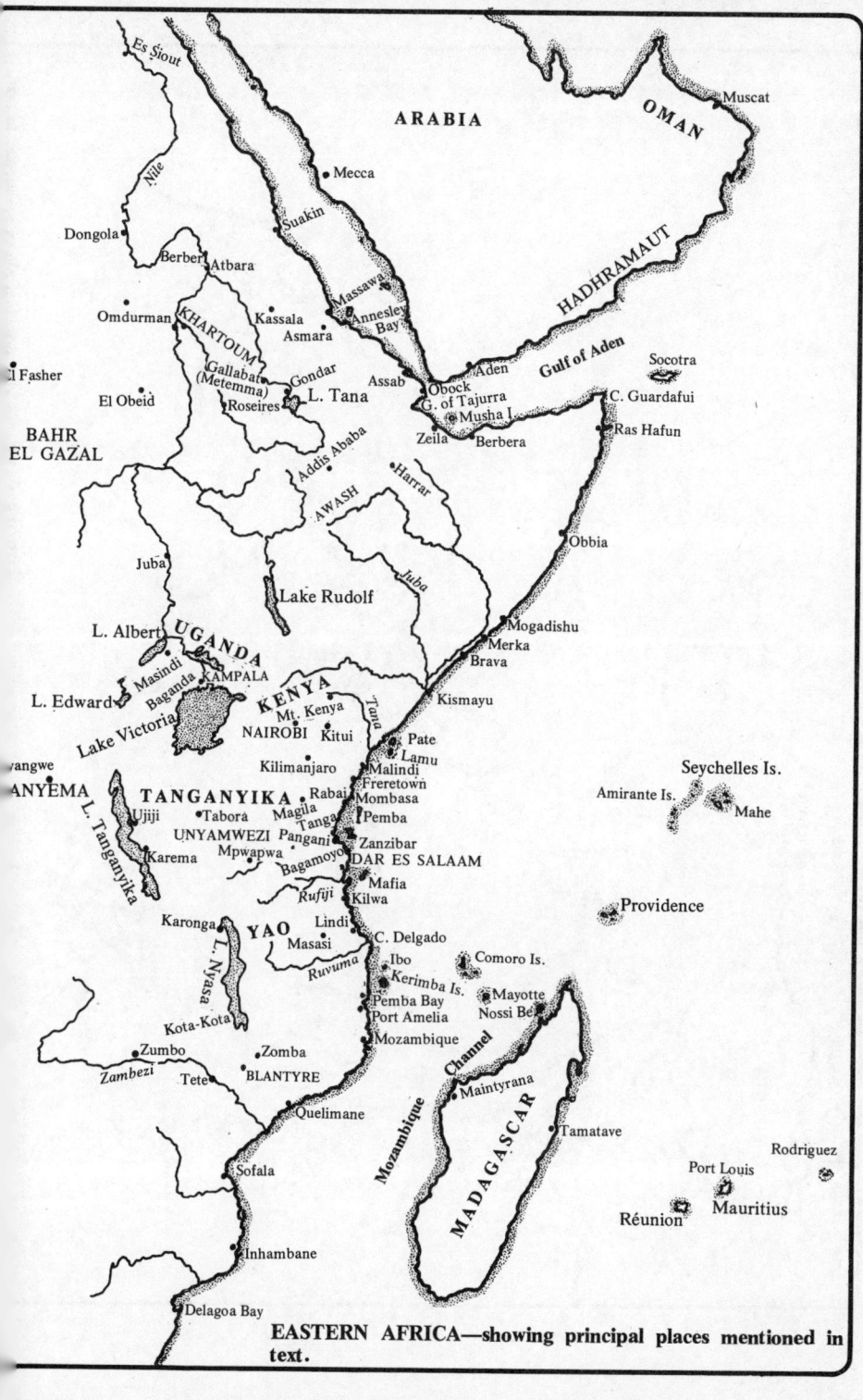

EASTERN AFRICA—showing principal places mentioned in text.

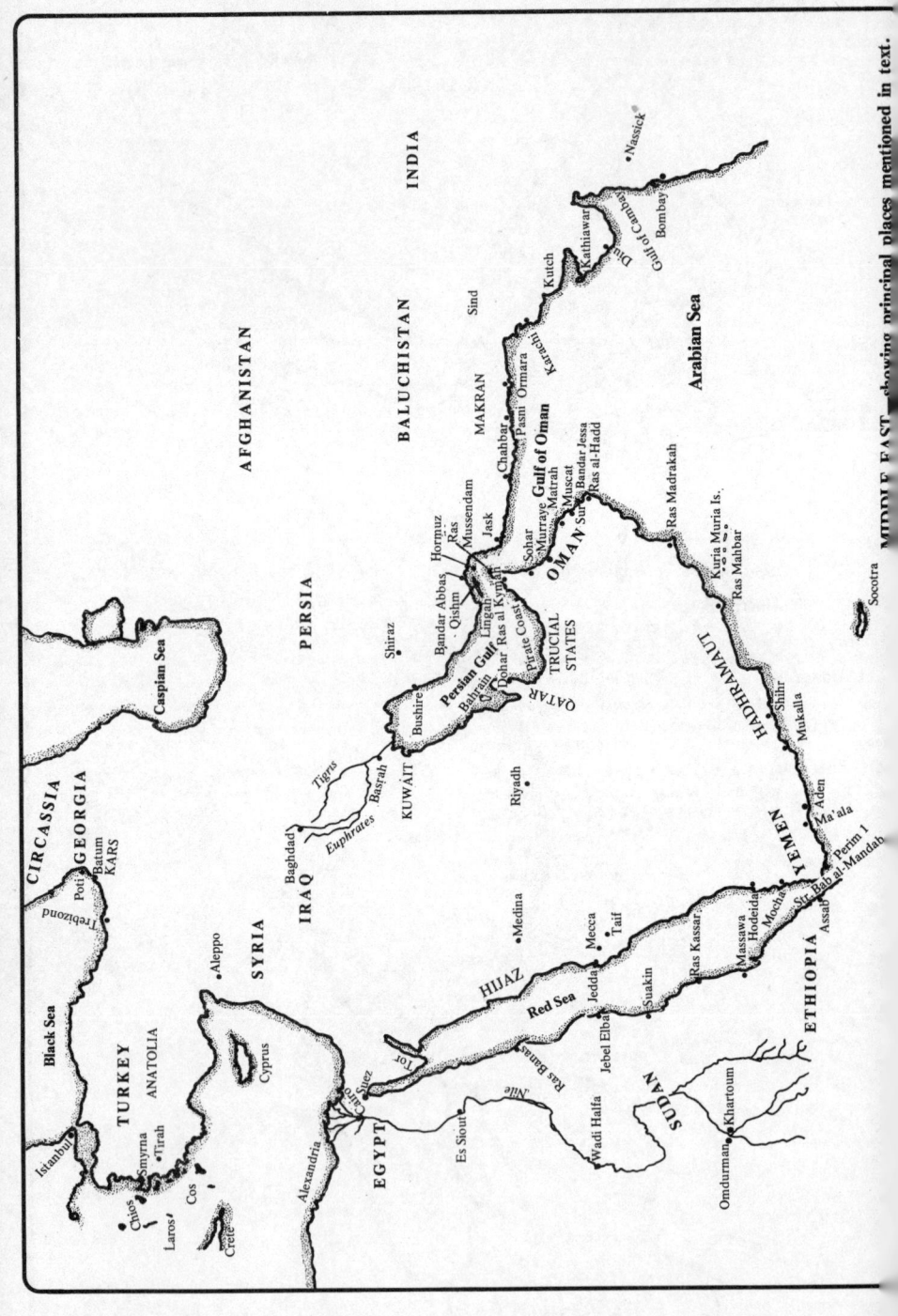

MIDDLE EAST, showing principal places mentioned in text.

Index

Abd al Malak, 5
Abbasid Caliphates, 121
Abd al Kuri, 73-4, 89
Abd bin Salim, 188
Abd ul-Hamid, 174
Abdul Majid, 127, 163
Abercromby, General, 41
Aberdeen Act (1845), 18
Abour Rosah, 140
Abu Bekr, 155-6
Abyssinia, 4, 7, 9, 49, 50, 52, 73, 85, 127, 130, 140-1, 145-6, 148-59, 167, 178, 188, 199, 262
Acholi, 133
Adalia, 167
Aden, 6, 22, 40, 55, 65, 71-5, 86-7, 89, 112, 153, 155, 161-2, 273
Aden, Gulf of, 1, 76, 130, 137, 152, 154, 156
Admiralty, 71, 73, 79, 82, 89, 201, 232-3, 235, 249, 258, 267
Admiralty Courts, 18, 24, 76, 83, 89, 99, 104-5, 119, 158, 169, 178, 267, 280
Adowa, 161, 198
African Institution, 39
African Lakes Company, 214-16, 218, 229
Aidan, 167
Ahmed bin Said, 48
Ahmed bin Sultan, 40
Ainsworth, J., 197, 290
Aintab, 168
Albert-Edward, Lake, 136, 201
Alexandria, 2, 3, 127, 138, 166-7, 173
Aleppo, 167
Ali, 5
Ali Bey, 9
Ali bin Said, Sultan, 225
Ali (son of Said), 246
Alids, 5
Ali ibn Muhammed, 4
Ali Pasha, Sherif, 142
Allington, C., 279
Almeida, Governor-General, 16, 24-5, 33
Almozeid, 5

Amenhotep II, 2
Americans, 47, 55, 123
American Civil War, 23
American flag, use of, 19, 20-3, 32, 43
Anatolia, 167
Anglo-Egyptian Condominium, 144
Anglo-German Agreement (1890), 217, 225
Anglo-German blockade, (1888-9), 223-4
Anglo-Portuguese Conventions (1890) (1891), 217
Angoche River, 12, 19, 20, 24, 211
Angola, 8, 11, 289
Ankole, 196, 195-6
Annesley Bay, 73
Anstruther, Sir R., 281
Anti-Slave Trade Conference (Paris 1867), 97-8
Anti-Slave Trade Conference (Brussels 1890), 222
Anti-Slave Trade legislation:
  Abolition Act (1807), 27, 268
  Abolition Act (1811), 268
  Anti-Slave Trade treaties (Anglo-Portuguese) (1817 et al.), 266
  Moresby Treaty (1822), 44-6, 50, 272
  Abolition Act (1833), 40
  Equipment Clause Treaty (1842), 18, 21
  Abolition Act (1843), 40
  Anti-Slave Trade Decrees (India), 40, 270-1
  Hamerton Treaty (1845), 53-4
  Anti-Slave Trade Decree (Turkey) (1846), 163, 175
  Anti-Slave Trade Decree (Persia) (1847), 163, 175
  Abolition Act (1849), 32
  Anti-Slave Trade Treaty (Anglo-Persian) (1851), 175
  Anti-Slave Trade Decree (Turkey) (1864), 165
  Anti-Slave Trade Decree (Zanzibar) (1873), 109-14, 116-17, 119, 227

Slave Trade Consolidation Act (1873), 277
Anti-Slave Trade Decree (Zanzibar) (1875), 117-18
Anti-Slave Trade Convention (Anglo-Egyptian) (1877), 137-9, 143, 157
Abolition Decree (Hova) (1878), 212
Anti-Slave Trade Convention (Anglo-Turkish) (1880), 158
Anti-Slave Trade Treaty (Anglo-Persian) (1882), 178
Anti-Slave Trade Treaty (Britain and Sultan of Mohilla) (1882), 178
Anti-Slave Trade Decree (Italian) (1886), 161
Anti-Slave Trade Decree (Zanzibar) (1888), 221
Anti-Slave Trade Decree (Turkey) (1889), 169
Anti-Slave Trade Decree (Zanzibar) (1890), 225-7
Anti-Slave Trade Decree (Zanzibar) (1891), 230
Anti-Slave Trade Convention (Anglo-Egyptian) (1895), 142
Anti-Slavery Decree (Zanzibar) (1897), 253-9
Anti-Slavery Decree (German) (1901), 203
Anti-Slavery Decree (Ethiopia) (1903), 151
Anti-Slavery Decrees (Zanzibar) (1907) (1909), 259
Anti-Slavery Ordinance (British) (1922), 205
Anti-Slave Trade patrol, 25, 72, 118, 227, 281
Anti-Slavery Reporter, 113
Anti-Slavery Society, 30-1, 97-8, 108, 117, 129, 136, 147, 151, 156, 158, 160, 163-4, 169-70, 220, 222-4, 230, 241, 249-51, 253, 256-8
Anuak, 146
Aqqad Bros., 127, 132
Aqqad, Sheikh al-, 126, 129, 281
Arabia, 1, 3, 6, 10, 68-70, 72, 74-6, 83, 85, 216, 262
Arabs, 1, 3, 4, 6, 7, 9, 12, 15, 19, 22-5, 32-6, 39-41, 47, 50, 52, 54-65, 76-8, 80, 84, 92, 94, 96-7, 107, 111-12, 115-16, 118, 134, 154, 172, 179-80, 182-205, 209-11, 213-15, 217-19, 226-31, 233
Araxes, 163

Arbain Road, 122, 126
Argyle, Lord, 108
Arusa, 149
Aruiwimi, 188
Ashabab, 147
Aswan, 138
Atbai desert, 147
Atbara, 145
Austria, 18, 166
Austrian Lloyd Steamship Company, 167
Austrian Mission and Agricultural Home, 142, 284
Australian Station, 118
Averet Bazaar, 168
Aynterad, 153
Azande, 127, 134, 284
Azizieh Company, 167-8

Bab al-Mandab, 48, 61
Bab Island, 152
Baddu, 194
Badger, Reverend G., 110, 282
Bagamoyo, 47, 61, 65, 90, 92, 100, 111, 116-17, 201-2, 261
Baganda, 172, 188, 193-6
Baggara, 140, 160
Baghdad, 175, 179, 264, 288
Bahia, 21
Bahrain, 4, 51, 55, 176, 179
Bahr el Ghazal, 124, 126-8, 133-5, 139-40, 144, 146, 172, 284
Bahr el Jebel, 284
Bainder, 167
Baker, Sir Samuel, 108-9, 125, 128-9, 132-3, 149
Baladhuri, al-, 5
Baluchistan, 50, 80
Banda Atjch, 71
Bandar Abbas, 41, 75, 176-7, 288
Bandar Jessa, 240
Bandawe, 188
Bani Shanqul, 145
Bantu, 9
Banyans (see Indians)
Barawa (see Brava)
Barcelona, 22
Barghash, Sultan, 102-3, 108-14, 116-17
Bari, 125, 133, 136, 282
Barotseland, 293
Barros, Joao de, 4
Baro river, 146
Bartholemy, D., 126
Barun, 145
Basra, 4, 54, 175, 271, 288

INDEX

Basrah (see Basra)
Basso, 150
Batinah coast, 176
Batoum, 164-5, 168
Battuta, ibn, 6
Baumann, O., 200
Bayuda, 123
Bazarut, 211
Beaver, Captain, 15
Bebutov, General, 163
Bedouins, 177
Beira, 12
Bemba, 213, 219
Benadir, 1
Benefield, Captain, 74
Bengal, 4, 40-1
Beni, 140
Berber, 129, 145, 149
Berbera, 7, 130, 153, 155, 161-2, 275
Bergman, M., 159
Berlin Act (1885), 224-5
Berlin Conference (1878), 220
Berlin Conference (1884/85), 220
Berlioux, M., 108
Bey, Ahmed, 128
Bismarck, 117, 220
Bissell, A., 38
Black River, 29
Black Sea, 162-4
Blankett, Commander, 38
Blantyre, 214
Blomfield, Captain, 78
Boers, 206
Bogos, 130
Bombay, 38-42, 50, 53, 66, 71-3, 85-7, 152, 209, 216, 286
Bongo, 25, 210
Bono, Andrea & Amabile de, 126-7
Bosanquet, Lieutenant, 17
Boteler, Lieutenant, 45, 272
Bourbon, 25-9, 31, 232
Bouring, R., 171-2
Bousted, Ridley & Co., 222, 231
Bowden, Captain Cornish, 23, 75, 84, 86-7
Brava, 51, 72, 74, 76-8, 154
Brazil, 8, 13, 17-21, 97
Britain, 8, 9, 11, 13, 16-18, 20-1, 24-5, 27-9, 31-2, 35-8, 40-3, 51, 53, 56-7, 68, 70, 72, 75, 80, 98, 100, 103, 118, 130, 147, 152, 155-7, 159, 161, 166, 178, 195-6, 211, 216-19, 228, 232-41
British and Foreign Anti-Slavery Society (see Anti-Slavery Society)
British Central Africa Protectorate, 219

British East Africa Company (see Imperial British East Africa Company and IBEAC)
British East Africa Protectorate, 117, 198
British India Steamship Navigation Company, 106
British West Indies, 18, 25, 30
Brownrigg, Captain I. C., 119, 236
Bruce, Captain W., 43
Brucks, 48
Brussels Act (1890), 173, 224-5, 228
Brussels Conference (1889/90), 224, 237, 239
Buchanan, J., 214
Buddu, 196
Buganda, 47, 90
Bukoba, 201
Bullard, Sir Reader, 169
Bunce, Commander B. H., 16, 19, 20
Bunyoro, 133, 136, 194-6, 290
Burkhardt, J. L., 171
Burton, R., 20, 48, 153, 172
Burtt, T., 256-7
Bushire, 54, 118, 173, 175-6, 179, 200, 288
Bushman, 2, 6
Busoga, 194
Buxton, S., 223
Buxton, T. Fowell, 17, 236
Buzurg, 6
Byzantine, 2

Caggenmacher, Herr, 130
Cairo, 55, 122, 126-8, 130-1, 137-8, 166, 168, 172-3
Cairo Home for Freed Women, 142-3
Calcutta, 39, 41
Caliph, The Third, 5
Cambay, 7, 44
Cameron, V. L., 133, 187-8, 289
Canning Award, 57, 275-6
Cape, The, 7, 8, 11, 15, 19-22, 24, 37-8, 71, 76, 85-9, 118
Cape Amber, 36
Cape Command, 19, 20, 45, 71-2
Cape July, 249
Carthage, 3
Carvalho, Major, 16
Cass, L. (Sec. of State, USA), 23, 267
Cassaba, 167
Castlereagh, Lord, 28
Caucasus, 163
Cavaignac, M. de, 41
Cave, Sir B., 252
Cavendish, Lord, 281

Central Africa, 11, 49
Ceylon, 3, 39, 40
Chabhar, 50, 173
Chanler, W. A., 197
Chewa, 213
Chikumbi, 217, 219
China Station, 118
Chinese, 3, 4, 23, 264
Chitesis (Chitesi's), 215
Christie, Dr J., 89
Church Missionary Society (CMS), 40, 86, 88-90, 92, 138, 183, 193
Churchill, H. A., 59, 60, 64, 82-3, 88, 99, 102-3, 154, 278-9
Circassia, 122, 143, 162-6, 169, 171
Clarendon Committee, 90, 99, 101-2, 107, 235, 279
Clarendon, Lord, 96, 99, 102, 166, 168, 208-9, 280-1
Clerk, Sir G., 114
Clarkson, T., 236
Cloves, 66, 89, 230, 250, 256
Cobbold, Captain R. P., 151
Cockburn, Admiral, 105
Cogan, Captain R., 48, 260
Coghlan, Sir W., 87, 176, 281
Colebrooke, Major, 30
Colomb, Captain P., 62, 64, 74, 78, 80, 84, 103-4, 242, 281
Colono, 13, 33
Colvile, Colonel C., 196, 290
Comité Français d'Emancipation, 129
Commission of Enquiry into the State of the Mauritius Slave Trade (see Eastern Inquiry)
Comoro Islands, 29, 32, 34, 36-7, 59, 60, 76, 90, 97, 118, 235, 238
Conducia Bay, 24
Congo, 183-4, 186-7, 189-90, 213, 220
Congress of Anti-Slavery Societies (Paris, 1890), 237
Constantinople, 162-4, 166-8
Cook, Captain, 17
Cookson, Consular Agent, 173
Corbett, Rear-Admiral, 158
Cos, 167
Cosmos Indicopleustes, 3
Cowrie shells, 191
Crassons de Medeuil, 11, 26
Crespigny, Hon. Vivian, 281
Crimean War, 20
Cromer, Lord, 143, 161
Cross, Dr, 218
Crum-Ewing, J., 281
Cuba, 13, 17, 18, 21, 23, 97
Cumberbatch, Consul, 167

Cumming, Admiral A., 113, 118, 154
Curzon, Lord, 240, 251, 253, 257
Cushites, 149
Cutfield, Commander, 84

Dallons, Captain P., 26, 38
Dalrymple, A., 38
Damascus, 156, 166
Danakil, 155, 157, 160, 173
Danaqli, 133, 141
Dangla, 123
Daraw, 138
Dar es Salaam, 60, 89, 100, 102, 106, 114-15
Darfur, 49, 121-2, 134, 172, 282
Dar-Nuba, 140
Decken, Baron von der, 65
Dècle, L., 200
Deep Bay, 218
Deim es Zubeir, 144, 284
Delagoa Bay, 12, 13, 20, 104, 208, 212
Delgado, Cape, 2, 3, 13, 34, 44, 208, 211-12
Delos, 3
Denha, 125
Derby, Earl of, 117, 131
Dervishes, 134, 136, 140-1
Devereux, W. Cope, 84
Dhows, 1, 60, 67, 69, 70, 72-3, 76, 276
Digo, 183
Dhabol, 264
Dinka, 125, 128, 283
Diogenes, 2
Dioscurus, 2
Disbrowe, Lt. Colonel H. F., 177
Diu, 8, 44
Diu, Battle of, 7
Djebbel Gudda, 152
Dohar, 177, 180
Dongola, 49, 126-7, 135
Drummond, Professor H., 215
Dufile, 136
Duruma, 183
Dutch, 8, 9, 26
Duval, Governor-General, 16

East Africa, 1, 4-6, 20, 23, 25
East African Coast, 1-8, 12-13, 26-7, 32, 34, 37-9, 42, 45-6, 65-7, 70-6, 79, 80, 84-5, 88-9, 92, 98-9, 119, 154, 161, 180, 183, 210, 232, 239, 258, 260-1
East India Company, 28, 37-40, 41-3, 65, 152, 154, 174, 288

INDEX

East India Station, 71-3, 118, 162, 236
Eastern Inquiry, 30-1, 232, 268-9
Egypt, 2, 3, 38, 79, 97-8, 117, 121-3, 131, 135, 142, 145, 148-9, 156, 160, 162, 164-6, 167, 172-3, 195, 261, 283-4
Egyptian Steamship Company, 167
El Fasher, 122, 134, 140
El Obeid, 125, 135, 140, 146
Elgon, Mt., 197
Eliot, Sir C., 258
Elliott, Sir H., 168
Elphinstone, Mountstuart, 42-3
Elton, Captain F., 90, 114-16, 210-11
Eltz, Baron von, 201
Emin Pasha, 135-6, 194
Emmerton, E. A., 18, 61, 64
Enfield, Viscount, 281
Engagés, 32-5, 269
English Point, 85
English River, 13
En Nahud, 122
Epirus, 3
Equatorial Province, 136
Eritrea, 150
Es Siout, 122, 126, 138
Ethiopia (see Abyssinia)
Eunuchs, 3, 39, 52, 122, 135, 140, 165, 169-74, 287
Euphrates, 4, 175, 277

Fairfax, H., 280, 282
Far East, 6
Far East Station, 73
Farler, J. P., 256
Farley, Reverend J. R., 116
Farquhar, Sir R., 28-9, 30-1, 39, 42-3
Fars, 176
Fashoda, 128-9, 132, 141
Fatiko, 133
Fatimids, 121
Fazil Mustapha, 168
Fazogli, 129, 140
Felkin, R. W., 195
Fellowes, Lieutenant, 89
Firearms, 13, 192
Fisher, Captain, 27
Foot, Captain C. E., 214
Fort Jesus, 9, 10, 46
Fort Manning, 219
Fountaine, Lieutenant, 94
Fowler, R., 281
France, 9, 11, 13, 18, 21-2, 25-7, 31-41, 64-5, 90, 92, 98, 102, 107, 110-12, 130, 147, 151, 155, 166, 224, 232-41, 267-8

Franco-Prussian War, 184
Fraser, Captain, 90
Free Church Mission, 214, 218
French Congo, 146
French East India Company, 25
French Flag, 28-9, 32, 35, 39, 78, 93, 100, 118-19, 220, 232-41, 258
Frere, Sir B., 24-5, 36, 62, 73, 86-7, 90, 103, 105, 108-14, 117, 131-2, 223, 235, 281
Freretown, 90-2
Fuladoya, 91, 280
Fungani, 68

Galla, 84, 148-51, 153-4, 159, 166, 176, 182-3, 285
Gallabat (Metemma), 125, 141, 149-50
Gallonsier Bay, 74
Ganda (see Baganda)
Gama, Vasco da, 7, 9
Gambela (Gamelab), 146-7
Gardner, Captain, 234
Gazi, 229
Gedaref, 139, 150
Germans, 11, 107, 187, 199-205, 215, 217-19, 221, 223, 229, 247, 252, 291
German Anti-Slavery Society, 218
German Catholic African Society, 201
German East Africa, 196-7, 199-205, 231, 249, 252
Georgia, 122, 162-4
Gessi, R., 134-5, 139, 172
Gezireh, 145-6
Gilpin, C., 223, 281
Giriama, 183
Gladstone, W. E., 113, 139
Goa, 9, 11, 37, 39
Gojjam, 149-50
Gombroon (see Bandar Abbas)
Gondar, 149
Gondokoro, 123, 125-7, 129, 133
Gordon, C., 133-5, 137-9, 151, 156, 159, 173, 195
Gorringe, Colonel, 146
Grant, Captain J. A., 128, 194
Granville, Lord, 90, 109, 112, 160
Gray, E., 282
Greek slaves, 122
Guardafui, Cape, 2, 71, 75-6, 86, 94, 104, 130, 154
Guillain, Captain M., 31-2, 47, 51
Guilleme Père, 187
Guinea, 8
Gurney, R., 103
Guising, Commander, 150

Habash (Habashi or Habashat), 148, 188
Haboba, 140
Habr Gerhajis, 152
Habr Toljaala, 152
Hadhramaut, 1, 8, 69, 86, 259
Hadimu, 255
Hague Tribunal, 240-1, 295
Haines, Captain, 274
Hajee Furruj, 177
Hales, J., 154
Hamdi Pasha, 168
Hamid, Sayyid, 251-2
Hamerton, Colonel A., 32-3, 44, 48, 50-5, 260, 275, 277
Hamitic, 6
Hardinge, Sir A., 200, 231, 240, 242-8
Hardy, Lieutenant, 38
Harem, 169-74, 186, 193, 253, 287
Harrar, 130, 149, 153, 283
Harris, W. C., 51, 151, 170
Hart, Captain, 47
Hassan bin Omar, 202
Hastings, Lord, 39, 42
Havana, 22-3
Hawes, A. G. S., 214-15, 227
Hawish road, 155
Hay, Sir J., 280
Heath, Commodore L., 59, 75, 87, 99, 104, 281
Hedjaz, 156-7, 159-60, 164, 176
Hell, Admiral de, 32
Hermias, 170
Hicks, General, 135, 140
Hill, Sir C., 253, 282
Hillyar, Commodore C. F., 57, 72, 75, 81, 104, 281
Hima, 194, 196
Hippalus, 1
Hirth, Mgr., 290
Hodeida, 155-6, 159, 161
Hollis, Sir C., 205
Holmes, Consul, 164
Holmwood, Consul F., 116
Holy Cross Mission, 126
Holy Ghost Fathers, 90
Hong Kong, 71
Hormuz, 7, 10
Horner, Père, 91
Husain, 5
Hutchinson, E., 281
Hutley, W., 191
Hutu, 182

Ibrahim Bey Foussi, 128

Ibrahim Pasha, 122
Ibrahim Wad Mahmoud, 146
Ibo, 15-17, 24, 35
al Idrisi, 6
Ile de France, 25-7
Imeretia, 162
Imperial British East Africa Company (IBEAC), 90-2, 197, 221, 226, 248, 250
India, 4, 5, 8, 9, 15, 31, 35, 38-41, 44-5, 48, 50-1, 64, 67, 106
Indians, 12, 47, 56, 60, 65, 78, 105, 111, 113-14, 123, 211, 226, 234, 249-50, 254, 256-7, 276, 282, 296
Indian Navy, 71, 73, 120, 152-3, 175-6, 274, 285
Indian Ocean, 2, 6, 7, 9, 13, 25, 27, 30, 32, 40, 45, 65, 71-2, 94, 235
Inhambane, 12, 17, 72, 210
International Slavery Bureau (International Maritime Bureau), 225, 239, 293-4
Iraq, 5
Iringa, 204
Isenberg, C. W., 151
Islam, 1, 4, 5, 7
Ismail, Khedive, 97, 109, 117, 123, 129-31, 136-9, 164, 283
Ismail, Wad el Andok, 140
Isna Province, 132
Italians, 123, 130, 145, 150, 161, 173, 198
Ituri River, 184
Ivory, 3, 6, 27, 65, 96, 100, 122, 184, 186, 289

Jadder, 176
Ja'liyin (Jaalin), 123, 141
Jask, 50, 76
Jawasmi, 41-3
Jebel Elba, 147
Jedda, 140, 155-60, 162, 167, 173, 274
Jellaba, 134, 146
Jibuti, 151
Jimma, 149
Johanna, 29, 33-4, 36, 90, 104, 234
John, King, 150-1
Johnston, Sir H., 189, 201, 216-19
Jones, Rear-Admiral, 236
Juba River, 4, 25, 71, 90, 130, 153-4
Juma Merikani, 192
Jumbe, 213, 217

Kabarega, 133, 136, 194, 196
Kabunda, 214
Kaffa, 150

INDEX

Kagera River, 194, 196
Kagwa, A., 193
Kaka, 132
Kakika, 135
Kakwa, 283
Kamba (see Wakamba)
Karachi, 40, 50, 79
Karema, 222
Karonga, 214–15, 218–19
Kars, 163
Karusco, 127
Kassala, 145, 147
Katanga, 20
Kathiawar, 40, 54
Kavirondo, 195
Kaye, Sir W., 280–1
Kayser, Dr. 203
Kayuni, 218
Kelat, 176
Kemball, Captain, 173, 175–7
Kennaway, Sir J., 281
Kenya, 182, 197
Keppel, G., 274
Kerimba, 13
Ketkas, 127
Khalid, Sayyid, 251–2
Khalifa, 136, 140–2, 160, 252
Khalifa, (Sultan), 224, 246
Khartoum, 123, 125–30, 132, 138, 140
Kibwezi, 92
Kikuyu, 182, 197
Kilifi, 118
Kilimanjaro, Mt., 3, 197, 200
Kilwa, 5–7, 22, 25–7, 34–5, 37, 42, 45, 47, 50, 52, 54, 56–8, 60, 62, 76, 79, 81, 106–7, 111–12, 114–16, 154, 176, 202, 215, 261, 278, 292
Kilwa Kivinja, 110–11
Kimberley, Lord, 251
Kimweri, 187
Kinglake, A. W., 122
Kinnaird, J., 281
Kirk, Sir J., 88, 92, 103, 106, 108–14, 116, 130, 137, 155, 223–4, 261, 273, 280
Kirolane, 211
Kisanja, 212
Kisiju, 114–16
Kismayu, 5, 116–17
Kitab al-Ajaib al-Hind, 6
Kitab al-Zanuj, 5
Kitangole, 196
Kitchener, Lord, 144, 160
Kiungani, 90
Kiwale, 115
Knoblecher, I., 125

Koki, 196
Kopa Kopa, 214, 216
Kordofan, 122–3, 125–6, 134, 140, 144, 146, 172
Kota Kota, 215, 217, 219
Krapf, Reverend J. L., 54, 183
Kroomen, 80
Kuku, 283
Kuria Muria Islands, 74
Kutch, 40, 105
Kuwait, 69, 176

La Bourdonnais, 25
Lacerda e Almeida, F. J. M., 11
Lado, 133, 136, 141, 146
Lagos, 72, 105
Lambermont, Baron, 224
Lamu, 1, 5–7, 22, 25, 37, 45–6, 51–2, 58, 60, 74, 76–9, 88, 90, 104, 106, 114–15, 154, 229
Lamu Award, 224
Lancaster, Sir J., 37
Langenberg, 201
Langheld, Captain, 201
Lansdowne, Lord, 199
Laros, 167
Latuka, 128, 136
Lavigérie, Cardinal, 222, 237
Laws, Dr, 181
Lefevre, S., 281
Leopold, King, 223–4
Levantines, 123
Levesque, Reverend, 193
Libertos, 268
Linant de Bellefonds, E., 195
Lincoln, President, 23
Lindi, 33, 54, 90, 111, 202, 236, 261
Lingah, 69, 173, 176–7, 179
Lisbon, 9, 15
Livingstone, D., 8, 17, 34, 62, 64, 86, 94–7, 103, 108–9, 185, 188, 206–10, 214–15, 222, 234, 289, 291–2
Livingstone Mission, 181
Lofulla, M., 126
Lol River, 127
London Missionary Society, 29, 191
Lourenco Marques, 12
Lualaba River, 187
Luanda, 206
Lubirianzi, 188
Lucereau, M., 155
Lugard, F. G., 91–2, 181, 185, 189, 195–6, 215–16, 226–8, 247, 250
Lundahl, Madam Emily, 150
Luo, 283

Lupanzula, 189
Lurio River, 212

Ma'ala, 69
Mabla, 152
Macdonald, Admiral R., 116, 261
Macdonald, Major, 196
Machakos, 197
Machesa, 217
Mackay, A. M., 193-4
Mackenzie, Sir D., 249-51
Macguire, Captain C., 217
Madagascar, 13, 20, 23-4, 27-9, 30, 32-6, 39, 42, 44, 50, 59-60, 71, 73, 75, 94, 97, 100, 210-11, 234, 236-8, 262
Madeira, 15
Madeira, Abreu de, 16
Madi, 133, 135-6
Mad Mullah, 162, 198, 252, 258
Madras, 85
Mafia, 5, 22, 37, 52, 88, 203, 291
Magassi River, 115
Magila, 90, 116
Magnesia, 167
Mahdi, 135-6, 139-43, 159-60, 283
Mahé, 84, 88-9
Mahon, Colonel, 146
Maintyrana, 36
Majid, Sultan, 22, 55-60, 100, 102, 275, 281
Makololo, 206-7
Makongeni, 280
Makran, 48, 50, 180
Malabar, 76
Malcolm, Captain G., 137
Malindi, 4, 6, 7, 37, 46, 80, 92, 117, 229, 264
Maltese, 123
Malzac de, 125
Mambari, 293
Mamelukes, 121, 283
Manda, 5
Manganja (Manganya), 65, 207, 213
Mangapwani, 118
Mangbetu, 124, 127, 133, 172
Mangoche, 219
Manilla, 188
Manning, Cardinal, 138, 223
Manyuema, 183, 187-90, 192
Mapazetas, 13
Mariano, 207
Marseilles, 22, 32, 153
Marshoud, Sheikh, 145
Masai, 4, 182-4, 197, 200, 287
Masani, 19

Masasi, 90
Mascarenes, 265
Mascarhenas, 15
Mashona, 213
Masindi, 133
Masnah, al, 177
Mass (Buona Ventura), 22
Massawa, 129-30, 147, 150, 155, 157, 161, 171, 281
Masudi, al, 4, 6
Matabele, 212-13
Mataka, 209
Matapwiri, 215, 219
Mathews, Sir L., 117, 223, 231, 242, 244, 246, 249-50
Matrah, 177
Mauritius, 22, 27-9, 30-2, 39-43, 71, 88, 153, 266-7, 269
Mayo, Lord, 108
Mayotta, 34, 101
Mzitu (Mavitu or Maviti), 209-10, 292
Mazrui, 46, 229
Mbarara, 197
Mbe, 182
Mbuta, 189
Mbweni, 90
McCausland, Lieutenant, 116
McKillop Pasha, 130
McLeod, L., 144
McMurdo, Captain, 145-7
Mecca, 53, 140, 147, 156-9, 160, 162, 167, 173, 175, 178, 261, 289
Medina, 147, 156, 167
Mello, Antonio de, 15
Mende, 193
Menelik, King, 151
Merka, 78
Metemma (see Gallabat)
Meyer, 151
Mgungara River, 116
Middle East, 1, 8, 38-40, 44, 50, 66, 70, 97-8, 101, 114, 120, 171-3, 261
Miganda, 65
Miles, Major, 114
Milius, Governor, 29
Mirama, 12
Mirambo, 186-7, 212
Mitylene, 167
Miyana, 65
Mkokotoni, 59, 118
Mlanje (Mlanji), 212, 214, 216
Mlozi, 214, 216-17, 219, 227
Mocambe, 24
Mocha (Mokha), 48, 155, 159, 161
Mogadishu, 5, 6, 76, 170, 264

INDEX

Mogee, 176
Mohammed, 4, 5
Mohammed Ali, 121, 123
Mohammed Kumfereh, 160
Mohammed Nossair, 147
Mohammed Taha, 128
Mohilla, 35
Mola, 197
Mo Lin (see Malindi)
Mombasa, 6, 7, 9, 12, 27, 37, 46, 60, 70, 85, 91, 111, 116, 118, 235, 259, 273
Monomotapa, 12
Moraes, 210
Morgadas, Senhor, 14
Moresby, Captain Fairfax, 39, 43, 152
Morice, M., 25–6
Morocco, 241
Mozambique, 7-9, 11-19, 21, 24-5, 33, 50, 70, 90, 94, 99, 110, 210-11, 216, 267
Mozambique Channel, 16, 19, 23-4, 35, 60, 67, 84, 211-12, 234
Mpenda, 215
Mpwapwa, 190, 261
Msalema, 213
Msimbati Island, 278
Mtesa, 172, 187, 193-5
Mtotila, 190
Mtowa, 189
Muddu (see Baddu)
Muhammed el Fadhl, 170
Muhammed Kurra, 170
Mukalla, 48, 69, 75, 112, 120, 176
Mukhtara, al, 4
Mukopi, 193
Mumoni, 197
Munza, King, 172
Muraviev, Count, 163
Murchison, Sir R., 209, 228
Murraye, 75
Musa Pasha Hamdi, 128
Muscat, 7, 10, 34, 38-50, 54-5, 65, 72, 75, 79, 80, 84, 89, 100, 102, 106, 108-9, 112-13, 118, 175-7, 233, 240-1, 258, 274
Muscat Dhows Arbitration Award, 241
Musha Island, 152, 155
Mussendam, 76
Munzinger, W., 130
Mwananyani, 217
Mwanga, King, 194-5
Mwemba, 213
Mweru Lake, 190
Mzilikazi, 212
Mzimba, 219

Naaman, 156
Nabob, 15
Nair, Mimr, 123
Namwanda, 219
Napier, Lord, 73
Napoleon I, 27, 41, 71, 121, 282
Napoleon III, 34
Narses, 170
Nassick, 40, 85–6
Natal, 90, 92
Ndorobo, 182
Nejd, 171
Nepean, Sir E., 41–2
Ngoni, 182, 186, 212-16, 218-19, 292
Nikon, 3
Nkonde, 215–16, 219
North Africa, 172
Nossi Bé, 32, 101, 234
Nourse, Commodore, J., 45, 232
Nsama, 190
Nubia, 121, 123
Nuer, 125, 283
Numidians, 2
Nyangbara, 283
Nyangwe, 187-90, 192, 210
Nyanja (see Manganja)
Nyasa Lake, 183, 201-2, 207-9, 211-19, 227-8, 292
Nyasaland, 60, 65, 95–6, 114, 182
Nyasera, 219
Nyika, 183, 248
Nzawi, 197

Obock (Obokh), 155, 161
O'Connor, N., 281
Ohrwalder, Father J., 284
Oldfield, Commander R. B., 76-7
Oman, 5, 6, 9, 26–7, 32, 37–9, 40-2, 44, 46-50, 54, 60, 65, 67, 70, 74-6, 79–80, 96, 104, 185, 188, 223, 233, 274
Oman, Gulf of, 175-7, 238
Omdurman, 140-1, 143, 145
O'Neil, Lieutenant H. O., 211-12, 216
Ormara, 50
O'Sullivan, Dr R., 113, 242, 244
Ottoman, 7
Owen, Captain, 13, 45–6, 55, 85, 98, 170, 272
Ozi River, 116, 154

Pajula, 283
Pall Mall Gazette, 250
Palmerston, 50, 52-4, 94, 164, 232
Pangani, 46, 116, 183, 197, 200, 203, 261

Paris Anti-Slavery Conference (1867), 166
Parr, Commander, 36
Pasni, 50
Pate, 5, 6, 37, 45-6, 78, 170
Patterson, Captain R. R., 213-14
Pearl divers, 180
Pease, J. A., 251
Pelly, Colonel L., 75, 177
Pemba, 5, 12, 16, 24, 46-7, 52, 56-7, 59-60, 66, 76, 111-13, 116, 118-19, 154, 202-3, 229-30, 236, 239, 242, 244, 246-7, 249-50, 253-9
Penazzi, Count Louis, 150
Pentagoa, 278
Perim Island, 40, 152, 155-6, 161
Periplus, 3, 4, 263
Persia, 9, 45, 50, 62-3, 85, 100, 156, 174-80, 264, 289
Persian Gulf, 1, 4-6, 38-48, 51-2, 55, 59, 60, 67, 69, 71, 75, 80, 83-4, 97, 99, 103-4, 107, 163, 173-80, 223, 238, 240, 264, 274-5, 278, 288
Peters, K., 194, 200
Petherick, J., 125-8
Pigott, J. R. W., 250-1
Pirate Coast, 38, 41
Playfair, Consul R. L., 23-4, 56-7, 59, 75, 78, 155, 234
Pliny, the Elder, 2
Plowden, Consul, 166
Pokomo, 183
Pompeii, 2
Poncet, Androise & Jule, 126
Portal, Sir G., 196, 221, 224
Port Amelia, 13
Porters, 222, 289, 293
Port Louis, 26, 32
Port Sudan, 147
Port Tola, 278
Portuguese, 4, 6-21, 23-7, 33-5, 39, 43, 49, 64, 107, 110-11, 192, 206-17, 237, 291, 293
Portuguese East Africa, 13, 15-17, 22, 24, 36, 211-12, 260
Poti, 165
Prager, Captain, 218
Prason, 3
Prazeros, 13-15, 266
Prideaux, Captain, 183
Prior, J., 13, 27, 65
Providence Island, 39
Prussia, 18
Ptolemy's *Geography*, 3
Pungwe River, 12

Purvis, Commander H. R., 278
Putnam, H. P., 49

Qapudan, Salim, 123
Qatar peninsula, 127, 180
Qishm Island, 179
Quambola, 197
Qua Qua River, 12
Quelimane, 12-14, 17, 18, 33-5, 207, 211, 217, 265-7
Quintuple Treaty, 18

Rabai, 90-2, 183
Radama, 28-9, 42, 44
Ranavolana II, 32
Raouf Pasha, 139, 283
Rashaida (Rasheida), 145, 161
Rashid, 190
Ras al-Hadd, 75-6, 120, 175
Ras al-Madraka, 74, 76
Ras Banas, 140
Ras al-Khymah, 177
Ras Hafun, 69, 78
Ras Kassar, 147
Ras Mahbar, 74
Red Sea, 2, 7, 45, 52, 71, 75, 97, 104, 123, 137, 140, 142-3, 147, 150-1, 154-9, 160-2, 274
Regis & Company, 32
Reitz, Lieutenant, 46
Rejaf, 125, 136, 141
Réunion, 22, 30-5, 90, 234, 236
Reute, Emily (Salma bin Said), 59
Rhodes, C., 216
Rhodesia, 213
Rigby, C. P., 38, 48, 55-6, 64-5, 72, 85, 101, 103, 177, 214, 260, 276, 281
Right of Search, 232-41, 267
Rionga, 136
Rio de Janeiro, 13, 14, 18, 19
Rising, Lieutenant, 81
Riyadh, 177
Robinson, W., 280
Rodd, Sir Rennell, 231, 238
Rodriques Island, 29
Rohl River, 126-7
Romans, 2
Roscher, Dr A., 65
Rosebery, Lord, 231
Roseires, 146
Royal Navy, 58, 65, 71-2, 74, 78
Rothery, H. C., 280-1
Ruanda, 182, 200
Rudolf, Lake, 197, 199
Rufiji River, 278

INDEX 321

Rukn-ud-din Barbak, 4
Rumaliza (Mohammed bin Khalifan), 244
Rumelia, 167
Russell, Lord, 23, 127, 234
Russia, 18, 162-4
Rustchuk, 168
Ruvuma River, 10, 12, 25, 96, 207-9, 213, 260, 292

Saadani, 116
Sabaean, 69
Sabaki River, 91-2, 195, 197
Sabi River, 213
Sadler, Sir J. H., 199
Said Abou Sadecka, 160
Said bin Habib, 186, 192
Said Ibrahim, 146
Said Sultan, 260, 275
Saif bin Sultan, 48
Saint Andrew, 36
Saint Helena, 20, 40, 71, 88, 271
Sala, Count della, 138
Salisbury, Lord, 212, 219, 223, 251-3, 257
Salonika, 166-7
Samanga, 115
Samburi, 197
Samh, 177
San Antonio River, 24
Santos, Father Joao dos, 170
Sao Paulo, 12
Scala Nuovo, 167
Schaeffer, Colonel, 138, 142
Schele, Baron von, 199
Schimpfer, Dr., 157
Schweinfurth, G., 127, 146, 194
Scott, Sir J., 142
Scott, Sir W. (Lord Stowell), 232
Scylax, 2
Sebebwane, 180
Sebowa, 207
Select Committee (1870/1), 35, 88, 101, 103-8, 168, 209, 233, 235, 281
Semboja, Chief, 116
Semliki River, 189
Sena, 8, 14
Seneca, 2
Seneeko, Queen, 32
Senerefu, King, 121
Senga, 213
Sengo, 219
Sennar, 122-3, 125
Seward, Consul, 73
Seward, W. H., 23
Sewjee, Messrs. Jairam, 66

Seychelles, 25, 27, 29, 39, 71, 75, 87-90, 106, 267
Seymour, Captain, 157
Seyyid Said, 38, 40-8, 50-4, 275
Seyyid Hamoud, Sultan, 246
Seyyidieh, 259
Shaftesbury, Lord, 138
Shaka, 212
Shamyl, 163
Shangul, 140
Sharja, 176
Shihr (Sheher), 8, 69, 120, 176
Shilluk, 125-8, 133
Ships:
 Albatross, 272
 America, 22, 24, 280
 Andromache, 45
 Antelope, 232
 Ariel, 76-7
 Aurélie, 33
 Aurora, 167
 Barracouta, 272
 Bittern, 159
 Blanche, 230
 Bouvet, 237
 Brazileno, 29
 Brisk, 22
 Briton, 89
 Bullfinch, 72
 Caledon, 27
 Caridat, 35
 Castor, 16, 34, 54
 Charles et George, 33
 Ciceron, 23
 Cleopatra, 19, 20
 Clive, 176
 Columbine, 36, 72, 235
 Condor, 216
 Cossack, 72
 Coureur, 29
 Crecian, 20
 Daedalus, 38
 Daphne, 72, 83, 114, 116, 280
 Dart, 20
 Dee, 54
 Delight, 29
 Dryad, 74, 154
 Duke of Tetuan, 267
 Edward Bonaventure, 37
 Enarea, 149
 Eolo, 16
 Esperance, 22
 Falkland, 176
 Formosa Estrella, 22
 Forte, 72
 Good Hope, 265

Gorgon, 72, 76
Gyptis, 167
Immanuela, 88
Imogene, 47
Industry, 29
Inferne, 240
Jagstrust, 265
Jose, 88
Kangaroo, 164
Kingfisher, 120, 161
Lady Nyasa, 209
Lapwing, 179
Le Succès, 39
Laura, 33
Le Louis, 232
Leven, 46
Leveret, 17
Lily, 88
London, 56, 72, 119, 236, 282
Lyra, 22, 25, 55-6, 72, 85, 276
Magicienne, 269
Mahalen, 167
Manuela, 22
Margaraita Quintera, 22
Ma Roberta, 207
Mascareignes, 33
Mazurka, 34
Menai, 39
Mercury, 265
Minnetonka, 267
Morning Star, 166
Nestre, 161
Nisus, 13, 15, 65
Nymphe, 72
Orestre, 167
Orestes, 16, 89
Osprey, 150, 160, 178
Pantaloon, 25, 72
Pelorius, 157
Penguin, 22, 25, 72, 74, 86, 94
Persian, 22
Philomel, 114, 178, 239
Piedmontese, 56
Pigeon, 179
Pioneer, 207
Progresso, 267
Racehorse, 27
Rapid, 59, 72, 89
Red Breast, 258
Rifleman, 114
St Abbs, 94
Salamantea, 35
Schibiya, 167
Scout, 162
Seeadler, 162
Semiramis, 286

Sidon, 72
Star, 86, 154
Sylph, 38
Tantah, 167
Teazer, 72
Ternate, 38
Thetis, 85
Tigris, 175-6
Tribune, 163
Undine, 84
Wasp, 58-9, 72, 81-2, 84, 87
Wissmann, 218
Wolverine, 72
Shiraz, 5, 264
Shire River, 207-9, 211-12, 214, 217, 228
Shirwa Lake, 215
Shoa, 50, 151
Shoa Roman Catholic Mission, 159
Shubar, 176
Sicard, Major, 207
Sidis (Shankalla), 50, 148, 166
Sierre Leone, 89, 280
Sind, 40
Singapore, 203
Siu Siu (See Wee), 78
Siua, 143
Slaves:
    Enslavement of women, 290
    Exports to Middle East, 274-5
    Freed slaves, 280
    Freed slave settlements, 280-1
    Pledging of children as slaves, 290
    Slave markets, 113, 277
    Slave numbers, 260-2, 284, 296-7
    Slave prices, 277
Slave Trade Commissioners, 20, 267
Slave Trade Department (Egypt), 137, 142, 145, 161-2
Smee, Captain, 38, 55
Smith, Consul, 253
Smith, Mackenzie & Co., 222
Smyrna, 166-7
Sobat River, 133, 146
Socotra, 67, 73-8, 89, 90, 104, 152, 273
Society for the Abolition of Slavery (German), 200
Sofala, 5-8, 12, 211
Sohar, 152
Sokia, 167
Somali, 50, 56, 149, 152-4, 182-3, 198, 252, 261, 275, 278
Somaliland, 1-3, 7, 51, 71, 75-8, 94, 159, 162
Somaliland (French), 232
Songea, 205

Soter (Ptolemy I), 2
Sotik, 197
South Africa, 12
South Africa Company, 229
South America, 13
Spain, 21-2, 24, 29, 41, 50
Speke, J. H., 128, 193
Stamboul, 171
Stanley Falls, 188, 190
Stanley, H. M., 117, 184-5, 188, 190, 221
Stanley, Lord, 60
Stanton, Consul-General, 128
Steere, Reverend E., 281
Stigand, 69
Storrs, Sir R., 242
Strabo, 2
Stratford de Redcliffe, Viscount, 163, 166
Stuhlmann, F., 189
Suakin, 129-30, 140, 145, 147, 159-60
Sudan, 2, 121-4, 129, 131, 135, 138-47, 149, 156, 159, 166, 172, 220, 261
Sudan-Abyssinian Delimitation Commission (1902/3), 146
Sudanese, 137, 196, 218
Suez Canal, 94, 97-8, 130, 152, 162, 167
Suhar (Sohar), 177
Sulivan, Captain G. L., 20, 79, 84, 86, 103
Sulaiman, 5
Sulaiman (Son of Zubeir), 139
Suleiman, the Magnificent, 159
Sumatra, 71
Suna, 47, 193
Sunley, Consul, 234-5
Sur, 48, 59, 175, 177, 238-40, 258
Swann, A. J., 190
Swahili, 1, 5, 7, 9, 37, 65, 68-9, 185-6, 188, 196-8, 246, 264
Syria, 5, 264

Tabora, 47, 184-5, 186, 189, 202, 289
Tabwa, 190
Tagamoyo, 188
Tagus River incident, 33
Tahaly, 125
Taif, 157
Tajurra, 150, 152-5, 166, 173
Tajurra, Gulf of, 154-5, 159, 174, 262
Taka, 129, 150,
Takaungu, 197, 229
Talbot, Commander, 20
Talbot, J., 281

Talodi, 145
Tamatave, 27
Tambala, 219
Tambara, 14
Tanaland, 198, 259
Tana River, 149
Tanga, 90, 116, 202
Tanganyika Lake, 47, 96, 98, 183, 186-8, 190-1, 201, 210, 212, 216, 222-3, 227-8
Taweisha, 134
Taylor, Consul, 165
Teleki, Count, 197-8
Tenterden, Lord, 136
Tete, 8, 207-8, 265
Tewfick Pasha, 156
Theodore, Emperor, 130, 149-50
Theophilus, 2
The Times, 136
Thutmose, 2
Thwain, 60, 275
Tigrai, 149
Tippu Tip, 189-90, 192, 201
Tirah, 167
Tite, Major, 16
Tomkinson, Captain, 27
Toora, 126
Tongo, 213
Tor, 162
Toro, 196
Treaty of Adrianople (1829), 162
Treasury, British, 20, 81, 101, 107
Treaty (British-USA 1862), 95
Treaty of Ghent, 21
Treaty, General (1820), 42
Treaty (Madagascar 1865), 94
Treaty of Paris (1814), 27-8
Trebizond, 163
Trucial Oman, 50-1
Tuchila, 219
Tucker, Bishop, 195, 242
Tucker, Captain, 235
Tukuni, 278
Tumbatu, 255
Tungi, Bay of, 211
Turkana, 199
Turkey, 75, 79, 97-8, 134, 137, 140, 148, 155-60, 162-76, 178, 220, 238-9, 241
Turki, Sultan (Sayyid bin Said), 103, 108, 112
Turks, 8, 121
Turquel River, 199
Turu, 287
Tutsi, 182

Ubanghi River, 134
Uganda, 92, 129, 133, 135, 185, 187, 193-7, 202, 231-2
Uganda Railway, 198, 221, 248, 257, 290
Ujiji, 186-7, 189, 191, 202, 210, 222
Ukambani, 197
Ukerewe Island, 200
Ulu, 197
Ulungu, 186
Umayyads, 5
Umfussi, 211-12
Unyamwezi, 110, 183, 192, 212
United States, 21, 105, 107, 225, 234
Unyanyembe, 185, 186-8, 190, 192, 195, 261
Urundi, 186, 200
Universities Mission to Central Africa, 90, 256
Usambara, 116, 183, 187
Uthman, 5

Vaudey, A., 125
Vayssiere, A., 125
Velhace, 24
Victoria Falls, 209
Victoria, Lake, 186, 195, 200-1, 212
Vidal, Captain, 272
Vidal Frères, 22
Vince, A., 125
Vivian, Lord, 105, 223, 280

Wadelai, 136
Wadi Halfa, 123
Wadigo, 285
Wahabi, 43
Wakamba, 182, 197
Wakefield, Sir E., 179-80
Wajiji, 183, 186
Walker, Rear-Admiral, 72, 233
Waller, H., 64, 97-8, 103, 131, 221, 234, 279
Wanyamwezi, 186, 189, 192
Washington Treaty, 23
Wasin Island, 77, 116, 258
Wataveta, 183
Wateita, 183

Waters, R. P., 17
Webi Shibeli, 153
Wele River, 134-5
Wellsted, J. R., 49
West Africa, 9, 11, 72, 118
Wharton, Captain, 114
White Fathers, 196, 200-1
Wilberforce, W., 43, 236
Williams, Brigadier-General, 163
Williams, Sir F., 281
Willoughby, Sir J., 221
Wilson, Captain, 76
Wilson, C. I., 195
Winton, Sir F. de, 229
Wise, Commodore, 23
Wissmann, H. von, 190, 201, 218
Wylde, A. B., 140, 158, 172, 286
Wylde, W. H., 286
Wyle, W. W., 280
Wyndham, P., 281
Wyvill, Commodore, C., 15, 19, 20, 54

Yacout, 38
Yao, 65, 182-3, 207, 213, 217, 219, 292
Yemen, 6, 70, 155-6, 176
Younghusband, Sir F., 242
Yussuf Bey, 172

Zambezi, 8, 12, 13, 183, 187, 190, 192, 206-9, 211-13, 228
Zambia, 213
Zanj, 6, 265
Zanzibar, 4-7, 12, 20, 22-4, 27, 30-50, 52-66, 76-80, 82, 86-91, 99, 100, 104-13, 118-19, 130, 154, 176, 178, 183-4, 186, 189, 203, 205, 210, 213, 215, 220-31, 233-40, 265, 274, 276-7
Zarafi, 217
Zebedeeh, 158
Zeila, 7, 130, 150, 152-6
Zingion, 3
Zombo, 217
Zubeir Pasha, 134, 145, 284
Zulu, 183, 212
Zumbo, 265
Zwemmer, Reverend S. M., 179

DATE DUE

HT1327
.B34

Beachey

The slave trade of eastern Africa